HISTORY OF ANCIENT
GREECE

D0958302

HISTORY OF ANCIENT
GREECE

JEAN HATZFELD

Revised by
ANDRÉ AYMARD
Professor at The Sorbonne

Translated by
A. C. HARRISON

Edited by
E. H. GODDARD

W · W · NORTON & COMPANY

New York · London

938
H568h
1966

First published in the Norton Library 1968
by arrangement with Oliver & Boyd Ltd.

This is a translation of *Histoire de la Grèce*
by Jean Hatzfeld, revised by André Aymard, and
published in Paris by Payot, 1963.

Books That Live
The Norton imprint on a book means that in the publisher's
estimation it is a book not for a single season but for the years.
W. W. Norton & Company, Inc.

ISBN 0-393-00247-0

W. W. Norton & Company, Inc., 500 Fifth Avenue, New York, NY 10110
W. W. Norton & Company Ltd, 10 Coptic Street, London WC1A 1PU

PRINTED IN THE UNITED STATES OF AMERICA

3 4 5 6 7 8 9 0

INTRODUCTION

Professor Jean Hatzfeld was one of the foremost historians of Ancient Greece as well as one of the most arresting writers of his generation. Even though the advances of scholarship and research, especially in the early periods of Greek history, would have caused him to alter some of what he originally wrote, his work has a timeless quality and his attitude was most enlightened, for he displayed how history ought to be written, how it can be much more than a mere catalogue of wars, politics and constitutions. His *History of Ancient Greece* enjoyed a wide popularity for its keen and lively narration and description, for its attention to social and economic patterns, and for its inclusion of matters of cultural and artistic interest. The book has also another outstanding merit, for its pursuit of Greek history does not terminate with the death of Alexander the Great in 323 B.C., as do most works, but proceeds as far as the absorption of Greece into the orbit of Rome in the second century B.C.

Hatzfeld's book was revised by A. Aymard, another leading French historian of Greece, and the second edition in French, which appeared in 1962, has again enjoyed wide popularity, not least among students of the English-speaking communities, and so it was decided to translate the work for the benefit of such students. The death of A. Aymard in 1964 prevented his participation in this edition and so his views on some of the later developments could not be ascertained. The present publishers of the English edition, however, have sought to incorporate a number of modifications which Aymard would probably have accepted in the light of recent research, not only in the field of Minoan and Mycenaean studies and in the decipherment of the Greek 'Linear B' script, but also in later periods.

It is hoped that the reader will find in this concise volume a lively and stimulating introduction to Greek history and that he will be led on to further reading and search for knowledge, for which purpose a select bibliography has been appended to the English edition.

D. J. MOSLEY
Dept. of Ancient History
University of Sheffield

ACKNOWLEDGMENTS

We have pleasure in acknowledging the courtesy and assistance of the following in giving us permission to reproduce the maps:

Greece and Asia Minor . . . . The Clarendon Press, Oxford: from *History of the Ancient World, The Orient and Greece*; by M. J. Rostovtzeff.

The Peloponnesian War . . . . Cambridge University Press, London: from Vol. 5 of *Cambridge Ancient History*.

The Second Athenian Naval . . . Cambridge University Press, London: Confederacy . . . . . . from Vol. 6 of *Cambridge Ancient History*.

The Conquests of Alexander . . . Methuen & Co. Ltd., London: from *A History of the Greek World*, by M. L. W. Laistner.

CONTENTS

*   *   *

MAPS

I

THE AEGEAN SEA

Greek history is the story of a people who during the first centuries of the second millennium B.C. established themselves in the south of the Balkan peninsula. Their civilisation came to extend over what is now known as Greece, the coastal regions of the Black Sea and of Asia Minor, and the Aegean islands, and spread to southern Italy, Sicily and points even further west. The Greeks had a common language and tradition but they were never united as one country or nation and the name 'Hellas' signifies a culture and civilisation rather than a state or nation. They began to describe themselves by the common name of 'Hellenes' ('Greek' comes from the Roman term) perhaps as late as 800 B.C. The mode of life and the physical environment of their widely dispersed and independent communities were similar, and so in ancient as in later, times the sea was not a dividing influence.

Geography is in agreement with history on this matter. The subsidence which, in the quaternary period, formed the bed of the Aegean Sea in a continent which had already taken, in the main, its present shape has not altered its unity. It is solely for convenience of exposition that the western shore of Anatolia is considered in geographical treatises to be part of Asia. Homer never had the notion of calling the two shores of the Aegean by different names; Herodotus was astonished at the arbitrary bounds that science was already setting up in his day between Europe and Asia. The traveller who goes aboard ship in the evening at the Piraeus to wake next morning at Smyrna does not think he has changed continents: he finds the same light, the same reddish, bare slopes that he left the evening before. Such an impression is not deceptive. The mountain ranges, the geological formations, are continuous from one shore to the other; and if the sunset colours Hymettus and Mount Mycale with the same mauve tints, it is because both these mountains belong to the same crystalline massif. They also share the same climate, the same vegetation, and to a certain extent the same rain-belt. On the other hand, the landscape changes as soon as you leave the Asiatic coast to penetrate into the interior: a hundred and twenty-five miles from the sea you come to the plateaux and steppe-lands that make the Anatolian peninsula a fragment of Asia surrounded by a coastal belt of Mediterranean type. But Phrygia, Galatia, Lycaonia have played but a short and inconspicuous part in Greek history; we can therefore neglect them in this preliminary study which is limited to that region in which for twenty centuries Hellenic civilisation was developed.

The Aegean Sea owes its existence, as we have seen, to a subsidence which broke up a continent of relatively recent formation and whose structure was very complicated. This geological catastrophe also produced a coast-line of astonishing diversity. The sea invaded the valleys, turning them into fiords which penetrate deeply into the interior of the land-masses, and into innumerable bays; the mountain ranges push out into the sea in peninsulas which are elongated into capes that are in turn prolonged by strings of islands. In no other part of Europe do we find coasts so capriciously indented; even those of Dalmatia and of Norway with their fiords all lying in a uniform direction do not present such variety. The length of the coast-line compared with the area it contains is very considerable; for continental Greece (excluding Macedon) and the Cyclades (excluding Crete) it is some 1937 miles for an area of 31,505 square miles. This is thrice the minimum circumference for such an area; whereas in other peninsulas (Italy for example) the coastal development barely reaches twice the minimum.

The physical formation is such that the sea is never far away. You rarely get out of sight of it in journeys through the interior and no point of the Peloponnese is more than 33 miles away from it (38 miles in central Greece). The sea makes the background for the finest and most characteristic landscapes in Greece, its absence is felt as a veritable privation; and we know with what cries of joy the mercenaries of the Anabasis saluted it as they came down from the high plateaux of Asia Minor.

The Greeks soon familiarised themselves with the sea. Coming from a continental area, even having no word in their language to designate it, but borrowing its name from the peoples previously established around the Aegean basin, they rapidly became the best sailors of the Mediterranean. The inhabitants of certain mountain provinces, the Arcadians among others, who naïvely showed their fear of long sea-crossings (right up to the Roman epoch), appeared ridiculous to their neighbours. How could people not respond to the invitation of an element which you could observe to be so calm in those broad sheltered gulfs, and which was strewn, even in the main sea, with strings of islands which the extreme clarity of the air made seem still nearer than they really were? In favourable weather a sailing-boat could go from the Piraeus to Smyrna or to Rhodes without ever losing sight of land, putting in every evening as was the custom in primitive coasting-trade. And in these indented coasts numerous sheltered bays opened out, usually protected from the north wind which blows almost constantly during the good season.

The variety of disposition of such harbours responded to the successive needs of Greek navigation. A striking example is the peninsula of Acte near Athens, with its four ports, from the open roadstead of Phalerum where the Greek sailors used to draw up their ships upon the sandy beach even until the beginning of the fifth century, to the Piraeus where ships of deep draught can today discharge their cargoes at the quay.

The sea which washes these shores is subject to a meteorological system which presents some remarkable characteristics. During the summer the heat of Libya and the high plateaux of Asia Minor cause a flow of air to those regions that takes the form of steady north and north-east winds, well known to the Ancients by the name of Etesian winds, and to the modern Greeks, who have retained for them their Turkish name 'Meltem'. In winter, on the other hand, the weather-chart is complicated, and there are frequent and sudden changes. Hence no regular transit is possible for sailing-ships in winter, a season when in fact navigation has always been reduced to a minimum in the Aegean, up to the nineteenth century. In summer, on the contrary, the constancy of the winds has particularly facilitated commercial traffic in which, from the fourth century to our own times, financiers have not hesitated to invest considerable capital. Moreover, the indented and mountainous coasts and the irregularities of the climate have multiplied local winds – sea-breezes and land-breezes – of which the inhabitants have learned to take advantage in each district of the Mediterranean, but which spring disagreeable surprises on those who are ignorant of them. These local winds have played a certain part in the annals of Greek naval exploits; the morning wind that the Athenian Themistocles could foresee, but which was unknown to the Phoenician and Carian sailors of the Great King, contributed to the triumph of the Grecian fleet at Salamis.

The lands which border on the Aegean Sea, like most of the Mediterranean region, are of relatively recent formation and their relief has not yet been much worn down by erosion. The structure is very complicated, and only their geology reveals the existence of a continuous mountain chain, a prolongation of the Dinaric Alps, whose general direction is from north-west to south-east, but which undergoes a considerable divergence towards the east in the neighbourhood of the Aegean, where certain islands (Crete in particular) indicate its new orientation, which in Asia Minor turns definitely north-eastwards. This west-east direction has played a great part historically by providing a series of barriers which have often protected Greece against invaders from the north, and have made it easier to maintain her independence: the Geranian mountains of the isthmus of Corinth, which were the last hope of the Peloponnesian states during the Persian wars; the line of Cithaeron and Parnes, the rampart of Attica; Oeta with Thermopylae; Othrys; Olympus and the Cambunian mountains where the Greeks thought to stop Xerxes in 479; finally the ranges of Upper Macedonia with the help of which the Salonica front was established during the first world war.

On the other hand the complicated relief of continental Greece, unequalled in any other region of Europe, has had a most unfortunate effect on its history. On a land thus segmented, the Greek nation has been parcelled into a dust of little peoples, all jealous of their independence, which was usually easily defended, and of their autonomy, which made them incapable of accepting not only a common domination but even the notion of any extensive federalism. All attempts at union, provoked by some pressing danger, have been precarious and often too late. The tormented surface of Greece has in all ages made hard the development of a road system, which is the thing that gives any unified nation its framework. It was by sea that essential communications were maintained, and only poor roads led to the inland towns. Even the Romans did little to modify this state of affairs; the only road they built in the Balkan peninsula, the Via Egnatia, a military and administrative road, does not cross Greece proper. Even today it is hard to say that the position has entirely changed; where the railway has failed to penetrate, often only rough tracks link villages and even towns. From this point of view there is a great difference from Asia Minor where broad valleys, followed by royal roads in the time of the Achaemenids, and later by Roman roads, assure easy communications between the coast and the towns of the interior.

The rare plains that are met with in this mountainous country, which the orientation of the mountain ranges generally leaves with an opening to the sea towards the south or east, have usually acquired great political importance. In the smallest of them there was soon developed a close unity around a central town – Argos, Sparta, Athens, and later Thebes – cities which all played a considerable part in Greek destinies. In the largest of them the vaster idea of Hellenic unity was elaborated; almost realised at the beginning of the fourth century by a Thessalian chieftain, Jason of Pherae; actually realised for a few years by Philip of Macedon and his son Alexander.

The soil of Greece in general is rather poor. The foreigner coming from the West is struck by the bare aspect of the limestone mountains, worn by atmospheric agencies and growing little but tufts of thorny shrubs. Even in the valleys the layer of humus is a thin one. Patient toil alone has succeeded in maintaining the meagre fields on the slopes, by the walled terraces which give the Cyclades to this day so unusual an appearance. Only by careful irrigation can the agricultural prosperity of the plains be assured. Landed property was parcelled out in the classical period, and boundaries scrupulously marked, as was necessary on an infertile soil which demanded such great efforts. In those parts where

serfdom did not intervene to falsify the situation, a rural element constituted the solid basis of the population – a class strongly attached to tradition, inimical to war (which devastates the land or at best takes away the
labourer from his field), and opponents of the merchants and the town
artisans. In the fifth century, at Athens, Aristophanes puts on the stage
this class of small landed proprietors, hostile to changes and friends of
peace. Only Thessaly, a more fertile region, saw the development of a
system of large estates, which reappeared in more recent times and which
has been the root cause of certain social discontents and agitations.

A land of extensive properties, Thessaly is also one of the rare regions
of Greece where stock-raising on the grand scale evolved. Its horses were
famous and its cavalry played an important military part. In the remainder
of Greece, apart from Epirus, the soil was devoted to agriculture. By
dint of great pains the olive flourished there, frequently under the protection of severe laws, as did the vine which no doubt the Greeks made
known along the shores of the Western Mediterranean, and the fig-tree.
Some of the plains grew wheat, but when these were in the neighbourhood
of large urban centres, the corn harvest was often insufficient to feed the
whole population – in the classical period, at any rate. And so the great
cities had, from an early period, to have a corn-policy which sometimes
determined their expansion and their history. It was in order to have
enough wheat that many towns made such sacrifices on behalf of their
Black Sea colonies, that Athens so carefully maintained her alliances in
the Crimea, and attached such importance to control of the Straits, where
her fortune was several times at stake.

Timber was also needed. It may be asked if the shores of the Aegean
have been poor in forests ever since the days of antiquity. In recent times
improvidence has caused deplorable effects in this matter. Even now,
after all the efforts made in the reign of George I, forests fill no more than
9·3% of the country's area. (In Italy, 15·7%.) But from classical times,
herds of goats and the charcoal-burners have carried on their ravages;
brushwood invaded the slopes; in Attica alone the number of place-names
that include the notion of bush is symptomatic of this process. Thus the
cities, which needed timber for their private and public buildings and for
their fleets, were obliged to have it brought from the northern regions of the
Aegean, from Chalcidice, Thrace, the Troad, Mysia, or from the Black Sea.

Poor in arable land, in meadows, in forests, the countries which border
the Aegean possess useful or precious minerals in abundance. The excellent clay which is found in so many places in continental Greece, in the
isles and along the Asiatic coast, has since the days of the Minoan civilisation favoured a great development of pottery, remarkable both for the
size of some of the pieces produced and for the beauty of their decoration.
In the Greek epoch in certain centres there grew up a flourishing ceramics
industry, essential in a country which exported oil and wine, and real

artistry was shown in its products, which master-potters were proud to sign. The most lovely kinds of marble are to be found in the crystalline formation which extends from Attica to the Ionian coast. This magnificent material, harder than ordinary limestone, but easier to work than granite, has from a very early period appealed to architects, who in the classical period preferred it to the finest limestones or the most compact tufas. It allowed Greek sculptors, as did Carrara marble those of Florence, to display a care for truth and a passion for perfection which have never been surpassed. The extraction of clay or marble from quarries open to the sky has never presented any great difficulties. On the other hand the numerous metalliferous deposits of the eastern Mediterranean lands have not been intensively exploited either in antiquity or our own days for lack of timber and owing to the difficulty of getting a sufficient supply of pit-props for the mine galleries. Only a certain number of valuable metals, whose value justifies a very high cost of production, have given rise to thriving industries – copper in Cyprus, silver in Thrace and Attica.

In these regions of comparatively recent geological origin the soil is still unstable. Earthquakes are frequent. The present condition of the ruins of Delphi shows their violence, and it is not certain that the miracle which saved the sanctuary of Apollo from the Gauls in 278 was not an opportune seismic movement. In Asia Minor some towns, destroyed by great catastrophes in the Roman epoch, were a source of anxiety to the imperial government. These phenomena had their influence on Greek scientific and mythological ideas. A soil so unsure owed its mobility, they thought, to the sea which surrounded it and on which it floated. Poseidon, god of the restless waves, was also he who carried (γαιήοχος) and who shook (ἐννοσίγαιος) the earth, and who shattered the mountains with a stroke of his trident. The volcanoes, however, to which certain islands of the Cyclades owe their actual configuration, were all extinct by the historical period, except those of Methana and Santorin; while that of Lemnos, whose eruptions the Latin poets of the decadence describe so gravely, was merely a peat-bog. Hephaestus was the god of fire long before he became god of volcanic phenomena, about which the Greeks acquired their knowledge in the western Mediterranean.

The climate of the Aegean area is remarkable for its dryness – not that the rainfall is insignificant, but the actual precipitations of rain are violent, infrequent, and only in the winter months. This being so most of the rain drains off and disappears without being absorbed by the land. Hence the torrents, with a furious flow during a few hours each year and dry the rest of the time; hence the small number of true rivers in Greece proper and even in Asia Minor, and the lowness of their normal levels which makes them unfit for navigation; hence the importance of springs, welcome to the labourer as to the thirsty traveller, indispensable to the very existence of cities, and protected by heavy penalties against any befoulment. A town without fountains, said the Greeks, does not deserve to be called a city; and the ban on cutting off the water supply of a besieged town was for the Greeks an elementary principle of the law of nations. The art of irrigation was known in Homer's time; and on the outskirts of Athens the tiniest trickles of water were collected with as much care as on a Spanish *huerta*. Today, after a century of civilised government, this countryside probably looks little different to what it did in the fifth century.

This dry climate is also a hot one. In summer almost all continental Greece, part of the Cyclades, and the Asiatic coast, like Sicily and central Spain, have to endure African temperatures; and the average for July exceeds 26° (C) or 79° (F). A blazing sun suspends all economic and social activities for some hours each day. Fortunately the sea is almost always near at hand, and thanks to the Etesian winds or to local and daily breezes the heat rarely becomes overpowering. Even nowadays the Greeks from Egypt come to Phalerum or the Cyclades to find the cool hours that the heavy summer weather of the Delta denies them. In winter, on the other hand, if the average temperature is fairly high, there are some hard days. An Athenian winter rarely goes by without frosts or even some brief snowfalls. The doctors of antiquity had already realised that a climate where cold and heat thus alternated was favourable to the growth of an active and vigorous race. The beneficent effects of sunlight and sea-winds have prevented the spreading of endemic diseases. The Greece of antiquity never knew epidemics comparable to those which ravaged western Europe from Roman times to the eighteenth century. The deadly effects of the plague of 430 B.C., a localised outbreak from which important districts including the Peloponnese were able to protect themselves, were due to a momentary and abnormal over-population created during the hot season at Athens by the invasion of Attica by the Peloponnesian armies. Even malaria, the scourge of the Mediterranean shores, was not rampant in Greece or around the Aegean Sea except at the mouths of the rivers Achelous, Axios (Vardar), Maeander, and in the neighbourhood of a few marshes.

In such a country, where hours of cold and rain are few, and interrupt but briefly the series of radiant days, tempered as these often are in summer by north winds or sea-breezes, the population is tempted forth and kept out of doors by the pleasant open-air life. Hence we notice in ancient Greece the modest size of private dwellings compared with the splendour of its public buildings, on which all the efforts of architects and sculptors were concentrated and which themselves were adapted to a rainless climate. There are porticos around the open squares or surrounding the sombre room in which were enclosed the gods and their treasures, and

GREECE & ASIA MINOR

Miles

0   50   100

1 : 3,750,000

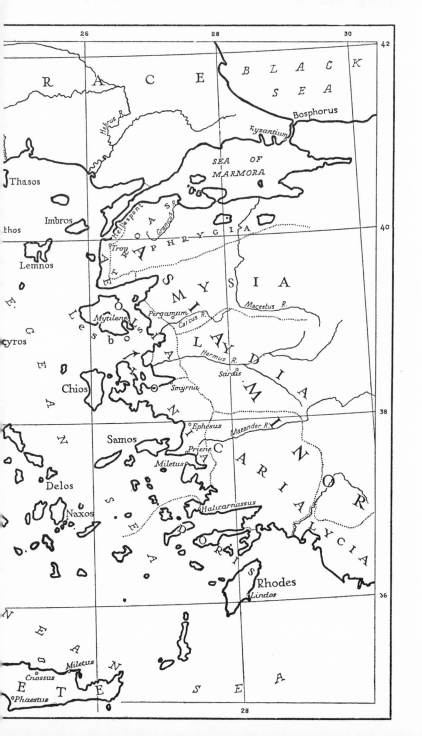

the theatres are open to the sky with magnificent landscapes to serve as backcloths. This life in the street and market-place developed in Greece, as it did in all Mediterranean Europe, a profound feeling of equality which, even if it was not everywhere written into the law, was almost always reflected in manners and customs. A social hierarchy cannot always easily resist the ceaseless mingling of the various classes; and still today the Greek peasant uses the familiar second person to whomever he may be talking; and in some Greek cities this idea of equality acted in support of the most radically democratic institutions that mankind up to the present day has anywhere developed.

Geography does not explain the whole of history. In the same country different peoples may manifest divers qualities. The Turks, planted for five centuries on the coasts of the eastern Mediterranean, have never availed themselves of the facilities it offers for sea-borne commerce; the mountain barriers which the Balkan peninsula opposes to invasion from the north have not saved Greece from being overrun frequently; today, in spite of its marble and clay, it has not produced any original art. But the two races which in ancient times succeeded one another on the Aegean shores were well enough endowed to bring to fruition the possibilities offered by the climate, sea, and soil. The Minoans, from the second millennium, were the great sailors of the eastern Mediterranean, and reached a high degree of economic organisation in which there sprang up delightful art-forms. Following them the Greeks were for five centuries the masters of the maritime trade of the ancient world. Their country saw the birth of free and rival cities in which the least citizen had his rights protected by law. Their religious beliefs and their political organisation, and the open-air festivals these involved, led to the finest flowering of art and literature that the ancient world ever knew.

II

THE AEGEAN CIVILISATION

The Greek-speaking peoples were not the first to occupy the regions where later Greek civilisation was to develop: the southern part of the Balkan peninsula, the islands of the Aegean Sea, and the western coasts of Asia Minor were inhabited long before the arrival of the Greeks. These earlier inhabitants have left traces of their activities, which are too variable in nature, characteristics, and importance for it to be affirmed that this pre-Hellenic population was a homogeneous one. On the contrary it seems probable that it was already made up of elements that differed from one another both in their origins and their level of civilisation. While remarkably little is known of Old Stone Age settlements in these regions, the excavations of the last half century have discovered settlements of the New Stone Age at different points in continental Greece and on the Asiatic coast. From the third millennium before our era, some agricultural areas, such as Boeotia and especially Thessaly, were quite thickly populated; but by people living a humble existence, at first in miserable round or oval huts, and then in small rectangular houses. These folk made by hand, with a rather roughly prepared clay, pottery whose decoration, painted or incised, remained rudimentary. They built neither palaces nor cities but only small townships, sometimes defended by a poor wall of stones and earth, and had a somewhat primitive agriculture which was aware of wheat and the fig-tree but still without knowledge of the vine or olive.

The same, however, was not true of the Aegean isles, and certainly not of Crete where a brilliant civilisation flourished for fifteen hundred years. There can be no question here of attempting to write its history; how can history be composed when the facts are unknown, or the facts be ascertained when the only 'documents' available are walls, paintings, vases, and some brief only partly deciphered texts? The ceramic discoveries made in Crete have been systematised in chronological divisions; but though these are useful for the classification and display of such finds, they are naturally arbitrary, and there is no reason why they should correspond with definite events. Into what errors should we not fall if we had to reconstitute the political and military history of Britain from the study of British furniture?

Some precious landmarks are, however, supplied by objects of Egyptian origin which have been found in excavations in Crete and can be precisely dated, and by some Cretan vases found in Egypt, in tombs which can be dated with certainty. They show that a first period of Minoan civilisation ('Early Minoan') began in the third millennium; that the brilliant 'Middle Minoan' period which is the highest point of that civilisation, at least from the point of view of its art, and probably politically too, corresponds to the first half of the second millennium; while finally 'Late Minoan', a period of artistic maturity, is to be put approximately between 1500 and 1100. The presence in the deposits of that epoch and later of numerous brachycephalic skulls replacing in ever larger numbers the dolichocephalic earlier type, is testimony of the arrival of a new race of men which it is tempting to identify with the Greek tribes leaving the continent to colonise the Aegean islands.

On the other hand, thanks to the abundance of archaeological discoveries made in the last sixty years and to the care with which they have been classified it is easier to study the Minoan as well as the Mycenaean civilisation, whose centre certainly appears to have been Crete, from where it spread outwards into the islands and along the shores of the Aegean Sea. The basis for the Minoan civilisation appears to have been a very strong economic position. The temperate and relatively humid climate of Crete favoured its agricultural development; in the Roman period the island was a veritable granary, and in our own day in spite of two centuries of relative neglect, the plain of Messara is strikingly verdant. During these early periods of civilisation corn, the vine, and the olive were grown, as is proved by the cellars of the palaces of Knossos, Phaistos, and Gournia. A vase found at Ayia Triada, which has become famous as 'the harvesters vase', shows the labourers of a great farming estate, returning in procession from their work, no doubt singing a hymn in honour of the agrarian gods, and carrying on their shoulders forks very like those still used by the peasants of the island in winnowing.

Industry, too, flourished. The beautiful products of Cretan potters found their way to Egypt and Italy. A local industry worked the copper brought in ingots from Cyprus, and learnt during the Middle Minoan period to change it into bronze by an admixture of tin. It was perhaps colonists from Crete who established themselves in the Cyclades, until then empty or sparsely populated, to exploit their natural resources – especially the quarries of obsidian on Melos. An active commerce was the result and the complement of this industrial development. Cretan ships, under the spur of trade and adventure, scoured the Aegean in all directions. Their long boats did not restrict their activities to carrying the products of the great island to neighbouring shores; it was the Cretan fleet and not that of the Phoenicians which in 1482 in the reign of Thutmose III carried the timbers of Lebanon to Egypt. At the same time it assured to the Cretans that command of the sea, that 'thalassocracy', of which Greek historians of the classical period have preserved the memory: Herodotus and Thucydides agree that King Minos was the first to possess a naval force in the eastern Mediterranean.

Their social and political organisation appears to have been quite advanced. The existence of several systems of writing, one recently deciphered, bears witness to a state of affairs in which orders could be readily transmitted, and financial and commercial transactions were easy and common. At several points in the island the ruins of actual towns have been discovered with agglomerations of houses, and with streets narrow but well-paved and carefully drained. Their aspect could not have been very different from that of the little towns with white square houses which to this day give their special character to the appearance of the Cyclades. On the other hand, it cannot be doubted that the great palaces of Knossos and Phaistos, the villa of Ayia Triada and so forth, were the habitations of powerful lords whose extensive lands made them self-sufficient, like the typical Roman villa, and included agricultural and industrial buildings – barns, mills, oil-presses, pottery-kilns, and studios for sculpture.

It is not easy to tell whether these dwelling-places, which are practically contemporary with one another, belonged to the same master, and whether there really existed a sovereign, or a dynasty of sovereigns, named Minos who united the island under one rule, and in addition was master of the Aegean and imposed tribute as far as distant Attica. Possibly Crete may have been divided into several principalities living in accord with one another; the legend of Minos may well have been the creation of myth-makers, a story supported principally by the existence at various points around the Mediterranean of trading posts which in historical times bore the name Minos. In any case, and in spite of the armouries and guard-rooms that have been found at Knossos and Phaistos, the absence of a surrounding wall points to a peaceful state of affairs, at least during the most brilliant period of Cretan civilisation, i.e. from about 1700 to 1400. No doubt Crete was not then torn by the dissensions between city and city which made its history during the Hellenic period so deplorable; and at the same time its insular situation and marine supremacy gave it security. During several centuries Crete enjoyed, and for much the same reasons, an existence as privileged as that of England from 1689 to modern times: no revolutions, no invasions, a rich agricultural and industrial development. Neighbouring nations knew it had to be reckoned with and respected its independence; and though on the tombs of certain great personages of the eighteenth Egyptian dynasty (fifteenth century) ambassadors are represented from the land of the Keftiu – that is to say from Crete – bringing Minoan vases, these must be regarded as gifts between allies rather than as tribute from a vassal state.

In such favourable conditions manners and customs were easy and joyful. Life was pleasant in these palaces, these villas with shady rooms and sunny porticos opening on delightful landscapes. These princely habitations were also equipped with modern conveniences, bath rooms and water closets with piped water. Various entertainments, boxing contests, bull-fights, wrestling matches took place in a great arena which was lined with tiers of seats and had room for large audiences. There was considerable luxury too, if not in the dress of the men which consisted simply of a loin-cloth, at least in that of the women. Frescoes, statuettes, and engraved stones show very low-cut corsages, jackets very tight at the waist, flounced dresses, aprons, complicated and coquettish hair-styles – in short a modern wardrobe, modern both in style and in the importance of sewing and 'dress-making'. In this it was very different from the true Hellenic costume where the almost exclusive use of the brooch (*fibula*) was to impose a simplicity of line.

The abundance of monuments representing women seems to indicate that they had a considerable part in social life and enjoyed a great deal of freedom – a plausible hypothesis so long as we do not give it too much precision and importance by talking, when there is no textual support for it, of a matriarchal organisation of Minoan society. All this agrees with what little we know of their religion and the part played in it by a goddess in multiple forms. Numerous archaeological discoveries have given us information about Minoan religion, or at least its external forms. The Minoans seem not to have built temples for their gods. There were only open air sanctuaries, sacred groves and caves; and in the palaces, tiny chapels, one might almost call them oratories, where the sacred objects of their cult were kept. These include no large statues, but only little statuettes, of which many may have been merely votive offerings representing the worshipper rather than the god. Their religious rites certainly included blood-sacrifices in which animals – bulls and horses – were consecrated, bound, and sacrificed, and their blood collected in vessels, while the playing of clarinets and lyres accompanied the ceremony. Dances – symbolic performances in which snake-charmers or persons pulling up (or planting?) sacred trees appeared – perhaps also the bull-fights, all made part of Minoan ritual.

Behind these exterior forms of their cult we should like to be able to perceive the real nature of their religion and how they thought about their gods. But such documents as we possess, in the absence of any decipherable text, excite rather than satisfy our curiosity. Their interpretation is uncertain, and we still do not know whether the scene represented on the famous sarcophagus at Ayia Triada is to be interpreted as an agrarian rite or an offering to a dead hero. Similarly the hypotheses that have been put forward about the sacred nature of the pillar (or shield) so often depicted on incised stones or mural paintings, or of trees, cannot be confirmed. At most we can offer a few likely theories, based both on Cretan documents and on survivals that have been preserved in the myths of the Greek period.

The bull certainly played a great part in Cretan religion; its horns figure frequently in paintings and have been found in several chapels. A divine animal, it was also a god, the god out of whom the Greeks later on perhaps evolved the wise King Minos, and certainly the bull-headed monster, the legendary Minotaur, and again the 'Cretan' Zeus who so often takes the form of a bull. The double axe, which is sometimes depicted, recalls that brandished by the God of Thunder who was worshipped by the primitive peoples of Asia Minor. His Cretan name 'Labrys' followed by a typically Aegean suffix gave its name to the Lab(r)yrinth, the house of the double axe, without doubt the palace of the Minoan lords and perhaps the very one which has been unearthed at Knossos, where indeed the double axe figures abundantly. Representations of the god in human form are rare. More frequent are those of a goddess living on the high places, a tamer of wild animals. Her aspects are numerous and contradictory; and no one can be sure whether she is a goddess of fecundity recalling the *Magna Dea* of the religions of Asia Minor, or a 'gentle virgin', Britomartis, the forerunner of the Greek Artemis.

Nor is it easy to know exactly what the Minoans thought about death. Corpses were usually buried, not burnt, in graves, tombs, or sarcophagi. It seems, too, that the practice of a 'second funeral', which is still found in several parts of Greece today, was very widespread. The funeral furnishings found in the tombs and scenes which seem to show offerings being made to the dead make it almost certain that the Cretans believed existence to be prolonged, at least for a certain time, after death.

When it comes to appreciating the talent of Minoan artists, however, and the technical skill of their engineers and workmen, we need have no recourse to such interpretations and often very dubious guesswork. The artifacts are there, in what is so often a surprisingly good state of preservation. Palaces are there, with their plans clearly to be traced and their ruins which justify plausible and sometimes accurate reconstructions of their missing elements. There are mural paintings, bas-reliefs in stone or earthenware, statuettes, vases, weapons, and jewellery. As architects the Minoans were great builders and their constructions often cover considerable areas. The palace of Knossos has sides over a hundred yards long. The architects faced all sorts of complications, knew how to build storeys one above another with windows and balconies, and ingenious porticos squared off so as to allow a room to have two favourable or picturesque outlooks at the same time. But the rather over-ambitious terms used by archaeologists should not make us forget that this large-scale architecture is lacking in grandeur. As the walls were built of inferior materials, and the columns were of wood, their buildings had to be of only modest height and breadth, especially as the Minoans seem not to have known, or to have made little use of the principle of the roof-truss and the roof with double slope. At Knossos, the hall of the double axes which seems to have been a place for ostentation and splendour, had a span of only twenty-four feet between its walls; and the throne-room measured only thirteen by nineteen feet. Made up as it was of cubic constructions set side by side, the Minoan palace could be indefinitely extended, but in a somewhat shapeless manner and without any organic plan.

The Minoan decorators have given archaeologists a charming surprise. No one could have expected to find in such early civilisation so much flexibility, life, and grace. In addition to a most advanced technique which enabled them to make very large and complicated pieces of pottery, and to obtain a tolerably wide range of colours – among others that fine black glaze of which the Greek potters later rediscovered the secret – it must be realised that Minoan artists had two essential virtues: a very accurate eye and perfect freedom of hand. There is nothing stereotyped or conventional about their work except in the latest period, already somewhat debased and probably under Egyptian influence in what is known as the 'palace style', because the pottery seemed to take its inspiration from the highly stylised decoration which they found in the most recent palace at Knossos. Until then the painter or modeller trusted only to his practised eye, which caught to perfection contours and movements, and to his sure hand which reproduced them with subtlety.

Valuable as are these qualities in floral design they are even more so in depicting animal forms. The Minoan painters, potters, and jewellers were animal-painters of the first order: galloping bulls, furious ibexes, cats about to pounce, and all manner of sea-beasts well-known to these islanders – dolphins, flying-fish, octopuses – were all rendered with a fluent and spontaneous outline that has been compared to that of the prehistoric cave-paintings of France and Spain. But the talent of Minoan artists goes no further than this. They lacked a feeling for perfection and for determined effort, and certainly failed when faced with the difficulties of representing the human form. In depicting robed women, the interest of the costume, which painters, modellers, and engravers all took pleasure in showing to be sumptuous or coquettish, could disguise serious mistakes: but not when it was a matter of naked or half-naked men. If the gesture is often well and amusingly caught, the drawing is arbitrary and the anatomy sketchy. When we regret that Minoan art should have disappeared completely we sometimes forget that the Cretan artists, in spite of their happy skills in perception and execution, were not capable of that detailed observation and patient progress which enabled their Greek successors to recreate with unequalled mastery the splendour of the human form.

The study of linguistics confirms these archaeological discoveries. It tells us that many Greek words are derived from roots which are neither Indo-European nor Semitic, and which must be regarded as borrowings from a forgotten language, most likely spoken by the inhabitants of certain regions where the Greeks afterwards established themselves. It was these people who taught the Greeks to name both the sea (θάλαττα) and such products of the Aegean coastal lands as the vine, the olive, the fig-tree, cypress, rose, and lily; and also some manufactured articles, for example bath (ἀσάμινθος). (A bath has been unearthed in the palace at Knossos.) The Greeks also borrowed from their predecessors many place-names: those ending in -σσος (-ττος) and -νθος, or -νδος are found over a considerable area which presumably corresponds with that inhabited by peoples belonging to the earlier civilisation. They are to be found in Attica, for example, in the Peloponnese, in the Cyclades, in Crete naturally, at Rhodes, in the south-west of Asia Minor where they are particularly numerous, and as far away as Cyprus. This island, rich in copper, must have been from the second millennium onwards a secondary centre of industry and commerce where Cretan, Egyptian, and Semitic influences intermingled. Ever since that period Cypriot products showed the complex character that they were to retain throughout Greek history. It would be risky to go further and affirm an identity of race between all the primitive inhabitants of continental Greece and the 'Aegeans'. A theory linking the 'Aegeans' with all primitive peoples around the Mediterranean – Iberians, Ligurians, Libyans – is one of those which, in the present state of our knowledge, it is as difficult to prove as to demolish.

The Greeks preserved only a faint memory of the peoples who preceded them in the regions where they finally established themselves. Their historians knew that before the arrival of the Greek tribes, different parts of continental Greece, of the Cyclades and the coast of Asia Minor had been inhabited by Pelasgians, Leleges, and Carians. But from what they wrote only one certainty emerges, that the Greeks had a notion, founded on some obscure tradition or on archaeological discoveries such as Thucydides (1.8.1) tells us were made on the island of Delos, that they were not the first occupants of their country. From such belated testimony information more precise than that cannot safely be drawn. If we maintain that the first inhabitants of Greece were really called Pelasgians, and that we must call the people Pelasgians who built the Cretan palaces and spoke the language with words in -σσος or -νθος, we are forgetting that the evidence of Greek authors about this distant past is based on far-fetched conjectures whose arbitrary elements we can at times detect. The Greeks originally employed the term 'Pelasgian' to indicate, not on the basis of their ethnic characteristics but merely of the districts in which they lived, certain peoples that cannot now be declared either to have been or not to have been of Greek race.

If we must thus give up any idea of learning the name of those who occupied the shores and islands of the Aegean before the coming of the Greeks, we can at least affirm that their successors owed them a great deal. The Greeks had little previous acquaintance with the sea, and it was the Aegeans who taught them the art of navigation. It was they who showed them how to cultivate the vine, olive, and fig-tree which were to play an essential part in Greek economic life. The Greeks probably found in some parts of continental Greece and the Cyclades, and certainly in Crete, forms of organisation superior to those under which they themselves had lived before arriving in these regions; for example, wide territories obeying a stable centralised government, rulers established in rich palaces, cities where law and order were maintained, and commercial and administrative relations facilitated by the use of writing.

In religion their borrowings are less clear, but it is at least likely that many features of the Greek gods, even those whose character is most indisputably Hellenic such as Zeus, are to be explained by their Cretan origin, and that Hellenic ritual was influenced by that of the Aegean peoples. As to art, we shall see that the Mycenaean nobles who settled in central Greece and the Peloponnese employed Cretan decorators. But this reflection from Minoan art was extinguished towards the end of the second millennium. In the drab conditions in which Greece lived from about that time these delightful examples and clever techniques were forgotten; and when, after a long period of obscurity, Greek art began to make its first attempts we find in it no traces of the architectural principles or methods of the Cretan artists nor yet of their peculiar imagination.

III

THE GREEKS AROUND THE
AEGEAN SHORES

We have seen in the previous chapter that the shores of the Aegean were inhabited, until the second millennium, by peoples who spoke a language that had no obvious or close relationship with Greek or any other Indo-European or Semitic tongue, and who had attained a high degree of economic and social organisation, and of artistic culture. Now the earliest written documents to be found in Greece, including both the Homeric poems (which without doubt assumed towards the eighth century the form in which we now have them) and the earliest inscriptions, show us these same regions to have been inhabited for quite a long time by Greek-speaking populations with a civilisation very different from that which had reached its highest development in Crete. Hence we may conclude that it was in the course of the second millennium that the tribes from which the Greek people was constituted arrived and established themselves in the south of the Balkan peninsula, in the islands of the Aegean, and along the western coasts of Asia Minor.

The language of the newcomers was closely related to those of the western group of Indo-European peoples, in particular the Italici, the Celts, and the Germans. We cannot fix with any precision and certainty the date and circumstances of the separation of this branch from the main trunk, in spite of the excellent work done in recent research, but it is not unreasonable to suppose that the separation occurred about the beginning of the second millennium, at a time when an important group of Indo-European tribes were spread over the plains of the middle Danube. From thence the valleys of the Morava and the Vardar, which eventually join, run down to the shores of the Aegean Sea, separated by only a low ridge. This route, evidently easy – indeed it is followed today by the railway from Belgrade to Salonica – may not have been the only one. The first Greek tribes that came to settle in the north-west corner of Asia Minor could well have reached Thrace from the Dobrudja by the valleys of the Tundzha and the Maritza. The roads of the western side of the Balkan peninsula along the valleys of the Drina, the Lin, and the Drin, while they cannot be entirely excluded, can only have served as communications in favourable weather and for brief migrations. The exodus of the Serbs during the winter of 1915-16 showed the hardships which a people crossing the mountains of Albania would have to endure.

Of this primordial event in their history the Greeks, it will be realised, retained no memory. Their records certainly show them to have been aware that migrations of their tribes took place in the interior of continental Greece and from one side of the Aegean to the other, but the idea that they could have come from another continental region was quite foreign to them. It is useless to search their writings for the slightest evidence as to the causes of this migration, its duration and its character. Only linguistics and archaeology provide a basis for the hypotheses which are summarised below.

What were the economic, social, and intellectual conditions of these tribes when, separated from their parent stock, they first debouched into the Balkan Peninsula? Certainly it would be useless to try to find in them the first manifestations of the wonderful gifts which the Greeks later displayed: those qualities could only develop in the course of a prolonged evolution, and we shall see that at the end of the second millennium, at a time when the Greeks were already firmly settled in Boeotia and the Peloponnese, their civilisation was almost entirely a borrowed one, at least as far as their art goes.

Nor were all the invaders of equal standing, or destined to make the same progress. The Epirots, though apparently of Greek stock and language, seem never to have participated in Hellenic civilisation. (The Illyrians and the Thracians were of Indo-European origin, but not Greek.) The Macedonians only entered into the Greek heritage very late, and the Aetolians later still. The most that can be done is to attempt to determine the common stock of civilised notions that these tribes brought with them. They practised the growing of wheat and the raising of cattle, which already bears witness to settled habits and allows us to suppose that they had stable institutions before their migration into Greece. It is not impossible that they knew how to work in copper, and even in bronze. Ever since the beginning of the second millennium Hungary had been an important metallurgical centre, whose workshops produced objects in copper and bronze of original artistic merit. In the Near and Middle East copper had been worked for a remarkably long time.

The harsh rainy climate in which they had long lived had led them to use building methods very different from those they were going to find in the Aegean world. Their huts, like those of other inhabitants of central Europe, were covered not with flat roofs but with ridge-roofs having a double slope to shed the rain-water. They introduced the gable into Greece, where it remained common, whereas in the Cyclades the flat roof has been retained to this day. From the humble gable-end of these primitive cabins there probably developed the pediment which gives the Greek temple its unique appearance. Moreover, the new arrivals soon proved themselves to be good builders, and from the middle of the second millennium were skilled in the construction of formidable walls, as at Mycenae, at Tiryns, and at Orchomenus; and could build a whole apparatus of defence for which they certainly found no model in the Cretan palaces.

Their social organisation was based on the strongly-knit family, monogamous as far as can be ascertained. Simple though one may suppose it to have been, it may have comprised, even at this early stage, brotherhoods (φρατρίαι) whose members were united by their belief in a common ancestry, expressed in the cult of a common hero; and over these brotherhoods, the small number of tribes who together made up the nation. The fact that three tribes – the Dymaneis, the Pamphyloi, and the Hylleis – were to be found, later on, following further waves of migration, in many 'Dorian' cities, allows us to believe in a Dorian nation in which this division into three tribes existed from its arrival in Greece. As to the way in which these groupings were governed no precise explanation can be formulated. Some rudimentary kind of hierarchy among the warriors, analogous no doubt to that found among the Germanic tribes, may have led by the beginning of the second millennium to the feudal régime of which the Mycenean civilisation seems to betray some traces. On the other hand, the names for the sovereign ruler (βασιλεύς, ἄναξ) were not drawn from the Indo-European word-stock, and it is not impossible that the kingship, of which the earliest written Greek documents have preserved the memory, might have been a borrowing from the Aegean civilisation.

Different though the culture of the new arrivals may have been from that which was flourishing on the shores of the Aegean at the beginning of the second millennium, they must obviously not be thought of as a horde of savages. One essential fact shows that their civilisation cannot have been inferior to that of the average of the peoples established in Greece, in the Cyclades, and on the coasts of Asia Minor before they came: their language so completely replaced that of the previous occupants that only a very few words representing the more common substances or objects have actually survived, and there has been the greatest difficulty in recovering a few elements of these earlier languages. In marked contrast with this we have the barbarian invasions of western Europe which from the third to the sixth century of our era submerged Romanised Gaul and Italy, but failed to introduce into the languages of those countries more than a few hundred specialised terms.

These people from the north must have arrived in Greece at an early date – certainly not later than the first half of the second millennium. It is most likely that they first penetrated these regions not in the form of a single invasion, but – as happened with the barbarians in the Roman Empire – in successive waves preceded perhaps by a gradual infiltration. In fact, by historic times we find the Greek language divided into regional forms of speech of which the Ancients had already noted the existence and which their grammarians had grouped into dialects. Modern linguists, making some changes in this traditional classification, have regrouped Greek forms of speech into Arcado-Cypriot, Aeolian, Doric and Ionic Attic. Macedonian was in all probability a language closely related to Greek, but no written text in it has survived to make this clear. (Illyrian and Thracian, neither of which was known from any long texts, were certainly independent Indo-European languages. Thracian was quite closely related to Phrygian, and probably also to the pre-Roman language of Dacia.) The Greek languages, dovetailing sometimes with particular features of social organisation such as the division into tribes mentioned above (p. 21), were spoken by groups of tribes which made their appearance in Greece at successive dates. Indeed one would be wrong to assume that the invaders all spoke a uniform language which was only differentiated after their settlement in the country.

The first arrivals probably were those who spoke the dialect called Arcado-Cypriot, and who gave themselves the name Achaeans, Ἀχαιοί. They penetrated as far as the Peloponnese of which they occupied the major part. The coming of new invaders, Ionians or Dorians, forced some of them to take refuge in the mountains of Arcadia, where they maintained their hold right into historical times. Written documents of those invaders have been found at, among other places, Mycenae and Pylos ('Ano-Englianós') in the Peloponnese, and Knossos in Crete. The partial decipherment of the Mycenaean 'Linear "B"' script confirms that these people spoke Greek, but sheds little light on variations in dialect.

The Ionians certainly occupied territories in continental Greece much wider than those to which we see them reduced in historic times: the existence of an Athens and an Eleusis on the shores of Lake Copais, and an Ionian dodecapolis (federation of twelve cities) in Achaea, of which historians of the classical period retained the memory, suggest that Ionians were settled for a time in Boeotia and in the Peloponnese. Later their domain in Greece proper was restricted to Attica and Euboea. On the other hand they colonised some of the Cyclades and thence spread along the coast of Asia Minor in the region which in historical times was known as Ionia.

The Aeolians chose for their home the fertile plains of Thessaly and Boeotia, and no doubt the well-sheltered harbours of the Gulf of Pagasae and the Euboean channel served them as starting-points for journeys to Lesbos and the Aeolian coast of Asia Minor.

Last to arrive were the Dorians, by the end of the twelfth century. Their traditions recalled that they had long dwelt to the north of central

Greece in the region of which the mountainous Doris was the centre. They worked round the flanks of those districts where the Aeolians had already founded solid agricultural settlements – Thessaly and Boeotia – to spread out over central Greece, and probably crossing the Gulf of Corinth, over Achaea and the whole of the Peloponnese, where they isolated the Arcadian population in their mountains. Thence short sea-crossings took them to Melos, to Cythera, into Crete where they submerged their Arcadian precursors, to Rhodes, and even to the south-west corner of Asia Minor. Modern historians have not thrown any clearer light on the coming of the Dorians by identifying it with the return of the Heracleidae, perhaps an invention of the Greek mythographers. Neither this confused double explanation, nor the theories of the mid-nineteenth century which see in the Dorians the purest representatives of the 'Aryan' race coming to regenerate a Greece already defiled, nor yet those of today which present the Dorian invasion as a brutal catastrophe that blotted out the Achaean civilisation, have any certain foundation in the actual state of our knowledge. The Homeric epics tell us nothing of any such events; and the fact that in the historical epoch, in 508, one of the kings of Sparta proclaimed his Achaean origins confirms at least that the Dorian invasion left in existence some important traditions of Achaean civilisation.

All the regions which the newcomers occupied were already inhabited by peoples who had been able to establish lasting settlements there long before the arrival of the Greeks. The coastal towns of Asia Minor from Smyrna to Halicarnassus all have names which cannot really be explained as of Greek origin, so we may surmise that they replaced ancient townships perhaps founded by the Carians. As to Crete, we know what a magnificent civilisation had developed by the early second millennium. As can be proved from various Egyptian points of reference, Crete was still prosperous about the year 1450: but it seems that we must date only a little later the burning of the palaces at Knossos and Phaistos, as well as the Mycenaean invasion, which was followed in its turn by the Dorian invasion. It will be seen in the following chapter what relations the indigenous inhabitants were able to establish with the invaders, and the way in which the new arrivals were influenced by the Aegean civilisation.

The arrival of the Greek tribes had its repercussions throughout the Aegean basin. Egyptian texts, which after 1400 no longer mention the Keftiu (i.e. Cretans of the Minoan civilisation), begin to refer to attacks on the shores of the Delta in which certain seafaring folk took part, who from the thirteenth century on are designated by the generic term 'Peoples of the Sea'. Their names have been paralleled by those of Greek cities or peoples known from the Homeric poems or the historians of the classical period. Several of these comparisons, especially that of the Akhaiwasha = Ἀχαιοί, have had a striking confirmation from the discovery at Boghaz-

Keui of Hittite tablets of the end of the fourteenth century which mention a country of Ahhiyawa (Ἀχαιϝα) situated, it would seem, at the south-east corner of Asia Minor, whose sovereign may also have controlled Laspa (Lesbos).

All these proposed identifications between the proper names found in Hittite and Egyptian documents on the one hand and those found in Greek traditions on the other are not of equal value; but texts and linguistics agree on the essential fact that Achaean settlements were in existence in the south of Asia Minor. Their military strength and the size of their fleet made them a serious nuisance to Egypt and to the Hittite empire.

We know of another conflict in the northern regions of the Aegean Sea, where the Aeolians became masters of Lesbos. In this area there occurred, in the second half of the second millennium, one of those events whose actual importance we cannot measure, but which by a special concatenation of circumstances acquire a symbolic value so great in the course of time that oral tradition perpetuates their memory for many centuries. From the third millennium there existed, at the north-west corner of Asia Minor, a town situated near the mouth of the Hellespont. So favoured a situation was bound to be much coveted, and in fact excavations have discovered under the mound of Hissarlik the superimposed ruins of several successive towns dating from the third and second millennia. The most brilliant was the second, which saw the flowering of a civilisation whose architecture, luxury, and various other characteristics remind us of that which developed from 1400 onwards in Argolis (cf. Chapter IV). This 'Troy II' disappeared in a great fire at some time in the third millennium. However, it was not the Homeric Ilium whose still later ruins, on the hillock of Hissarlik, are by no means so magnificent as the city the poet describes. This is no reason, however, for doubting the reality of the victorious siege which, about 1200 at the latest, was one of the most noteworthy episodes of the conquest of this coast by the Greeks, perhaps by the Aeolians. This success may have won them passage through the straits and access to the rich and mysterious regions of the north. We can understand how the capture of Troy became the type-event of the period during which the Greeks were taking possession of the Asian coast. And because it gives us this story, transmogrified as it may be, the Greek epic has a genuine historical value, for it is the earliest written document of Hellenic origin in which we can discover any recollection of this period of conquests.

IV

THE MYCENAEAN CIVILISATION.
MONARCHY, ARISTOCRACY, THE CITY

The Greek tribes, in establishing themselves in Greece, seem to have shared out the newly-conquered territory among the different families of which they were composed.

In several regions of Greece, in Attica in particular, a great number of villages (κῶμαι), which later became administrative districts (parishes, δῆμοι), had collective names in the plural (Φιλαίδαι, Βουτάδαι, etc.) which seem to indicate that originally they were the homes of family groups. This sharing out of the land was evidently complicated by the fact that the Greeks were not settling in an uninhabited country.

They found there peoples who had in certain regions, Crete for example, reached a high degree of civilisation.

We should like to have some idea about the relations that grew up between the newcomers and the earlier inhabitants of the land. In the classical period we find serfs in certain parts of Greece: Helots in Laconia, Penestae in Thessaly, perhaps Hektemoroi in Attica. It is tempting to consider them as descendants of the primitive inhabitants, enslaved by the invading Greeks, but this tempting hypothesis is unfortunately quite unproven. No text speaks of any differences of race, language, or religion between Helots and Lacedaemonians, between Penestae and Thessalians. The Penestae and Helots are no more the descendants of the first inhabitants of Greece, than the twelfth-century serfs in France were descendants of Gallo-Romans enslaved by the Burgundians and Franks. It is probable that after a brutal invasion conventional relations were established between the two races which paved the way for their eventual fusion. Some mythological stories perhaps reflect these events: on Olympus, the marriage of Zeus, the chief celestial deity and Indo-European by his name and nature (cf. Chapter VII) with Hera, the goddess worshipped by the original peoples of the Peloponnese, at first rebellious but finally tamed by her husband, mirrors the period when the northern conquerors wedded the daughters of the great native families, just as in the fifth century of our era the barbarian chieftains allied themselves in Gaul as in Italy with the great patrician families.

A complex civilisation was born of the contact between these two races. In continental Greece the new arrivals established themselves as powerful overlords, and built, in Boeotia (at Gla and at Orchomenus), in Attica, and especially in Argolis (at Tiryns and at Mycenae) fortresses in which an original architectural style is joined with a type of decoration clearly borrowed from the Aegean civilisation. The formidable walls, thirty-three feet thick in places at Tiryns, and sixteen at Gla, are provided with casemates, and bear witness to a state of affairs much less peaceful than existed in Crete at the height of the Minoan civilisation, and at the same time show a highly developed art of fortification. Whereas in the tombs at Mycenae and Orchomenus, which popular tradition had associated from remote antiquity with memories of Atreus and Minyas, the 'cupola' built of circular courses overhanging one another seems to be an application of a process imported from Crete. The isolated buildings which are to be met with in the precincts of Tiryns and Mycenae, covered with a double-sloping roof and having a façade divided into three by two columns corresponding to two rows of columns in the interior, are undoubtedly the development of an architectural type brought from the north, whence was eventually to be derived the great hall, the *megaron* described in the Homeric epics, and still later the Greek temple.

While they were undoubtedly originators in architecture, the Mycenaeans showed, on the other hand, almost complete lack of expertise in the plastic arts. The stelai of the Acropolis at Mycenae are of rough and awkward fashioning. And the overlords of these castles were glad to turn for their furniture and paintings to the island decorators who had preserved the tradition of Aegean art. The beautiful vases with floral and animal designs that have been unearthed not only in Argolis and Boeotia but in several spots in the Peloponnese and central Greece derived inspiration from Crete. And it was artists from Crete who adorned the castle of Tiryns with frescoes similar to those of Knossos and Phaistos.

Ruins, pottery, painting, jewellery – all the remains of the Mycenaean civilisation provide evidence of a warlike régime, which might perhaps be described as feudal. The lords' castles commanded plains or well-frequented roads, as at Mycenae. At the foot of their walls, in modest townships, lived farmers and artisans, mostly no doubt the ancient occupants of the land who must have been liable to forced labour. This is surely the only possible explanation of how those enormous walls can have been built, walls which the ancients called 'Cyclopean', since they could not persuade themselves that they were the work of men's hands. On the other hand these dependants could find shelter in the fortress, in case of invasion. The inhabitants of the castle, lords and men-at-arms, led a luxurious life in which Aegean influences were obvious. Hunting, wrestling, and bull-fighting were their favourite sports. The women wore elaborate costumes in the Cretan fashion; the men on the other hand kept to their national dress, a short-sleeved tunic, drawn in at the waist and reaching to mid-thigh – very different from the Cretan loin-cloth. Their accoutrements were derived partly from Crete: a great bronze sword, a tall semi-cylindrical shield made of wicker-work covered with leather, as well as another much older type of buckler shaped like a figure eight, now only to be seen in Mycenaean paintings and engravings of a religious character. For hunting and in war the lords made use of chariots after the fashion of the kings of Eygpt and Assyria.

Egyptian references enable us to date between 1400 and 1100 the culmination of the civilisation which has come to be called 'Mycenaean,' because it left in Argolis and particularly at Mycenae its richest remains. This date, the style of architecture and men's costume, various literary traditions, and finally the proof by the decipherment of their 'linear "B"' script that they used the Greek language, justify our conclusion that it was folk of the Greek race who built and inhabited these strongholds. Since the first Greeks who occupied the Peloponnese spoke the Arcado-Cypriot dialect, and were later driven out of most of the peninsula, or else absorbed, by other Greeks who spoke 'Doric', we quite naturally attribute to the former the splendour of this Mycenaean civilisation which was blotted out by the Dorian invasion. Since moreover the Homeric epic, which takes us back to the days when Mycenae, Tiryns, and Orchomenus were flourishing cities 'rich in gold', gave the generic name of Achaeans (Ἀχαιοί) to the inhabitants of the various regions of Greece, it was tempting to identify the Achaeans with the peoples speaking the Arcado-Cypriot dialect.

There has been talk of an 'Achaean civilisation' and even of an 'Achaean empire'. Such ideas should be accepted only with caution: the extension of the term Ἀχαιοί (in the Homeric poems) to include all the Greeks was merely, it would seem, a common literary convention, just as with the Argives (Ἀργεῖοι) and Danäi (Δαναοί). Nevertheless by the thirteenth century Mycenaean culture spread over central and southern Greece, Crete, Rhodes, and Cyprus, and it was far richer than that which followed. By that time, however, signs of internal decay were evident and the process was hastened by the invasion of the Dorians, a people who were Greek but who were culturally impoverished and unacquainted with the art of writing.

The relations between various conquerors were doubtless far from peaceful. Not only would the earliest established among the Greek peoples try to resist the intrusion of those who pushed into Greece behind them, but within the same nation wars between tribes and quarrels between families must have been frequent. In addition to other causes of conflict in a country where on the whole the soil is not very productive, the valleys and fertile plains must have been the objects of repeated struggles. Literary tradition had preserved the memory of these troubled times; combats between heroes of which the *Iliad* is full no doubt recall the inter-tribal wars, stories of which were later artificially grouped around the history of the siege of Troy (*cf.* Chapter VIII). During this warlike period the need was felt in every group for a strong military organisation and a concentration of power. Hence circumstances justified the maintenance of the authority which chieftains of the Greek tribes had held even before they penetrated into Greek territory. Entrusted during the war with command of the men capable of bearing arms, they perhaps found among the pre-Hellenic populations certain patterns on the basis of which they could extend their powers in times of peace. In various parts of the Aegean seaboard, and certainly in Crete, there perhaps existed more advanced forms of organisation in which 'kings' exercised religious and civil functions.

The Greek chieftains would be able to model their authority on that of these rulers, in the same way that they borrowed from them their titles of βασιλεύς and ἄναξ, and the luxury which prevailed in their castles, just as the Frankish chieftains took the titles of 'Consul' and 'Augustus', and set up the Merovingian monarchy after the manner of Imperial Rome.

This accounts for the composite character of the Hellenic kingship as it appears in the Homeric poems, though these give us, it is true, a belated and in many ways a distorted picture. It had divine right: the king, at first regarded as the incarnation of the tribal god, later became his descendant when more rationalistic ideas prevailed. Yet the power of this scion of the gods was none the less limited by that of the heads of tribal families, the γέροντες whom he had to summon to the Council (βουλή, γερουσία) whenever decisions that concerned the public interest had to be taken. In case of war he called up the army, directed military operations, and shared out the spoils; at all times he acted as intermediary between the gods and the rest of the community; and assisted by soothsayers and sacrificial priests he accomplished the rites by which the safety and prosperity of his subjects were assured. Finally he acted as judge in legal disputes, but the repression of crimes which would now be the function of what we call 'common law' was a matter to be regulated either by vendetta or blood-money, between the families concerned.

There were differences in the types of early Greek kingship, perhaps due to the survival of the 'tribal' type in peripheral areas in the second millennium, and to its re-introduction by the Dorian immigrants.

The kings were naturally tempted to strengthen so restricted a power and to extend their prerogatives. They seem to have found some support among those inhabitants of their territories who were excluded from the noble families of the tribe. This class, of diverse origin, no doubt included a part of the indigenous population, that which was of too low a station to intermarry with the conquerors, together with all those of doubtful or foreign extraction, bastards, banished men from other tribes, strangers coming from abroad. In this mass of no-account folk (κακοί, χέρηες), the kings hoped to find a means to resist the ambitions of the heads of families, who gave themselves such titles as the 'best' (ἄριστοι), the 'distinguished' (ἔξοχοι ἄνδρες) or 'those of good family' (Εὐπατρίδαι). The kings gathered together this population of the lesser breeds on the lands of their own private estates, and gave them guarantees against oppression whether by the nobles or by outside enemies. They also gave them an interest in public affairs by summoning them from time to time to an Assembly (ἀγορά, ἀπελλά, ἐκκλησία), in which they authorised them, if not to take an active part in the deliberations – a right of the elders or an élite – at least to demonstrate their approval or disapproval. In return the people owed them military service in time of war, and in peacetime a labour-tax besides payments in kind.

It was thanks to this statute-labour that the massive walls of the Mycenaean fortresses were built. At their bases were grouped the humble dwellings of the royal vassals; the tiny houses of which the slopes beneath the acropolis of Tiryns or Orchomenus still bear traces, convey some idea of what these villages must have been like which came into existence under the shadow of the royal citadel.

One can understand the motives which led the kings to establish these concentrations of population (συνοικισμοί) – a policy traditionally attributed to them, and with good reason, in several parts of Greece. The Greeks found models for such urban organisations among several of the peoples who were settled on the shores of the Aegean before they arrived. The fame of the 'hundred towns' of Minoan Crete was spread throughout Greece, and it was not so much their number as their very existence that must have aroused the admiration of the Greeks. It goes without saying that it was neither the purpose nor the result of these synoecisms to denude the countryside and to concentrate in one swollen township all the people of a region. Most of the great families would certainly refuse to move their place of residence, the tombs of their ancestors, and their family altars. In Attica, right up to the time of the Peloponnesian War, the largest part of the population lived in the country. But it was not the number of its inhabitants which gave its importance to the Greek city. The city was, above all, the place on which the community was centred, where their god was worshipped, where the king meted out justice, whither he summoned the Council of Nobles to the βουλή, the people to the *agora*. Its importance, and if one may so call it, its moral personality, are expressed by the name πόλις by which it is henceforth called, a term originally used only for the citadel where the king's palace and the sanctuary of the local deity stood. The *polis* was more than the amorphous conglomerations of the Euphrates or Nile valleys, more even than the town of the Latin races, which was first and foremost the military centre of the country, and of which the essential element was the rampart that surrounded and protected it. The city of the Greeks was primarily the religious and political centre of the community. It came to be the corporate manifestation of a political entity as much as a location for common defence.

The king was no more than the first among the nobles. Each of the nobles who acknowledged his authority also had his own domain, ἀγρός, which might well be as considerable as that of the king himself; and each wielded, within the often very extensive family of which he was the head, both religious and judicial powers. Together, these Eupatridae made up a material force much superior to the king's, able to outweigh and even cancel his authority. Indeed, primitive kingship carried within itself the seeds of its own destruction. First of all it seems that the sovereigns often led a sumptuous existence which impoverished their resources. Excavations at Tiryns, Mycenae, and Pylos have brought to light an ostentation in the furnishings of the royal dwellings, their jewellery, festivals, and tombs, which was quite out of proportion to the small size of the domains which might have belonged to the owners of these palaces. In the second place the king might die without leaving male descendants, and pretenders to the succession then wore themselves out in useless struggles. There was also in most cases a slow evolution which prepared the collapse of the royal power. Parts of the *Iliad* and *Odyssey* give us some idea of this intermediate period when the heads of the great families arrogated to themselves the title of βασιλεῖς, and when the son of a dead or absent king was no longer certain of succeeding his father.

Often, however, the nobles did not get rid of the kings, but only restricted their authority and their powers. In a number of towns βασιλεῖς are still met with in the classical period, and municipal tradition had not lost the memory of the days when these were recruited only from certain families, the descendants of former kings. But the power of such kings was restricted, except in some very conservative cities, and in general was limited to religious functions. Maybe there were scruples about modifying the arrangements which maintained the connection between the community and the gods, or maybe there was a feeling that the rôle of priest to which the king must henceforth confine himself was an inoffensive one. All other royal functions were exercised by magistrates who, together with the deliberative Council of Nobles and doubtless nominated by it, made up the executive authority: overseers (ἔφοροι) civil (ἄρχοντες) or military commanders (στρατηγοί, πολέμαρχοι).

We cannot fix a date when the aristocratic régime replaced the monarchy in Greece; and in any case it is most unlikely that the change took place everywhere at the same time.

It may have begun as early as the tenth or ninth century in the Ionian lands, where the population, throughout the course of Greek history, displayed a fondness for political and intellectual innovations and had less respect for tradition than elsewhere. The king is absent from the city that Hephaestus, according to Homer, portrayed on the shield of Achilles; and it was the elders who were pictured administering justice amid the people assembled on the agora and reduced as always to the rôle of noisy spectators. On the other hand the aristocratic revolution was not complete in certain islands of the Aegean until the sixth century. In Sparta, the maintenance of royal authority in an oligarchic constitution created a complex organisation which was big with future conflicts (*cf.* Chapter X). Some backward regions to the north and west of continental Greece retained their kings; in particular Macedon which, after remaining for a long period outside the area of Hellenic civilisation, became part of it in the fourth century and re-introduced the monarchic principle into it.

When the gleam of Mycenaean civilisation faded, to whose splendour archaeology bears witness, an obscure period followed about which the texts are almost silent and whose rare monuments are difficult to interpret and to date. It is, however, in the course of this epoch (which has some-what mistakenly been called the 'Hellenic Middle Ages') that the Greek nation was preparing the leap forward that it was to take from the eighth century onwards, the first manifestation of which was the colonial movement.

V

GREEK COLONISATION

One of the first results of the settlement of the Greeks in the south of the Balkan peninsula was to give this nation of landsmen a taste for and familiarity with the sea and its ways. We have seen (Chapter I) that the very structure of the regions where they had established themselves was an incitement to navigation. In addition they could take lessons in that art from the folk they found already installed, for the Aegeans at the beginning of the second millennium were the finest sailors in the eastern Mediterranean. The Phoenicians have often been credited with this initiation of the Greeks into seamanship, but against all probability. In the nautical vocabulary of the Greeks there is not one word of Semitic origin; and the long ships with their high prows, that figure on the Cretan gems and pottery, are very like the Greek ships shown on Athenian vases of the eighth century. The Semitic derivations which scholars have attributed to some Hellenic place-names, as evidence that there was some sort of Phoenician colonisation along the shores and even in the interior of Greece, cannot stand up to any serious linguistic investigation.

We have seen how the Greeks in the course of the second millennium spread themselves out over both shores of the Aegean. This movement preceded the colonial expansion and must not be confused with it. There cannot be a colony in the true sense of the word without a mother country, in this case a city. Now it is quite likely that the earliest Greek settlements in the Cyclades and along the coast of Asia preceded the foundation of the first classical cities in continental Greece. We reject the learned or nationalistic theories which have sought to attribute the foundation of Miletus, Thera, or Rhodes to Sparta or to Athens. Undoubtedly the Greeks who came to occupy the lower valley of the Maeander, for example, were closely related to those who established themselves in Attica; it is even possible that they actually came from Attica, but we cannot possibly assert on that account that Athens was founded before Miletus. Indeed it may even be questioned if urban organisation was not developed later in continental Greece than in the Cyclades or on the coast of Asia Minor, where the ancient towns of the Minoan or Carian civilisations may have served as models.

Colonisation, properly so-called, was doubtless preceded by a period of discoveries and adventures. In the north of the Aegean, coasting-trips or short sea-crossings led to the shores of Thrace, of the Propontis, and the Black Sea. To the west there must have been a very long-established coming and going between the two sides of the Strait of Otranto, for in clear weather the mountains of Epirus can be seen from the cliffs of Calabria, and Mycenaean relics have been found at the gates of Tarentum. From the beginning of the first millennium, at latest then, the Greeks had some knowledge of these distant lands; the Homeric poems, which do not mention any Hellenic city outside the Aegean basin, nevertheless show knowledge of Egypt, of the country of the Cimmerians with its long winter nights (i.e. South Russia), and of Sicily.

But colonisation in the true sense of the word had not begun so early. The very early dates which tradition has assigned to the foundation of certain cities are quite unsubstantiated. Though it seems paradoxical, the first foundation may well have been the most distant, that of Cumae by the Chalcidians about 750, on the bluff overlooking the rich Campanian plain in the west of Italy. These same Chalcidians did not occupy the straits of Messina and sites along the eastern coasts of Sicily (Naxos, Catana) until later in the second half of the eighth century, and the Corinthians founded Syracuse in 733. The Achaeans of the Peloponnese installed themselves in the south of Italy inside the Gulf of Otranto at Metapontum, Sybaris, Croton, and Tarentum itself. In the course of the seventh century all these settlements proliferated: the shores of the Gulf of Otranto, of Sicily, of the western side of Italy were covered with Greek towns; about the year 600, people coming from Ionia founded Marseilles which itself then set up trading-posts all along the Gulf of Lyons and into Spain. Colonisation also began, perhaps a little later, to the north of the Aegean in regions where the Greeks, owing to the climate and general aspect, felt themselves less at home than in Sicily or the south of Italy. Not before the beginning of the seventh century was Thasos founded by the Parians; not until 650 did the men of Chalcis occupy Chalcidice, and about the same time the sailors of Megara established themselves along both shores of the Bosphorus thus opening up for Hellenism the Black Sea along whose shores Miletus, in the course of a hundred and fifty years, founded nearly a hundred towns and trading-stations.

The causes which brought this colonial movement into existence are various. One of the most important, according to the Ancients, was lack of land (στενοχωρία). From this explanation the improbable conclusion has sometimes been drawn that the Greece of the first millennium was overpopulated. Neither tradition nor archaeological discoveries lead us to believe that Greek towns in the ninth or eighth centuries could have had a population too large for the resources of their territories. Even those which sent out most colonies were at this period only small cities with

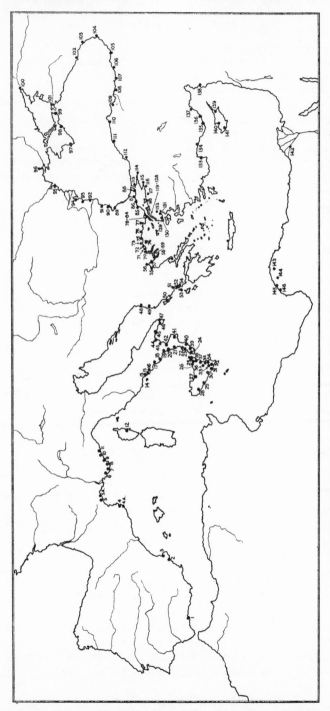

GREEK COLONISATION : only colonies founded between 800 and 500 B.C., and the earlier settlements in Cyprus, are shown.

KEY

L. = Latin   Mod. = Modern   Met. = Metropolis

Ionian Colonies
1. Maenace (Met. Massalia)
2. Alonae (Met. Massalia)
3. Hemeroscopeum (Met. Massalia)
5. Agathe (Mod. Agde, Met. Massalia)
6. Massalia (L. Massilia, Mod. Marseille, Met. Phocaea)
7. Tauroeis (L. Tauroentum, Met. Massalia)
8. Olbia (Met. Massalia)
9. Athenopolis (Met. Massalia)
10. Antipolis (Mod. Antibes, Met. Massalia)
11. Nicaea (Mod. Nice, Met. Massalia)
12. Alalia (Met. Phocaea)
13. Cyme (L. Cumae, Met. Chalcis)
14. Pithecusae (Met. Chalcis)
15. Dicaearchia (Met. Cyme)
16. Neapolis (Mod. Napoli, Met. Cyme)
18. Elea (L. Velia, Met. Phocaea)
24. Rhegium (Mod. Reggio, Met. Chalcis)
25. Zancle (Met. Chalcis: later dorised as Messana)
27. Himera (Met. Zancle)
36. Leontini (Mod. Lentini, Met. Chalcis)
37. Catana (Mod. Catania, Met. Chalcis)
38. Naxos (Met. Chalcis)
43. Siris (Met. Colophon)
55. Methone (Met. Eretria)
56. Therma
59. Mende (Met. Eretria)
61. Mecyberna (Met. Chalcis?)
62. Sermyle (Met. Chalcis)
63. Galepsus (Met. Chalcis)
64. Torone (Met. Chalcis)
65. Singos (Met. Chalcis?)
66. Assa (Met. Chalcis)
67. Sane (Met. Andros)
68. Acanthus (Met. Andros)
69. Stagirus (Met. Andros)
70. Argilus (Met. Andros)
71. Galepsus (Met. Thasos)
72. Oesyme (Met. Thasos)
73. Neapolis (Met. Thasos)
74. Thasos (Met. Paros)
75. Abdera (Met. Clazomenae)
76. Maronea (Met. Chios)
78. Cardia (Met. Miletus and Clazomenae)
80. Limnae (Met. Miletus)
81. Elaus (Met. Teos)
84. Pactye (Met. Athens?)

Ionian Colonies (cont.)
85. Bisanthe (Met. Samos)
86. Perinthus (Met. Samos)
89. Apollonia (Met. Miletus)
91. Odessus (Met. Miletus)
92. Callatis (Met. Miletus)
93. Tomis (Met. Miletus)
94. Istrus (Met. Miletus)
95. Tyras (Met. Miletus)
96. Olbia (Met. Miletus)
98. Theodosia (Met. Miletus)
99. Panticapaeum (Met. Miletus)
100. Tanais (Met. Miletus)
101. Phanagorea (Met. Miletus)
102. Pityus
103. Dioscurias (Met. Miletus)
104. Phasis (Met. Miletus)
105. Trapezus (Mediaeval Trebizond, Mod. Trabzon, Met. Sinope)
106. Cerasus (Met. Sinope)
107. Cotyora (Met. Sinope)
108. Amisus (Met. Miletus)
109. Sinope (Mod. Sinop, Met. Miletus)
110. Cytorus
111. Tieum (Met. Miletus)
115. Cius (Met. Miletus)
116. Myrlea (Met. Colophon)
117. Miletopolis (Met. Miletus)
118. Cyzicus (Met. Miletus)
119. Proconnesus (Met. Miletus)
120. Priapus (Met. Miletus or Cyzicus)
121. Parium (Met. Paros)
122. Colonae (Met. Miletus)
123. Paesus (Met. Miletus)
124. Lampsacus (Mod. Lapsaki, Met. Phocaea)
126. Abydus (Met. Miletus)
132. Scepsis (Met. Miletus)
135. Nagidus (Met. Samos)
136. Celenderis (Mod. Gilindire, Met. Samos)
138. Posideum (Met. Chalcis?)
142. Naucratis (Met. Miletus)

Achaian Colonies
17. Posidonia (L. Paestum)
19. Scidrus
20. Laus
21. Terina
40. Caulonia
41. Croton (L. Crotona, Mod. Cotrone)

Achaian Colonies (cont.)
42. Sybaris
44. Metapontum (Mod. Metaponto)
60. Scione

Locrian Colonies
22. Hipponium (Met. Locri Epizephyrii)
23. Medma (Met. Locri Epizephyrii)
39. Locri Epizephyrii

Dorian Colonies
4. Emporiae (Mod. Ampurias, Met. Rhodes)
4A. Rhoda (Mod. Rosas, Met. Rhodes)
5A. Rhodanusia or Rhode (Met. Rhodes)
26. Lipara (Mod. Lipari, Met. Cnidos and Rhodes)
28. Selinus (Met. Megara Hyblaea)
29. Acragas (L. Agrigentum, Mod. Girgenti or Agrigento, Met. Gela)
30. Gela (Met. Cnidos and Rhodes)
31. Camarina (Met. Syracuse)
32. Casmenae (Met. Syracuse)
33. Acrae (Met. Syracuse)
34. Syracuse (Mod. Siracusa, Met. Corinth)
35. Megara Hyblaea (Met. Megara)
45. Taras (L. Tarentum, Mod. Taranto, Met. Sparta)
46. Callipolis (Mod. Gallipoli, Met. Taras)
47. Hydrus (L. Hydruntum, Mod. Otranto, Met. Taras?)
48. Epidamnus (later Dyrrhachium, Mod. Durazzo (It.), Durrës (Alb.), Met. Corcyra)
49. Apollonia (Mod. Pollina (It.), Pojan (Alb.), Met. Corinth)
50. Corcyra (Met. Corinth)
51. Ambracia (Met. Corinth)

Dorian Colonies (cont.)
52. Anactorium (Met. Corinth and Corcyra)
53. Leucas (Met. Corinth)
54. Sollium (Met. Corinth and Corcyra)
57. Aenea (Met. Corinth)
58. Potidaea (Met. Corinth)
87. Selymbria (Mod. Silivri, Met. Megara)
88. Byzantium (Met. Megara)
90. Mesembria (Met. Megara)
97. Chersonesus (Met. Heraclea)
112. Heraclea (Mod. Erekli, Met. Megara)
113. Calchedon (Mod. Kadiköi, Met. Megara)
114. Astacus (Met. Megara)
133. Phaselis (Met. Rhodes)
137. Soli (Met. Rhodes)
143. Cyrene (Met. Thera)
144. Barca (Met. Cyrene)
145. Tauchira (Mod. Tokra, Met. Barca)
146. Euesperides (Met. Cyrene?)

Aeolian Colonies
77. Aenus (Met. Mytilene and Alopeconnesus)
79. Alopeconnesus (Met. Mytilene)
82. Madytus (Mod. Maito)
83. Sestus
125. Arisbe (Met. Mytilene)
127. Dardanus
128. Sigeum
129. Tenedos
130. Assus (Met. Methymna)
131. Antandrus
134. Side (Met. Cyme)

Colonies in Cyprus
139. Salamis
140. Soli
141. Paphos

---

quite a sparse rural population around them. And it must be noted that several of them – Miletus and Chalcis for example – were centres of fertile regions which could easily support a population a good deal denser than that which occupied them at the beginning of the first millennium. But although Greece in the eighth century was not overpopulated, the legal system under which it lived was the reason why its soil was not enough for all its inhabitants. We have seen that the Greek tribes shared out the lands on which they had settled among their constituent families. These family properties were inalienable and indivisible. Anyone excluded from the γένος – the exile, the foreigner, the bastard – could not hold any landed property; in each family even its descendants were limited to farming in common the fields assigned to their forebears. Such a system was unacceptable both to those whose birth or misdeeds had put them outside the family fold, and to the ambitious; and one can realise to what an extent the στενοχωρία drove both classes of outsider to seek abroad the land they were refused at home. The family régime of primitive Greece, as we have already noted, explains Greek colonisation in the same way that the rights of the first-born explain English and French colonialism in the seventeenth and eighteenth centuries.

Moreover, the life of Hellenic cities seems to have been most disturbed during the period that followed the destruction of monarchy. The struggles between the noble families and the royal families – for the latter were doubtless not easily resigned to the loss of their authority and prestige – seem to have resulted in a monotonous succession of revolutions. The last book of the *Odyssey* shows us one of these towns in which discord reigned – and Athena did not always appear at the critical moment to reconcile the combatants! A number of colonies, Cyrene and Tarentum among others, seem to have been founded by defeated parties who preferred exile to submission, and one of them which owed its origin to men banished from Cumae was given the characteristic name of Δικαιαρχία 'City where Justice reigns'.

Finally, Greek colonisation would not have been possible without that spirit of adventure characteristic of youthful peoples still in process of formation, a spirit which shows itself in a variety of forms in primitive Greece. The same motives that drove some men to found new cities in distant lands stirred others to seek the excitement and unforeseen thrills of a sea-pirate's life. In ruthless verses the author of the *Odyssey* sings of the joys of the guerrilla who loves not toil and domestic profit but ships, battles, spears, and arrows. The corsair's trade was a paying one in that Aegean sea with its ring of defenceless towns, and rewarded those who took to it with riches and glory unmixed with any reprobation. The Greek pirates, like those of Phoenicia, pillaged the Aegean coasts, carrying off anything that fell into their hands – corn, cattle, manufactured objects, and frequently human beings too. On Attic vases of the eighth century women are portrayed being carried off by a raider on to a ship about to sail: and abductions play quite a considerable part in the stories of the *Odyssey*.

When the advance of civilisation put an end to piracy, the Greeks satisfied their warlike and adventurous yearnings by serving as mercenaries. They are met with in Asia Minor in the service of Lydian kings, in Mesopotamia under the orders of the rulers of Babylon, and above all in Egypt where the appearance of the 'men of bronze' terrified the native populations and made it easier for the Pharaoh Psammetichus, who had taken them into his pay, to reorganise Egypt under his sway in the mid-seventh century.

The causes of the colonial movement enable us to understand the form that it took in its early days. What these banished men and malcontents went out to look for was above all good land. So we see them settling first of all in the fertile and thinly populated districts of the south of Italy where they built towns whose location depended chiefly on agriculture. Metapontum, Sybaris, Croton arose in the midst of fertile plains, where in spite of the unhealthy situation the early colonists were only too glad to be able to carve out great estates for themselves as did the first planters in Florida or Texas. In the same way in Sicily, the great wheat country of classical Antiquity, the Greeks settled at Naxos, at Catana in the prosperous region fertilised by the ashes of Etna, and at Leontini, the corn-growing centre of Sicily in the Roman period. Beyond the straits of Messina they founded Cumae in that Campanian paradise which to this day easily supports a population of abnormal density.

Thus new towns arose in these regions where man felt more at his ease than in Greece; in southern Italy, for instance, which was called 'Greater Greece' – towns which were to their mother-country what America was to the England of the eighteenth century; towns which built temples to the agrarian gods and later were to stamp magnificent coins with the image of Demeter or Korê.

But these new cities could not remain isolated amidst strange and often hostile populations. They needed to keep in touch with their mother-countries. They soon realised that they could provide an outlet for the products of the growing Greek industries among the barbarous tribes around them, and also send to Greece the raw materials and foodstuffs in which these virgin lands abounded. For this they needed ports; and so we see Greek colonists concerning themselves particularly with the configuration of coast lines and the direction of currents. After the farming townships came the trading-ports: in Greater Greece Tarentum, in Sicily Syracuse, on the Gulf of Lyons Marseilles, in the Sea of Marmora Cyzicus and Byzantium, and then on the shores of the Black Sea Sinope and Trapezus, the settlements of the Thracian Chersonese and of the Danube delta on the threshold of the richest cornlands of all Europe. These towns no longer, like Metapontum or Sybaris, turned their backs on a difficult and inhospitable coast. To suit the maritime, commercial, and military needs of the day they were established on an island or a peninsula commanding a good natural harbour; Syracuse and Tarentum are typical in this respect. Sometimes there was a groping hesitation before the really favourable spot was hit upon: the Megarians built Chalcedon at the mercy of unfavourable currents and on a site criticised as unsuitable even by classical geographers, some seventeen years before discovering the natural harbour of the Golden Horn, where they built Byzantium, the key to two seas and two continents.

But whether it was to agricultural settlements or to seaports, the Greek colonists took with them the religious and political habits of their homeland. They were no straggling and shapeless settlements which the Greeks established in Italy and along the shores of the Black Sea, but cities, each provided with its magistrates, its assembly, and its gods as in the metropolis. Nor would it be surprising if they took on a distinctively urban character even earlier than the towns from which they had issued. Isolated as they were among non-Greek populations, which were generally uncivilised and frequently hostile, they needed to be centralised and fortified. Tradition estimated the perimeter of the built-up area of Sybaris, which was destroyed about 510, at 50 stades (over six miles), a size unexampled among the cities of Greece itself in the sixth century. Acragas (Agrigentum), Poseidonia (Paestum) had walls completely enclosing the city at a time when, in Greece, only the acropolis of a town was fortified.

Whatever reason impelled a party of colonists to leave their motherland, the city they set out to establish outside Greece always kept up relations with its metropolis. To the mother-city it owed respect, which was shown by sending ambassadors on particular occasions; disputes between the two towns were avoided as far as possible, and commercial and sometimes military alliances were established between them. Although in principle the political independence of colonies from their mother-cities was always respected, the existence of numerous colonies was a source of prestige as well as wealth for the city from which they went forth, especially after the commercial character of such settlements began to be emphasised. And so the setting out of emigrants became an important event about which the gods were consulted. A city could officially intervene in deciding on the foundation of a colony, in nominating those to take part in the expedition, selecting its leader and even the magistrates specially appointed to share out the new lands among the colonists on their arrival.

Not all the Greek peoples took an equal share in this colonial movement. Neither did the Epirots, nor the Illyrians, nor the Macedonians – except during the late period of Alexander's successors – swarm overseas in this way. Although some colonies were founded by tribes leading a rural life in continental Greece – for example the Locrians, and the Achaeans of the Peloponnese – colonies were mostly sent out by well-populated cities, firmly established in their territories, having an advanced political and economic organisation, and acquainted with the ways of the sea. Such were Corinth, Chalcis and Megara, which played a great part in the Aegean long before Athens; Naxos, the commercial centre of the Cyclades; Paros; and finally Miletus, the heart of that Ionia where Greek civilisation reached its zenith during the seventh and six centuries.

Thus in less than three hundred years the Mediterranean had become a lake at least half Greek. This first expansion of Hellenism was only limited by that of other civilised and trading nations. At the same period, indeed, the Phoenicians – firmly installed on the Syrian coast where the Greeks could not hope to found settlements – had set up posts of a definitely commercial nature in Cyprus, in western Sicily, in Sardinia, and on the coasts of north Africa and Spain. The Etruscans spread themselves along the shores of the Tyrrhenian Sea where their corsairs were predominant (*cf.* Chapter XII). By the end of the sixth century most of the favourable spots in the Mediterranean basin were occupied, and this by itself was sufficient to check Greek colonisation. In fact, from 500 onwards to the time of Alexander, the movement stopped almost completely. The Athenian 'cleruchies' of the fifth and fourth centuries were usually established in countries long under the Hellenic sway, and were the response of a single city to its political, military, and social needs, and in no way represented the tendencies of a whole nation. They were constituted, as we shall see, on an entirely different pattern.

But another cause may have slowed down the Greek colonial movement. The system of family property disappeared and was replaced by that of individual ownership: political revolutions (*cf.* Chapters VI and X) improved the lot of the masses; and the fact that a greater number of men could own land and enrich themselves by trade and industry explains why the Greeks no longer needed to seek abroad the fortune they could now win at home.

But the effects of colonisation lasted longer than the movement itself. Its first effect was to create in foreign parts a feeling of Panhellenic solidarity stronger than in purely Greek territory. A colony was often made up of elements from several Greek cities, who in spite of their diverse origin made common cause when they found themselves living together, far from the metropolis, among people of an alien race. To Cyrene, where the men of Thera had established a settlement which soon grew rich by the export of African products, energetic rulers invited immigrants from all parts of Greece. The most striking example of these mixed colonies was the town of Naucratis in the Delta, mistress of the commerce between Egypt and the Greek world, founded by a regular consortium of towns on the coast of Asia Minor with whom Aegina had associated herself. There a 'Hellenion', at once citadel, warehouse and shrine, symbolised the unity of the Greeks in a foreign land, which was also expressed by the federal constitution of the city. Hellenic union was thus realised in certain colonies before the Persian wars made the need for one felt – for all too short a time – in the mother-country. In a similar way, five centuries later, Italian unity found its first expression in the merchant communities of *negotiatores* of the East.

In these new towns, often made up of the most active and enterprising people from their metropolis, Hellenic civilisation frequently made swift and brilliant advances. In these, however, not all the colonies took part in the same way. Many of them – established in harsh climates, amid hostile populations which they could not hope to assimilate – remained merely centres of commerce, more or less taken over by barbarians who often threatened their very existence. The towns of Cyrenaica were strongly influenced by the Libyan populations that surrounded them. Several of the Black Sea colonies never had more than a precarious existence, constantly threatened by attacks of the Getae and Scythians, and hence they played only a minor part in the history of Greek civilisation until the belated day when Mithridates, a semi-barbarian king, tried in vain to organise there the last resistance of a dying Hellenism. It was far otherwise in the west, especially in 'Greater Greece' and Sicily. Not only did the colonists find there similarities of climate and countryside, but the local populations – Messapians, Sicans, and Sicels, all of native Italian origin – opposed little if any resistance to Hellenic culture.

By the time of the Roman conquest Sicily had become a Greek island, towns and country alike. In these favourable conditions great cities developed in which political ideas, science, literature, and art soon attained advanced forms. The constitution of these towns, whose founders brought the principles of an aristocratic system with them from Greece, seems to have evolved rapidly. Tradition tells of legislators such as Zaleucus, Charondas, and Draco (cf. Chapter VI) – who introduced important reforms at an early stage. These clearly had their influence on subsequent development. The democratic spirit, with all its consequences, showed itself there at least as early as in the Aegean basin. From the sixth century onwards highly developed literary forms – the lyric and comedy (cf. Chapter XI) – were elaborated there; daring systems of philosophy found an enthusiastic welcome from a public eager for novelties; around Pythagoras and Parmenides chapels of enthusiasts gathered. There was a splendid artistic blossoming. Some of the most grandiose buildings of the sixth and fifth centuries are to be found in Greater Greece and Sicily; and standing before the most beautiful ruins in Greece, even the Acropolis of Athens, one cannot but remember the grave perfection of the temples of Paestum.

The peculiar character of Greek colonialism is thus explained simply by its origins. Greek colonies were neither military establishments nor, at least in principle, trading factories like those which the Phoenicians set up around the Mediterranean shore between the eighth and sixth centuries. They were essentially colonies of settlement. To this fact they owe the often magnificent development of their civilisation, and the part they played in the history of Hellenism. They remind us of some English colonies, among whose originators we also find convicts, adventurers, and malcontents, which now equal or outstrip the mother-country by the vigour of their economic and intellectual development and sometimes by the boldness of their social experiments.

VI

CHANGES IN ECONOMIC AND SOCIAL LIFE

In the domains thus extended by colonial expansion the conditions of life were modified little by little. This society based on agriculture slowly adapted itself to a more settled form of life in a new climate. The great family estates into which the land had been divided at the beginning of the occupation were broken up. Evolution was both economic and juridical in character, and gradually the ownership, first of buildings and finally of the land itself, was taken from the family and handed over to the individual. On the death of the father the children shared out his farm between them. Thus parcelled out, land increased in value and men tried to obtain a better yield from it. The wide expanses formerly given over to stock-rearing, acorn-harvesting, or forestry made way for fields of wheat and barley, olive-groves and vineyards. Experience crystallised into an agricultural technique: the Homeric poems mention a biennial rotation of crops, fertilisers, and irrigation. Nevertheless methods remained primitive; the plough described by Homer and even by Hesiod, and depicted on archaic terra-cottas, is doubtless as primitive as the swing-plough still to be met with in some districts of Greece or Macedon; its wooden coulter painfully scratched a thin soil. The labourer had to compensate by hard work for the lack of soil-fertility and farm equipment. Hesiod's *Works and Days* gives us a vivid picture of the hard life of the Greek cultivator.

But although agriculture was developing it no longer provided a mere means of existence. The creation of city-states modified this primitive subsistence economy in which each family, living on a wide domain, was self-sufficient and produced at home all the food and clothing needed by its members, in which the man of the household had to be stonemason, joiner, and shoemaker, and the woman cook, baker, and washerwoman; she also carded, spun, wove, and embroidered the wool. By the time of the *Iliad*, however, we see the shepherd and the farm-labourer going to the town to barter their milk and corn for the tools they needed. A long-distance commerce was added to this minor trading, as the Hellenic world grew wider and as more varied regions came under its influence. The Sicilian colonies exported their surplus of wheat and timber; Cyrene its spices and wool; the Aegean lands sent to the Black Sea settlements the oil, figs, and wine that the Greek, however far from his mother-country, could not do without, and in return obtained cereals and salted fish. Little by little a merchant-class grew up. There is no mention of them in the Homeric poems, where the word ἔμποροι, which later means 'merchants', still retains its old meaning of 'passer-by', and where large-scale commerce seems to be the prerogative of the great – for example of Mentes, king of the Taphians, who exports iron to Cyprus in exchange for copper. But as early as the seventh century Hesiod met in Boeotia rich merchants from Aegina, and knew the seasons when steady winds allowed regular sea-borne trade.

Such exchanges required the invention and diffusion of a system of weights and measures. It is likely that the early Aegean peoples had a system, maybe more than one. Those elaborated in the Hellenic world, like the Neo-Babylonian and Egyptian ones, were based on a unit of length calculated from a part of the human body (foot or forearm) and gave rise in turn to units of weight, volume, and capacity. Agreement was never complete in Greece as to the part of the body to be taken as the basis, nor as to its exact length, nor about the fixing of multiples and fractions. The Greeks wavered between the decimal system, the duodecimal system, the use of multiples of six, and multiplication by 2, 4, 8, 16, etc. Hence in the Hellenic countries there existed a number of complicated systems of measurement which, in spite of repeated efforts, were never satisfactorily unified or even made reasonably simple.

But to be able to weigh and measure was not enough. To meet the needs of trade the inconveniences of barter had to be overcome by the invention of a conventional medium of exchange. The language of the *Iliad* and *Odyssey* preserves the memory of very ancient times – perhaps before the Greeks settled in the Balkans – when the exchange value of an article, even of a human being, was calculated with reference to that of the most useful of all animals – the cow. The Cretan maidens depicted by Hephaestus on the shield of Achilles are called ἀλφεσίβοιαι because their marriage would earn many cattle for their parents. But by the time these poems reached their final form the custom had been established of using precious metals for exchange purposes – iron, copper, gold – either in the shape of weapons or in pieces, valued by weight. Through tradition and archaeological discovery we have become acquainted with pins (ὀβελοί, ὀβολοί) either in units or handfuls (δραχμαί, drachmas) of six. Such is the system that seems to have been in use in the eighth and seventh centuries. But a great step forward was taken, perhaps towards the end of the seventh century, when the ingots – reduced to small dimensions by the use of the most precious metals and hence easier to handle and transport – were stamped with a mark by the mint which made them, thus indicating their weight and value. There was no need to weigh and test them each time they changed hands: money had been invented, and this invention might well have been made in the west of Asia Minor, a region of intense commercial activity.

The half-Hellenised kingdom of Lydia first coined electron since this natural alloy of gold and silver was obtainable from certain alluvial deposits, notably the sands of the river Pactolus. Later the minting of silver coins of warranted value spread in Greece itself, where the metal was not too scarce. Finally the Lydian King Croesus was the first to issue gold coins. At the same time and progressively, minting became a state prerogative. The governments of the Greek cities took away the right of coinage from private individuals, and eventually reserved this valuable privilege for themselves. Various monetary systems were established: that of Aegina was adopted by most cities in continental Greece, that of the Euboean towns by Corinth, whose merchants spread it far and wide in Chalcidice, in Cyrenaica, in Sicily, and Greater Greece. Only very conservative cities such as Sparta kept their clumsy iron money right up to the fourth century. Apart from the towns of Asia Minor, Greek money was monometallic, differing in this from Lydian practice. The Hellenic countries were rich in silver-mines but poor in gold. It was from further east and at a later date that gold staters and darics appeared, and they were not in current use before the end of the fifth century.

Trade was not usually carried on by land. That there were roads in ancient Greece is indisputable; the Homeric poems mention them even if without precise details; and traces of causeways, said on dubious evidence to go back to Mycenaean times, have been found in Argolis. But these were nothing more than unimportant paths leading from the town to the fields or to neighbouring hamlets or to some popular shrine. Greece never had, either at this time or later, a network of roads comparable to that which Italy possessed from the third century onwards. It was by sea that the greater part of her merchandise was carried, and to meet new needs new naval methods were evolved. Alongside the privateer, whose speed and striking power varied according to the number of rowers, we see in vase-paintings heavier vessels propelled by sails and worked by a small crew like their descendant the modern caïque. These ships transported the more cumbersome cargoes cheaply but very slowly. Navigation was still a slow business and was subject to the natural hazards of the elements and the seasons.

Along with merchant shipping a fishing fleet developed. Sea-fish did not figure on the menu of the lords of Mycenae and Tiryns, but the Homeric poems, which recall the days when sea-fish was thought an inferior type of food, nevertheless do mention harpooning and net-fishing. Fish began to take an increasing place in the diet of the Greeks, and a number of towns (including those on the Black Sea) grew rich on the trade in salted fish.

It was not only agricultural and woodland products or raw materials that were carried in merchant ships. Greek manufacturing activity was stimulated by the growth of commerce. As the primitive domestic economy based on the family came to an end, craftsmen and specialised artisans appeared and often had sufficient orders to take on assistants and set up workshops making standardised articles. In the towns of Asia Minor, perhaps under the influence of oriental civilisations like those of Lydia or Assyria, weaving sheds were established whose fine and richly decorated products spread throughout the Hellenic world. Metal industries, too, made progress. The Greeks learned to smelt the iron ore that was plentiful in some parts of Asia Minor and in Laconia. Out of this came important modifications of weapons. The old leather shield was no longer strong enough to ward off spears and arrows with iron points. Henceforth the warrior's defensive armour consisted of a round shield, more suited for parrying blows, a helmet, a leather and bronze breast-plate, and bronze greaves. Tools of iron, but less frequently weapons, are mentioned in the later parts of the *Iliad* and *Odyssey*.

Numerous deposits of clay favoured the growth of a ceramics industry, and from an early period the decoration of pottery shows real artistic feeling. At first, especially in Attica, vases which were notable for both shape and size, and showing evidence of very considerable technical skill, display an original, if unsophisticated, type of decoration in which various geometrical patterns are used to frame landscapes with numerous figures. Later Corinth gave a strong lead to the rest of Greece in imitating oriental tapestries to produce a composite style, in which floral designs, fantastic animals, and mythological figures were employed in rich and imaginative combination.

Architecture and sculpture also improved, like pottery. Though it is of doubtful value to try to reconstruct Priam's palace or Odysseus's house from the rather imprecise details given in the *Odyssey*, excavations have shown that from the eighth century Greek architects knew how to cover large areas with the gabled roof.

The *cella* of the ancient temple of the Heraeum near Argos (seventh century) measures about 120 feet long by nearly 30 feet wide. Colonnades, formerly restricted to the façade, developed into peristyles around the whole of the buildings, giving them a more imposing appearance without becoming ponderous. Architects still used only wood, tufa, and limestone, finished off for economy's sake with unbaked bricks or sometimes terracotta. The sculptors, however, who had abandoned wood for stone tried working in marble, though to begin with they carved only stiff sheathed idols with arms held straight by their sides. The bas-reliefs in tufa and daubed with vivid colours that are found on the Acropolis at Athens show a remarkable effort to reproduce the most violent movements of both men and animals.

All this progress in commerce and technical skill had important social consequences. Power was no longer based solely on the possession of a large estate; hereditary properties were divided up and the law began to regulate sales; personal wealth was accumulated by trade, and the introduction of money made the handling of it easier. Some families obtained considerable incomes from trade which allowed them to play an important part in their cities. At Corinth the Bacchiadae – great patrons of the arts, great merchants, and chief magistrates of their city – are a striking example. It is hard to say whether a set of upstarts invented imposing genealogies for themselves or whether we are dealing with genuine aristocrats who had realised how to adapt themselves to changing social conditions; at all events wealth now became the accepted basis of political power, and the class-structure of the citizenry was based on its visible signs.

It is true that these signs are usually still clearly agricultural. At Athens, according to a classification that goes back possibly to the eighth century, the top category of citizens included anyone who could harvest five hundred bushels of wheat ($\Pi\epsilon\nu\tau\alpha\kappa\sigma\iota\sigma\mu\epsilon\delta\iota\mu\nu\sigma\iota$); the second class those who could afford the luxury of a horse ($'I\pi\pi\epsilon\hat{\iota}s$); the third, well-to-do peasants owning a pair of bullocks ($Z\epsilon\nu\gamma\hat{\iota}\tau\alpha\iota$); and below them the wage-earners ($\Theta\hat{\eta}\tau\epsilon s$). It was only slowly that another system of values better suited to the new conditions of a money-economy was adopted. Little by little, however, personal wealth exerted its influence on the social hierarchy, and the aristocratic régime that had replaced the monarchy was thoroughly transformed into a plutocracy. 'Money maketh man' ($\chi\rho\acute{\eta}\mu\alpha\tau$' $\dot{\alpha}\nu\acute{\eta}\rho$) the current proverb put it.

In a society so constituted the position of the lesser folk was a painful one. The rich could draw enormous incomes both from commerce and from their estates, which no law limited in size. Judging by the level of incomes indicated by property classification in Attica (some 900 square miles) many land-owners had more than fifty acres of arable land. Meanwhile the poor peasant lived on a patrimony just large enough to maintain his family, but his ownership was made precarious by bitter law-suits about the succession and by boundary disputes. The increasing use of money did not help matters. Being still rare in the sixth century, money had enormous purchasing power, and before Solon was not widely used in small denominations for internal trade. Hence there was a great fall in the prices of agricultural products. And so if, as a result of illness or a bad harvest, the peasant had to borrow to live he could only do so at extortionate rates of interest, and ended by pledging the only valuable he possessed – his land.

Mortgages, which have always been the scourge of the countryside, already existed in Greece at this period, probably in the form of sales subject to the vendor's right to repurchase. The first mortgage bonds that have been found in Greece date from the sixth century, but the usage to which they bear witness is certainly much older. If he was turned out of his farm, the peasant had no other security to offer than himself and his family. He lost his status as a free man and became no more than a serf. And although the economic conditions that prevailed in Greece from the eighth century onwards were not the only cause of serfdom, at least they favoured its extension and emphasised its oppressive nature.

This institution, which seems to have been unknown to the Hellenic tribes when they first arrived in Greece, and which is still not mentioned by Homer or Hesiod, was strongly developed before the sixth century. With some slight differences the Helots of Sparta, the $Πενέσται$ (servants) of Thessaly, the $Μνωῖται$ and the $Κληρῶται$ (serfs bound to the soil) of Crete, and perhaps also the $Πελᾶται$ (clients) and the $Ἑκτήμοροι$ (who had to pay to their landlord one-sixth of the crop) of Attica all had the common characteristic that they were bound to the land they cultivated, and had to pay a proportion of their annual harvest as rent. We have already seen (Chapter IV) that these people are not to be regarded as descendants of a primitive race enslaved by the Greeks. Probably a series of personal contracts – as happened in Europe from the sixth century A.D. onwards – bound the families of lesser folk to the nobles who, at least in earlier days, gave them help and protection in return for rents. But this system, patriarchal in the beginning, became most oppressive as time went by. The plutocracy debased the share-cropper into a slave, and created a class of miserable malcontents always on the verge of revolt. This disinherited proletariat in the end became a real menace to states such as Thessaly and Sparta, which remained firmly oligarchic and never made any attempt to give them back their lost liberty by radical reforms.

Alongside these serfs, the true slaves – brought back from some warlike expedition, or perhaps purchased from pirates in one of the slave markets that sprang up all over Greece, but especially in Ionia – began to play an important part in agriculture. In the *Iliad* the harvesters depicted on the shield of Achilles were still it seems free men ($ἔριθοι$), and alongside these day-labourers there was no lack in Greece of tied-debtors ($θῆτες$), men bound by a permanent contract to their employer. But the *Odyssey* shows us real slaves ($δμῶες$) who kept Odysseus's flocks or carried out domestic duties in his house. In towns the progress of industry led to the setting up of small workshops where free labourers and slaves were employed side by side. Law and custom alike usually assured the slave of an easy relationship with the family. At this period, it is true, he had still no hope of obtaining his freedom, but at least he was generally treated without harshness and sometimes with affection. He enjoyed a relative measure of independence, especially in rural employments, and could even accumulate a small capital for himself. The position of a slave in archaic Greece seems to have been more tolerable than in the Rome of Cato the Elder.

These new economic conditions favoured the growth of towns. The ports on the shores of the Aegean grew larger: e.g. in Ionia, Miletus on the Gulf of Latmus (the outlet for the Maeander valley) and Phocaea (which commanded the valley of the Hermus and served as port for industrial Lydia); in central Greece, Chalcis on the Euripus channel, which was so important when ships still hesitated to double the island of Euboea; Aegina, whose rovers and shipbuilders played an important part in archaic Greece (as did those of her neighbour Hydra in the eighteenth century A.D.); and on both sides of the Isthmus the two ports of Corinth, enriched by entrepôt trade and dues.

Megara, the founder in the seventh century of numerous colonies in Sicily and on the Bosphorus, was another prosperous city. Its future rival, Athens (whose harbour of the Piraeus had not yet been constructed) was at this time not yet a major power, although before the sixth century its population was already overflowing the walls of the Acropolis and settling in new districts, both to the south towards the Ilissus and to the north-west, where the potters and blacksmiths foregathered. In the Peloponnese, Argos had displaced Tiryns and Mycenae, and since it was in the centre of a fertile plain and in possession of the port of Nauplia it developed great commercial strength, as is shown by its creation, under King Pheidon in the seventh century, of a system of weights and measures adopted by a great number of Greek towns. Sparta, in spite of its distance from the sea, owed its power to its political constitution which seems from the beginning to have had a strong military flavour.

Despite the misery of this 'Iron Age' as it was called by its poets, when throughout Greece a depressed majority of serfs and day-labourers lived under the yoke of the opulent few who were enriched both by their great estates and by commerce, the natural play of events was leading to progress in the spheres of both morals and law. The increase of urban populations was strengthening the power of the city at the expense of the family system. A whole mass of legislation was built up in the Hellenic world from the seventh century onwards. Tradition has preserved for us the names of several of these legislators, such as Zaleucus of Epizephyrian Locri, Charondas at Catana, Draco of Athens, and Lycurgus at Sparta. There is some doubt about the historicity of the last named, and the accounts concerning him and Draco have assumed some almost mythological characteristics, but whether they really were the authors of the reforms attributed to them or whether these were the results of a slow and anonymous process, a new spirit in the law was certainly manifesting itself.

Ancient law, founded on family solidarity both when it imposed restrictions and where it gave responsibility, had to retreat before more modern ideas which see the individual confronted by the state. A bronze plaque, found at Olympia and dating from the end of the seventh century, has been rightly described as a 'first edition of the *habeas corpus* act'. It lays down the rights of the accused, forbids any illegal violence against him, regulates the action of the courts before whom he is to be tried, and limits the powers of the plaintiff, who is moreover quite definitely forbidden to seize the family or goods of the accused. At Athens the Draconian code, far from being 'written in letters of blood' as a late and ill-founded tradition asserts, went a long way in applying reason and humanity. Among the laws, more or less authentic, which are attributed to Draco, the most notable without doubt is the one which set up the court of the Ephetae alongside the Areopagus, and established a distinction both in law and in the penalties imposed between the crime of premeditated murder and that of involuntary homicide, thus proclaiming, probably for the first time in the ancient world, the importance in law of the doctrine of moral responsibility.

VII

THE EVOLUTION OF GREEK RELIGION

The characteristics of Greek religion cannot be summed up in a few formulae. It was never fixed in changeless dogmas, but on the contrary adapted itself constantly to the intellectual and moral evolution of the argumentative, curious, novelty-loving people who practised it. This makes the history of its origins particularly uncertain. The earliest written documents in which this religion can be studied are the Homeric poems and Hesiod's *Theogony*. These mention a number of gods with well-marked characteristics. It would be wrong to regard this clearly developed polytheism as a primitive state of the Greek religion. On the contrary, it was the result of a long elaboration. It may be presumed that behind these clear and well-ordered aspects there were others, older and more obscure, of which the Homeric poems have not been able to eliminate all traces. Some authors of the classical period, Aeschylus for example, bring out these features very clearly; and this is the only way in which we can account for some of the figured pictures and carvings, often of very late date, as well as for rites which maintained themselves, in modest, obscure, and popular forms, until an advanced state of Hellenism. In this chapter we shall seek to sum up the most likely hypotheses which have recently been put forward to explain these earlier aspects of Greek religion, and the successive modifications which gave it the form in which we find it at the opening of the historic period.

It has long been argued, and often with more ingenuity than science, that the religions of the peoples of classical antiquity, and those of other human groups which did not reach so advanced a degree of civilisation, can have nothing in common. It was little short of scandalous, some people thought, to point out resemblances between the beliefs of the Greeks and those of 'savages'. On the other hand is not the 'Hellenic miracle' all the more miraculous if it started from notions closely akin to those which we find today among Kaffirs and Red Indians, and yet the Greeks could arrive at conceptions of the greatest artistic, moral, and philosophic value?

We should not disregard the striking resemblances which the comparative method has shown us just because some scholars have used it wrongly or unwisely. We can, in fact, find some of the elements which are common to all so-called primitive religions in that of ancient Greece; in particular, the idea of divine beings who are no changeless gods, but can evolve, can be children, or in the prime of life, can grow old and die and be reborn. This is the origin of those baby gods who were transformed later on into Zeus or Dionysus; of those gods or heroes who suffer, die, and are reborn. Genealogies were invented to represent the relationships established between the god, the group who worshipped him, and their leader; and the theory of kingship by divine right was formulated both at the dawn of Greek history and later in its decline.

Finally, though it would be going too far to talk of totem-worship in Greece, we can hardly deny that there are traces of animal-worship. The Homeric vocabulary includes words which recall a time when Hera had the face of a cow, βοῶπις, and Athena that of an owl, γλαυκῶπις, before they became more reputable deities in a wholly human shape, but with an animal as their attribute – the eagle of Zeus, the owl of Athena.

All that was most precious to the tribe or city depended on this god, who was thus closely related to them – their flocks and herds, and their harvests. He could well have his dwelling in the land which nourished them all. At the seasonal festivals his followers invoked him and propitiated him by magic rites, in which a very crudely symbolised act of generation was supposed to ensure the fertility of the fields and cattle. This was the origin of phallic rites in the worship of Hermes, and later in that of Dionysus and the great goddesses of Eleusis. A sort of elementary physiology was intermingled with these religious ideas; the earth was thought of as a woman, at first virgin (Κόρη) later fertilised by the rains and storms to become Mother-Earth (Δη-μήτηρ). To fill the gap between her time and that of men of their own day they imagined generations of monstrous creatures born directly from the Earth – Titans and Giants. By a continuing process of assimilation of the divine to the human, the god of the tribe became its ancestor, a 'hero' whom people pictured to themselves in increasingly precise forms – a serpent to begin with, the most earthy of animals – and later a man. Little by little his story was elaborated, and as time went on his grave could even be pointed out: but numerous details betrayed his origin. At Athens, for instance, we still find the hero Cecrops who civilised the country represented in the paintings and bas-reliefs of the classical period with his serpent's tail.

Born of the earth, men returned to it after death. Like the ancestor of the tribe some became heroes, and like him objects of respect and worship. There was no interruption in communication between the living and the dead, and the agrarian festivals – for instance the Athenian Anthesteria – had a complex ceremonial in which magic rites and invocations called up the dead, and then afterwards other rites and spells sent them back to their subterranean dwellings. For the dead were ambivalent beings, respectable and kindly but to be feared, especially if unappeased. Hence the precautions taken to assure their well-being: embalming, offerings, blood, and sometimes even human sacrifice.

The Homeric poems have preserved a more or less precise record of all these practices, although by the time they received their final form the custom of burning the dead had already been introduced. In what circumstances cremation found its way into Greece we have as yet no means of telling; all we can say is that burial and cremation both persisted side by side into the classical period.

On top of this first stratum of divine beings, born of the collective sentiments and emotions of man, there was imposed a second, not so elemental, drawing its inspiration from a more disinterested observation of the world. Before the latest of the invading Greek tribes had split off from their Indo-European forbears they had already made a supreme god out of the celestial vault of the heavens which spans the universe (Vedic Djaus, heavens; Greek Zeus; Latin Diespiter, vocative Jupiter). When he reached Greece, Zeus conquered the old Earth-gods, Titans, and Giants, who tried in vain to resist him and to scale the towering cliffs that held on high his dwelling-place. But for a long time he was still looked upon as something of an upstart, proud of his recent success but still rather unsure of himself; and it was in this guise that he appeared even in the fifth century in the *Prometheus* of Aeschylus.

Zeus, the god of the heavens, is also the storm-god who wields the thunder, with Pallas the virgin-goddess at his side, holding the lightning-spear in her hand. At first she was the personification of brute-force and blind will-power; later she personified the reflective wisdom of the god: a fierce Valkyrie in the *Iliad*, she became in the *Odyssey* a wise counsellor of gods and men. She was the protector of cities, and of Athens in particular – hence perhaps the surname of Athena (Ἀθηναία, Ἀθηνᾶ) by which she is already known in the Homeric poems.

The Sun, the son of Heaven, who had been the object of a restricted cult under the too obvious name of Helios, became one of the great Hellenic gods under the name of Φοῖβος (the Brilliant), and later of Apollo, a title not yet clearly explained. His ambiguous nature, at once beneficent and terrible, derived from the effects of sunlight in the fierce climate of Greece. By his side was his sister the Moon (Φοίβη) known as Artemis, a name of similarly obscure origin. Under the vault of heaven stretch the surfaces of lands and seas supported and sometimes violently shaken by a powerful god, Poseidon (Ποσειδῶν), lord of the earthquakes. Originally worshipped in those districts most subject to earthquakes, such as Boeotia and the Gulf of Corinth, he kept his title of Earth-Bearer or Shaker (γαιήοχος, ἐνοσίχθων) throughout Homeric times, although his power had by then been limited to the realm of the ocean. Fire, which Greek philosophers later looked upon as an essential element in the universe, was also a god, leaping but deformed like the wavering flame – rather like the Germanic Loki. The importance of fire to the growing handicrafts of the potter and metal-worker made Hephaestus a special object of worship in the industrial regions of Asia Minor and Greece, where he became the ill-dressed patron of blacksmiths.

The religion of the Greek tribes must have been influenced by that of the peoples they found settled in Greece when they first arrived. It has been suggested that the heavenly gods were the creation of the Greeks who were 'Indo-Europeans and nomads', while the gods of the fields and the underworld owed their origin to the pre-Hellenic folk who were settled agriculturalists. But this simple and attractive hypothesis cannot be supported by any evidence from linguistics or archaeology. Demeter, the agrarian goddess *par excellence*, bears a definitely Indo-European name; while symbols of heavenly phenomena – the double axe of thunder, the lightning-lance, the sun, the moon – are all to be found among the pre-Hellenic populations of Crete and Asia Minor. Indeed it is very difficult to disentangle the elements that Greek religion owes to Aegean religion, for the reasons given in Chapter II. But it may be noted that the Cretan bull-god reappears in beliefs and myths about Zeus, Dionysus, and Poseidon; and that Britomartis of Crete and Asia Minor – the tamer of animals – has been identified, heaven knows how, with Phoebe-Artemis, the chaste huntress of the night.

On the borders of the Hellenic world we find a number of gods, some of whom established themselves in Greece while still maintaining their alien characteristics. Some tribes to the north of the Balkan peninsula who, like the people of central Europe later on, were much given to strong drink, worshipped a god of drunkenness, Bacchus-Bromios, or Dionysus, the son of Zeus and of the Earth, Semelê, consumed by the lightning of fertilising storms. Accompanied by a band of savage creatures, Satyrs and Sileni, and by Maenads (women possessed by the god), he penetrated into Greece, where from a drinker of beer he matured into a god of wine. In the Homeric poems he is still a newcomer with a very insignificant part to play.

From the north, too, there came a god obscure in name and character – Ares, who in the *Iliad* is still nothing but a pugnacious brute. He was coupled with Aphrodite, but she was no foreigner, as we can see from her distinctly Hellenic name and the importance of her cult in northern regions of Greece, especially in Thessaly. Nevertheless she only assumed her definitive form in the islands, and in Cyprus in particular, under a variety of influences – of which the most important was that of the Phoenician Astarte, Queen of the Heavens, who was in turn related to

Syrian and Chaldaean goddesses, and whose rites and effigies often expressed very crudely the ideas of fertility and generation. Until classical times Aphrodite was the only Greek goddess who undoubtedly owed something to Semitic religions. Thus Greek religion at the beginning of the first millennium was a very complex accretion of beliefs and rites, very diverse in nature and origin.

By a slow process this dense and composite material was gradually organised and given precision, until towards the eighth century it emerged as the Homeric and Hesiodian mythology. It is in this sense that we can say with Herodotus that Homer and Hesiod 'have made the theogony of the Greeks, given to the gods their names, attributed to each of them his domain, and defined his appearance'. In the course of this further evolution, the gods on the one hand finally and exclusively took on a human shape, and on the other separated themselves more and more from humanity. Religion lost its character as a communion charged with emotion, and became matter for learned expositions, literary elaboration, and artistic creation. The vicissitudes of the gods became dramatic events, analagous no doubt to those which disturb the lives of men, but placed in a distant past or in the inaccessible realms of Olympus. Ancient practices designed to ensure fertility were explained as respectable marriages, or at the worst as poetic love affairs or piquant episodes like the affair between Ares and Aphrodite. Complicated family-trees were drawn up. A hierarchy was established. The old and vague tribal gods attached to the soil became heroes with human attributes, who lived, suffered, and died, and whose mythical story – taking on a historical flavour – was reconstructed to accord with the rites with which they were worshipped. Sometimes, too, attempts were made to identify them with one of the great cosmic deities. Thus Agamemnon was a Thessalian god who had migrated in very early times to the Peloponnese, but later in the epic became a human being, at first triumphant but afterwards unfortunate, and still worshipped in Laconia under the name of Zeus Agamemnon.

The great Olympians, enriched in this way with borrowed functions, attributes, and anecdotes, constituted a society of immortals established, like the societies of men, on family and monarchical principles. Zeus, its father and king, lives in his palace on Olympus just as did Priam in his Trojan palace. And when he has to take some decision, he convenes the Assembly of the Gods (ἀγορά) as a constitutional monarch must do.

This brilliant mythology appealed to the Greek taste for clarity, but it no longer satisfied their curiosity. The old gods of the tribe, which had been imagined as constantly changing, provided a suitable explanation of the constant succession of natural phenomena which men saw around them. The new gods, fixed in an unchanging pattern, no longer appeared to account for this natural flux. Scientific thought awoke and sought to enrich religion with a wealth of philosophic notions. At the beginning of his *Theogony* Hesiod put an attempted cosmogony in which Earth, Chaos, and Eros – doubtless an ancient Boeotian god of fertility – are seen as the original principles of existence. Above the gods Homer placed the Fates (*Μοῖραι*) whom Zeus himself cannot alter and whose decrees he can but realise.

As theology became organised, so did a system of worship. When the Greeks first arrived in the Balkan peninsula their only priests were their tribal chieftains, who since they partook of the divine essence were the obvious intermediaries between the group and its god. Nestor, one of the most archaic figures of the *Odyssey*, himself sacrifices to Athena, with the assistance of his sons; and as we have seen (Chapter IV) after the disappearance of kingship, certain royal families retained their priestly functions. Even before that date it seems that a regular priesthood had been constituted alongside royalty. The *Iliad* mentions priests, both men and women, but strangely enough only on the Trojan side. The Greek army was accompanied only by soothsayers who interpreted the signs (in particular the flight of birds) by which the gods intimated their will to men.

At the same time as a sort of clergy was establishing itself, ritual was being defined and purified. Instead of the old magic rites intended to ensure the survival and prosperity of the tribe and its god, we see sacrifices made to him as a god who had developed into a well-defined figure more and more withdrawn from his faithful worshippers. The object of this practice was to obtain by an appropriate offering the benevolence of the deity towards the giver, and the god's effective aid in some particular need. Human sacrifices, bloodthirsty rites in which the victim was torn and devoured by the worshippers – understandable when the purpose was to communicate and commune with the god through the mediation of some carefully chosen being – gave place to innocent substitutes, sacrifices of animals, offerings of cakes, fruit, and wine. The periodic return of the festivals associated with the cycle of the seasons led to the creation of sacred calendars, whose rustic quality was gradually toned down as life in the city developed.

Finally worship was concentrated in buildings specially reserved for it. The primitive Greeks built no temples for their gods. They had only the domestic hearth whereon they prayed to their ancestors, and various consecrated places, often chosen because some natural phenomenon – a spring, a grove of great trees, exhalations, the fall of a thunder-bolt – indicated the presence of a god there. Some of these holy places maintained themselves until classical times; a circle of stones and an inscription protected them from profanation. Possibly the Greeks borrowed from the Cretans both their idols and the chapels in which they used to place images and symbols representing their gods. From the eighth century onwards, owing to the growth of anthropomorphic ideas which attributed to the gods the appearance and habits of their worshippers, these images turned into statues in human shape, often of great size, lodged in buildings which resembled those in which men dwelt, and large enough to accommodate both the god and the offerings consecrated to his use.

The Greek temple is basically an oblong room, like that of the megaron of the Mycenaean palace (*cf.* Chapter IV) and like the Christian church usually orientated from east to west. Two ranks of interior pillars held up the framework of the roof; an exterior colonnade surrounded the building and served to shelter the faithful worshippers who were not permitted to enter the habitation of the god. The ceremonies which they did have a right to attend or participate in took place outside, around an altar which was raised in front of the eastern face of the temple. This is the model on which the ancient temples of Hera at Argos and Olympia had already been built. To provide for the upkeep of temple-worship the priests owned sacred domains which they cultivated; valuable offerings also accumulated in the temple-treasuries.

And so there grew up places of pilgrimage to which worshippers flocked, especially as the god sometimes declared his will or revealed the future there. At Dodona, amidst the forests of Epirus, in a venerable sanctuary perhaps of pre-Hellenic origin, the priests interpreted the noise of the wind in the branches of great oaks as signs of the will of Zeus. At Delphi, not far from the road which to this day leads from northern Greece to the Gulf of Corinth, Phoebus-Apollo had come down from the north and displaced an ancient divinity born of the Earth and in the form of a serpent. His presence was manifested by exhalations, which caused nervous crises in certain special persons and inspired them to make utterances that were held to be prophetic. The new god drove out the old, but appropriated his oracle; and from all parts of Greece ordinary people as well as public deputations came to consult the Pythian priestess. Similarly at Olympia Zeus supplanted the local deities, and his cult was united with that of Hera, an ancient goddess of the Peloponnese. At Delos, the Ionians of the Cyclades gathered around the temple of Apollo: on Cape Mycale those of Asia Minor met near the temple of Poseidon. These earlier centres of religion, from which had been purged all senti-mental elements, (and one might almost say all religious elements, at least in the modern sense of the word) remained great sanctuaries, but played only a feeble part in the moral life of the nation. On the other hand their political influence was often very considerable, and their existence proved singularly favourable to the literary and artistic development of Greece.

VIII

THE BEGINNINGS OF GREEK LITERATURE.
THE HOMERIC POEMS AND HISTORY

The material progress which took place at the beginning of the first millennium favoured the intellectual development of the Hellenic nations and the Greeks began to make wider use of writing. An ancient tradition asserts that they owed their script to the Phoenicians. This we must accept, for there is a great resemblance between the signs of which both Phoenician and Greek alphabets are composed and between the names given to these signs. The writing in inscriptions found in Crete, Mycenae, Pylos, and elsewhere is derived from very different systems; the oldest Phoenician text actually known (an inscription from the tomb of Ahiram at Byblos) probably goes back to the thirteenth century, and is certainly earlier than the end of the second millennium. Nevertheless the Greek alphabet, as it appears in the very first texts preserved to us in which it was used, demonstrates a considerable advance on all other alphabets coming from the eastern end of the Mediterranean which have been actually deciphered. Though it reproduces only the *essential* sounds of the language, it does reproduce them all – including the vowels. Even a slight acquaintance with languages that use a less complete system – such as the Phoenician or Hebrew – will show the practical value of an alphabet that leaves nothing to guesswork.

The oldest texts in Greek script that have come down to us are inscriptions on stone or baked clay dating at the earliest from the seventh century; and the authentic portions of lists of winners at the games, of kings and priests, probably do not go back any further than the eighth century. Writing may have long remained the privilege not so much of a special caste as of a tiny minority of learned men. In any case it was widespread from the seventh century onwards. The fact that ordinary Greek mercenaries in the pay of the Pharaoh Psammetichus II could engrave on one of the giant statues at Abu-Simbel reasonably correct inscriptions, which tell us not only their names but also something of the Ethiopian expedition in which they took part between 594 and 588, makes it clear that about that time writing was in use among all classes of Greek society. It was employed, as was natural, particularly in towns with an advanced civilisation and with considerable economic development.

Hence it was most rapidly perfected in the Ionian ports where it also conformed most exactly to modifications in pronunciation; and by adopting
the Ionian alphabet in the fifth century, Athens imposed it on the whole
of Greece; while from the seventh century the alphabet that Chalcis had
transmitted to its colony at Cumae had spread to the Etruscans of the
Campania and thence to all the Italian nations.

The importance of such an innovation can easily be realised. Communication of all kinds, and particularly commercial relations, must have
been greatly facilitated – especially when we remember that this was a
nation that from the eighth century had spread from one end of the
Mediterranean to the other. Again, the government of social groups no
longer had to depend only on oral tradition; archives accumulated of
which the chroniclers soon made use; citizenship rolls with compulsory
registration were drawn up: the city became more conscious of its own
existence and of its past. But the consequences of the use of written
language are still more obvious from the literary point of view. Writing
allows the composition of voluminous works constructed on a vast scale,
and this had certainly not been possible when an author had to trust
entirely to his memory.

We may suppose, indeed, that Greek poetry was at first limited to
work-songs whose rhythm was composed, as with other Indo-European
peoples, on alternate long and short syllables, and to ritual chants accompanied by the lyre and clarinet, instruments borrowed from the
Minoan civilisation. Later the growth of an aristocratic society, which
was fond of luxury and pleasure, encouraged the composition of songs of
some length. Since the end of the Mycenaean period the narration of
pleasant stories in fine language served to amuse the nobles. These little
poems, declaimed to the accompaniment of music by professional bards,
who were received with hearty hospitality in hall and castle like the
trouvères of medieval Europe, were not in the least popular or spontaneous.
Intended first of all for the ears of the Thessalian nobles and then of the
important people in the ports of the Asian coast, they were composed in a
wholly artificial language half-way between the Aeolian and Ionian dialects, full of set phrases, many of which – stereotyped line endings, and
'stock' epithets – passed into the Homeric poems. Most important of all,
a dactylic line was employed which developed into the hexameter, a very
skilful metrical form of which no equivalent is to be found in other Indo-
European languages (except of course among the Romans who copied it).

We can get an idea of these little poems from those which Homer
has included in the *Iliad* – e.g. the rhapsodists' songs of the pleasant and
amorous adventure of Aphrodite and Ares, or the quarrel between
Odysseus and Achilles. The great events of times past, and in particular
the struggles which had led to the Greek possession of the shores of the
Aegean, were favourite topics for these set songs. One achievement

which was undoubtedly a real event – the capture of the fortress of Troy – supplied the bards with plenty of themes, and considering the importance of the expedition, its duration and consequences, we need not be surprised at their popularity. All the Hellenic peoples were believed to have taken part in it, and the 'Trojan War' came to stand for the whole story of the conquest, including the quarrels that had broken out among the Greek tribes in the course of their establishment on Greek soil. Once accept that the exploits and quarrels of Achilles, Diomedes, Agamemnon, Ajax, and Hector – who were originally all heroes of northern Greece – had taken place under the walls of the city that was so long besieged, and it was only a step to ranging some of them among the enemies of the Greeks and to including men like Hector, for instance, among the defenders of the citadel, although his name and character remained basically Greek.

Nor did the bards, in celebrating the prowess of the heroes, forget the gods. We may suspect, though we cannot prove, that they made some bold transpositions. Just as in the Germanic epic we see Siegfried the dragon-slayer alongside Attila and Theodoric and the Valkyrie, riders of the winds, so in the stories about the siege of Troy (which have a basis in historical reality) we may think of the adventures of Helen as those of a moon-goddess who, after being stolen away by evil powers, always returns more brilliant than ever. Similarly we may see in Odysseus-Ulysses a sun-god who disappeared into the country of the dead and the shades, the Cimmerians and Phaeacians, and who, on his return, like Phoebus Apollo slays his enemies with his pitiless arrows.

Thanks to the existence of writing, these poems, all dealing with the same limited range of subjects, could be grouped in extensive collections. This work was done in the course of the eighth and seventh centuries in response to the new conditions of religious and social life. These large-scale works were not intended to amuse solitary readers; they were recited at the great festivals which from this time forward gathered Greeks from all parts of the Hellenic world around some famous sanctuary. In these great pilgrimages, as at those of our own Middle Ages, a concourse of the curious crowded round to hear the bards chanting the exploits of heroes and the adventures of the gods. The festivals lasted several days, and the shorter poems of earlier days, which had been intended to please a few nobles at table, would have been quite inadequate. What was needed were long compositions, of which the recital could be spread over several sessions. Their hearers, without feeling obliged to listen from beginning to end, could enjoy hearing each day the sequel to the previous evening's recital, and notice that just as the rhythm remained uniform, and the style equal and sustained, so the characters conformed to tradition and remained characteristically themselves from one end of the story to the other. Achilles throughout remained passionate and violent, as liable to childish anger as to the most touching sorrow, while Odysseus, who became one of the most popular Greek heroes, was always bold, prudent, and inventive. Naturally in such conditions, the bards were willing enough to use as many as possible of the short poems with which oral tradition supplied them; and provided that the general plan of the work was not disrupted and the characters remained self-consistent, they were not greatly worried by slight factual inconsistencies into which such a method of composition might lead them. For instance, after the first book of the *Iliad* we should certainly have expected the story of a Greek defeat, yet the next six books are devoted to combats that turned out badly for the Trojans. What a pity it would have been, however, to omit the duels between Paris and Menelaus, Ajax and Hector, the exploits of Diomedes, and Hector's farewell to Andromache.

This also explains the somewhat clumsy piecings together, the contradictions that even in antiquity aroused criticism, and which have given rise in the last hundred and fifty years to the most varied theories about the making of the *Iliad* and the *Odyssey*. We have just seen that the conditions in which these poems were recited explain the irregularities in the flow of their stories; but on the other hand it cannot be doubted that they were given the admirable form in which we have them today by a group of poets who were living at the same time and were animated by the same spirit – or, an even simpler explanation, by a single poet whom the ancients called 'Homer'. This is to be inferred from their carefully constructed general plan, their unity of style not only in metre but in the methods of description, the general colour of the story, and the bearing of the characters, although the text was not established in any definitive form until the Alexandrine period.

We can thus see how far we can rely on the *Iliad* and the *Odyssey* as historical documents. They reflect several successive epochs. The oldest of the primitive dactylic songs may well have been composed before the end of the second millennium. They were contemporary with the decline of that Mycenaean civilisation whose centre was central Greece and especially the Peloponnese. The bards were powerfully influenced by the still recent memories of these cities 'rich in gold' and the power and ostentation of their kings. Hence the part played in the Homeric epic by Tiryns, Mycenae, Argos, Sparta, and Orchomenus, by the kings and heroes of Laconia and Argos, by Helen, Menelaus, and Agamemnon, whose presence might surprise us in the story of an expedition undertaken by the tribes of northern Greece, an expedition which, as tradition never forgot, set sail from Aulis, an Aeolian port. On the other hand the general editing of the *Iliad* and *Odyssey* most likely dates from the eighth or seventh century, and its author 'Homer', while making an obvious effort to keep his story in a distant past, has not been able to free himself completely from the influences of his own day. This accounts for the various and easily understandable contradictions in his description of certain objects and in his account of manners and customs. A characteristic example of this will be seen later on in the description of weapons; and a study of the various political, social, and religious techniques and formalities described in the two poems has revealed many similar discrepancies. These are explained and allowance can be made for them when we know the story of how these poems were composed. We must not be astonished to find, sometimes in the same passage, lines which take us right back to the Mycenaean period (when the only metal used for weapons or in industry was bronze, and when rich kings ruled the land as by divine right) and yet other lines which indicate that men knew how to work in iron and that royalty was no more than a memory.

The same thing is by no means true of the poems attributed by literary tradition to Hesiod. They bear the impress of a clearly defined period, of that 'Iron Age' when the conditions of life were hard and Greek thought began to be conscious of the questions that so imperfect a world puts to men. Moreover the spread of writing was creating, from the seventh century onwards, a public not of listeners but of readers looking for information as much as amusement. His *Theogony* is plainly a serious effort to bring order into the charming but absurd confusion of Greek mythologies and to explain the origin of the world. More characteristic is his *Works and Days*, whose purpose was to instruct the hard-working and ill-used class of small land-owners. Their toilsome existence is described with a harshness which contrasts strangely with the poetic form of the poem that was borrowed wholesale – vocabulary, style, and metre – from the Homeric epics, and this in itself proves how immediately successful these poems had been.

Archilochus of Paros (*c.* 650), on the other hand, turned his back on this learned and ornate technique and sang in an iambic rhythm, which was definitely popular in character, and went back to the times before the Greeks detached themselves from their Indo-European origins. The language he used was closely akin to the current Ionian as spoken in the Cyclades and the ports of Asia Minor, and he tells of the chances and changes of his life as a poet and a soldier, in poems which express the violent passions and the spirit of adventure that drove so many Greeks to seek their fortunes as mercenaries or colonists from one end of the Mediterranean to the other. We have seen what variety and vitality were already displayed at this early date in a literature that under an oppressive plutocratic régime and within the space of two centuries could produce long and learned epics redolent of a heroic and sumptuous past, didactic poems with a realistic and rural flavour, and lyrics in which the individual temperament found free play. We can imagine its further development as conditions became more favourable with the improvements in general well-being and advances in democracy and in civic pride.

IX

THE FORMATION OF THE GREEK STATES

We have seen how the city (the *polis*), set up under the monarchical régime, had strengthened its constitution under aristocratic rule despite the evils of government by the nobles and the rich, and the serious social disequilibrium which this had created. One of the first signs of such growth in power was to be a better organisation of the city's military strength.

The Greeks, like the Celts and Germans, were a warlike nation. In stirring lines the *Iliad* expresses the pride of the warrior and the joy of battle. But there had been many changes in weapons and tactics since the Greeks first penetrated into the Balkans. The Homeric epic has retained the evidence of this progress. The primitive poems celebrated the exploits of the individual hero who advanced on foot or in his chariot (the memory of the chariot may have been a relic of Minoan civilisation) to meet a worthy foeman, and from behind his leather shield 'as tall as a tower' challenged him to a single combat with its shifting fortunes and doubtful issue. Thus fought Ajax, son of Telamon, one of the most archaic figures in the *Iliad*. But improvements in metallurgy were to modify these straightforward methods. Offensive weapons of iron made stronger defensive armour necessary, and this was both more complete and allowed more mobility. Such armour, which could now be made in quantity, ceased to be the privilege of a few warrior nobles. All the citizens could be similarly equipped – hence the files of bronze-clad men that we see marching to battle in the *Iliad*; hence those 'men of bronze', the pirates and mercenaries from Caria and Ionia, whose appearance terrified the population of the Nile Delta in the middle of the seventh century.

The rich now monopolised the expensive privilege of maintaining a horse and serving as cavalry, usually more brilliant than useful, for the infantry was already 'queen of battles'. Strict discipline ensured its cohesion and power; and Homer contrasts the silent and impeccable march past of the Greek battalions with the noisy mob of Asiatic armies.

Such troops were necessarily used as instruments of conquest, and from the eighth century we see a number of cities enlarging their territories and establishing veritable states. The most characteristic example is that of Sparta, where military organisation was reinforced, as we shall see (Chapter X) by a peculiar social system. Sparta began by conquering all the little towns in the Eurotas valley in which, if tradition is to be believed, lived a people of Greek but not of Dorian descent, akin to those who had formerly taken refuge in the mountains of Arcadia. Once conquered, these 'inhabitants of the environs' (*Perioikoi*) constituted a special class in the Spartan state, distinct from the serfs strictly so-called (Helots). They enjoyed personal liberty, and were liable for military service. With its army thus augmented, Sparta could launch out on a greater enterprise. On the other side of Mount Taygetus lay the plain of Messenia, in ancient days as in ours one of the most prosperous and pleasant plains in all Greece. This was bound to whet the appetite of its covetous and warlike neighbour. It was seized by Sparta after a first war of aggression in the second half of the eighth century. But the Spartan state was always a poor administrator, and scarcely a century had passed before Messenia was in full revolt, probably in the second half of the seventh century; it required a second war to reduce the country.

The story of the conflict was embellished in popular tradition with romantic episodes, whose central figure was King Aristomenes, the heroic defender of Messenia; and the country remained a very uneasy conquest for the Spartans.

It was cornlands, too, that Athens coveted and conquered. From an early period she had extended her rule beyond the narrow plain whose boundaries her kings used to be able to scan from their palace on the Acropolis. This plain was bounded on the west by Mount Aegaleos, to the north by the ridges of Mounts Parnes and Pentelicus, and to the east by Mount Hymettus. At an early date Athens had become mistress of the mountain region of Attica where – still unsuspected – lay the mineral treasures of Laurium, and had laid hands on the little rural federation of which Marathon was the centre, thus securing a foothold on the shores of the Euboean channel. In the seventh century she annexed the city of Eleusis, and there in a broad plain rich in corn had stood, perhaps ever since Mycenaean times, a sanctuary sacred to the corn deities which, under the skilful administration of Athens, was to become one of the great religious centres of Greece. The bay of Eleusis is commanded by the island of Salamis on which a small independent state had established itself more or less under the influence of Aegina and Megara, the great ports of the Saronic Gulf. Athens seized it to make her conquest of Eleusis quite secure. At this time she was still ambitious for territorial conquests only. It was left to the sons of Peisistratus to show her the sea ways, and until the fifth century the poor roadstead of Phalerum was to satisfy her as a port.

In Boeotia, an essentially agricultural country, none of the small towns which were the heirs of the castles of the Mycenean period, and had grown up on the lower slopes stretching round the depression of Lake

Copaïs, had managed to assert its superiority over the others, in spite of a long succession of futile quarrels. And thus, about the seventh century, the original and fruitful idea was born of a federation at once religious, political, military, and economic in its scope, which found expression in the provision of common sanctuaries, common magistrates, a common army, and from the sixth century at latest, a common coinage.

Another federation, far more powerful, established itself in Thessaly and almost imposed its organisation on Greece as a whole, in which case its destiny would have been radically altered. The Thessalian aristocracy, originally grouped into four regional associations, ultimately set up a single federal state with a president and four regional rulers elected by the nobility. This federation had at its disposal considerable military strength which consisted mainly, as was to be expected in a stock-raising area, of an excellent cavalry force. Before long it wanted to take an active part in Greek affairs. It subdued the small mountain tribes which bordered the Thessalian plain, and then others which had gathered around the Malian Gulf and whose religious centre after a time became the shrine of Delphi. The federation intervened, as Macedon was to do two hundred and fifty years later, in the conflict that broke out between this group and the Phocian town of Cirrha which claimed control of the road leading from the sea to the Delphic sanctuary (beginning of the sixth century). Cirrha was destroyed and its territory made sacred to Apollo. Possibly some years later, but still in the seventh century, Thessaly took an important part in a war between the two great Euboean ports Chalcis and Eretria for possession of the Lelantine plain.

Several other towns in the Hellenic world were likewise drawn into this conflict by affinity of race or commercial rivalry, but it was the Thessalian cavalry which won the victory of Chalcis. This cavalry, however, does not seem to have had enough infantry support, and when the brilliant Thessalian squadrons tried to penetrate into central Greece the Theban hoplites inflicted a crushing defeat on them near Thespiae about 540. This defeat, together with a rebuff they sustained in the mountains of Phocis, put an end to Thessalian ambitions for a long period. So ended the first attempt of a great northern state to unite all Greece in a single federation. Later Thessaly herself and then Macedonia were to renew this great enterprise but with varying success.

In a Greece thus distracted by wars, the spirit of aggressive nationalism, and jealousy between one town and another, must have been to some extent restrained by economic contacts and a variety of religious organisations. In addition to the bonds between mother-state and colony, commercial connections necessarily linked city with city and state with state. These resulted in agreements which, now that writing existed, could be put down in precise terms and their maintenance insisted upon. The oldest treaties between Greek towns of which we possess authentic texts date from the fifth century, but older ones certainly existed. No international trade would have been possible if the persons of merchants and ambassadors had not enjoyed certain guarantees in foreign lands. Thus grew up the ingenious idea of the *proxenoi*, a development of the laws of family or individual hospitality which were common to many Indo-European nations. In return for material advantages or honorific titles one town would appoint a citizen of another town to act in his own town as host (πρό-ξενος) to the nationals of the town which appointed him. This office is very like that of our consuls and the institution certainly existed from the sixth century and perhaps even earlier.

The idea must also have occurred among peoples who were neighbours or of the same race to accept arbitration in, or at least some regulation of, conflicts between cities. And so alongside political and military states and federations, we find leagues of a peaceful and religious character. These consisted of cities whose representatives met at stated times in some common sanctuary, each however still preserving its independence and autonomy. Such a league was called an 'amphictyony', its members being 'those who dwelt around' (ἀμφικτίονες, ἀμφικτύονες) the shrine. Thus the temple of Poseidon on Cape Mycale served as meeting-place for the Ionians of the Asian coast; Delos for those of the Cyclades; Calauria for various towns in the neighbourhood of the Saronic Gulf. Better known was the amphictyony of the coast-dwellers along the Malian Gulf whose representatives first met at the shrine of Demeter at Anthela (Thermopylae).

At first it seems to have done little more than require from its members respect for certain elementary principles of the law of nations: thus it was forbidden in time of war to destroy a member-town or to cut off its water-supply. But its aims increased as the circle of constituent states extended. As a consequence of events of which we know nothing, it began about the beginning of the seventh century to take an interest in the sanctuary at Delphi, then in the full vigour of its development, and while it allowed the local priests to remain, it took over the administration. It did not entirely abandon Anthela, but most important gatherings henceforth took place at Delphi. On the basis of some ethnic fictions which served to disguise political ambitions, new states such as Athens, the Boeotians, and the Dorians of the Peloponnese asked one after the other to be allowed to join the league, so that it soon enjoyed a tremendous prestige.

The council of the amphictyony, made up of deputies from the participating nations, bade fair to become a tribunal with power to adjudicate in international disputes, and whose decisions and authority no people in Greece could challenge or disregard. Ambitious states often tried, with more or less success, to turn the influence of the Delphic Amphictyony to their own profit, and the Thessalians who, owing to their geographical position, always had a preponderant share in the affairs of this league, used it from the beginning of the sixth century to interfere in the affairs of central Greece.

In certain sanctuaries a notion with a wider scope than that of such limited federation found expression. The festivals which the neighbouring peasants celebrated at these shrines included races and wrestling matches, as rustic solemnities so often do. At first neighbours were attracted, and then competitors and spectators from further afield. The taste for bodily exercise, perhaps inherited from the Aegeans, which induced the Greek army to assemble around the tomb of Patroclus, or the Phaeacians in their market-place, there to watch foot races and chariot races, wrestling, boxing, and discus-throwing, drew Greeks from all parts of the Hellenic world to Delphi, to the isthmus of Corinth and to Nemea. At Olympia in particular a movable harvest festival, celebrated in high summer every four years, was from the seventh century onwards a *rendezvous* for athletes, runners, and charioteers from Greece, Asia Minor, and Sicily. At these games, skilfully exploited by the men of Elis, the spirit of emulation and comradeship grew up together with some ideas of fair play – a common result of sporting activities when properly conducted.

The various games – Olympic, Pythian (Delphic), Corinthian, and Nemean – preserved a feeling of Panhellenic solidarity which descent from a common stock and the sharing of a common language would not by themselves have been enough to maintain. This solidarity does in fact find expression in Homer, although none of the great festivals is named there. By a fiction which was not to become a reality until several centuries later under Alexander the Great, Homer imagines all the nations of the Greeks united under a single command to take part in a military expedition. And even if we cannot be sure that the names the poet arbitrarily gives to the confederates – Ἀργεῖοι, Δαναοί, Ἀχαιοί, or even more explicitly Παναχαιοί – preserved the memory of a Greece which was really united at the time of the Mycenaean civilisation, at least the concept of a union of all the Greeks was clearly one that the public would understand and appreciate.

But from the seventh century we can see words appearing which are not just the inventions of a poet but terms in current and sometimes even official use, which imply the unity of the Greek nation. The names of Hellas, and Hellenes, which were originally those of a small mountainous district bordering the Malian Gulf and its inhabitants, were first used, perhaps at Delphi, by the members of the Amphictyony to indicate their own league; then, as the league extended, to designate Greece and all the Greeks. Hesiod and Archilochus already speak of Panhellenes, and at the beginning of the sixth century an inscription shows that the umpires at the Olympic Games called themselves *Hellanodikai* (Judges of the Greeks). These names that originated at the great sanctuaries, under the double influence of federal organisation and solidarity in sportsmanship, were to last as long as the nation they designated. In spite of its geographical dispersion and political fragmentation they express its underlying unity during more than six centuries, and until the time when a strange combination of circumstances was to bring the old Homeric name of Achaeans (Ἀχαιοί) into the foreground of Hellenic history once again and turn mainland Greece into the Roman province of Achaea.

X

DISAPPEARANCE OF THE ARISTOCRATIC SYSTEM: TYRANNY AND DEMOCRACY

The oligarchic system under which the Greek cities were living at the beginning of the sixth century had resulted in a situation of social unbalance and general discontent. The old noble families could not, without disquiet, see low-born persons making themselves so rich by industry and commerce that they could put themselves forward for public office! Besides this, the aristocracy by constant inbreeding was becoming less vigorous; some families of the *Eupatridai* (the well-born) were dying out; and from the sixth century onwards at Athens those who took part in the political life of the city were a very restricted group. This narrow aristocracy, furthermore, was divided against itself, and in their internal quarrels the weaker party naturally turned for support to the lower classes. The latter felt their power to be growing, for in the new conditions of industry and of weapons and armour, victory must lean more and more towards the 'big battalions' which could only be recruited from the mass of small land-owners, town artisans, and country farmers. Yet the political framework of the city took no account of this shifting of power. The lesser folk were still excluded from the aristocratic council and from high municipal offices, and restricted to ineffective demonstrations of the market-place. Denied any effective political rights, they were continually in danger of losing their civil rights as well, and lived in constant fear of the slavery into which a grasping creditor could throw them.

It was during the sixth century that the old type of constitution, based on the aristocratic system and the principle of family solidarity, disappeared from a great many Greek cities, and a new system of government better adapted to the facts of the situation established itself. This evolution, which no doubt involved internal stresses unrecorded in history, had as one of its main stages a wholly new form of government which was called 'Tyranny', a name which to begin with carried no implication of arbitrary or oppressive rule but simply meant that power was wielded by one man, not according to principles of divine right and heredity as had been the case with the old monarchy, but based on personal prestige, the favour of the lower orders, and a strong military organisation.

Tyrants of the seventh and sixth centuries, even when of aristocratic family, were in principle defenders of the people's rights; it was the people who first gave them their extraordinary powers, which, it must be admitted, their successors often abused. Several of their number created or maintained democratic constitutions. And they too, like the founders of the very numerous colonies, were typical of the spirit of initiative and adventure that characterised the youth of the Greek nation, and led their cities in policies of wide territorial expansion, while at the same time they secured their economic development and architectural embellishment.

The Age of the tyrants in its early stages was a period of prosperity and splendour for the Greek cities that several of them (Sicyon for example and perhaps even Corinth) were never again to experience. Hence it is not surprising to find this form of government in the districts where Hellenism was most enterprising and bent on innovation. In Asia Minor, in the early sixth century, Thrasybulus was Tyrant of Miletis, Pythagoras of Ephesus. At Mitylene a middle-class philosopher named Pittacus held power, as elected 'Aisumnetes'. In Samos, about 530, the tyrant was Polycrates, an ostentatious sovereign and a great builder after the oriental style, who held the island under his rule and made it a strong maritime power, capable for a time of holding the balance between his powerful neighbours the kings of Persia and of Egypt.

Elsewhere, among the western Greeks, tyranny appeared during the first half of the sixth century in Leontini and Agrigentum, vigorous and prosperous cities of Sicily, and later in Cumae and Sybaris. In Greece proper the same type of régime had established itself in ports of the Gulf of Corinth, where a strong population of merchants, workmen, and sailors – controlled by rich and intelligent leaders – was able to keep the old noble families in check. At Sicyon, Orthagoras founded a dynasty which lasted nearly a century, during which Cleisthenes may have abolished the old aristocratic framework and established new 'tribes' on a more democratic and egalitarian basis. At Corinth, the Bacchiadae were overthrown by Cypselus who was succeeded as tyrant by his son Periander. The latter had a widely differing reputation among the ancients, some of whom represent him to have been a bloodthirsty brute and others a philosopher worthy to figure among the Seven Sages of Greece. In any case he did a great deal for the growth of Corinth, both territorially and as a sea-power, and above all by the reduction of Corcyra (Corfu) a former colony of Corinth and mistress of commerce in the Ionian Sea and along the coasts of Epirus and Illyria. He also founded, amongst other colonies, Potidaea, the key to Chalcidice and its forests, so useful to a city whose principal source of wealth was its fleet.

In this period of general transformation Sparta began to attract attention by the stability of its political organisation. This city presents a very special case in the history of Hellenism. Hitherto it appears to have had a political, economic, and artistic development parallel to that of the other Greek cities. But at some not clearly defined moment, perhaps about the beginning of the sixth century, it appears to have hardened into a rather peculiar organisation of which certain features were to be maintained to the end of ancient times. It is not at all easy to get a clear idea of the Spartan constitution when the historical period opens; no doubt many of the aspects attributed to it by late writers really date from much more recent periods. For instance it was doubtless only from the third century, at a time when the attempts at agrarian socialism being made by Agis and Cleomenes demanded an appeal to a glorious past, that tradition imputed a communist trend to the reforms of Lycurgus. What is certain is that right up to the Hellenistic period Sparta must have preserved an essentially oligarchic social system. The number of citizens with full rights, i.e. of true Spartans, was strictly limited since they alone possessed a domain in the city's territory, and this was divided into theoretically equal plots, all of them in principle hereditary and inalienable. To each of these plots several families of serfs or Helots were attached, and these were theoretically the collective property of the state.

Between the Helots and the full citizens were the Perioikoi who comprised all the other free and independent communities in Laconia, preserving personal liberty, but enjoying no political privileges. As a general rule there was no movement between these three classes; only very exceptional circumstances occasionally decided the government to grant freedom to some contingents of Helots, without however raising them to the status of full citizenship. This rigid framework corresponded to political institutions which were just as fixed. From the beginning of its history and until the end of the third century, by a strange anomaly there were at the head of Sparta's government not one king but two. One belonged to the family of the Agidae and the other to the Eurypontidae, and these two kings, alongside the five ephors, maintained real authority in peace, and had command of the armies in war. Over against this executive power, the function of policy-making belonged in essence to the aristocratic senate, the Gerousia, composed of thirty life-members including the two kings. The Assembly (Apella) of first-class citizens appears to have been reduced, from the sixth century onwards, apart from the election of ephors and senators, to the mere business of registering decisions.

These singular arrangements, whereby both an effective royalty and democratic institutions were maintained inside an aristocratic form of government, had important consequences for the history of Sparta and of Greece. It is understandable that a powerful spirit of solidarity and discipline should exist among a set of men holding first-class citizenship and restricted in number. This *esprit de corps* was maintained by some peculiar customs, for instance that of having meals in common in civil as in military life, and the harshly athletic education given to their children. Some of these practices survived as long as Hellenism; even in the fourth century A.D. young Spartans underwent flagellation at the altar of Artemis-Orthia. Before degenerating into an out-of-date formalism, however, these customs had for several centuries fostered great military virtues, and in days when the technique of war was still rudimentary they assured the triumph of the Spartan infantry on the field of battle.

This was not always a good thing for Greece, for the same causes that gave Sparta her power and prestige also distorted her activity. These few thousand Spartans, isolated amid a crowd of Helots and Perioikoi, never felt safe. The hatred of the lower classes showed itself time and time again, and often with great violence, in conspiracies and revolts. But there was no thought of conciliating them, and even the reformers of the third century would not risk improving the conditions of the Helots. Never sure of peace at home, Sparta's foreign policy could only be hesitant and cramped. In the face of the great perils that often threatened Hellenism she proved slow to take action, frequently failing to realise what was happening. She came to Marathon too late; she almost prevented Salamis; she took no part in the struggle against Philip of Macedon, and never even foresaw the threat from Rome.

Moreover, the complexity of her executive power often paralysed her, owing to conflicts between the two kings and between kings and ephors, five annually elected officials. These typified the Spartan mentality, and in their quarrels with the kings, who were usually more magnanimous and better informed than their compatriots, almost always defended the inviolability of the aristocratic system at home, and in foreign affairs the short-sighted policy of landsmen whose outlook was limited by the boundaries of the Peloponnese. Finally, in adhering to the principle of a rural aristocracy who disdainfully left commerce, industry, and even the management of their own estates to the inferior classes, Sparta condemned herself to idleness and stagnation. She stayed outside the great intellectual and economic currents that flowed through the Hellenic world with life-giving power. And it was a fact with grave consequences that this city, made up of three or four mediocre townships, scornful of work of any kind, ill-informed as to the general interests of Hellenism and untouched by its finest activities, should have had the best infantry in Greece at its disposal from the seventh century until the battle of Leuctra.

Owing to the magnificent development of Athens in the fifth and fourth centuries, to the careful study that had been made of its institutions, even in ancient days, and perhaps also to the clarity and boldness of the ideas that its statesmen had already put forward in the sixth century, the story of the city's political evolution from that date is particularly well known. At Athens a first scheme of reforms was carried through by a man with whom we leave the realm of legend and enter that of history. Solon's personality is no longer one that can be resolved into a congeries of myths, though the stories we have of his life and doings are embroidered with sentimental and romantic anecdotes several of which are of considerable antiquity. As early as the middle of the fifth century Herodotus could regale his readers with details that are more amusing than probable of an interview between the great lawgiver and Croesus King of Lydia. Fortunately we have a source of incontrovertible evidence in the works of Solon himself, poems in which he summed up his career and political achievements in clear language of studied simplicity. He belonged to a noble family of middling wealth, and must have been a merchant in his youth, in which business he gained a very keen sense of economic realities and a taste for practical measures.

The nine archons (board of chief officials) were chosen by the aristocratic Council of the Areopagus (composed of ex-archons). But public opinion forced the election of Solon as president in 594-3. There was a general craving for peace, after a series of struggles of which we know little between the *Eupatridai*, who wished to keep not only all their privileges but the benefits of an outdated system of law-making as well, and the revolutionaries who demanded a complete remodelling of the constitution and the re-distribution of lands. To this latter radical measure, which many other reformers in later periods were to advocate in Greece, Solon would never agree. But soon after his election he imposed another reform which had results almost as important. He deprived creditors of the power to reduce an insolvent debtor or any member of his family to slavery. The boldness of this reform can be appreciated if we remember that in Britain imprisonment for debt was not suppressed until 1869. And we can realise its political consequences if we note that this law, which was made retrospective, resulted in the enfranchisement of many citizens of the middle and lower classes who then swelled the ranks of opponents of the *Eupatridai*.

To this reform Solon added another which, in spite of its renown, remains for us somewhat obscure and which surprised ancient historians by its revolutionary character. He ordered, we are told, the cancellation of debts! We can ill imagine how the Athenian economy, rudimentary though it may have been, could have endured the disturbance which so radical a decree would cause. The terms used by the ancients to indicate this operation were χρεῶν ἀποκοπή (cancellation of debts) and σεισάχθεια (the shaking off of burdens). The fine verses in which Solon boasts of having cleared the land of Attica of the mortgage-stones that disfigured it, seem to indicate a reform that was above all agrarian in nature and aimed chiefly at relieving the debt-burdened small land-owners.

This cancellation of debts was easier to apply since Solon had also modified the Athenian systems of weights and coinage. Until his time Athenian coinage had used the standards of Aegina, the largest commercial town on the Saronic Gulf whose mina was 630 grams of silver. Solon adopted the lighter Euboean mina and drachma (one mina = 431 grams of silver) which necessitated the recasting of the existing coinage and a fall in the purchasing power of the new drachma. This was a great advantage to the small rural land-owners who could sell the produce of their fields at higher prices, and with the increased number of coins could more easily pay off their debts. At the same time this system, in bringing the Attic drachma into line with that of Euboea, which circulated not only in Euboea but at Corinth, in Sicily, and in the Black Sea colonies, greatly facilitated trade between Athens and some of the greatest commercial centres of the period.

The interest taken by Solon in trade was shown again by his law, which, while forbidding the export from Attica of important commodities such as wheat and figs, allowed the export of oil and incidentally led to the development of Athenian pottery and of the port of Piraeus.

To round off these economic and financial reforms, further measures affecting the laws and constitution were introduced. A law gave, or at least confirmed, the right to make a will, declaring that if a man had no legitimate male heirs he could make whatever testamentary disposition of his goods he wished. This favoured the spreading of both capital and the ownership of land, and counteracted the monopolising of fortunes encouraged by the old family organisation. By authorising any citizen to require satisfaction on behalf of an injured third party Solon struck an equally heavy blow at the ancient legal procedure of 'composition', thus strengthening the authority of the state and extending its judicial competence. This measure must have had important juridical consequences. A new kind of court became necessary to try all the civil cases, which were less and less often settled by transactions between the interested families. Hence came that very modern creation, the *Heliaia*, a new tribunal, a regular jury chosen by lot from the mass of citizens without distinction of wealth or class.

All these changes tending to ensure the ascendancy of the state over the family at the same time weakened aristocratic institutions. The old Council of the *Eupatridai*, which sat on the hill of the Areopagus, and had been both a supreme Court and a political assembly, had had its powers in criminal trials limited by the creation in the seventh century of the Court of the *Ephetai*. Now there arose side by side with it this new popular jury of the *Heliaia*. Its political powers, too, were reduced along with its judicial functions. It lost the right to nominate the archons. In any case, though the ancient authors do not state the fact, it is difficult to believe that Solon's reforms were not sanctioned by a vote of the old Assembly of the whole city ('Εκκλησία) gathered in the Agora, which must have undertaken to safeguard the new constitution, to the great advantage of its own authority and prestige.

As we have noted, these 'laws of Solon' did not disrupt the Athenian city-state. They retained its framework, the four ancient Ionian tribes, and, with some modifications, the old electoral organisation; eligibility as magistrates was made the privilege of the three wealthiest classes, the other participating only in the Court of the *Heliaia*, the popular Assembly, as well as the elections by which each tribe elected ten members by universal suffrage and from whom the archons were then chosen by lot. This queer system was an attempt to reconcile democratic principles with the tradition that attributed a sacred character to the chief magistrates as having inherited royal powers. Moreover, it is probable that Solon's reforms, such as the right to make wills, or even the abolition of slavery for debt, were only the result of an evolution in public manners and opinion begun long before his time. Yet it remains true that Solon's legislative activity was fraught with important consequences. It favoured the development in the countryside of the small land-owner, and in the towns of a middle class of merchants whose number was increased by the many naturalisations of which Solon's legislation showed itself very tolerant. Thus it prepared the advent of a sort of 'Third Estate' of peasants, traders, and craftsmen which was to make Athens glorious in the fifth and fourth centuries, and whence sprang some of its greatest statesmen from Themistocles to Demosthenes.

We do not know how long Solon's legislative activity continued. A single year was probably not enough to set his programme going, and the different dates that are given for his period of office as archon may support the conclusion that he held it for more than a single year. Once his final laws had been voted and engraved on the κύρβεις – the great wooden tablets pivoted on a vertical axis which stood under the portico surrounding the Chief Archon's house at the side of the *agora* – and were hence accessible to all citizens, Solon seems to have retired from public life. From that moment legend seized upon him and made of him a wandering philosopher, fabricating constitutions for other Greek cities, or explaining the principles of Greek wisdom to the proud kings of the East. In any case there is no reason to doubt either his retirement or his departure from Athens. Perhaps he foresaw the practical difficulties that would follow the putting into effect of his laws; and in fact the thirty years that followed were full of strife. The *Eupatridai* sought to defend their old privileges or at least to retain those that Solon had left to them; while the lesser folk, country labourers and town artisans, as they became more numerous and more active, tried to get some share in the government. An attempt at proportional representation, with five archons chosen from the *Eupatridai* and four from among peasants and workers, had no success.

In 632 the Athenians had prevented the establishment of a tyranny by

Cylon, but such a danger had not been averted for ever. For in 561 there were three parties opposed to each other: the nobles (or *Pedieis* recruited among owners of estates in the Athenian plain (*Πέδιον*); the moderates, the *Paralioi* made up of well-to-do middle-class men and merchants, particularly those living in the little ports growing up along the southern shore (*Παραλία*) of Attica; and finally the 'popular' group, the *Diakrioi*, which included mostly shepherds and agricultural workers employed on the great estates stretching across the north-east of Attica (*Διακρία*). To these were soon added a whole set of malcontents, debtors freed by Solon's laws, and citizens of dubious origin. Each of these factions was led by an aristocrat (as happened so often in Rome from the second century onwards): the *Pedieis* had Lycurgus as chief; the *Paralioi* had Megacles of the family of the Alcmaeonids; and the leader of the *Diakrioi* was Peisistratus. He came from Brauron in eastern Attica, had gained popularity by leading a successful campaign against Megara, and by reoccupying the island of Salamis, which had first been conquered in the seventh century, then lost, then retaken, and lost again. He was the favourite of the popular Assembly, and after an attempt on his life he persuaded them to vote him a bodyguard for his protection, with whom he established himself on the Acropolis, the former home of the kings. Athens, too, had her tyrant, but not for long, since his opponents rallied to force him out of Attica. Within five years the factions led by Lycurgus and Megacles, who had united to expel him from Athens, disagreed amongst themselves, and Peisistratus (with the help of Megacles) contrived to return to Athens. The new arrangement was not successful, however, and Peisistratus again established himself as tyrant, but soon had to withdraw in 555 and settle in Thrace, from where he kept a close watch on how things were going, and prepared his eventual return in 546.

Abroad Peisistratus was able to obtain considerable wealth from the silver mines, which then enabled him to bid for really effective political and military support, and hire mercenaries. Then when the attention of Sparta and those who were most hostile to tyranny was diverted towards Argos, Peisistratus, who had kept an eye on the turn of events, judged that the moment had come for his return to Athens. Crossing the Euripus channel he found an army of his partisans awaiting him in his faithful *Diakria*, and with these – reinforced by contingents from Euboea, Boeotia, Argos, and his friend Lygdamis, he easily gained control of Athens.

Established once again on the Acropolis, with the support of his guards, Peisistratus used his power with moderation and skill. Like all usurpers who seize power after a period of internal struggles he found a policy of external conquest the best way to divert the energies of his fellow citizens. He was the real founder of Athenian greatness, the forerunner of the imperialist generals of the fifth century, and like them was wise enough to realise that his country's future lay on the sea.

Athens had begun to take an interest in maritime affairs: a class of sailors and shipbuilders had grown up there, and the *naukrariai* – a kind of co-operative naval outfitting corporation, each of which undertook to provide the state with a vessel properly equipped and maintained – attained political importance. They played a considerable though ill-defined part in the suppression of Cylon's abortive *coup d'état*. It was probably Peisistratus who guaranteed free passage in the Saronic Gulf for Athenian ships by taking possession, and this time for good, of the island of Salamis. He realised the necessity of ensuring untrammelled importation of corn for a city with little fertile soil of its own and a population turning more and more to commerce, industry, and shipping. So he assured safe communication with the wheat-lands of the Black Sea area by establishing ports on the Dardanelles. In the Hellespont the Athenians had some time previously won a foothold at Sigeum, in about 590, in the Thracian Chersonese, he encouraged the settlement of Athenian colonists under the leadership of Miltiades, an aristocrat who was rather too enterprising and ambitious to be allowed to stay in Attica. At the same time Athens secured a foothold in the Cyclades by placing Naxos, the most important island, under the authority of the Tyrant Lygdamis, a friend of Peisistratus, while Delos – the religious centre of the Cyclades – also came under Athenian influence.

At home Peisistratus seems to have ruled in the spirit of Solon's reforms. He avoided any great change in the constitution and does not seem to have troubled to obtain the confirmation of his extraordinary powers from the Popular Assembly. The archons were no longer to be chosen by lot, and he could thus secure places in the College of Archons each year for himself, his relatives, and friends. This, in turn, allowed him to take the necessary measures to ensure civil peace and to foster prosperity in Attica. Quite rightly, he had a strong feeling that in a country that was still basically agricultural, the best guarantee against revolution was a peasant-class contented with its lot. Two clever schemes were introduced with this intention: first, a kind of agricultural credit-bank to lend small land-owners the funds necessary to improve their equipment or augment their holdings; secondly, the institution of circulating tribunals to save the peasant those journeys to town which, whatever his country, make the course of justice unpalatable to him. This care for their interest helped to persuade the Athenians to accept the financial measures necessitated by the grand scale of his military expeditions abroad and his building programmes at home.

An income tax of five per cent was introduced, and the treasury was also enriched by the output of the silver mines of Mount Pangaeus, where Peisistratus had obtained a private estate during his exile – a considerable source of wealth and influence. Doubtless he also began to draw revenues from the silver mines of Laurium, which were much more lucrative in the fifth century because of their nearness to Athens.

On the death of Peisistratus (c. 527) no problem seems to have arisen as to the succession. His two older sons, Hippias and Hipparchus, were established on the Acropolis and stayed there, sharing between them the duties of government chiefs. Hippias concerned himself with administration and politics; Hipparchus supervised religious affairs and their natural complements in literature and the fine arts. This arrangement lasted without mishap until the conspiracy of Harmodius and Aristogiton. Party spirit so soon distorted accounts of this event that ever since the fifth century it has been hotly disputed whether it was a plot of young enthusiasts aflame with love of liberty, or merely an act of personal revenge. Whichever it was, the attempt failed; the inoffensive Hipparchus was assassinated, but Hippias, who really wielded the power, survived.

Danger had soured his temper, and he became a violent and suspicious tyrant. He thought of leaving the Acropolis to secure himself in the fortress of Munychia, where the neighbouring ports of the peninsula of the Piraeus would have given him a safe line of retreat and easy embarkation in case of revolt. But he had no time to realise these projects. The Alcmaeonids, banished since Cylon's attempt, felt that the moment had come for their return to Athens. A first attempt, in which a squadron of young exiled noblemen tried to push into Attica and establish themselves at Leipsydrion on the slopes of Mount Parnes, did not succeed. This repulse decided the Alcmaeonids to ask help from other states. This was an easy matter for them, for they were related to several great families in Greece, and in constant communication (until the capture of Sardis in 546) with the kings of Lydia, who had been the chief manipulators of money in the Aegean lands during the first half of the sixth century. The Alcmaeonids themselves were clever financiers, and had acquired a reputation all over Greece by undertaking a splendid reconstruction of the temple at Delphi after it had been destroyed by fire in 548. In this pious undertaking they no doubt made a good deal of money and certainly many useful friends, especially at Sparta, whose attention was very opportunely called to Athenian affairs by a pronouncement of the Delphic oracle.

Little by little during the sixth century, Sparta had become the chief state in Greece. Beyond the territories directly under her sway she had built up a league which a number of Peloponnesian cities – Elis, Corinth, Sicyon – had joined one after another. How this federation worked in the sixth century we do not really know; the bonds that held it together must have been very loose. But Sparta, mistress of two-fifths of the Peloponnese and provided with the best infantry in Greece, must have played a preponderant part in it, though she failed to use it to attain any bold or far-sighted political ends. Her ill-balanced internal situation limited her outlook. Nevertheless she could not easily tolerate Athenian expansion, in which the sons of Peisistratus were allied to her old rival Argos and to Thessaly, whose cavalry maintained its great prestige. Perhaps also she imagined, with that misunderstanding of realities which so often marked her policy, that by bringing back the Alcmaeonids she would be promoting the re-establishment in Athens of an oligarchic system which was sure to function in her favour. She decided to intervene in Attica and marched her soldiers in as the defenders of liberty. After a preliminary defeat when the Spartan infantry was routed by the Thessalian cavalry, a great expedition got the better of Hippias, who was besieged on the Acropolis and had to surrender (510). He left Attica and took refuge at Sigeum, where we shall come across him again at the time of the Persian wars.

Athens was free. And the party returning there triumphant was in no humour to restore for someone else's benefit a form of government which had served its time. We shall see later (Chapter XIII) why tyranny was maintained in Ionia until the beginning of the fifth century and in Sicily even longer; but in continental Greece at least it was rapidly disappearing from the cities where it had established itself during the sixth century. At Corinth for example Psammetichus, the nephew and successor of Periander, had in 584 been assassinated during a riot, and a government of moderates had been put in his place. The Alcmaeonids took this lesson to heart, and especially Cleisthenes, who at this time was the most outstanding member of that great family and highest in favour with the Athenian populace. The confusion which had developed in the aristocratic party since the expulsion of Hippias gave him an opportunity to suggest some important constitutional changes to the Athenians. They were founded on one of those administrative revolutions to which reformers in all countries have always attached great importance, since they break up the framework which served to support the old political system.

Cleisthenes replaced the four traditional Ionian tribes with ten tribes of a purely artificial character. These were no longer local divisions, but each comprised three *trittyes* (sectors of territory), one situated in the city, a second on the coast, and the third inland. Each of these *trittyes* consisted of a number of parishes or demes. In the eyes of the state every Athenian citizen belonged only to the deme where he was domiciled and to the tribe to which that parish belonged. From the end of the sixth century it became customary, in legal documents, to add to the name of any citizen an indication of his parish, from which his tribe could easily be deduced. This new organisation was intended to do away with the regional spirit that had brought Peisistratus to power and had facilitated his return.

Henceforth the old groupings by families, phratries, and aristocratic tribes, which had acted as centres of conspiracy and supports for an out-of-date and biased law, were lost in the mass of citizens, a mass that had increased by the admission into the city of foreigners, freedmen, and slaves whom the new régime had been very willing to receive: or if they survived it was only as inoffensive parochial associations of a mainly religious character.

The ten tribes also became the basis for the creation of the Council (βουλή) of five hundred members, fifty selected from the citizens of each tribe, chosen by lot. Each group of fifty (*prytaneis*) acted during one tenth of the year as an executive committee responsible for the prompt dispatch of current business. By organising this regulating body recruited so democratically, Cleisthenes no doubt deprived the old Council of the Areopagus of much of its political activity. The new body, together with the People's Assembly, made up a two-chamber system like that of republican Rome, or even analagous to that in modern constitutional governments; but with this difference, that the regulating power of the *Boulê* was largely negative, since its chief function was to prepare laws and decrees to be submitted for the approval of the Popular Assembly. The latter now played the preponderant part in the city's political life; and it is curious to see, in the earliest Greek tragedy which we possess (*The Suppliants* by Aeschylus) the people of Argos being consulted by their hesitant king and deciding (by a popular decree, like those pronounced by the Athenian Assembly), the fate of the fugitives who are imploring his protection.

The radically democratic constitution achieved by the fifth century did not yet exist, however. Although the people were in control of the legislative power in the *Ekklesia* and the *Boulê*, and of judicial power through the tribunal of the *Heliastai*, they were still excluded from the executive. At the end of the sixth century the great civil and military offices of state were still reserved for the two highest electoral classes. Yet the progress achieved during the century was obvious and the aristocratic party was growing restive at the successive restrictions to its prestige and authority. It decided to resist, and found a rather unexpected and still unexplained ally in Cleomenes, one of the kings of Sparta, who entered Attica at the head of a small army, established himself on the Acropolis and demanded the banishment of Cleisthenes and his chief supporters. Such was the fame of the Lacedaemonian infantry that at first the Athenians offered no resistance. But when it looked as if the new constitution was to be tampered with and the Council of the Five Hundred to be abolished, the populace rose in revolt and besieged Cleomenes on the Acropolis, where after three days he surrendered.

But now Sparta's military pride was offended. A great expedition was planned, in which the members of the Peloponnesian League and also the Boeotians and Chalcidians joined, fearing no doubt that the Athenians had become too enterprising since Peisistratus had become tyrant. The concentration of allied troops took place in the plain of Eleusis. Here for the first time was shown the weakness of Greek confederations, as well as the inconsistency of Spartan policy. The coalition broke up before battle had been joined. The Corinthians absolutely refused to take part in this expedition, through their hatred of tyranny. The two kings of Sparta could not agree with one another. The Boeotians and Chalcidians, seeing this disunion, went home. They were pursued by the Athenian army, which had no hesitation in giving battle first to the sturdy infantry of the Boeotian League and then to the powerful cavalry of Chalcis (506 B.C.). Their victories gave all Greece reason to reflect. A great assembly of the Peloponnesian League gathered at Sparta, and in spite of the presence of the ex-tyrant Hippias, who had been specially invited by the Lacedaemonians, was unwilling to interfere with the young democracy which had displayed its military prowess in so brilliant a fashion.

XI

GREEK MANNERS, ART, AND SCIENCE
IN THE SIXTH CENTURY

In spite of the political disturbances which afflicted so many Greek cities during the sixth century, the progress of commerce, industry, and the democratic mode of government encouraged the growth of private fortunes. A middle-class of land-owners, merchants, bankers, shipbuilders and manufacturers developed and grew rich in many towns, and was eager to display its affluence. Thus elegant styles of living, that the population of the Ionian ports had borrowed from the great towns of Lydia, spread throughout Greece. The Athenians of Pericles's day recalled the times when their grandfathers had long tunics of fine linen for town wear and golden ornaments in their hair. Women's dress was still more refined. They wore tunics of light wool or muslin, pleated and embroidered, many-coloured shawls, and elaborate hair-styles with long tresses, curls, and fillets.

No great progress in comfort, however, went with these refinements in dress. Both literature and archaeology reveal that the Greek home remained small and undistinguished in style until the Hellenistic period. But one can have a pleasant life in a modest dwelling. The poets and vase-painters depict very lively banqueting scenes, with female musicians and dancers in attendance. These were recruited all the more easily owing to the increase of slavery. The lawful wife, as may well be imagined, was absent from such festive gatherings. And indeed, although the situation of the free woman seems to have improved from the legal point of view following the reforms of the sixth century, which in some cities (Athens among them) gave her the right to own land and specifically protected the orphan girl who had no brother, her social position had deteriorated. This was particularly noticeable in the Ionian lands where the influence of oriental manners was stronger. Women were shut up in the *gynakeion*, and completely excluded from political and intellectual life unless their literary or artistic talents enabled them to win fame and disregard convention.

And as private luxury increased, the public embellishment of the cities continued. The sense of security had increased, thanks to the armies and fleets which had suppressed brigandage and piracy and had allowed the towns to spread over the plain and move nearer towards the sea. In Athens an industrial quarter developed to the north-west of the Acropolis along the road leading to the commercial centres of Boeotia and the isthmus of Corinth – on the very spot where to this day we can see the stalls and workshops of the bazaar. Ephesus came down from the heights of Coressus and established itself right on the shore of the bay which the deposits of the river Caÿster had not yet silted up.

The tyrants flattered the municipal pride of their subjects by contributing to the adornment of their cities. Many of them planned, and at least partly carried out, programmes of great public works. The matter of a water-supply was vital to these growing cities. Aqueducts were built at Megara and Samos, fountains erected at Corinth and Athens. The *agora* at Athens, the centre of its economic and political life, was finally laid out in the middle of the new quarter of the town and surrounded with porticos and public buildings. Later, perhaps in the time of Cleisthenes, solid foundations were laid on the slopes facing the Acropolis to uphold the terrace of the Pnyx, where the Popular Assembly of the new democracy had its meeting-place.

The greatest improvement in architectural beauty and majesty, however, was in the temples built to honour the gods. Around the shores of the Mediterranean, from Selinus to Miletus, temples were erected surpassing in size and wealth any previously to be seen there. That of Olympian Zeus, which the sons of Peisistratus began to build in a suburb of Athens and which was not completed until six centuries later, had a *cella* more than fifty feet wide and columns with a diameter of nine feet at the base. On the Acropolis, the ancient temple of Athena with a length of a hundred feet (*Hekatompedon*), which had seemed marvellous to Solon's contemporaries, was now surrounded with a colonnade: by the end of the sixth century the foundations were laid down of a much vaster building, which was to be carried on and completed by the architects of the following century. This increase in the dimensions of buildings was accompanied by similar progress in constructional methods and the evolution of new architectural styles. The bonding of walls improved and the use of the bevel square made possible those faultless and most decorative combinations of polygonal stones, of which the retaining walls of the terrace to the temple of Apollo at Delphi are the finest example. The shafts of pillars became more slender and their appearance was further refined by fluting; the ovolos of capitals were raised and made more vigorous, marble began to be used for decorating pediments. Architects tried new formulae. Alongside the purely Hellenic style that came to be known as Doric there arose, first in Ionia and afterwards in the Cyclades and as far as Delphi, graceful edifices of smaller size. These could be entirely of marble and had façades enhanced with a very ornate decoration, often inspired by oriental designs and picked out in striking colours.

They were adorned with voluted capitals, sometimes supported by graceful caryatids, with palm-leaf, lotus flower and convex mouldings, and friezes with sculptured figures full of movement and life.

Sculptors gave up working in soft stone to devote themselves to marble, more difficult to manipulate but more enduring and with a seductive splendour. Their tools and techniques slowly adapted themselves to the new material. The cult of gymnastic exercises drew their attention to the beauty of the human body, and as a result of persistent effort they learned to reproduce its form, its structure, and even its movement. Statues, which at first had been immobile with arms held stiffly against the body, showed movement and animation. On the pediment of the colonnade to the *Hekatompedon*, Athena has overthrown a giant and is about to transfix him as he collapses at her feet. Together with male nudity artists learned to reproduce with minute accuracy the coquetry of women's attire. At Delphi, at Athens, bas-reliefs and statues in lively colours give us the very image of the fashions worn by Ionian women as the sixth century was drawing to its close.

At the same time the metal-founders of Samos discovered how to cast large statues in bronze, and their methods were not improved upon to any extent until the Renaissance. Progress was made, too, in the minor arts. If the jewellery of the sixth century is not as splendid as that of the Mycenaean epoch, the wider use of money favoured the engraver's art in the commercial centres of Asia Minor, of Euboea, and the Saronic Gulf. In Attica, where potters had discovered an excellent clay, they became numerous enough to give their name to one of the new quarters of Athens (Ceramicus). They manufactured vases and cups, with figures standing out in a fine black glaze against a background reddened by firing; and thanks to their variety of shape and perfection of pattern, these displaced throughout the Mediterranean area the vases that had been mass-produced without much care and without art in the potteries of Corinth.

In towns thus embellished by architects and sculptors, religious ceremonies could take on a magnificence of style that the tyrants were only too anxious to develop. Thus the Peisistratids gave a new splendour to the cult of Athena, protectress of the city, and rivalled the Delphic and Olympic Games with the *Panathenaia*, celebrated like those other festivals every four years. In these city fêtes, as formerly in those of the castles and the great pilgrimages, literary entertainments played a great part. Certainly the old poetic forms were much appreciated, and it was to facilitate the recitation at the *Panathenaia* that Hipparchus had a particularly careful edition of the Homeric poems produced. At Sparta, right up to the Hellenistic period the warlike elegies of Tyrtaeus, which used a language very like Homer's and in a similar dactylic metre, were chanted on military occasions. But a more or less modulated recitation accompanied by discreet chords on the lyre was considered most suitable for the epic or elegy.

In the districts where Doric was spoken the people were particularly fond of the old hymns, melodies, and dances that constituted part of the old worship. Out of these a new form grew up in which poem, music, and dance were inseparable. In a language as artificial as that of the epic, but with a generally Doric turn of phrase so as to be understood by the public they were addressing, authors of very diverse origin wrote works to order and for money at Sparta, at Corinth, in Sicily, at Athens, commissioned either by a city or by a rich private patron. Authors came from many parts of the Greek world – Alcman from Asia, Simonides from the Aegean, Stesichorus from Sicily, Ibycus from Italy. Their poems, judging by the very inadequate fragments that have come down to us, seem to have been of an erudite and impersonal nature, and their chief charm would doubtless have been in the actual performance when their complicated rhythms were enlivened by lyre and flute, and the balance of the stanzas was emphasised by the evolutions of the chorus.

Some agrarian cults, that of Dionysus among others, with their notions about life and death, suffering, resurrection, and the mystical intoxication which they fostered, produced works of a special character. While it is unfortunately impossible for us to appreciate the worth of the 'dithyrambs' composed in the sixth century at the instigation of the tyrants of Sicyon and Corinth, we do know what a wonderful literary movement was to develop from the rustic poems sung in the agricultural demes (parishes) of eastern Attica by the brotherhoods of the 'He-Goats', worshippers of Dionysus. An important improvement was introduced when a master of the chorus – the ancients credited Thespis with this change – added to the chorus a 'replier' ($\upsilon\pi o\kappa\rho\iota\tau\eta s$) who took the part of the suffering hero: the song of the Goat ($\tau\rho\alpha\gamma\omega\delta\iota\alpha$) thus became an action ($\delta\rho\hat{\alpha}\mu\alpha$). And so in making Athens the centre of worship of Dionysus the Peisistratids were preparing the way for the wonderful development of tragedy in later days. The more ribald element in these rustic festivities, which included the carrying in procession of a phallus as symbol of fertility, and ludicrous disguises and a regular exchange of gibes and mocking couplets, assumed a literary form in the works of Epicharmus who lived in Sicily at the other end of the Greek world towards the close of the sixth century.

Alongside this poetry intended for the city festivals, other literary types developed designed to please a more restricted public. The gay life being enjoyed in Ionia encouraged the composition of songs of good cheer, sung to the lyre; in these Anacreon excelled. Their themes – love and wine – were commonplace enough, but their charm lay in their lightness of touch, and in the graceful turns of phrase. Nearer still to the popular tongue as spoken in the Ionian ports were the satirical iambics of Hipponax of Ephesus.

In the Aeolian regions, on the other hand, poetry maintained the air of personal communication that Archilochus had given it. Alcaeus, and above all the poetess Sappho, in a style which was simple without being commonplace, sang of the passions and torments of love with a penetrating sincerity and conciseness that only Catullus has equalled in Latin and Heinrich Heine among the moderns.

'What is not verse is prose', and Greek prose existed from the moment when, thanks to the invention of writing, cities could maintain archives, lists of magistrates, and compendia of laws. These documents, which municipal vanity tended to amplify by extending them into the distant past, were to be found from the seventh century, specially in Ionian districts. Together with oral tradition, they became evidence for genealogies and chronicles based on entirely artificial calculations which counted every thirty or forty years as a 'generation', and whose arbitrary conclusions long cluttered up the history of the early centuries of Rome and Greece. Such 'inquiries' (ἱστορίαι), out of which history developed, are not the only ones in which the curiosity of the Ionians exercised itself. Hecataeus of Miletus not only wrote a *Genealogy*, but also a *Journey round the Earth* illustrated with a map. The universe no longer seemed only a collection of things either dangerous or profitable, the former to be avoided and the latter to be used, but began to be considered as an object for disinterested study. It is true that the physicists of the sixth century, like all the scientists of antiquity, had no conception of experiment or of the experimental method, by which the phenomenon under consideration can be analysed and its various elements isolated.

On the other hand they displayed a curiosity constantly on the alert, an attentive observation, and a great effort of logic. For the first time in the history of human thought there appeared the idea, perhaps mistaken but certainly fruitful, that it was vital to look for a primary element of the universe, which might be water as Thales of Miletus held, or perhaps air as Anaximenes thought. And since it was not merely a matter of asserting this principle, but also of showing how everything arose out of it, Anaximander, who believed in the existence of a primitive, indeterminate element (ἄπειρον), came to formulate crude but daring theories which link up with Laplace's hypotheses on the origins of the solar system and those of Lamarck on transformism. These meditations on first causes led Xenophanes, another Ionian, to form the idea of a unique and perfect god who no longer had any connection with the gods of human shape and passions that make up the polytheism of Homer and Hesiod. He left Colophon for Greater Greece and attracted disciples there, among them

Parmenides who was the first to suggest the opposition between intelligible reality (ἀλήθεια) and appearance (δόξα), and prepared the way for the metaphysical constructions of later centuries.

Another great philosopher, Pythagoras of Samos, also abandoned the Ionian public for that of the towns in southern Italy, which were perhaps more interested in serious speculations, and explained to enthusiastic audiences at Croton the properties of numbers and space. He took from arithmetic and geometry the exclusively utilitarian character they had always held in Egypt and Babylonia, where they had never been much more than ready reckoners for commercial and financial transactions, or empirical methods for orientating sacred buildings and working out a permanent land-survey. He enunciated the laws which regulate the relations between numbers themselves, and a large number of theorems about lines, angles, and areas. Applying his results to acoustics, and especially to astronomy, he was the first to affirm that the earth is a sphere and not a disc, and to attempt a geometrical explanation of eclipses, for which astronomers at that time knew only the Babylonian tables, based on observations maintained over several centuries.

It was not only by means of books that the thoughts of these sages were disseminated; indeed it is by no means certain that Thales or even Pythagoras ever wrote anything down. They were the originators of those traditions of oral teaching that lasted as long as Hellenism. In such a transmission by word of mouth it was quite natural that scientific instruction should be accompanied by moral considerations, though these, it is true, were not accepted with the same enthusiasm throughout the Hellenic world. In the eastern parts, during the sixth century, a practical and pedestrian set of principles prevailed, which had nothing systematic about them. The maxims into which this wisdom was condensed were attributed to a number of sages (σοφοί) of whom several, it must be noted, had been statesmen – Solon, Bias, Pittacus, Periander. Later, tradition quite arbitrarily declared that they had constituted a College of seven members, whence had issued those famous sayings – 'Man, know thyself', 'Nothing too much', etc. – which spread throughout the Aegean area and were sometimes engraved on the façades of temples and public buildings. In greater Greece, on the other hand, in the small coteries that gathered around Xenophanes, and especially around Pythagoras, a very lofty if obscure morality was elaborated in which strange notions about numbers, based on the master's marvellous arithmetical discoveries, were reinforced by ideas about physical and moral purity and the immortality of the soul.

These doctrines corresponded to new needs that neither the rationalistic explanations of the Ionian physicists nor the traditional religion could satisfy. As the condition of their cities improved, men could see that the condition of the world was very far from matching the ideal of justice set forth by their legislators, that evil was often triumphant, and that in this world one did not always witness the punishment of crime and over-weening pride. The idea of personal responsibility, as it grew clearer, was opposed to the older notions that had got round the difficulty by visiting the sins of the fathers very heavily on the children. So arose the idea of the pains that the wicked would have to endure after death, which gave point to the vague current conceptions about the vital spark ($\psi v \chi \acute{\eta}$), and the obscure and diminished existence it led after the destruction of its body. Hence also, in order to escape the pain of these punishments, precepts of moral conduct were formulated and accompanied by regulations often borrowed from very ancient rituals.

Brotherhoods were founded whose members conformed to these rules of conduct. In particular we know of one that owed its origin to Orpheus, a poet-musician from Thrace, like Dionysus, but who rewarded his adepts only with an ecstatic calm and not with the intoxication of beer and wine. We are ill informed about the actual state of Orphic doctrines in the sixth century, and it is uncertain whether the admixture of Egyptian influences later to be found in them already existed at that time. It can, however, be affirmed that the notions of the immortality of the soul, of rewards and penalties in the hereafter, of moral and physical purity, which have always constituted the foundations of Orphism, were already widespread at that date at any rate among poets and the learned. They had an influence on incipient Pythagoreanism: late lines in the *Odyssey* describe the torments of great sinners in the regions of Hades; and the feeling that purification was necessary after sin, though still unknown to Homer, was so strong among Athenian statesmen in the sixth century, that ceremonies of col-lective purification were celebrated at Delos, and even at Athens.

Religion felt the influence of these new ideas. Though some sanctuaries – Delphi among others – long opposed them, others skilfully learned how to adapt themselves; and particularly and naturally those where the old agrarian cults based on beliefs about death and resurrection were cele-brated. Hence those 'secret initiations' where an audience previously subjected to rites of purification was then allowed to witness ceremonies which ancient authors have kept secret, but which we may suppose were intended to express the vicissitudes, sorrows, and joys that awaited the soul after the death of the body. At Eleusis, where the legend of the maiden Korê, carried off but afterwards restored to her mother Demeter, had taken a particularly moving form, the priests arranged for representa-tions of a sacred drama and added comments upon it. A kind of Passion-play was produced in a great hall with tiers of seats, built in the time of the Peisistratidae; its symbolic value was heightened by clever staging.

These 'mysteries', which seem to have been an innovation of the seventh and sixth centuries and not a really ancient form of religion, certainly played a great part in the history of the growth of moral ideas in Greece. They were accessible to all who were willing to undergo initiation ceremonies, without distinction of race, city, family, or social rank, and in a striking form they spread throughout all classes of society various ideas about good and evil, and comforting doctrines on death and human destiny. The Hymn to Demeter, composed in the early sixth century, says:

> Happy is the man who in this earthly life has been able to witness these sacred ceremonies; but for him who has not participated in these holy rites a very different fate is in store, even when he shall be no more than a corpse in the dank subterranean darkness.

The Hellenic people of the sixth century provide a spectacle of remarkable intellectual activity. In law, ethics, science, and art, they were everywhere innovators, and everywhere their innovations proved fruitful. Classical Antiquity did no more than develop and perfect the types of architecture, sculpture, and poetry which had been originated in this period. Until the eighteenth century A.D. the science of western Europe was founded to a great extent on the principles first laid down by the natural-scientists of Ionia. From this time, too, the Greek people have a special place among the trading and military populations around the shores of the Mediterranean. Not only does the democratic daring of her municipal constitutions distinguish her from the monarchic and feudal states that surrounded her, but the liberty which was the rule in most of her cities gave full scope to freedom of thought and to original talents. Whereas in Egypt, and in Babylon, the astronomers, geometricians, architects, and sculptors were merely anonymous officials anxious above all that their activities should conform to established rules, in Greece the philosophers, poets, and artists, down to the modest 'artisans of art', were well-marked personalities, working without restraints of any kind and sometimes with the material and moral encouragement of an enlightened 'tyrant'. And their work clearly displayed not only their scientific curiosity or their devotion to beauty but also the independence of their individual temperaments.

XII

GREECE AND THE GREAT MEDITERRANEAN NATIONS AT THE END OF THE SIXTH CENTURY

Brilliant though it was this civilisation had its weak spot. It was founded on the individual city. The tiny autonomous city, owning a very modest area of land, was the state for which legislators drew up their constitutions, for whose gods the architects and sculptors laboured, for whose festivals the poets composed their works. This civic spirit was usually opposed to the kind of mutual concessions that alone make great federations possible. Associations acquiring any real economic and military unity were few and of restricted scope. As for the idea of a political union embracing all the Greeks, it would doubtless have appeared as absurd to a contemporary of Peisistratus as that of a United States of Europe would have done to a nineteenth century Englishman. The most important of these little towns had no more than 30,000 citizens at the end of the sixth century. They possessed only small armies of foot-soldiers, seldom supported by cavalry, and very modestly equipped. Cities built near the sea had only small fleets, in which the larger warships with two or three ranks of rowers (biremes and triremes) were still exceptional, and which consisted chiefly of ships partially decked and with a single rank of rowers. During the eighth and seventh centuries vast highly centralised empires were being developed on the frontiers of Hellenism. They had at their disposal huge military and naval forces with equipment that had been perfected by the experience of long-range expeditions.

The Assyrian armies by the eighth century had powerful and complicated siege engines which the Persian Empire inherited, while in Greece the technique of siege warfare remained rudimentary until the fourth century. Syrian sailors, under orders from the kings of Nineveh, had built biremes, fully decked and armoured, at the same early date. These powerful states constituted a serious danger to the Greeks, and the towns on the outer fringe of Hellenism were soon to feel its effects. From 710 onwards the rulers of the Greek towns in Cyprus thought it prudent to pay homage to Sargon II of Assyria. In the seventh century the danger became clear.

At this time, as in later periods, the Greeks occupied only the coasts of Asia Minor. In the interior, which was not Hellenised until after Alexander, the Lydian Kingdom had been developed by the seventh century along both sides of that great artery, the valley of the Hermus, and had been raised to a high degree of prosperity by the dynasty of the Mermnadae. This fertile country, rich in gold, which the Homeric poems praised for its industry, needed an outlet to the sea, and so relations were established at an early date between the kings of Sardis and the bankers and shipbuilders of the Ionian and Aeolian ports. From the first half of the seventh century, Gyges (the earliest historical king of Lydia) seems to have undertaken a methodical policy of alliance and conquest in relation to the Greek cities of Asia Minor.

A common danger also drew Greeks and Lydians together at about the same date. The Cimmerians, a horde of barbarians from the northern shores of the Black Sea, had invaded Asia Minor early in the seventh century. About 650 they entered Lydia, routed the army of Gyges who was killed in the battle, took the lower town of Sardis, threatened the Greek cities, and destroyed Magnesia and the temple of Artemis near Ephesus. This invasion, the forerunner of those which from the third century A.D. onwards threatened and laid waste Greece, then Gaul, and finally the Roman Empire, made a deep impression on the Hellenic populations of Asia Minor. Battles between Greek hoplites and Cimmerian horsemen were long the theme of poets and artists. The wave of invaders went on to lose itself in the east and to break against the power of Assyria; and Gyges's successors, Ardys, Sadyattes, Alyattes, and especially Croesus were able to rebuild their empire and definitely resume possession of the Aegean coast-line. One after another the towns of Ionia and Aeolis fell into their power.

Lydian overlordship was not oppressive, however. The Greek cities paid tribute and provided contingents in time of war, but they remained autonomous under the control of their own magistrates or tyrants, and lived under a kind of protectorate based on treaties both commercial and political in character. The Lydian kings moreover were fascinated by the pleasant lively Greek spirit. They married into the great Ionian families, and became indebted to the bankers of Priene and Ephesus. They welcomed Greek philosophers and artists, and displayed great piety towards the gods of the Greek cities whose temples, not only in Asia Minor but even in continental Greece, received their offerings. In the fifth century gifts in solid gold from Gyges and Croesus were still being displayed at Delphi.

But in the hinterland behind the Lydian kingdom on the Iranian plateau, a formidable empire, whose military might alarmed the kings of Sardis, was established in the seventh century. The revolution of 549, which replaced the Median dynasty in this empire by a Persian family, seemed to Croesus a good opportunity to extend his rule beyond the river

Halys. He was defeated, taken prisoner, and Sardis was captured (546). All the Greek towns of the coast, except Miletus which had proclaimed its neutrality, fell into the hands of Cyrus, king of the Persians, after a useless attempt at resistance.

The new conquerors proved to be less susceptible to Hellenism than the Lydians had been. The Greeks and Persians never realised the kinship between their languages – indeed the Greeks always classed the Persians as 'barbarians', that is to say people who spoke an incomprehensible jargon. Nor did the Achaemenid kings seem to have appreciated the charm and splendour of the Ionian civilisation until the fifth century. Nevertheless, Persian rule during its first fifty years made no great change in the position of the Greek cities in Asia. The Persian government demanded no heavier tax payments than those made to the Lydians, and – ruling through the Persian satrap in whose district these towns were situated – interfered very little in their internal affairs. So far from hindering the economic and intellectual development of the Ionian and Aeolian cities, this régime brought them a prosperity that they did not again experience until the Hellenistic period. We have already noted their splendid artistic and literary achievements by the end of the sixth century.

By his conquest of Lydia, the king of Persia had obtained control of the fleets owned by the Greek ports of Asia Minor. The fall of the Neo-Babylonian Empire in 539 secured the additional support of the Phoenician fleets. Persia therefore became at once a great maritime power, and the peoples of the Aegean coasts were soon made aware of the fact. A combined expedition of land and sea forces subdued Egypt to the will of Cambyses the son of Cyrus in 525. Greek influence had been growing in Egypt since the seventh century; Greek mercenaries in the pay of the Pharaohs had pushed up the Nile valley as far as the cataracts of today; while in the Nile Delta Greek commerce flourished, and the prosperity of Naucratis under the favourable rule of the Pharaoh Amasis foreshadowed that of Alexandria.

There again the change of ruler did not noticeably modify the fate of the Greek population. There is no need to stress the economic importance of the Nile valley, but the fall of the Egyptian empire had been preceded by the submission to the Achaemenid dynasty of the petty kings of Cyprus with their fleets. Even more serious for the Greeks and more significant was the subjection of the Hellenic islands off the Asian shore, and in particular of Samos. Here Polycrates, an intelligent tyrant, had built for himself what may be termed a small empire supported by a powerful fleet, and he was the first of the Greek chiefs of state to try playing an active part in the great international rivalries of his day. But he knew the limits of his own power, especially as he had to reckon with the hostility of the Samian aristocrats at home. He allied himself at first with Egypt, but abandoned this alliance in face of the Persian attack, and even sent some ships to support Cambyses. He did not benefit from this treachery, however, for the satrap of Lydia had him assassinated, and after a brief attempt at independence Samos fell under the protection of Persia. Thus the Persian Empire extended beyond the confines of Asia Minor, became a threat to the islands of the Aegean, and even menaced the cities of mainland Greece.

At the other end of the Mediterranean Hellenism was equally threatened. There, too, the Greeks were divided in the face of powerful enemies. The most dramatic example of their disunity was given by the fall of Sybaris. This town, perhaps the most prosperous in southern Italy, was defeated and mercilessly razed to the ground by its neighbour Croton.

While the Greek cities were thus tearing one another to pieces, the Phoenician colonies in Africa, Sicily, Sardinia, and Spain grouped themselves together under the leadership of Carthage and constituted a strong empire with the boldest seamen and best equipped fleet of all the western Mediterranean at its disposal. At the same time a great Etruscan federation was being formed, stretching from the valley of the Po to the Campagna. True, its aristocratic régime was steadily opposed to any centralisation on the model of oriental despotisms; but the great armies that its nobles could raise from their vast domains were always ready for invasion and pillage, and were a constant menace to neighbouring territories, while its sailors went privateering all around the Tyrrhenian Sea.

No doubt wherever the Greeks were firmly settled they could offer an unshakeable resistance. The hoplites made a good stand against the Etruscan infantry, which though well-armed had no civic spirit to sustain it, as was clearly shown in 524 by the vigorous Greek defence of Cumae. But if Hellenism could maintain its position without much difficulty it could no longer extend it: the Phoenicians and Etruscans now prevented any new colonisation. In Corsica, a colony from Phocis (Alalia), founded about 565 and reinforced later by Phocians anxious to avoid Persian domination, was destroyed by the Carthaginians and Etruscans acting in concert, despite a naval battle in which its sailors had had the advantage. Its inhabitants were fortunate in that the people of Poseidonia (Paestum) in Campania allowed them to found the town of Elea near their territory. In Sicily some Lacedaemonians, already driven by the Carthaginians out of Tripolitania, where they had tried to establish themselves, were dislodged by the Phoenicians at the end of the sixth century from Mount Eryx, where they had taken shelter. These sad convoys of adventurers and emigrants wandering from one end of the Mediterranean to the other were proof enough that the days were gone when Hellenism could install itself as a conqueror on the shores of Italy, Gaul, and Spain. Even powerful Massilia (Marseilles) was obliged to come to terms with the Carthaginians, by now established in Spain, and limit its zone of influence to Cape Artemisium (Cape de la Nao).

Thus, about the year 500, the Greeks found themselves threatened or at least held in check, in both the eastern and the western Mediterranean. The results of three centuries of territorial expansion, and of remarkable moral, artistic, and scientific progress, might well be compromised. The enemies of Hellenism at this time did not seem capable of assimilating her thought, as the Romans were able to do five centuries later. The Lydian Empire, so well permeated with Greek culture, had perished; the Etruscans, though much taken with Athenian pottery, borrowed from the Greeks only the alphabet used in Cumae, fashions of dress, some conventional decoration, and a taste for certain frivolous amusements; while the Carthaginians and Persians had so far been unaffected by Greek civilising influences. The issue now to be decided was whether the Mediterranean basin would be shared between a set of merchant-aristocracies and a military despotism, or whether Hellenism could carry to victory the principles of individualism, art, and philosophy which at the end of the sixth century constituted her magnificently original contribution to the world.

XIII

THE REVOLT OF IONIA. MARATHON

At the end of the sixth century the Greek world was living under a paradoxical system. Its most prosperous districts, those in which urban civilisation, economic organisation, and artistic and scientific development were most advanced, were not free. The Greek cities along the coast of Asia Minor owed obedience to the king of Persia, and were dependencies of the satrapies of Sardis and Dascylium. Although the authority of the satraps was exercised mildly, this situation had two serious drawbacks for the Hellenic cities. Firstly, Persian rule favoured the continuance of the outworn system of tyranny. Rather than deal with the ever-changing representatives of restless democracies, the satraps naturally preferred to conduct negotiations with petty potentates, each solely responsible for the attitude of his city, and whose loyalty could easily be encouraged. Secondly, King Darius had succeeded Cambyses, after the defeat and death of a usurper. The revolts at the beginning of his reign had forced him to organise his empire more rigidly and to require heavy contributions in money and men from the provinces. While the adventurous spirit of the Ionians led them to take part in his military expeditions without much demur, the regular taxation which Darius substituted for the 'voluntary gifts', raised now and again by his predecessors, made his government far from popular. In addition to payments in kind, the districts along the west coast of Asia Minor had to pay into the royal treasury, good years and bad alike, no less than two hundred Babylonian talents (say 50,000 gold sovereigns). This tax, bearing on a number of Greek towns, must have been a considerable financial burden.

This unpopular sovereign had, however, established his authority on such solid foundations that any attempt at revolt and liberation seemed foredoomed to failure. A strongly centralised government with a network of royal roads and posting stations; a discreet but effective oversight of the satraps by secretaries, 'the eyes and ears of the king'; strict accounting by the Treasury made easier by the minting of an imperial coinage; the existence of a standing army, small maybe, but of picked troops; garrisons sheltered in strong fortresses to keep each province in subjection – all these devices welded countries stretching from India to the Aegean Sea into the most formidable state ever set up in the neighbourhood of the

Mediterranean. Such a power and one so well organised was not seen again until the rise of the great Hellenistic monarchies.

Nevertheless this vast empire had weaknesses which were chiefly due to its very size. When the swiftest couriers took several days to get from Sardis to Susa one can imagine how slowly news, orders, and especially troops went from place to place. Still more serious was the composite character of this enormous Empire. There was no bond of language or culture between the Hindus of its eastern provinces, the Medo-Persians, Assyrio-Babylonians, the Syrians, the Phoenicians, the natives of Egypt, the peoples of central Asia Minor, and finally the Greeks of the coastal cities.

We can perhaps form some idea of this heterogeneous empire by comparing it with the former Austro-Hungarian monarchy with its Slavs, Magyars, Italians, and Germans; and as in pre-1914 Austria, the authority of one man alone maintained any unity in such a composite body. These weaknesses might possibly escape the attention of the passive population of the Nile valley or Mesopotamia, accustomed for centuries to tremble before the rod of the oppressor, whoever might be in power. Not so for the Greeks, who were impatient of a rule so contrary to their political customs, and were very capable of noting its weak spots. They were only waiting for a favourable chance to throw off the yoke.

This chance was to be offered them by Darius himself. For reasons still unknown he undertook, about 512, an expedition into Scythia. Perhaps he was attracted by the fabulous but indefinitely located riches of the Ural mines; perhaps he wished to gain possession of the fertile black-earth regions of southern Russia, whence the Hellenic countries were already by this time beginning to provide themselves with wheat. At all events he set great store by this enterprise, and paved the way for it by a naval expedition that subdued the Greek towns around the Hellespont and explored the northern coasts of the Black Sea. He was determined to take personal command. It was a combined land and sea operation, as was the Egyptian campaign of 525, and that of thirty years later led by Xerxes. While the infantry and cavalry crossed the Hellespont on a bridge of boats built by Greek engineers from Byzantium, the fleet, consisting mainly of Hellenic contingents, sailed along the Euxine coasts and up the Danube. A second bridge was thrown over the river by the Greeks, in whose charge it was left after the army had crossed. At the head of his troops Darius pushed deep into the Scythian plains, and for the first time the very immensity of the steppes was victorious over an organised army. The Scythians laid everything waste in front of Darius; eventually, tired of advancing over scorched earth, he was only too glad to cross back again over the Danube bridge without hindrance. The Greek cities along the Hellespont were not mistaken in considering this to have been a definite failure, and seized the moment to make a first attempt at revolt. But Darius's rear-guard suppressed any such impulse towards independence, and went on to subdue the peoples of Thrace, including the Greek towns along the coast, as far as the river Strymon. On the far side of this river, in Macedon, where a dynasty of intelligent sovereigns had for more than a century past been building up a well-organised, centralised state, King Amyntas had to do homage to the Great King who now became his neighbour.

But 'the abscess was festering', as Herodotus said. Back home, the Ionian sailors could boast how they had held the safety of the king and his army in their hands. They even said that Scythian horsemen had suggested to them that they should break up and abandon the bridge left in their charge. Histiaeus, the tyrant of Miletus, who had held the guards to their duty, received striking testimonies of the king's gratitude, was put in charge of a Thracian district rich in mines and forests, and bidden to the court at Susa. His nephew Aristagoras replaced him at Miletus. Uncle and nephew are both excellent types of the Ionian adventurers – sailors, business-men, war-leaders, and pirates as occasion served.

About 500, Aristagoras proposed to Artaphernes, satrap of Lydia, that they should conquer the Aegean islands beginning with Naxos, at this time the richest of the Cyclades, as we can judge from the ruins of the monuments that were erected in the sanctuary of Delos. No doubt he wished to carve out for himself a maritime empire under Persian protection as Polycrates had done previously. Contrary to all expectation, the expedition failed. The democratic party which, as in so many cities of continental Greece, had taken the place of a régime of tyranny, had been able to organise a vigorous defence of the island, and after four months the Persians were obliged to raise the siege (in 499). This time it was no question of a distant reverse: only a few hours sailing-time separated Naxos from the ports of Asia Minor, which could thus have day to day information about the progress of the campaign. Twice in fifteen years the Persian Empire had exposed its weakness in the face of a resolute enemy. Revolt broke out. The tyrants of the Ionian cities, the firmest supporters of Persian rule, were expelled, and to everyone's surprise Aristagoras, who had probably been long preparing this stroke, assumed the leadership of the revolt. Better still, he offered to beg help from the Greeks of the European mainland for their brothers in Asia Minor, and set out for the Peloponnese.

Sparta, the greatest military power in the Hellenic world, but without much inclination for distant expeditions, and ill-informed as to what was happening outside European Greece, refused her aid. Aristagoras met with much more success in two cities that commerce, and affinities of race and language, kept in close relationship with Ionia. Athens supplied twenty ships – a great contribution from her young fleet – and Eretria sent five. In the spring of 498 the Ionian forces, together with those from the two cities, set out from Ephesus towards Sardis, which they occupied and burnt. Only the citadel, in which the Persian garrison had taken refuge, succeeded in holding out.

The capture of Sardis made a great stir. The revolt spread all along the coast, to the cities of the Hellespont and the semi-barbarous peoples of Caria, which was a reservoir of infantrymen with a great reputation for their valour and equipment. Finally it affected the Greek towns of Cyprus, which also supported the insurgents with their fleets. In the same way, four centuries later, Asia Minor was to rise in a single day against the Roman legions at the call of Mithridates. This was some compensation for the departure of the small Athenian contingent, recalled for reasons unknown after Sardis had been captured.

On the other side, the court at Susa awoke to the gravity of the situation. The region in revolt against the king's authority, if not the richest, was the most civilised; and Darius must have known the worth of Carian infantry, the manoeuverability of the Ionian fleet, the skill of Greek engineers, since he had employed them. He weighed up the situation with sound judgment and realised that he must defeat the insurgents by sea, so the mainspring of his plan of campaign was a naval expedition. While royal contingents from the satrapies of Asia Minor were arriving to hold the Ionian infantry in check, to force it to evacuate Sardis and even to defeat it near Ephesus, a Phoenician squadron was despatched to Cyprus, where it landed an army of occupation. Although the Greeks won a sea-battle, the Hellenic infantry was defeated ashore and Cyprus fell once again under Persian domination. The insurgents thus lost the ships and the bases which would have enabled them to carry the war to the Syrian coasts. The following year the towns on the Hellespont and in Aeolia fell into the hands of the king's armies. In Caria, on the other hand, the people's resistance took on the character of a holy war and ended, after two bloody battles, in a Persian repulse.

But, as Aristagoras realised, the matter must finally be settled at sea. When he learned in 496 that a new fleet was being built in the shipyards of Phoenicia he decided that the situation was desperate, and left Miletus for Thrace and the domains of his stepfather, Histiaeus. There he planned to convey his threatened compatriots, but he was killed while fighting the natives. The insurgents had lost an energetic leader, the only one capable of holding them together. After his departure, Persian intrigues were able to sow disunity among the Greeks. When the Phoenician fleet appeared before the harbour of Miletus the game was already half won. As soon as battle was joined close to the little island of Lade, the fleets from Samos and Lesbos deserted and the remainder of the Ionian fleet was vanquished. Miletus was besieged by land and sea and taken by assault in 494. Its defenders were butchered, the town and its temples pillaged and burnt, and the greater part of its population carried off to Babylon as was the custom in oriental wars.

This was as resounding a catastrophe as that which sixteen years earlier had destroyed Sybaris at the other end of the Hellenic world. Miletus never completely recovered. The principal city of Ionia, the centre of Greek civilisation, had to play a lesser role for a couple of centuries and saw its port, from which so many bold seamen had once set out, gradually silting up. Not until the Hellenistic epoch was she to regain at least some of her prosperity, though not her former prestige.

The revolt was over. A few chieftains still tried for a few months to keep the seas: Dionysus of Phocaea, who had attempted to organise the defence of Miletus, practised piracy in Sicilian waters: the aged Histiaeus, who had been suspected by both sides, and after going to Byzantium had made a serious attempt to revive the revolt, was eventually captured in Asia and put to death by the Persians. But on land the taking of Miletus put an end to all thoughts of resistance. The satrapies of Asia Minor were reorganised, the making of a new valuation survey had made possible a more equitable system of taxes, and some cities were authorised to maintain the democratic constitutions they had set up for themselves since 498.

These were adroit concessions, but recent events had shown Darius that more drastic measures were required. For six years a few Greek cities had held in check his ablest generals and boldest sailors. The defeat of the Hellenes had been due not so much to their military or technical deficiencies as to their lack of unity and the abstention of the European Greeks. Should a new rising take place, and the latter give it more support and organise a more united effort, the outcome might prove very different. The existence of a free Greece, still in course of evolving a complete democracy, was incompatible with the continued expansion of the Persian Empire in the Mediterranean. To put an end to this dangerous state of affairs the authority of the king must be established from one side of the Aegean to the other.

Darius might well think the prize at which he was aiming was scarcely worth winning – a country still on the whole rather poor, dependent for part of its food on the wheat of the Black Sea countries, and for its clothing on tissues imported from Asia Minor, with a restless, argumentative population that was impatient of all control! Certainly its sailors were brave enough, but its fleets were small by comparison with those of Ionia and Phoenicia. Yet the tranquillity of all Asia Minor was at stake, and the moment seemed opportune. Sparta and Athens, the towns of continental Greece that could have rallied around them the forces of Hellenism, were struggling against difficulties of all kinds. Sparta laboured under a highly stratified social and economic system. Though she had come victorious out of a struggle with her old rival Argos, the quarrels between ephors and kings, and within the two royal families, caused a perpetual uneasiness. One of the kings, Demaratus, whose position had been made untenable by his colleague Cleomenes, victor over Argos, had to leave Sparta and Greece in 491-0. Welcomed by the king in Asia he was able from a distance to foment intrigues there in favour of the Persians. For other reasons the same kind of thing was happening at Athens, where the aged Hippias, who had also become the king's vassal since he had fled to Sigeum, still had influential friends: one of his relatives had even held the office of archon. The party that supported tyranny would naturally have welcomed Persian suzerainty, and was still powerful enough to suppress the performance of a tragedy on the fall of Miletus, and was able to count on quite considerable support in Athens and Attica.

A first Persian expedition passed through the Hellespont in the summer of 492; the fleet kept along the coast, supported the movements of the land army and ensured its provisioning. But its leader Mardonius, Darius's son-in-law, met with unexpected difficulties: in a violent assault on his camp in Thrace he himself was wounded; and his fleet was half destroyed by a sudden tempest from the north-east, while rounding the dangerous peninsula of Mount Athos. Nevertheless the expedition was able to re-establish the king's authority in Thrace and Macedon and consolidate his power by garrisons under the command of experienced soldiers.

The disadvantages of these cumbersome land campaigns had however, been made very apparent. It would obviously be more effective to strike a direct blow at cities such as Athens and Eretria, which had taken sides in the Ionian revolt by sending reinforcements to the rebels. In the spring of 490 an expeditionary force, whose size we do not know but which was made up of good infantrymen from the central provinces of the Empire and a contingent of cavalry, was embarked in Cilicia under the command of Datis and Artaphernes, and having coasted along the south shores of Asia Minor struck boldly out for central Greece. In passing, it subdued Naxos, which secured for Darius the command of the Cyclades and the Aegean Sea, and then disembarked on Euboea where Eretria was taken by assault and pillaged. A short crossing then took the Persian army on to the shores of Attica. Hippias, who was taking part in the expedition, had advised this as the place for disembarkation. He recalled that it was the spot at which his father Peisistratus, returning to Attica, had been able to assemble an army of his partisans. A sandy beach, sheltered from north and east winds, gave suitable harbourage for the Persian fleet, and the plain of Marathon would eventually afford an open space for the cavalry manoeuvres against which the Athenian infantry would be powerless. The land army pitched camp near the shore and waited until Athens, which Hippias felt sure would be torn by internal dissensions, should lie at the mercy of the royal troops.

But the situation on the other side of Mount Pentelicus was not as the old tyrant had anticipated. The spring elections of 490 had brought to power a Polemarch and *strategoi* (military leaders) of the republican and patriotic group who were resolved to resist any return to tyranny and to maintain the complete independence of Athens. There was one resolute soldier in particular in the college of *strategoi*, Militades the nephew of that energetic Miltiades who had formerly headed the Athenian party which undertook the conquest of the Thracian Chersonese, and had there been able to carve out for himself a small independent princedom. In this family the spirit of the great adventurers of the preceding century was perpetuated. After the Ionian revolt had been crushed in 493, Miltiades had had to leave the Chersonese in haste, and had taken refuge at Athens, narrowly escaping the Phoenician galleys. His influence can be felt in the energetic steps taken by the Athenian government to meet the approaching Persians. General mobilisation was ordered, and messengers sent to Sparta and to Plataea, a small Boeotian town allied to Athens, asking for reinforcements. Sparta promised its support, and Plataea without delay sent several hundred men.

Within a few hours of the Persian landing an army of about ten thousand, mostly hoplites, crossed the passes of the Pentelicus range and posted themselves at the foot of its eastern slopes. With their backs to the mountain, easily provisioned from Athens which was only six hours' march away, they could keep close watch on the enemy camp. By the end of a few days Datis was obliged to realise that not a single deserter had appeared in the Diacria: Athens was proving resolute in its self-defence. Datis no doubt wished to try conclusions before reinforcements could arrive from Sparta. The Marathon plain was fever-stricken at this season, and without shade or drinking water, so he decided to re-embark his troops and lead them direct to Athens itself. The Athenian generals, realising his intentions and on the initiative of Miltiades, ordered an immediate attack. The Persian cavalry were already aboard ship. The Athenian hoplites went into action, crossed at speed the dangerous zone where the Persian archers might have taken a heavy toll, and attacked the enemy formation. The contingents of the royal infantry put up a strong resistance, their centre stood its ground and was drawn on to break through the centre line of the Athenians to be enveloped by the strong and mobile wings of the Athenian forces. A panic ensued in which the royal troops embarked in disorder, and the fleet hastily moved off, leaving seven ships, the wounded, and six thousand four hundred dead behind.

The Persian defeat was decisive and complete. When next day the fleet, having doubled Cape Sunium, appeared off the roadstead of

Phalerum the Persians dared make no new attempt at landing since Miltiades and his army had returned before them and were ready for them. The attack had failed, and the Persian fleet returned to Asia.

The defeat was a shock to Darius, and was proportionately more significant than the actual numbers of men and amount of material lost. The central provinces of his empire doubtless never even heard of the battle of Marathon, but Ionia, and more surprising still the islands of the Cyclades (only recently conquered), made no attempt to rebel. The Persian Empire, however, still had the threat from an independent Greece hanging over its flank, and her victory would swell Greek pride.

The moral consequences of the battle were considerable indeed. At Marathon, Athens which had previously measured her strength only against Boeotia, Megara, or Chalcis, had now proved the valour of her infantry, and their tactical mobility in spite of heavy equipment. Conditions had certainly been very favourable, but their superiority over lightly armed troops was obvious. Athens had also been able to judge the good results of its new régime. The principle of the nation in arms, the spirit which inspired her troops, the working of the institutions which had put a Miltiades in the leadership, had all contributed to give her the victory.

XIV

THE GREAT INVASION OF XERXES

It was only too likely that the Persian government would not rest content with an admitted defeat, yet so far as we can tell Athens, which had felt the first shock from the Persians, was the only Greek city to foresee their return to the attack. Her whole policy from 490 to 480 seems to have been influenced by such a thought. This fear must be held responsible for a certain number of measures which appear at first sight to run counter to the normal development of the system introduced by Cleisthenes.

During the whole of this decade, the external danger had serious internal consequences in Athens. The army had to be a first priority: important reforms were made in its organisation, and in particular the powers of the *strategoi*, the generals, were enlarged at the expense of those of the polemarch who henceforth played no part at all in the actual conduct of military operations. On the other hand the experiences of the last few years both in Athens and in Asia Minor had shown that the Persian government could find no surer support among the Greek states than a tyrant. Old Hippias, it is true, had died shortly after the battle of Marathon, but there remained in the city plenty of his relatives, 'and besides them numerous influential and ambitious personalities. One of these might at any time take advantage of the situation, and precisely by reason of the Persian danger, find means to restore for his own benefit the hated system of government.

Hence came the odd institution called ostracism. In winter and spring each year two meetings of the popular Assembly were summoned, the first to decide if there was any citizen who was a threat to public liberty, the second to indicate such a citizen by a majority of votes and thus condemn him to seven years' exile, but without confiscation of goods or loss of political rights. The peculiar and archaic character of the procedure for ostracism makes one wonder if it was not really an ancient religious practice revived for the occasion. In any case, the first time it functioned was in 487, and its victim, as might be expected, was the relative of Hippias who had been archon a few years earlier. Among other important people who suffered this fate in subsequent years were three members of the influential Alcmaeonid family. Ostracism, as an exceptional device, may have proved useful during these years of crisis, but it lasted until the end of the fifth century and lent itself to serious abuse, as can easily be imagined.

Neither the reorganisation of the army nor the banishment of domestic enemies, however, were sufficient safeguards. Darius had put down the Ionian rebellion by his use of sea-power, and all the indications were that he intended to base his next expedition on a powerful fleet. Athens at this time had only a mediocre naval force, and two events were soon to manifest its weakness. Immediately after the battle of Marathon Miltiades tried to liberate the Aegean islands from Persian domination, since their excellent harbours would provide bases for enemy squadrons. His expedition was repulsed in its attempt to take Paros. On his return, his political enemies charged Miltiades with responsibility for this failure, and after a trial the victor of Marathon was condemned to pay a heavy fine; shortly afterwards he died of a wound received during the siege.

Failing mastery of the Aegean, Athens wished to make sure at least of supremacy in the Saronic Gulf. For this she needed to subdue Aegina, the old trading city whose raiders threatened all the coasts of Attica, and where an aristocratic party favourable to Persia was in power. A democratic rising in the island seemed a good occasion, but here again the expedition failed, in spite of the help of a Corinthian squadron. And so Athens remained vulnerable from the sea in spite of her brave seamen and the favourable configuration of her coasts.

This was fully realised by a man who was to play a vital part in the history of Athens, and who was probably the greatest statesman she ever had. Coming from a family of merchants, without much education or much fortune either, at least in his early days, Themistocles was a born leader and had all the essential qualities of a statesman – a sound estimation of future events, rapid and sure decision, and a real genius for improvisation. His wisdom was in evidence in the interval following the fall of Miletus and before Marathon, when, showing great foresight and using his powers as archon, he caused supplies to be voted for the development of the harbour of the Piraeus in 493-2, where a well-sheltered roadstead was available to harbour the ships of war which the great maritime cities of the Greek world had now begun to build.

Important changes were taking place in the arts of navigation during the sixth century. Warships were henceforth decked over and fitted with an ingenious system of tiers, the details of which we do not fully understand, which allowed for two or three times the number of rowers without greatly widening the hull. These long swift biremes or triremes, with their large crews of nearly two hundred men (one hundred and fifty of whom were rowers) and their imposing superstructures, were naturally of deeper draught than the boats of earlier times, many of which could be pulled up on to the beach every evening. Deeper harbours now became necessary to take these larger vessels. The use of anchors which had spread in the course of the sixth century enabled them to be safely moored. The Piraeus, deep enough for modern steamships, was ideal for the up-to-date fleet which Themistocles intended to build for Athens, and a happy combination of circumstances helped him to realise this project.

From the sixth century the Athenians had exploited the lead and silver mines of Mount Laurium, but after 485 the discovery in this area of the deeper but much richer Maronean lode caused a financial revolution in Athens. These mines placed at the disposal of the state funds of one hundred talents in the first year. Themistocles did well in persuading the Assembly to vote that these revenues should be used for building a great fleet, a decision that was to have enormous consequences for the future of both Athens and Greece. The speed with which the policy was carried out was also admirable, for by 480 Athens had two hundred triremes, and this made her the most powerful maritime city in the Hellenic world.

Meanwhile the Persian government set about the preparation of an immense armed force, a task which Darius, who died in 486, was not to see completed. His successor Khshayarsha (called Xerxes by the Greeks and so continued in subsequent tradition) was described by them as impulsive and indolent. At the beginning of his reign, however, he proved to be active and intelligent in dealing with the grave problems which confronted him on his accession – a newly created empire that was far from unified, a serious question to be solved in the Aegean, a nationalist rebellion in Egypt, and another at Babylon. He moved to suppress the Egyptian and Babylonian revolts, without relaxing his preparations for a European campaign. The repulse at Marathon had shown that Hellenic insolence could not be conclusively repressed merely by putting an expeditionary force on the shores of Greece. So Mardonius's plan of campaign was revived with improvements and amplifications. The land forces were to reach central Greece by way of the Hellespont and Thrace, while the fleet, keeping along the coast, was to maintain supplies and support the army's operations if the need arose. The expedition was carefully prepared, the coasts were reconnoitred, Greek and Phoenician engineers were commissioned to throw two bridges of boats across the Hellespont, and to dig a canal across the isthmus of Mount Athos so that the fleet need not round this dangerous cape. Ration depots were organised in Thrace and Macedon. In addition, a diplomatic offensive in Greece itself secured at least the neutrality of Crete and Argos, and – so it seems – the support of the priests of Delphi, for they issued a series of defeatist oracles to soften up public opinion.

In the spring of 480 the royal troops crossed the Hellespont, where the fleet had come to meet them. As to the effective strength of the army we must admit ignorance. The figures given by Herodotus (seventeen hundred thousand fighting men) who was writing about half a century after the event are certainly an exaggeration, but the estimates of modern historians are arbitrary and sometimes ridiculously low. It seems likely that several hundred thousand men crossed from Asia into Europe, including infantry, cavalry, ships' crews with siege-material, a huge baggage train, and the masses of impedimenta that weighed down all the armies of antiquity – and especially oriental armies. We can see why the royal troops took nearly three months to march from the Hellespont to Thermopylae (about 375 miles).

The combat troops, though the contingents were of very unequal value, included the best cavalry in the Mediterranean area, and infantry recruited from the warlike mountain peoples of the Empire. But we can imagine the difficulties which would arise in the handling of such heterogeneous troops with their diverse languages, customs, and armaments. Still more difficult must have been the problem of rations in the infertile Balkan peninsula, so waterless during summer and practically without roads. An army could not live on the country, which was scarcely capable, except perhaps Thessaly, of feeding its own population. Just as modern armies depend on railways and motor-lorries, so that of Xerxes was dependent on the fleet, once it had crossed into Greece. If it were cut off from provisioning by sea, it would be condemned to privations and disease, as was realised after the battle of Salamis. Of this Xerxes was fully aware. His fleet comprised a large number of transports of every class and several hundred warships, but many of these may well have been of old or inferior design.

This expeditionary force, in spite of weaknesses due chiefly to its enormous size, was the most formidable war-machine ever set up on Mediterranean shores. Certainly it completely surpassed anything that the Greek cities had ever been able to realise or even contemplate. Imagine then their feelings when news reached them, via the Ionian ports, of the great troop-concentrations taking place in Asia Minor in the autumn of 481. Soon after the end of that year representatives from those Greeks who were determined to co-operate and resist foregathered at Corinth: a significant event in Greek inter-state relations. Yet although a kind of 'sacred union' was decided on, which put an end at least provisionally to the conflict between Aegina and Athens (among others), examples of individual selfishness could be seen elsewhere. Several peoples and cities made declarations of neutrality, including those from the west who were less directly threatened. Gelo of Syracuse agreed to help, but only on terms which were patently unacceptable.

Even among the states of Greece proper several were quite inclined to submit to the Persians. After all, what had happened to Ionia was not an encouraging example. But fortunately for Hellenism and the Mediterranean civilisation, Athens and the towns of Euboea (which knew they could expect no mercy), and Sparta (which foresaw that Persian domination would end her liberty and her supremacy in the Peloponnese) succeeded in persuading a majority of the assembly to decide on resistance.

This resolution once taken, agreement was necessary on how to put it into effect. Sparta and her allies had an underlying idea, to which they clung until 479 – that the Peloponnese alone should be defended by fortifying the isthmus of Corinth. This scheme would have allowed the Persians to establish firm bases in the abandoned regions, and for this reason (which was reinforced no doubt by the protests of the Athenians) the Spartans decided to take part in an expedition designed to protect Thessaly.

In the spring of 480, as soon as they learned that Xerxes had crossed the Hellespont, contingents of Athenians, Boeotians and Peloponnesians encamped in the Vale of Tempe. But they soon realised that this position could be outflanked by land and by sea, and that the attitude of the great land-owners thereabouts was uncertain. They therefore retired on the approach of the enemy – abandoning to him the granary of northern Greece and the contribution which the Thessalian cavalry might have made.

The royal army, joined by Thracian and Macedonian contingents on its ponderous way from the Hellespont, continued to advance without meeting obstacles other than that of keeping itself supplied with drinking water. Its first encounter with Greek forces did not occur until it reached southern Thessaly. The council of war at Corinth had decided to send out a new expedition to defend central Greece. The idea of defending the line of Mount Othrys was abandoned, since it could be turned by an easy pass. Instead they chose for their stand the road by Mount Oeta, which with its confused spurs and gorges was easily defended and quite impassable for an army encumbered with a heavy supply-train; this time the Greek fleet was to support their land army. A band of ten thousand hoplites was sent towards the Malian Gulf. The Peloponnesians had furnished only four thousand of these, once again demonstrating their ulterior motive of keeping the best of their troops for the defence of the isthmus of Corinth. The remainder of the fighting men were from Boeotia and central Greece. However, one of the kings of Sparta, Leonidas, was in command of the little army. Athens, on the contrary, had made a truly magnificent effort. One hundred and forty seven Athenian ships left the Piraeus and made towards the Malian Gulf. Aegina, the ports of Euboea, of the Peloponnese, and the western Cyclades, sent reinforcements so that the Greek fleet boasted two hundred and seventy one ships, many of recent construction.

The Greek armies took up their positions at the end of July. Leonidas occupied the pass of Thermopylae – Hot-Spring Gates – so called from the hot sulphur springs which gush out in the district. In 480 there was only the width of a carriage-way between the escarpments of Mount Oeta and the sea, though later deposits of silt from the river widened the shore. The fleet, theoretically under the command of the Spartan Eurybiades but effectively controlled by Themistocles, was moored broadside on in the bay of Artemisium to the north of Euboea. The first detachments of Xerxes's cavalry made contact with the Greek hoplites before the Persian fleet had left Therma (Salonica), where it had been concentrated. As soon as he was informed of the state of affairs, Xerxes ordered his ships to sail in haste towards Euboea. But the rocky coast of Magnesia along which they had to travel provided little shelter. One morning they were surprised while at anchor by one of those north-east gales that are so frequent in summer in the Aegean. Disaster overtook them. With the loss of a great number of vessels that had not been able to put out to sea in time and had been dashed against the reefs, the Persian fleet managed to reach the shelter of the Gulf of Pagasae, whereupon Xerxes gave orders for attack by land and sea. At sea the Greek triremes showed their superior manoeuvrability in two partial engagements which cost the Persians a great many ships.

During this time the royal infantry made a number of vain attempts to force the pass where the Greeks grimly held on. Another summer storm is said to have destroyed a naval division ordered to sail round Euboea, carrying troops intended to take the Greek army in the rear. Several days later Xerxes was told of the existence of a mountain track, practicable for light infantry without baggage, by which the position of Thermopylae could be outflanked. Leonidas knew of this path, but his troops were so few that he could only spare for its defence the Phocian contingent of one thousand. Surprised at daybreak by the Persian column, this small force withdrew, and at sunrise the news of their flight spread through the Greek camp. As to what happened at this moment we are ill-informed. Most of the detachments from central Greece seem to have retreated hastily along the coast to avoid certain destruction, abandoning Leonidas and his Peloponnesians, who remained faithful to their charge and were slaughtered on the spot. The presence of the Greek fleet near Thermopylae was thus rendered useless. It moved away towards the Saronic Gulf to renew contact with the bulk of the Greek forces now massed near the isthmus of Corinth, and came to anchor off Salamis.

Thus the selfish policy of the Peloponnesians and the system of 'small parcels' had ended in catastrophe. Central Greece lay wide open. In Boeotia the great land-owners had never been keen on resistance, and gave Xerxes a favourable reception. This rich countryside was to serve the Persian army as a base of operations, with Thebes as its general headquarters, for a full year. During this time the government of Athens evacuated town and countryside: everyone who could fight went aboard the ships, the rest took refuge on the isle of Salamis, at Aegina, or in the Peloponnese. Xerxes found Attica deserted, and merely had the satisfaction of laying waste the suburbs of Athens and pillaging and burning the temples of the Acropolis, where a handful of defenders had tried to put up a resistance. His fleet, however, doubled Cape Sunium without hindrance, and – no doubt fearing to be trapped in the Piraeus – moored in the road-stead of Phalerum.

Thus the two fleets again confronted one another. Once more, in accordance with tradition, two entirely different plans of campaign were opposed to each other in a series of tragic councils of war; the Athenians asked that the fate of Greece should be settled immediately and on the sea, while the Peloponnesians wanted to reserve their fleet and await the royal army behind the defensive line which had been hastily built to bar the isthmus of Corinth. The Spartan plan was absurd, for in a few hours the enemy could have landed in the territory of Argos, where they would have found allies and an excellent base from which to take the defenders of the isthmus in the rear.

Not without difficulty, Themistocles forced a decision to accept the naval combat which Xerxes, on his side, was anxious to offer. The season was advancing, the task of provisioning the royal army was becoming more and more difficult, and it was clear that the issue could not be decided as long as three hundred Greek triremes remained intact and grouped together at Salamis.

One evening at the end of September the Persian fleet received orders to leave Phalerum and sail in the direction of the island where Greek hopes were concentrated. What manoeuvres were carried out that night by the Persian fleet we do not know, but doubtless their object was to encircle the Greek squadron. Still less have we any clear idea of the course of the next day. What appears certain is that the Greeks at an early stage of the encounter emerged from the bay of Salamis, took up battle formation in spite of all enemy efforts to prevent them, and drove the Phoenician division drawn up opposite them on to the coast of Attica. They fell into disorder, aggravated by a land-breeze which sprang up, and the Phoenician and Ionian vessels, weighed down by troops intended for a landing party, crashed into each other and damaged one another in the narrow strait. Few escaped, and those who did took refuge at Phalerum, from where they fled as soon as they could towards the Hellespont. A detachment of picked foot-soldiers, disembarked the previous evening on the little island of Psyttaleia, was massacred.

Thus in a few hours an expedition came to grief which until then had succeeded beyond all hopes. An enormous army had been transported without hindrance from Asia into Europe, the whole north-east of the Balkan peninsula had been brought to obey Xerxes, and at last the insult of 490 was avenged. Attica was conquered and laid waste and her very gods outraged. But with his fleet worn down and demoralised Xerxes no longer had command of the sea. The supply position became impossible, the wet season was at hand, and he very wisely resolved to transport his army back into Asia as soon as possible. He took personal command of the retreat, which was made difficult and dangerous by bad weather, hunger, and by revolts in Macedon and Thrace inspired by news of the battle of Salamis.

But the future had to be safeguarded. An army of occupation was left behind in Thessaly under the command of Mardonius. Some fifty thousand of infantrymen, chosen from among the best of the imperial recruits and supported by good cavalry, were augmented by contingents from central and northern Greece. Hence in spite of the victory at Salamis the situation of Greece remained precarious. Attica had been devastated and was still threatened, indeed Mardonius invaded and pillaged it again in the spring of 479. As soon as Xerxes, learning from experience, should have fitted out an up-to-date squadron and taken advantage of the bases which Thessaly and Boeotia afforded him, the whole matter would once again be in the balance.

Athens on the other hand, the pivot of Greek naval defence, was unable to rebuild her fleet with the enemy still at her gates. Her people were tired of their precarious existence, and before the battle of Salamis had threatened to leave the land of their ancestors and seek a new father-land in Italy far from the Persian peril. All these reasons finally persuaded the Peloponnesians to give up their plan of defending the isthmus and to seek a decisive battle in central Greece. This time they made a great effort. Early in the summer an army of thirty-five thousand men, including the Athenian forces, crossed Mount Cithaeron under the command of Pausanias the regent of Sparta, and camped on its northern slopes near the little town of Plataea, overlooking the Boeotian plain.

For the first time the best troops of Greece and Persia faced one another on land in very large numbers, though the Persians had a superi-ority in cavalry. By a series of moves Mardonius was able to draw Pausanias down on to the plain and put him in a difficult situation, for enemy cavalry harassed his hastily fortified camp and cut him off from his supplies. Pausanias resolved to alter both his position and his order of battle, an imprudent operation which was carried out not without con-fusion, since he decided to make the move by night. Contrary to his expectations the movement was not completed by first daylight, and when Mardonius had information of what was happening in the Greek ranks he judged that the moment had come for decisive action. His cavalry and his archers bore down upon the Spartans. The latter formed up under a hail of arrows, and by an energetic counter-attack threw back the royal infantry that were following up the mounted troops. Mardonius was killed during the fight. On their side, the Athenians vigorously repulsed the contingents raised in central Greece. The Persian army was quickly thrown into confusion, and suffered severe losses of men. After this defeat there was nothing for the Persians to do but take the road back to the Hellespont.

Meantime the Greek fleet did not lie inactive. After Salamis they had been restricted during the remainder of the autumn, and by the approach of the winter season, to keeping a watch over the Cyclades. In the spring of 479 they came back there, and at Delos had news both about the dispositions of the Asiatic Greeks and of the enemy squadron which was guarding the Ionian ports. This decided them to make towards Samos and thence to the Gulf of Latmus, where the royal fleet, at the news of their arrival, drew its ships up on to the shore at the foot of Cape Mycale. These archaic tactics were a complete failure. The Greeks landed, routed the enemy crews (all the more easily because the Ionian contingents came over to their side as soon as the battle began) and burnt the Persian ships. The islands and cities of the coast then drove out their tyrants and their Persian garrisons. A naval division appeared in the Hellespont in the autumn and wasted no time in recovering Sestos from royal control. Powerless and discouraged, Xerxes had to look on from Sardis, and then from Susa whither he later retreated, at this series of disasters and the total defeat of his expedition.

While Athens and Sparta were driving the fleets and armies of the king of Persia out of the Aegean basin, similar events were happening in the western Mediterranean. A dynasty of intelligent tyrants had organised for their own benefit the same kind of unity in Sicily as that to which the Greeks had been impelled with so much difficulty by the Persian danger. At the beginning of the fifth century Hippocrates, the Tyrant of Gela, had brought the towns along the eastern coast of Sicily under his authority. His ambition was to establish himself at Syracuse, where there was an excellent deep-water harbour like that at the Piraeus, and much better suited as a base for an up-to-date fleet than the open roadstead at Gela.

This project was carried out by his cavalry general Gelo, who succeeded him in 485, and took advantage of internal dissensions that divided the Syracusans at that time to intervene as peacemaker, and establish his seat of government in that city. A series of marriages united his family with that of Theron, tyrant of Agrigentum, and so the chief Greek cities of Sicily all came under the sway of one dynasty. By its possession of squadrons of triremes, a sturdy infantry and, what no city in Greece proper could boast, efficient cavalry, this confederation became a formidable military power to its neighbours, the Carthaginian colonies of western Sicily.

Their metropolis was stirred by the danger, and about 480 sent a fleet with a land-army under Hamilcar's command, which disembarked at Panormus (Palermo) and laid siege to Himera. During these operations the Carthaginians were attacked by Gelon's cavalry and completely routed. It was as fine a victory, and as full of consequences, as those which had been won in Greece. For contemporaries, the triumph at Himera ranked equal even to that of Salamis. By her victory Syracuse became the centre of Hellenism in the western Mediterranean. In 474, it was her fleet under the command of Hiero, the brother and successor of Gelo, which defeated an Etruscan squadron that was threatening Cumae, and thus preserved the liberty of the Greek cities along the Italian coast and made the Tyrrhenian Sea safe for Greek ships.

Thus in the east and in the west the dangers which had threatened Hellenism were averted, some of them for ever. Never again did European Greece see a Persian army; not for seventy years did Carthage renew her attack on the Greek cities of Sicily; and the battle of Cumae appears to have annihilated the Etruscan navy. Great armies until then always triumphant, fleets manned by experienced sailors, had broken themselves against these tiny militias and against squadrons fitted out by towns with the most modest resources. Numbers, organisation, the fame of past victories, the real merits of some of their leaders such as Mardonius (who seems to have outmanoeuvred Pausanias at the battle of Plataea) all these counted for little compared with the sailing qualities of the trireme and the arms and armour of the Greek infantryman, and with the spirit which animated these citizen-soldiers. At Salamis, if the story of one of the combatants is to be believed, the Greek sailors could be heard exhorting one another to free their fatherland. Such words would have made little sense in the ears of Xerxes's men, and even less to Hamilcar's mercenaries.

We have already asked ourselves what would have happened if Xerxes had won. Having become a Persian satrapy Greece might still have known great economic prosperity, as Ionia did in the sixth century, possibly even some artistic and intellectual development. But she would most probably have experienced the obliteration of that idea of the city-state which, from Asia Minor to Sicily, had secured the triumph of Hellenism, and which was to develop so magnificently during the fifth century.

XV

END OF THE PERSIAN WARS.
THE ATHENIAN EMPIRE

Greece was free. But she had experienced, for the first time since the arrival of the Hellenic tribes in the Balkan peninsula, a terrible invasion which would not be forgotten for a long time. Some districts had been laid waste, others exhausted by the presence of enemy armies during long months. The Aegean Sea, formerly alive with the coming and going of trading vessels, had been deserted; and finally in the tragic weeks before the battle of Salamis the independence of the Greek states had hung in the balance. Nor could anyone be sure that the government at Susa would not renew its onslaught. Its fleet of course had been annihilated for the time being; the best soldiers of Media and Persia had fallen in central Greece; Xerxes was demoralised and said to be wasting his time, first at Sardis then at Susa, in unworthy court intrigues.

But the few tens of thousands of men whom Thermopylae, Salamis, Plataea, and the retreat had cost the Persians could easily be replaced in an empire whose population, at the most modest estimate, was thirty million. The shipyards of Ionia and Phoenicia could build a new fleet within a very few years. It needed only an energetic king, some worthy successor to Cyrus and Darius, to mount the throne and Greece would again be in deadly peril. Such a danger must be ended once and for all.

Not that there was any occasion for the Greeks to venture into distant Asia to shake the enemy Empire to its foundations. That idea did not take shape in Greece for another century and a half, and it required exceptional circumstances to put it into action. But it was a matter of the first necessity for Greek control to be restored at once to the islands of the Aegean and its eastern coasts, which had served as bases for the enemy squadrons; to resume command of the Hellespont, which two great hostile armies had been able to cross without hindrance within the last twenty-five years; to punish those cities and peoples of Greece itself who had assisted the Persian invaders.

But the union created by danger did not long survive victory. Immediately after the battle of Plataea the successful allies had agreed together to punish Thebes for her treachery. The city was taken by assault and the Boeotian League dissolved; but by the following year the Peloponnesians, who had been less directly threatened and tested, again displayed their lack of enthusiasm for distant expeditions. They did indeed send a detachment of infantry to Thessaly, where they engaged in a fruitless and inglorious campaign, and they contributed twenty of their ships to the great armada which drove the Persian garrisons from the Carian islands, from Cyprus, and from the Hellespont. The fleet contained triremes from Athens, from the Aegean islands, and from the ports of Ionia, yet it was commanded by Pausanias the king of Sparta, the victor of Plataea. He was an unpopular leader, and like most of his compatriots little conversant with naval affairs. His vanity, since his success, had made him unbearable, but he had at least the merit of standing firmly against the ephors in support of a bold sweeping policy.

This absurd situation could not last. After the taking of Byzantium some of the Ionian crews mutinied. Sparta recalled her king, and the Peloponnesian ships abandoned the expedition. An Athenian leader now took command, an event which had important consequences. At Artemisium, at Thermopylae, at Salamis, and at Plataea Lacedaemonian leaders had been at least nominally in command, such had been Sparta's military prestige. Now, however, she dissociated herself from the struggle against the common enemy. And indeed her government of land-loving aristocrats was ill-fitted to carry on so distant a war. Its direction naturally devolved on the young democracy of traders and sailors who, for the past fifteen years, had been fully aware of the enormity of the Persian peril.

Athens began by uniting all the cities which were carrying on the conflict into a league, quite similar to those that had been set up in the preceding two centuries in various parts of Greece, but on an altogether vaster scale, since it stretched from the Hellespont as far as Caria. Its original, and for several years its only objective was to police and keep watch over the Aegean Sea; so its chief need was to possess a fleet and to be able to maintain it. Some of the confederate states were to supply ships together with their crews, others were to pay contributions in money to a common treasury at Delos in the temple of Apollo. The mere fact that Athenian magistrates were entrusted with the management of these funds and appointed 'Treasurers of Greece' (*Hellenotamiai*) is evidence as to how far Athens occupied a pre-eminent position from the beginning of the Delian League. Their title shows clearly that the money was intended for a common purpose, and even though it was always an Athenian who was put in command of military operations, nevertheless all common business was decided upon by the periodic assemblies, to which representatives of all members of the league were summoned, to begin with at any rate. The first conception of such a confederacy ought probably to be attributed to Themistocles, but its organisation was entrusted to Aristides, a man less shrewd than the victor of Salamis, but honest and methodical and endowed with all the qualities of a good administrator.

The league very soon took action. Under the command of Cimon, the son of Miltiades, it cleared Thrace of the Persian garrisons which had been left there, and freed the islands of the Sporades from the pirates who had infested the northern Aegean since time immemorial. Pausanias was driven out; his success had completely turned his head, he had even established himself at Byzantium against the wish of Sparta, and he was making it a centre of intrigues with the court at Susa. Fresh reports showed that Xerxes had shaken off his lethargy and that a new fleet of two hundred vessels was about to be launched from the Phoenician shipyards. Cimon sailed to meet it, and, putting in where Greek triremes had never previously dared to venture, destroyed the enemy squadrons at the mouth of the river Eurymedon on the coast of Pamphylia (468 B.C.).

These were notable victories, and the city that had carried on the war so energetically reaped most of the benefit. Athenian settlers were sent to Scyros and to Ennea Hodoi in Thrace near to Mount Pangaeus, whose rich mines and forests Athens had coveted. The capture of Byzantium cleared the way to the Black Sea for ships to and from the Piraeus. Athens had reached that dangerous turning-point at which a government, after a dearly-bought victory, can no longer draw the line between the needs of national defence and the appetite for further conquest.

The imperialist party had at its head the young general Cimon whose victories had made him the most popular man in Athens, while his family's glorious past, his ostentation and generosity reinforced this popularity. Themistocles, trying to swim against this current, lost all prestige. His enemies were not content with getting rid of him by ostracism (471), but took advantage of his absence to rig up an accusation against him that was sure to succeed in a city whose national feeling had been inflamed by recent dangers, and still more recent victories. It was alleged that, like Pausanias who had returned to Sparta, he was maintaining treasonable relations with the Persian court at Susa. Absurd stories, which nevertheless obtained credence, were circulated that he had negotiated secretly with Xerxes immediately after Salamis. Pausanias was put to death, and Themistocles had to fly from Greece and take refuge in Asia Minor, where in fact the Persian government now gave him a friendly reception and handed over various towns to him, notably Magnesia, where he died.

His departure left a clear field to his adversaries, but their policy, in which greed for gain was joined to the spirit of conquest, began to disturb the rest of Greece. In Thrace the natives annihilated an expeditionary force sent to seize the mining establishments of the Pangaeus area; and Thasos, discontented at the Athenian design to appropriate this rich district which previously had been hers alone to exploit, tried to secede from the league. She was blockaded from the sea, and was compelled to surrender her ships and pay tribute. A few years earlier Naxos, the former mistress of the Cyclades and hence unwilling to be consigned to an inferior rôle, had been reduced (after an unsuccessful revolt) from the status of an ally to that of a subject. In fact the nature of the Athenian confederation was changing little by little, and becoming an empire with Athens at its head. Other cities had to submit to the same fate as Naxos and Thasos, some perforce and others by their own fault, since they were only too willing to be rid of all military obligations and trust to the Athenian fleet for the protection of the Aegean Sea.

Sparta, always slow to bestir herself, at last perceived that there had been an ominous change in Greece. She had already been astonished to see Athens, immediately after Salamis and while still half in ruins, using the débris of her houses and temples and even her tombstones to surround not merely the Acropolis, but the whole city and then the Piraeus with solidly fortified enclosures. Athens had thus proved her determination to take full responsibility for her own defence, and to achieve a position from which henceforth she could treat with any state in Greece as an equal. Sparta was coming to realise that alongside the Peloponnesian League there was growing up an empire which might well soon be a danger to herself and a threat to the independence of all Greece; an empire which was already mistress of the sea, which had great wealth at its disposal, and was led by a bold and energetic city.

During that time, however, Sparta's hands were not free. Messenia was in revolt and her population had taken up arms, concentrated their forces on Mount Ithome, the traditional refuge for the people of that district, and were defying the Spartan infantry. This was the time chosen by Cimon's party at Athens to put forward a grandiose plan intended to increase the size of the Delian League but at the same time to calm Sparta's misgivings. An Athenian army was sent into Messenia to help to crush the rebellion, and then subsequently a fleet was ordered into the seas around Cyprus. On the death of Xerxes, nationalist movements had broken out in various provinces of the Persian Empire, and in particular in Egypt. This seemed a good opportunity to damage Persian interests by destroying naval bases in Cyprus, which was important for the defence of the Phoenician coast, and by encouraging the revolt of Egypt from the Persian yoke. This task seemed all the easier because an army sent into Egypt by the young Persian King Artaxerxes had been cut to pieces.

The vast scheme broke down on all sides. In Messenia the Athenian army failed to seize the fortress of Ithome; and since the suspicious Spartan government grew doubtful about relations between the insurgents and the Athenians they sent the Athenians home with a good deal of discourtesy (462). Instead of strengthening an alliance between the two great cities, this affair created greater bitterness between them than ever before. Athens made an alliance with Argos, Sparta's old enemy, and with the Thessalians. Cimon, who had advocated the Spartan alliance, was ostracised, and his party, discredited by the murder of Ephialtes (*see* p. 127) lost control of the government.

Sparta, on her side, encouraged the envy and ill-will of all those cities which were disturbed by the progress of the Athenian empire: Aegina, which had formerly been mistress of the Saronic Gulf; Corinth, disquieted at seeing her neighbour Megara come under Athenian influence, and the Piraeus become the chief port in Greece; and Thebes, still unreconciled to her downfall. Athens was ready to face threats from all sides, and at the same time found means to fit out another fleet, in spite of having sent the expedition against Egypt. It defeated Aegina's navy, laid siege to the town, and ended by forcing its surrender under conditions which incorporated it in the Athenian empire, required a heavy annual tribute of thirty talents, and put an end for ever to its maritime power. The Corinthians, who had ventured as far as Megara, suffered a bloody reverse. In Boeotia, it is true, an Athenian detachment at Tanagra came up against a large Peloponnesian army which had been sent to central Greece on some futile pretext, and after a tough struggle was defeated. But two months later, when the Peloponnesians had gone home, the Athenians returned as masters, and Boeotia (all except Thebes) fell again under their influence. The Athenian fleet even sailed along the coasts of Laconia and intervened with success in the north of the Peloponnese (456-455).

Athens seemed to have nothing more to fear from her enemies. By land, now that the 'Long Walls' united the city's fortifications to those of the Piraeus, she was invulnerable behind ramparts that could defy the poor siege-weapons which were all that Greek armies at that period had at their disposal; and she could reprovision herself by sea. But in 454 news of a terrible disaster came to disturb her serenity. A division of the Athenian fleet, joined with the rebels in Egypt, had sailed up the Nile and delayed over-long at the siege of Memphis. The government at Susa, awakened from its lethargy, had been able during this time to fit out a great expedition which penetrated the Delta channels, defeated the rebel Egyptians, and after a siege of eighteen months annihilated the Greek squadrons. A second naval division dispatched from Cyprus was destroyed at the mouth of the Nile. Not merely was the great Athenian expedition thus brought to nothing, but the total loss of the two fleets seemed to put the clock back some thirty years, to the days before Salamis when the Aegean lay wide open to the Phoenician ships.

Following Themistocles's policy, Athens sacrificed her concerns on land to those at sea. To be able to rebuild her fleet she concluded a five-years' truce with Sparta, and abandoned the alliance with Argos and all claims on the Peloponnese. No doubt Cimon, who had returned from exile, was the author of this reconciliation. Within five years of their Egyptian disaster, the Athenians were able to send a new fleet under Cimon's command to Cyprus where it defeated the Phoenician fleet in two battles, by land and sea. Cimon died on this expedition, but the honour of Athens was saved and the Aegean Sea once more free from danger.

To consolidate the position, the Athenians resolved to come to an understanding with the Persian Government which, for its part, was only too anxious to put an end to a costly and quite useless war.

The King agreed to accept the existing situation. He gave up all rights over the Greek cities of the western shores of Asia Minor. In return Athens renounced her oriental policy, and Cilicia, Egypt and Cyprus fell once more, and for over a century, into Persian control.

This modest treaty gave Athens a free hand in the Aegean and in European Greece. After the death of Cimon, Pericles became the most prominent among the *strategoi*, and consequently had the real direction of the city's foreign policy in his hands. He was a grand-nephew of Cleisthenes and so belonged to the Alcmaeonids, a family which had played a considerable part in the financial and political world of the Hellenes for over a century. Not a great soldier and not keen on distant expeditions, he dreamed of making his city the preponderant power at home in Greece. Yet he knew quite well that Athens was exhausted by thirty years of warfare, during which the flower of her people had fallen on the battle-fields of Europe, Asia, and Egypt. In a single one of these years (459 or 458) one Athenian tribe lost one hundred and eighty men on campaign in Cyprus, Egypt, Phoenicia, Aegina, and Megara.

All these sacrifices had won for Athens only glory without peace. Her enemies, her allies, her subjects threatened her on every side. Boeotia rose against her, overwhelmed at Coronea the weak army which Pericles had sent out, and reconstituted the Boeotian League which for the next half-century was to hang in hateful enmity on the flanks of Attica. Then Euboea and Megara revolted and drove out or massacred their Athenian garrisons. Finally the truce with Sparta expired in 446, and a Peloponnesian army invaded Attica and encamped at Eleusis. Never since Salamis had Athens seen an enemy so close at hand. This state of affairs could not be allowed to continue. Pericles offered peace. The Lacedaemonian rulers agreed to conclude a thirty years' convention by which Athens was to give up all claims on Megara and the Peloponnese, and Sparta was to relinquish Aegina and the island of Euboea, which in the meantime Pericles had won back for Athens.

Their respective popular assemblies ratified this treaty both at Athens, where they were tired of war, and at Sparta where it was realised that, protected by her landward walls and mistress of the sea, Athens could endure a lengthy conflict.

The great events of the last half century had shifted Hellenism's centre of gravity. In the seventh and sixth centuries the Ionian cities in the east were the leaders of Greek civilisation. After the Persian wars they fell into a semi-obscurity, whence they did not emerge until after Alexander's day.

Henceforth peace and war in the Greek world depended on the cities of continental Greece, Sparta and Athens, and on those of the west, particularly Syracuse. These three great cities were soon to be engaged in a tragic struggle, but for a short time a kind of equilibrium seemed to be established between them. Based on this, and on the safety from Persian attack now secured, Greek civilisation from the middle of the fifth century attained its most perfect form.

XVI

GREEK AGRICULTURE, INDUSTRY, AND COMMERCE IN THE MIDDLE OF THE FIFTH CENTURY

Too often has it been said that 'iron calls to gold'; and as witness to the truth of this deplorable saying, the economic development of Greece after her fifth-century victories is often quoted. Yet it is also obvious that there are some fruitless victories. It would be truer, then, to say that iron sometimes goes with gold: in other words the manifestations of the vitality of a nation in the full tide of prosperity may well include both military and economic prowess.

In the Greece of the fifth century economic activity was much less a consequence of the victories of Marathon and Salamis than the continuation of a movement already begun in the sixth century. The Persian wars did not induce economic revolution in the Greek world. Most regions, most cities, kept the same economic organisation as had previously existed there. In Laconia, in Thessaly, indeed throughout central Greece the system continued by which a small number of families shared all the land between them and had it cultivated by serfs or lower-class citizens. As can easily be understood, such a system of great estates did not encourage improvements in agricultural technique. Even in the most civilised parts of Greece the fallowing of land every other year persisted until the end of the fifth century: and the substitution of metal ploughshares for wooden coulters was merely a consequence of the metallurgical progress of the preceding centuries.

Nor was there any important innovation in industry. Fifth-century vases are no more perfect in shape or glaze than those of the sixth century, and any superiority they may have is due only to better decoration; on the other hand the textile manufactures of Asia Minor, disastrously affected by the Ionian revolt and its consequences, disappeared without being replaced in Greece itself by any similar factories. This caused a curious change in dress, which the increasingly democratic way of life also favoured. In much the same way as woollen cloth took the place of silks and velvets in western Europe in the nineteenth century A.D., so the fine linens and muslins of the sixth century B.C. were replaced for both men and women by simple garments in plain wool, the undershirt (*chiton*) worn long or girded up with a belt, and the cloak (*himation*) draped in broad simple folds.

Whole regions of Greece, moreover, were condemned to economic stagnation by poor inland communications, for roads remained primitive, except near great towns and around frequented shrines or at the crossings of such isthmuses as those of Corinth and Boeotia. Hence cartage difficulties kept up the cost of transport for heavy, cumbersome, or fragile commodities to such a high level that the prices of goods carried might be more than doubled. Districts far from the coast or with poor harbour facilities were condemned to a limited industry with products for local consumption only; nor could any large concentrations of population be supported there, since, being on a poor soil and unable to import corn from outside, they would be constantly threatened by famine. So these 'continental' regions remained backward, and for a time played only a minor part in Greek history.

In Arcadia, in Phocis, and in Aetolia ignorant peasants or shepherd-brigands dwelt in widely scattered hamlets. Even Thessaly, in spite of her rich harvests, had little surplus for export and took but a slight share in the development of the country. Sparta alone remained a great power, owing her prestige to special institutions which enabled her to have the finest infantry of all Greece, and to a well-devised system of alliances which kept some of the outstanding Greek maritime cities under her influence. But this paradoxical situation could not long be maintained. The last third of the fifth century, it is true, was to be taken up by her conflict with the growing power of Athens in which, thanks to help from Persia, she emerged as victor. But within a generation or so of that victory she was to decline to a humble status.

The coastal towns, on the other hand, continued to make great progress. Only those of Crete had declined after the sixth century from their former prosperity. This decadence, disturbed by various obscure quarrels, was to last as long as Hellenism, and remains one of the puzzles of Greek history. Other maritime cities benefited by the advances in nautical science made during the sixth century. Those affecting war-vessels have already been noted, and their consequences included the building of great fleets which, besides assuring the defeat of the Persians, temporarily wiped out piracy. For thirty centuries pirates have been the scourge of the eastern Mediterranean, and have been reduced only when the great maritime powers have seriously set about repressing them.

The mercantile marine, too, improved its equipment: heavier vessels of up to three hundred tons burden were built and furnished with anchors, and were able to make faster and bolder sea crossings. The risks of shipwreck and of serious delays were still very great on journeys made without maps, compasses, or lighthouses, even although fewer merchant ships sailed in winter. And marine insurance, which began to function in the fifth century in the form of loans on 'bottomry', amounted to the enormous rates of between twelve and one hundred per cent. Nevertheless, ships were now numerous enough and crossings sufficiently frequent to ensure genuine competition, which brought down passenger fares – two drachmas from Athens to Egypt – and even heavy merchandise freights were very low. Cities which had the advantage of good ports naturally benefited from this state of affairs, and could extend their population without fear of famine. They could also produce abundantly in the certainty of being able to find export markets, since at this time supply seems always to have fallen short of demand. Of the four million inhabitants who constituted the Hellenic world in the mid-fifth century, it can be estimated that about two-thirds lived near the sea – in eastern Sicily, Greater Greece, the gulfs of Corinth and Athens, the Cyclades, and the western shores of Asia Minor. Henceforth the economic history of Greece was to be that of her great ports: Athens, Syracuse, Rhodes, Delos, Alexandria, and Byzantium.

In the fifth century the cities that made most progress were those situated along the sea-routes leading to Italy, the Black Sea, Egypt, and Phoenicia. In the west, Syracuse overflowed from the small island of Ortygia on which it had been founded, and with additional population transferred to it by its tyrants as it were artificially, spread on to the mainland in the suburb of Achradina. Along the trade-route to the Black Sea area, whence were brought cereals, building timber, salt fish, and slaves, a series of important cities was echelonned: Thasos, Abdera, Lampsacus, and Byzantium. In the archipelago Paros seems to have superseded Naxos in the fifth century, and both were later outshone by Delos. Finally there was a string of great ports along the straits and bays that join the Aegean to the Adriatic: Corcyra, mistress of commerce in the Ionian Sea; Corinth, the chief *entrepôt* trading station of Greece, with its two harbours on the two seas and a thriving industrial centre producing quantities of perfumes, coarse pottery, and textiles; and finally Athens which became the economic capital of Greece, especially after the downfall of Aegina.

In Attica, with an area less than that of a small English county, there was in the middle of the fifth century a population which cannot be estimated at less than a quarter of a million, including slaves. This population-density of three hundred per square mile, which was truly remarkable for the Mediterranean world at this period and only surpassed in certain parts of the Nile Valley, was not due solely to the existence of two great urban centres. Nearly half the inhabitants of Attica lived in the countryside and were still attached to the soil. The social evolution which had taken place there during the sixth century had had the effect of parcelling out the land and creating a class of small land-owners. The land which they continued to cultivate with old-fashioned methods did not yield heavy crops of cereals, except perhaps in the Eleusinian plain and in some parts of the Mesogaea, so that Attica was far from self-sufficient. By this period great quantities of grain were having to be imported from Euboea, Pontus, and perhaps Egypt and Sicily too. Her preoccupation with this problem of ensuring food supplies influenced her foreign policy and perhaps partly induced her to undertake two disastrous expeditions at forty years' interval: that against Egypt and that to Sicily.

On the other hand the dividing up of the land favoured market-gardening and fruit orchards; Athens, then as now, was surrounded with gardens, vineyards, and olive groves. On the forested slopes of Mount Parnes there lived a vigorous race of woodcutters and charcoal-burners. The population were greatly attached to their land, and dwelt there without affluence yet not in poverty; the organisation that Cleisthenes had given to each deme evidently did not prevent its inhabitants from being thinly scattered. Even the ancient Attic towns of Marathon and Oinoe declined to the status of obscure communes; Eleusis was nothing more than a religious centre; and only exceptional circumstances made Thoricus, the centre of the Laurium district, a densely-populated town.

Athens herself, however, had developed enormously. It is almost certainly no exaggeration to estimate the inhabitants who normally lived in peacetime within Themistocles's new enclosure at over 100,000. In the Mediterranean world only Syracuse and Carthage could rival her. Athens was indeed a great city, yet not a beautiful one, in spite of the marvellous monuments which arose there in the course of the fifth century. Until the Roman epoch she maintained a modest appearance, with narrow winding streets bordered with small houses. The other great cities of Greece, Sicily, and Asia Minor were probably very much the same in appearance. Only the Piraeus, a completely new town, had been built on a regular plan from about 450 onwards, and was thus the first example of 'town planning' in the Hellenic world.

The inhabitants of these great cities lived by trade and industry, yet industry and commerce were still conducted on a modest scale in fifth century Greece. Labour was cheap, tools still primitive, profits modest. In these conditions production was distributed over a number of small workshops, each with a master employing a limited number of workers. Only towards the end of the fifth century do we find workshops employing more than a handful of workers. The 'industrial' quarters in large towns of the Hellenic world should be pictured as looking very like the streets in the bazaars of modern Turkey or even present-day Greece with their wide-open shop-fronts of coppersmiths, shoemakers, weavers, and wood-turners. Two industries, however, required both a rather more ambitious establishment and a more numerous personnel – the shipyards and the mines. Yet fifty-nine small shipyards existed in the single town of the Piraeus in the course of the fifth century. In mining, too, small concessions were the rule, each employing perhaps sixty slaves for the extraction, washing, and smelting of the ore – at least this was so at Laurium, the only mining centre about whose methods we have much information.

Industrial conditions naturally affected commercial methods. To begin with the manufacturer was often also the salesman, and retailed the products of his labour himself. The same reasons that favoured the small work-place also favoured the small shop. Industry, with little capital, working with a limited labour force and primitive tools and materials, manufactured only in small quantities. Standardised production was almost unknown in a period when each worker was still a craftsman; there was no stockpiling and hence there were no wholesalers. Only the traffic in food-grains, owing to the capital required and the risks involved, was out of the reach of the small trader, and had the effect of encouraging the growth of a class of large-scale importers in the seaports, closely supervised, however, by the city authorities, who energetically repressed any attempts at cornering supplies.

Commerce was none the less active for being piece-meal. In the port of the Piraeus alone, a tax of two per cent on all imports and exports brought in about thirty talents in a year, which indicates a total trade movement of considerable proportions. This was early in the fourth century, after a war and a financial crisis! Even in the midst of the Peloponnesian War goods of all kinds were still pouring into the Piraeus from all corners of the Mediterranean, and envious states were annoyed to see Athens thus become a cosmopolitan market, but other great cities of the Greek world achieved comparable status a century later.

In an economic system which retained many archaic characteristics in spite of its prosperity, one innovation became definitely established in the maritime towns if not elsewhere, and that was the use of a convenient kind of money. Gold was mined in the Strymon area and silver obtained in quantity from the mines of Laurium. The gold deposits were not in fact particularly productive, and the relative value of this metal compared with silver remained high – about fourteen times greater – which hindered its use as currency. Instead it was hoarded, not as in Asia Minor or Persia in the treasure-chests of rich individuals or of the king, but in the temples where it constituted reserves of wealth, either in the form of ingots or pieces of jewellery, which could be utilised in a crisis but in normal times lay unproductive. The Greece of the fifth century used gold currency only in times of emergency, but silver coins circulated abundantly in the commercial cities. Issues increased, but for both political and economic reasons the number of mints diminished.

By the middle of the fifth century most secondary states had lost or given up the privilege of minting their own coinage. The Attic drachma which circulated throughout the Athenian Confederacy, and indeed all over the Mediterranean world, won its way as against other currencies by the fineness of its metal and its constant weight, which was maintained unaltered even in the most critical periods of the Peloponnesian War. Its diffusion was in direct relation to the enormous flow of currency which owing to special circumstances was concentrated in this city. Not only were private fortunes amassed there by commerce and industry, but Athens received money tributes from over two hundred subject towns, whose original assessment amounted to some 460 talents a year, although less was collected. Part of this was paid out again in civil allowances, in pay to the land and sea forces, and in expenses of all kinds. Hence there occurred a regular movement of money such as no other Greek city and probably no other Mediterranean state had previously known, and which consequently led to a very active mintage.

The increase in the amount of money diminished its purchasing power; in other words, prices rose. It is not easy to formulate any general rule on this matter, for the increase was much less felt in backward areas than in the commercial towns, and the difficulties of communication caused almost incredible divergences between different regions. In Attica wheat doubled in price between Solon's time and the end of the fifth century. During this time cattle, not being subject to foreign competition, increased in price tenfold, but an ox, which was worth between fifty and a hundred drachmas at Athens in 410, had still cost only two or three in rural Sicily soon after the Persian wars. The same reasons for the rise in prices accounted for a fall in the rate of interest, which apart from marine insurance settled at about twelve per cent, the normal figure throughout Antiquity both in Greece and Rome. These conditions favoured the creation of credit. 'Men of the counting-house' (τραπεζῖται), who formerly restricted their activities to money-changing, which was highly profitable in a country that had no fixed monetary unit, now undertook the investment in industrial or commercial undertakings of their own funds and those entrusted to them: and thus towards the end of the fifth century banks came into existence.

All this emphasised the contrast between inland and maritime districts in Greece. It would be imprudent to try to envisage the commerce and industry of fifth-century Greece as in any way comparable to those of civilised countries in modern times. However archaic the economic organisation of the most advanced cities of ancient Greece may have been, the bulk of their populations consisted of hard-working folk, and it is not astonishing to find in them the spirit which usually prevails in countries where work is respected and encouraged. This spirit was not normally found in the inland regions. Pericles, who belonged to one of the noblest Attic families, congratulated his fellow-citizens on the fact that for them wealth was not a motive for pride but a stimulus to activity, and that they considered it a reproach, not to be poor, but only if they did nothing to escape poverty. It was only later on that a reactionary movement of an aristocratic and intellectual kind was to introduce a distinction between various callings, denigrating some of them as unworthy of a self-respecting man; in this way citizens were kept aloof from these trades, so that little by little slaves replaced them in the workshops, and foreigners took over the management of industrial and commercial affairs. Nevertheless the dividing up of the making and selling of goods between large numbers of small concerns favoured personal initiative much more than our great factories do. Greek art of the fifth century, even in its most modest manifestations, is always marked by a pleasant individualism.

XVII

THE ORGANISATION OF DEMOCRACY IN THE FIFTH CENTURY

In political and social organisation as in economic affairs profound differences separated the Greek states one from another in the fifth century. In regions which had a reactionary régime, a minority of great proprietors continued to own the land and were the only citizens entitled to exercise full civic rights. In Thessaly and the Cretan towns a few hundred land-owning squires decided among themselves who should wield executive power, and dealt with the problems of policy that arise from time to time in such rudimentary states, at the occasional meetings of their assemblies. Conditions were not very different in Sparta. The leading rôle played by this city as head of the Peloponnesian Confederacy sometimes evoked rather more animation in the monthly sessions of the Assembly – which gave its decisions on the matters which the Council of Elders submitted for its approval by shouts of acclamation – and imposed much responsibility upon the ephors, the leaders of the city's executive. But Sparta remained an aristocracy, of some 2,500 Spartans, who alone had full citizenship, and controlled tens of thousands of *Perioikoi*.

In the great maritime and commercial towns on the other hand the democratic system continued to develop. We can observe this from one end of the Hellenic world to the other, in the ports of Asia Minor which had recently been liberated, as in those of Sicily and Italy, although tyranny had in its favour there the prestige of its victories over the Etruscans and Carthaginians. At Agrigentum, at Syracuse itself, in spite of the military trappings with which the successors of Gelo surrounded themselves and in spite of the artistic splendour of their reign, Thrasybulus – the last of Gelo's brothers – was driven out by a popular revolt (466 B.C.). In Greece, communities such as Argos and Corcyra had democratic constitutions. Of the great trading cities the régime of Corinth alone retained traces of its old oligarchic organisation. Historians and philosophers sang the praises of democratic liberties, and Herodotus boasts of the Greek cities where equal rights and freedom of speech held sway.

At Athens, about whose political evolution we are particularly well-

informed, the constitution introduced by Cleisthenes had come triumphantly through the test of the Persian wars. During the fifth century its
democratic character was accentuated. It had, as we know, retained some
traces of earlier systems. In particular there was the old-fashioned council
with its aristocratic tendencies, which continued to meet on the Areopagus,
and was composed of former archons who had served well in that office.
Besides its judicial functions it retained the right of general supervision
over the constitution, and as a result of the Persian wars it had been able
to extend this so effectively that the anti-democratic party could claim for
the council the honour of having saved the city in 480-79. Reforms were
nevertheless carried through. A law passed in 462 left to the Areopagus,
of all its judicial functions, only that relating to cases of premeditated
murder. Ephialtes, the author of this law which the aristocrats for a long
time held to be sacrilegious, was assassinated subsequently, but his reform
endured.

Eligibility as archon was originally restricted to the first two classes of
citizenship. In 457, however, the *zeugitai* (third rank citizens) became
eligible for these posts whose real importance had been greatly reduced,
but which still kept much of their former prestige; and next the *thetes*
(fourth class citizens, or wage-labourers) were unofficially given access to
the magistrature. And it should not be forgotten that the post of *strategos*
(military leader) whose importance will be shown later, was accessible to
all citizens who were landed proprietors; there were in fact remarkably
few practical restrictions to eligibility as *strategos*. Thus the movement
begun by Solon had led to a régime which may seem to us still imbued
with a plutocratic spirit, since the *thetes* continued to be excluded from
certain public offices, at least in theory, but which in reality had pushed
the egalitarian principle to limits far beyond those yet reached in any
other Greek city.

It must be understood, however, that this principle applied only to full
citizens. The inferior status of women, defensive measures adopted against
aliens, and the scandal of slavery, did not cause Athenian democracy any
qualms. Woman, whether as daughter, wife, or mother of citizens, had
no other function in the city than to perpetuate its families, and from the
legal point of view spent all her life in tutelage. She was accorded respect
in the home, but was completely excluded from intellectual, artistic, and
political life. If a woman such as Aspasia may have had some influence on
Athenian affairs as Pericles's mistress, we should remember that she was a
foreigner, born at Miletus, and if not a courtesan at any rate led what we
should call an irregular life.

As for foreigners they were entirely excluded from political activities.
Strict precautions were taken to prevent their presence at meetings of the
Assembly. Moreover, the city-state of antiquity was more exclusive than
most modern democracies. Naturalisation was infrequent and not easily

obtained; and at the most prosperous period of the fifth century Pericles persuaded the Athenians to pass a law refusing citizenship to anyone both of whose parents were not Athenian-born (451-0 B.C.). These regulations did not arise out of snobbery; the fifth century Greek certainly considered himself superior to the non-Greeks who spoke gibberish ($\beta \acute{\alpha} \rho \beta \alpha \rho o s$) but not to citizens of other Hellenic towns. Nationalism, for example the attempt to create opposition between Ionians and Dorians, did not arise until the Peloponnesian war, and then, as so often happens, a racial theory was called in to justify it. But Greece more or less consciously realised the disadvantages of overpopulation, and this feeling expressed itself in some cities, even before it had been expounded and justified by the philosophers, in the voluntary restriction of births, and at Athens by this defensive legislation against the foreigner. Again, in a city which paid fees for certain public services, which compensated war-victims, and even in times of crisis gave poor-relief (thus anticipating the costly doles of the following century) it was important to limit the number of those with a claim to state aid.

In any c⌣ ˎ a certain ease of social customs, combined with economic necessity, softened this apparent intransigence. Athens had become the chief commercial centre of Greece, and the Piraeus the foremost seaport in the Aegean. An ever-growing population, both Greek and non-Greek, came to settle in Attica. The law refused them the right to own land ($\gamma \hat{\eta} s \ \acute{\epsilon} \gamma \kappa \tau \eta \sigma \iota s$) and thus excluded them from agriculture; but they were to be found, more and more numerous, as craftsmen, merchants, shipchandlers, bankers, artists, and philosophers. The need to maintain a prosperous Athens made it essential not to inflict any unnecessary hardship on these domiciled aliens (metics). They were protected against any arbitrary act, and a certain liberality, in manners if not in institutions, allowed them to enjoy all the amenities of social life. In consequence the state required them to pay taxes and give military service. More than once in the course of the Peloponnesian War they were to be found fighting in the fleet or even with the ranks of Athenian infantry.

The number of slaves also increased as well as foreigners, and slaves accounted for probably a quarter of the whole population of Attica. They were used in the mines as well as the public services, and even in agriculture, though in much smaller numbers. They also competed with freemen employed in the small workshops, but the effects of such competition were mitigated by the gradually extending custom of paying them a wage which seems often to have approximated to that paid to freemen. Hence the existence of this large servile population did not upset the interplay of supply and demand as much as might be thought, nor lower the standard of living of the workers to any noticeable extent. Slaves were protected by law against ill-treatment, and their situation on the whole was not intolerable. Enthusiasts for 'the good old days' vainly regretted that nothing now marked out the slave in the streets of Athens, and that he had lost the habit of giving way to free men. But things were very different for slaves in the mines where the work was hard and dangerous; the only slave-revolts which Athens experienced in the course of her history occurred in the mining region of Laurium.

The idea of equality applied only to citizens. They alone had a share in public affairs, in which all of them could take part as of right from the time they reached adult status. Material conditions at Athens favoured the application of these principles. The social changes of the last one hundred and fifty years had levelled fortunes and abolished agrarian pauperism, and an urban proletariat had taken its place only to a slight extent. The average wage of a workman – one drachma a day towards the end of the fifth century – assured him of food and shelter for himself and his family, in that land of frugal living in the open air. By contrast a capital of 60,000 drachmas was already deemed a large sum. Exterior signs of wealth were not too obvious; dress was fairly uniform, the finest houses beginning to be built at this time in the suburbs were still quite modest, and the greatest luxury of the rich was to have good agricultural equipment on their farms. The general simplicity of manners, due to climate and other circumstances, made political equality seem natural.

The form chiefly taken by this participation in public affairs was that of legislative activity. Four times a month, apart from exceptional occurrences, meetings of citizens were convened on the Pnyx, at which all matters affecting the safety and prosperity of the state were considered. Even though the number of those present was seldom more than a small proportion of the free men of Attica nevertheless many Athenians in the end came to be well informed about the conduct of state affairs.

The part played by the Assembly (*Ekklesia*) in the political life of Athens, the liveliness, and occasionally the tragic turn taken by some of its meetings should not, however, make us forget the limitations imposed upon its powers. Sometimes it is tempting to believe that the Athenian state was ruled by a popular assembly, all-powerful and irresponsible, and led by a handful of demagogues. Yet, apart from the fact that the voting on a new proposal was a serious matter and could entail serious consequences for its sponsor, in principle the Assembly could take a decision only on a resolution previously drafted ($\pi\rho o\beta o\acute{v}\lambda\epsilon v\mu a$) by the Council of Five Hundred. The limited number of members of this Council, its division into *prytaneis* which became in effect standing committees whose members could get down to serious work, the fact that the presidency of the Assembly was in the hands of the *prytaneis*, were all so many guarantees that the government would not be too much swayed by the masses in the popular assembly. The moderating influence of the Council (itself democratically constituted) was no fiction, and during the fifth century on most serious occasions the Assembly of the people rarely failed to respect parliamentary procedure.

Over against these legislative assemblies there existed an executive body. This was not to be found in the college of the nine archons and their secretary. Their function was more and more reduced to the performance of certain religious and honorific ceremonies and the instigation of some special kinds of legal prosecution. The generals (*strategoi*) had taken their place as the effective government. Unceasing wars and the need for the fleet to ensure both the safety and the provisioning of Attica gave the very greatest importance to military and naval questions, and to the officers appointed to handle them. The ten *strategoi* who were the real elected representatives of the people, since they were chosen by popular suffrage, formed a kind of Council of Ministers. Frequently one among them played a preponderant part which can be compared with that of the President of the Council in modern parliamentary democracies, that of the 'first citizen'. It should be noted also that the Athenian democracy, which is often represented as having been fickle and incapable of a settled steady policy, had experience of long ministries quite as much as modern states with their better regulated constitutional machinery. Themistocles, Cimon, Alcibiades, Nicias were each *strategos* for several years in succession. Pericles exercised those functions from the death of Cimon in 448 to the year 429 almost without interruption. For these twenty years – after a brief abortive attempt by the oligarchic party at opposition had ended in the ostracism of their leader – the normal working of Athenian institutions made Pericles their prime minister in all but name.

He was the son of Xanthippus, who had distinguished himself as a general during the Persian wars; by his mother was related to the Alcmaeonids, and was a grand-nephew of Cleisthenes. Pericles thus belonged to the Athenian aristocracy, but to a section who believed that a democratic constitution was not incompatible with the city's prosperity, and were determined to go on cultivating their taste for intellectual elegance. Liberal-minded, interested in science, the friend of philosophers and artists, indifferent to traditional morality in his own private life, Pericles owed his position to his personal reputation, to the consciousness he had of his own worth, and – it must be also said – to his absolute integrity, a quality which at this period had already become rare. A happy mixture of tact and candour allowed him to lead the Assembly and to respect the susceptibility of the democracy, at the same time yet to impose his own will upon them. As we shall see, this did not always result in the wellbeing of Athens. In home affairs he seems to have used his influence especially to ensure the free play and normal development of Cleisthenes's constitution. His chief reform, which consisted in getting an allowance of two obols each session paid to jurors for attendance at the court of the

Heliaia, was simply a logical consequence of the democratic principle. This was to be extended later to citizens for attendance as members of the Council, and in the fourth century even of the Assembly. The satirical jests of Aristophanes ought not to make us forget that such an arrangement is no more shocking than the payments and allowances we ourselves give to our civil servants and members of Parliament.

In a well-ordered democracy everyone ought to contribute towards state expenditure in accordance with his ability, but in truth this principle was imperfectly applied in Athens, which never had a genuine budget, in the sense of a properly balanced account of receipts and expenses. Even at the height of the fifth century her financial system still showed clearly the marks of a time when she was nothing more than a small town defended by a little army whose soldiers equipped and fed themselves. The direct and permanent tax which Peisistratus had tried to establish had not survived the days of the tyrants. It reappeared in another form, as a small capital levy, only in years when the safety of the city required an exceptional effort. In normal times indirect taxes at moderate rates (but very productive owing to the activity of the port and market of Athens), the fines inflicted, the rent of public estates, and the farming out of the mines at Laurium, provided enough revenue to meet ordinary expenses.

In 454 after the Egyptian disaster the allied treasure was moved to the Acropolis, and not long afterwards Athenian statesmen yielded to the temptation to dip into it for the city's internal expenses. This scandalous procedure enabled them to carry out an enormous building programme at home on the Acropolis, and at the same time to conduct large expeditions abroad, without imposing additional taxation on Athenian citizens. However, the principle that heavier sacrifices should be borne by the larger fortunes was put into effect from the beginning of the fifth century by the regularisation of the 'liturgies' or public services. These seem to have been based upon an old custom, but details of how the system worked are not available for dates earlier than the fifth century. A certain number of citizens chosen in rotation from among the very rich were required to undertake the cost of maintaining the triremes of the battle-fleet, and of costumes and training for the choruses who performed at festivals. These were heavy charges, often running into thousands of drachmas, and if they had to be met more than once could ruin any private fortune, although we should remember that anyone designated could challenge a citizen whom he considered to be wealthier to take his place. This system, which inevitably led to abuses and lawsuits, nevertheless helped to ensure the naval strength of Athens and the glorious flowering of her drama for a century and a half.

More equitably applied was the principle of compulsory military service. Every citizen was liable in time of war to serve in the army (the first three classes of citizen) or in the naval crews (the fourth class). Moreover, the achievement of adult status was preceded by a period of communal retreat, which young Athenians used to a great extent for military exercises. A remarkable spirit of equality prevailed throughout the infantry, and alongside it only a small cavalry corps, showy but not very effective, recalled the existence of the old class structure.

Freedom of thought and speech was limited only by the interests of the state, and the notion of state interest was very adaptable and capable of surprising variations in different circumstances. It is astonishing, for example, to see the same city that had tolerated the enormous irreverences of Aristophanes towards the end of the fifth century, condemn Socrates to death for criticisms of its institutions and gods that appeared to be much more discreet. In normal times opinions, and particularly political opinions, could be freely expressed. The difficulties that had to be faced in setting up an opposition party in the Athenian democracy must not be exaggerated. In fact, the most diverse opinions were voiced not only in the Assemblies but also in the college of *strategoi* to which citizens of very different tendencies might, by the workings of universal suffrage, find themselves elected, and in which, during the Peloponnesian War, pacifist moderates like Nicias sat alongside demagogic aristocrats like Alcibiades and nationalistic democrats like Cleon.

Parties at Athens had a definitely political character. The social complexion which parties nowadays assume in most civilised countries would have been quite foreign to them. The moderate size of even the largest fortunes of those days, the absence of large-scale industry, the friendliness of manners, prevented even the poorest from seriously wishing for a society in which conditions of life would be the same for everyone. The notion of a financial communism, still more of an agrarian communism, would not have had the slightest chance of success in an Attica that was still semi-rural. The jests of Aristophanes in his *Assembly of Women* about common ownership of property were directed against theories that had been elaborated in aristocratic intellectual circles after the terrible shocks administered by the Peloponnesian War. What really divided Athenian parties were what may be called constitutional differences. In mid-fifth century a strong majority made up of peasants, workers, merchants, and liberally-inclined aristocrats was in favour of the natural extension of Cleisthenes's reforms, that is the extension of full participation in public affairs to an ever-growing number of citizens, with the financial consequences inseparable from such a policy.

The opposition, grouped naturally around a few Eupatrid families, would have liked a return to the good old days of privileged castes. An intellectual movement, which was later to find expression in Platonism, supported these aspirations and deplored the fact that in the Athenian state 'everyone was eligible for everything'. The ideas of the parties naturally evolved, and the Peloponnesian War in particular produced notable changes in both their programmes and their composition. At times, however, they assumed a tone of vehemence, displayed in extreme form in 461 in the murder of Ephialtes. The tact of Pericles kept it in check for a time, but it broke out again all the more fiercely the more the security of Athens was threatened. It is useless to deplore the bitterness of these struggles which were the almost inescapable price of a libertarian régime. And violent as they were, party quarrels did not constitute the fundamental weakness of Athenian democracy.

The evil lay elsewhere. Athens, no longer recognising privileges of birth, had never concerned herself to establish a new *élite* apart from the nobles and the rich. During the whole of the fifth century there is no evidence that any serious attempt was made to organise what we should call a system of public education. The middle-class Athenian entered upon his civic duties equipped with only the most rudimentary culture. There was no secondary education, still less any advanced education. Only a few great families who carried on a tradition of intellectual culture could indulge in the luxury of a resident tutor, or offer hospitality to some wandering sophist. As long as Athens remained a small city this lack of systematic instruction had no serious drawbacks, and the fact that certain noble families gave proof of their democratic inclinations allowed their members over a long period to play an important part in the state. During the fifth century, however, Athens became an imperial city, and to an ever greater extent needed competent men to conduct a national business which grew more and more complex. Such competent men, by a sad contradiction, could only be recruited from unreliable quarters.

By the end of the century culture and reaction had become synonymous. If Thucydides is to be believed, Cleon expressed quite brutally the mistrust felt by democracy for the over-intelligent and highly educated (ξυνετώτεροι). Such a state of mind led to the handing over of power to men of no ability and no morals. The Athenian populace which distrusted aristocrats ought also to have distrusted lower-class men, who became statesmen merely by the luck of the draw or the vagaries of universal suffrage. No doubt the venality of such politicians has been exaggerated by public ill-feeling, which did not spare even a Pericles; indeed it seems that the Athenians lived in a state of chronic suspicion of anyone to whom they entrusted power. This attitude is shown not only by the number of prosecutions for peculation recorded during the fifth century, but also by the close watch kept over magistrates during their terms of office, by the very detailed accounts they were obliged to render, and by the over-complicated legal organisation which distorted the intrinsic virtues of the jury system, and turned the Athenian courts into a queer and costly machine which produced negligible or bad results.

Still more serious was the lack of co-ordination, due to historical circumstances, between the internal organisation of Athens and her position in the Hellenic world. The constitution devised by Cleisthenes was suitable for a small town acting as the centre of a homogeneous little state, but as the Athenian empire was expanded no attempt was made to adjust its system of government to the new conditions. And when the only body through which the allied cities could express their wishes – the periodic meetings of their representatives – finally disappeared, the whole conduct of all the League's business then devolved upon the political Assemblies of Athens, on her law courts and officials. Their work was greatly increased, and it seemed natural that the contributions paid by the allies should be used to reward it.

From this practice, however, arose the notion which became more and more firmly fixed in the Athenian mind that the League existed mainly for the benefit of Athens, to provide for her expenses and her pleasures. A corollary to this idea was that the number of contributory towns should be increased to ensure the financial well-being of a few thousand Athenian citizens. This dangerous error was propagated by their leaders, even by Pericles. Thus Athens became an imperialist democracy from the middle of the fifth century. But such an unnatural hybrid could not survive, and even the most vehement demagogues knew this perfectly well. Not only did this imperialism hasten the end of a league founded on the principles of freedom and autonomy, but in the internal affairs of the city it lay behind the political revolutions at the end of the century, which were to complement the military defeats. For it originated a new alignment of political groups, it undermined public morality and the proper working of the constitution, and made it easy for a set of dangerous demagogues to get hold of the reins of office.

XVIII

RELIGION, FESTIVALS, AND THE FINE ARTS
IN THE FIFTH CENTURY

The Persian wars served only to reinforce some of the various spiritual principles which had contributed, long before that great conflict, to the moral strength of Hellenism, and in particular the idea of the city-state. The Greek thought of himself as being a member of a social corporate body dwelling in a limited territory, usually with a modest township as its centre. The fact that such a community was no longer personified in a unique being, a king or tyrant, nor even in a small group of aristocrats, made not the slightest difference to the importance of this concept. On the contrary, democratic institutions, while they ensured to everyone a part in the still primitive machinery of government, had the effect of increasing every citizen's sense of responsibility and civic pride.

The moral principles of the Greek of those days were determined by the laws of the city, his gods were the gods of the city: the Athenians of the fifth century were as devoted to their gods on the Acropolis as they were to the constitution of Cleisthenes, and in this sense they have been called the most pious of men. This municipal religion, free though it was from all sentimental elements, drew great strength from its basis in a narrow patriotism.

A separatist feeling of this kind was obviously unfavourable to the growth of the Panhellenic idea, which, in spite of the lessons of the Persian wars, made no progress whatever in the course of the fifth century. Pericles was the only man who made any serious attempt to bind the states together, and he met with scant success. We have seen how the Delian League based on Athens and Delos had soon turned into a central-ised empire, which the sovereign-city exploited for her own benefit. We shall, it is true, see the old Peloponnesian alliance rebuild itself to oppose Athens: but this grouping was nothing more than a wartime association which did not long survive the Athenian defeat. The Boeotian League, which was revived in spite of and in opposition to Athens, never spread beyond the limits of Boeotia. Only a few great shrines, by virtue of the traditions that clung to them, the periodical contests which took place there, and the fairs that established themselves at their gates, sustained any feeling of solidarity among the Greek peoples. Even here, the temple of Apollo attracted chiefly the islanders and men of the Aegean coasts, while Olympia appears to have been patronised mainly by those of the west.

Delphi did, however, remain essentially a Panhellenic sanctuary; its Priests had cleverly extricated themselves from their awkward predicament after Salamis by issuing a series of antedated oracles, in which they claimed to have advocated the policy followed by Themistocles, and spread a fabricated account of a miraculous cataclysm that had routed the Persian detachment sent to pillage the temple. They thus obliterated the memory of their attitude during the Persian wars. Commemorative tripods were set up in the sanctuary to celebrate the victories of Salamis, Plataea, Himera, and Eurymedon, not far from the shrine in which Athens, in 485, had consecrated a tithe of the spoils from Marathon; and Delphi became once more a centre of influence and intrigues where the great powers of the Hellenic world contended with each other for first place. Here, from 448 onwards, Sparta and Athens confronted one another, Sparta sending an army to restore to the priests of Delphi the administration of the sanctuary usurped by the Phocians, and Athens trying once again to dispossess the priests, in favour of the Phocians whom she wished to secure as allies in case of war with Boeotia.

So municipal patriotism strengthened the gods of the city, while the Panhellenic idea increased the influence of the great sanctuaries. It is useless to look for any other basis of their prestige or to try to find in them any trace of moral teaching at this period. At Delphi itself the sentiments of the priests as expressed in their oracles were in the main only manifestations of the most cautious opportunism. In all Greece only the sanctuary of Eleusis continued to offer, through the ceremonies of the Mysteries, a moral and consolatory doctrine. But the need for such spiritual comfort, which had encouraged the development of Orphism in the seventh and sixth centuries, was less strongly felt in an epoch of moral stability and material prosperity, which are conditions decidedly unfavourable to mysticism. It is noteworthy that the Thracian and Asiatic cults, which were so much more in keeping with emotional tendencies than were the purely Hellenic religions, made very little progress in the fifth century, and then only among the cosmopolitan populations of a few seaports.

To honour the gods of the city or nation, to bring them offerings and embellish their dwelling-places, thus became an essentially patriotic act. In the fifth century the Greek cities treated their temples as their great and almost their only luxury, for they contented themselves with quite modest buildings as municipal offices and places of assembly, much inferior for example to those of the great commercial cities of Flanders, Germany, and Italy in the fifteenth century A.D. Yet the temple of the fifth century was no great improvement in plan or construction on that of the sixth. It remained, in essence, a rectangular room with a colonnade in front or all around. Architects continued ignorant of the principle of vault or roof-truss, and were thus no better able than their predecessors to give any considerable width to this room. Even in the colossal temples built in Sicily in the first half of the fifth century, and in any case left unfinished, the width of the *cella* never exceeded seventy feet. Wherever the religious ceremonies required the construction of a vast square edifice – for instance the room of initiation at Eleusis – the architect could only comply by raising a whole forest of columns which could hardly fail to irritate spectators. Similarly, no new solution had been found for the problem of lighting, and the open door was the only way in which light could penetrate into the temple's interior. Obviously there had been no technical evolution comparable, for instance, to that which between the tenth and fourteenth centuries A.D. made the building of bolder and more and more luminous cathedral naves possible throughout western Europe. Even the general principles of decoration had been hardly modified. The architects of the fifth century, like those of the sixth, were acquainted only with the Ionic and Doric orders, and the Corinthian pillar found at the back of the *cella* in the temple of Bassae in the Peloponnese, built about 420, is an isolated example.

The increase of public wealth, however, additions to the labour-force, and above all the growth of national and civic pride, made possible and encouraged the realisation of architectural schemes much vaster than those of former days. At Olympia the new temple of Zeus was erected by the Eleans between 468 and 457, majestic and isolated, on a vast artificial esplanade. At the Heraeum of Argos, the old temple of Hera (burnt down in 423) was rebuilt shortly afterwards at the summit of a series of terraces communicating one with another by a monumental staircase.

This passion for building manifested itself more than anywhere at Athens. The *strategoi* of the fifth century, besides the various structures required for commerce and national defence – the long walls joining Athens to the port of the Piraeus, the arsenals, docks, porticos, and warehouses of the Piraeus – had great works put in hand at the shrines of Eleusis, at Rhamnus, at Cape Sunium, and above all on the Acropolis at Athens, which had become the religious centre of the Athenian Empire.

Upon this venerable spot, at the time when Pericles began to direct Athenian affairs, there stood only unfinished or temporary buildings bearing witness to the Persian invasion. The colonnade around the old Hecatompedon had crumbled into ruin; there was nothing left of the great temple of Athena, which had been begun under Cleisthenes and on which work had been resumed between the battles of Marathon and

Salamis, except the foundations on which the fire of 480 had left its tragic mark; the old shrine of Athena and Poseidon-Erechtheus had been destroyed.

After Salamis, the plateau of the Acropolis had been extended and made more regular in plan by embankments supported by strong retaining walls. On this vaster terrace Pericles planned to reconstruct the temples which were unfinished or in ruins, and to give them a splendour befitting the sovereign city. For the first time in Greece, marble was used not merely for small shrines but to build huge edifices from base to pediment. The quarries of Mount Pentelicus, which had already been worked for a century or so, provided blocks of close-grained marble well suited for building purposes and within one day's cartage of the site. From about 450 onwards the Acropolis became one vast builder's yard. On it were erected in succession the great temple of Athena which was later to be renamed the Parthenon or temple of the Virgin-Goddess (447-438); a monumental porch or Propylaea (begun in 438) to replace the more modest gateway built by the Peisistratids; and finally the Erechtheum (begun about 435). By rare good fortune Athens had no need to call upon foreign artists to direct these great works: the architects Ictinus, Mnesicles, Callicrates, and Philocles were all sons of the city.

In the fifth century sculpture was a branch of architecture. Anywhere that a temple was being built, as around the cathedrals of the Middle Ages, stone-masons' yards would be found where the artists and craftsmen worked, and from which masterpieces emerged, in most cases anonymously. The most celebrated of these work-places was that which produced the statues and bas-reliefs to decorate the Parthenon. Pericles had entrusted the oversight of the sculpture for this temple to an Athenian named Pheidias, who had achieved some fame in Cimon's time by casting and setting up an enormous bronze statue of Athena at the entrance to the Acropolis. It is not possible to decide just how much of the design and craftsmanship of the Parthenon sculptures are to be attributed to him. In any case it is quite clear that all of them could not have been by the same hand, nor even have come from the same workshop. The metopes are still rather clumsy, but the frieze, which by a fortunate innovation was designed to run the whole length of the *cella* wall so that the colonnade diversified it with a most interesting play of light and shade, gives evidence of the highest decorative artistry; and what is left of the pediments shows them to have been the work of a great master.

For the ancients, however, Pheidias was renowned above all as the creator of the two enormous statues of Athena and Zeus in gold and ivory, and placed, the one in the *cella* of the Parthenon in 438, and the other in that of the temple of Zeus at Olympia a few years later. Modern taste is offended by these monstrous figures nearly forty feet high, consisting of a wooden framework covered with a costly shell: but they need to be imagined as viewed from a distance by the crowd of worshippers, who from their position outside the temple could see through the open doors only a gleaming image in the dark interior of the *cella*.

Designed as part of great architectural schemes and generally for the open air, the sculpture of the first two-thirds of the fifth century was mainly intended to create a sense of stability. On the friezes and pediments, which usually took their subjects from mythology (or exceptionally, as on the Parthenon, from the more majestic occasions of civic ceremony) vigorous movement was generally avoided. A feeling for broad stylisation shows itself in the treatment of the human figure and of the garments, for the sculptors, in accordance with the newer fashions, had ceased to depict the more coquettish and elaborate styles of the preceding century. Any suggestion of pathos was avoided, as being no longer in keeping with these grand compositions; and if there is a certain *gaucherie* in the fixed smile of the warriors on the pediments of Aegina, which are perhaps the belated products of a provincial type of art, there is no doubt that the stylised and summary method of indicating passion in the combatants of Olympia is not due to any lack of skill, but arises from some definite principle.

Painting, too, was used in the mid-fifth century as an integral part of the architectural effect. The essential features of buildings were emphasised by a use of colour which was very probably less startling than was customary in the sixth century; and painted frescoes were now often added to give animation to the interior of a temple or the inner wall of a portico. These vast compositions have completely disappeared. We know that the painters of those days – Polygnotus, Panainos, and Micon – employed a very limited range of colours, much poorer than the Italian primitives had at their disposal, and had no idea how to make their figures 'stand out'. They probably contented themselves with representing human figures pleasantly grouped and painted in flat tints against a rudimentary landscape. Their work, however, had one outstanding merit – a firm and accurate draughtsmanship, a quality which even the most modest decorative artists possessed in Athens.

This is demonstrated in a striking way in the ceramics of the period. From the end of the sixth century Attic pottery had reached a rare state of perfection. A fortunate innovation had reversed the use of colours, so that the fine black glaze was used for the background and red for the figures. In this new technique, about the year 500, a master-potter Euphronius was already making vases on which the paintings, whether actually his own or executed under his direction, display an admirable purity. A little later the studios of Douris and Hiero produced vessels in delicate, sensitive shapes, decorated with mythological or family scenes. These displayed with an astonishing sureness of touch the finest qualities of thought and emotion.

Municipal or national patriotism, besides finding this permanent expression for itself in the temples of its gods, enjoyed regular periodic manifestations in the city festivals and those of the great sanctuaries. The 'Games' at Olympia, Delphi, Nemea, and the Isthmus of Corinth were powerful attractions for crowds of pilgrims eager to inspect the temples and the offerings which turned them into regular museums, and above all to be present at the trials of strength and skill in which competitors from every quarter of the Hellenic world measured themselves one against another. The sporting events in which students of British or American universities vie with one another, in spite of the numbers and enthusiasm of their spectators, give only a feeble idea of these festivals in which their religious character was marked by literary and musical displays of a special kind. In honour of the gods, of the heroes, of the victors at the games, poets composed choruses accompanied by music and dances, which were intended for performance either in the sanctuary during the period of the festival or on the return of the victorious athletes to their native towns.

In the first half of the fifth century a Boeotian, Pindar, belonging to that rural aristocracy which had played a considerable and often an unhappy part in public affairs for two centuries past, was supreme in these lyric compositions. His triumphal odes are not the easiest of Greek poems to understand and appreciate. They were written in an artificial and complicated vocabulary and were full of allusions which we can often understand only with the aid of voluminous commentaries, and they switched from narrative to personal praises or to general considerations in a series of abrupt transitions typical of this kind of composition. Pindar's poems owed their success to the magnificence of their imagery, to the nobility of their religious and moral ideas, and also – it should not be forgotten – to the popularity of the music and dancing which accompanied them. The triumphal and heroic odes of the Ionian poet Bacchylides are less difficult and are graceful if somewhat commonplace, so that they provide us with more pleasing examples of the great choral lyric. This aristocratic poetry was out of date in a Greece which had moved towards democracy. It lived on until about the middle of the fifth century by favour of a few great families, and in particular of the Sicilian tyrants, but after this period it fell into a decline which the richness of its settings and music could not disguise or reverse.

From the early years of the century it had also to compete with a kind of poetry which did not express merely the pride of a few noble families, but that of a whole city. We have seen the great efforts made by the Peisistratids when they were in power to provide Athens with magnificent festivals. Democracy continued these traditions, and during the whole of the fifth century the Panathenaea and above all the Dionysia were celebrated with tremendous pomp, increased by the spirit of emulation which inspired the citizens who were called upon to contribute from their personal wealth to make these ceremonies more and more striking. The Panathenaea, in spite of the splendour of the procession which was its chief event, exercised no direct influence on literary development.

It was far otherwise with the festivals of Dionysus. From 534 at least tragedy was a form sufficiently distinctive to be allotted a part in these ceremonies alongside the ancient dithyramb, and from the end of the sixth century it constituted the chief attraction at the old ceremony of the Lenaea, and especially at the Great Dionysia which had become the characteristic festival not only of Athens but of the whole Delian League. Tragedy is a definite literary *genre*, with its own laws deriving from its religious origins and the material conditions of its performance. Tradition dictated that its subject-matter had to be taken from legends having as their main theme the suffering or death of a hero. Tradition, likewise, retained the chorus which was still the main *dramatis persona* in Aeschylus's tragedy *The Suppliants*, and was long destined to contribute largely to the moral unity of the play.

It was because of these religious associations that innovations were so few and so timid, for they would be thought to involve changes in the sacred ritual. In the same way these origins explain the absence from tragedy of certain spectacles and emotions which would have seemed shocking and intolerable in a religious ceremony; for instance the direct representation of murder was avoided as was that of amorous passion, at least until the advent of Euripides; and even though the exact meaning of the rites which underlay these dramatic performances may have been long forgotten, the notion survived that tragedy ought to convey symbolic and moral values.

Tragedy was also conditioned by the setting in which it had to be produced. In the fifth century the choruses and actors played their parts on a circular stage surrounded by wooden tiers, and situated in the precincts of a shrine of Dionysus at the foot of the Acropolis. Production in the open air with very primitive settings, the distance between the actors and their audience, the ritual masks they wore, all contributed to impose on the art of tragedy a kind of stylisation. Action had to be simple with no qualms about using broad effects, the characters needed to be boldly drawn without any attempt to indicate fine shades of meaning, which would have been lost on that audience, for the several thousand spectators who would be watching the performance of a tragedy did not in any way constitute an *élite*. To suit this huge crowd, of which only a tiny minority could hope to read the play later, and none of whom (at least in the fifth century) could see it performed a second time, the essential thing was clarity, clarity of action and of language. True, in the parts chanted by the chorus the influence of great lyric verse could be seen in the artificial vocabulary, though even there the tragic authors made it sound a little less unfamiliar; but the 'dialogues' were in Attic Greek, slightly flavoured with Ionian, and this would be easily understood by the citizens of Athens as well as by allies and subjects of the imperial city. Finally, the spirit of competition which the Peisistratids had given to the dramatic performances, with carefully chosen judges, excited the emulation of authors, and for a whole century kept their production at a very high level.

All these conditions combined to make the tragedies of the fifth century a very original art-form, particularly representative of the Greek mind by its admixture of the solemn with the realistic, of truth and stylisation. Some remarkable poetic geniuses were able to pour their own spirit into the framework thus laid down. Aeschylus, born about 525, who fought at Marathon and Salamis, is one of the noblest of Greek men of genius. No one has been better able to bring out the terrible splendour of the legends which provide the themes for his tragedies; no one has shown better insight in discovering, by a remarkable intuitive effort, their underlying symbolic value; nor has anyone else been more adept at drawing from them the profoundest moral lessons – and this perhaps is not surprising in a man born so near the sanctuary of Eleusis. In his dramas, which are composed in the grand manner if somewhat stilted and over-wrought in style, we are shown how power and fate join issue with justice, how lack of moderation causes right to 'get out of place', how crime begets vengeance; and how in the end 'new laws' and 'new gods' are born. In this respect Aeschylus links up with the great sixth century, which was so deeply preoccupied with moral problems.

Sophocles belonged to a less care-laden generation. Born about 495, of a merchant-family in easy circumstances, he was eighteen when the nightmare of Persian invasion was banished. His most productive years happened to fall in a relatively peaceful period, and he died in 406 before his country's defeat. In these circumstances, and since he enjoyed a cheerful disposition, he had a well-balanced genius that was peculiarly fitted to make tragedy into a true art. The firm structure of his plays enabled him to produce effects whose intensity still astonishes us even today; and while he maintains his idealism, he can affect his audience with the most realistic details. He contrives a contrast which skilfully opposes energy to weakness, love to duty; and his easy mastery is demonstrated both in the language of the dialogues and in the lyric passages which are the fine flower of Attic poetry.

Like tragedy, but going back much less far (only to 486) comedy had a place in the programme of the Dionysian festivals. Its development had been much slower. By the middle of the fifth century, when Aeschylus had composed all his masterpieces and Sophocles was at the height of his genius, comedy had produced nothing but a few clumsy attempts. The old entertainment of the Attic peasants, in which a chorus of drunkards would challenge the crowd while a *compère* played up to them, was not enough to originate a new art-form, even with its mimic combats and jesting tirades. Foreign influences, however, came to add to its substance. In the Peloponnese, at Megara, in Sicily, the cult of Dionysus had led to the production of plays in which clowns took part, representing simple types like those of Italian marionettes or our own Punch and Judy shows. The clowns of Megara found their way into Attic comedy. The poets Eupolis and Cratinus added, as best they could, to this background of jesting disputation a primitive kind of plot in which these comic characters could develop. Hence arose a hybrid *genre*, the chief interest of which lay in its very forthright political satire.

It can be said that Greek art in the fifth century was to a certain extent based on religion. But religion itself was supported by national feelings and civic sentiment. It was the cities which built the temples and raised statues to the gods who ensured their prosperity; it was for the city festivals that the poets, tragic and comic, wrote. And the same motives which stimulated local patriotism at Athens encouraged the blossoming of a magnificent art.

XIX

SCIENTIFIC CURIOSITY AND
POLITICAL REACTION

These literary works composed for the festivals of a sanctuary or a city certainly do not represent the whole of Greek intellectual activity. Along with them other forms of thought, independent of municipal patriotism, continued to develop. In Greece, as everywhere, science was international. The sages and philosophers of the fifth century, except for Socrates and perhaps Empedocles, were great travellers. Compare the life of a Sophocles, an Aristophanes, of a Pheidias even, who never went further from Athens than Olympia, with that of Anaxagoras, or those of the great sophists whose existence was one triumphal procession from Sicily all the way to Asia Minor. This state of affairs naturally gave rise to an international language – literary Ionian – which was used until about 425 by the learned men of all the eastern Mediterranean lands, by Ionians and Dorians, such as Herodotus of Halicarnassus, Hippocrates of Cos, or Hellanicus of Lesbos: scholars of such diverse origins obviously needed a prose that could be generally understood. No town, no region in the fifth century, had a monopoly of knowledge. Sicily, Asia Minor, the Aegean islands, northern Greece all produced physicists, doctors, philosophers, and historians.

The political and artistic fame of Athens might mislead us on this point, for the city was for a long time merely a meeting-place for thinkers coming from every corner of Greece. It was not until the very end of the fifth century and, oddly enough, after the decline of her power had set in, that Athenian historians and philosophers demonstrated their originality within the shadow of her threatened walls. It is not surprising that this cosmopolitan learning was not greatly influenced by current events. Even the Persian wars made no definite break: the philosophers of the fifth century concerned themselves with just the same questions as those of the sixth had done, and produced similar answers. The problem of matter was what interested the Ionian Anaxagoras, and especially the Sicilian Empedocles in the first half of the fifth century. The latter had the brilliant intuition that all bodies were made up of a combination, in variable proportions, of a few simple elements. And as so often happened in Greek science, a potentially fertile idea, based however on insufficient experimental evidence, was expressed in imprecise formulae so that the theories of the four elements – fire, air, water, and earth – and that 'like attracts like', were dead weights upon chemical science right up to the eighteenth century A.D.

Other thinkers, continuing the tradition of Parmenides, took up once more the problem of knowledge. Protagoras of Abdera (c. 480-410) declared that 'man is the measure of all things', a celebrated statement that has been variously interpreted, but seems in any case to sketch an incipient theory of relativity. The Sicilian Gorgias, in the second half of the century, with a more radical turn of mind showed that 'being' is unknowable. Such theories, in a different setting, might have led to the negation of all science. But the active curiosity which was a characteristic element of the Greek temperament reacted against these nihilistic tendencies. The boldest systematisers, the most subtle critics, still retained their taste for exact ideas and for observation. Gorgias was a geometrician; Empedocles studied facts which nowadays form part of chemistry or biology; Anaxagoras conducted modest experiments in physics.

This state of mind led to the elaboration of a theory in which Greek intellectual daring and love of clarity were exemplified. Two philosophers, Leucippus and his disciple Democritus (second half of the fifth century) from the town of Abdera where Protagoras was born and which was an active centre of science, thought out a coherent and systematic explanation of matter. Behind the conventional qualities of things as experienced by the senses they postulated the existence of atoms, differing from each other only in form and in the way in which they moved and linked up with one another in space. The universe of the senses was thus reduced to an infinite number of combinations of shapes and movements; and so the discrepancies between the problem of knowledge and the problem of matter, which had been pointed out a century before, were now resolved. Galileo and Descartes were to take up again this geometrical conception of the universe: of all the systems elaborated by Greek thought, the atomic idea provided chemistry with its most useful and most fruitful hypotheses.

The theories of the fifth-century physicists did not amount to sciences in the modern sense. An experimental method was still lacking, and those who thought out the theories, experienced observers as they were, never devised any but the most elementary experiments. Nor did they have the attitude of scrupulous caution towards nature which is characteristic of the modern scientist, and their presumption was further increased by their certainty that they could grasp the whole of human knowledge. At a period when the total number of scientific notions was limited and when books were scarce, there was no separation of the sciences and no division of labour between scientists. Plato made fun of the know-all *savants* of his day.

Medicine alone, and for obvious reasons, constituted an art (*techne*) with its specialists inspired by a truly scientific spirit, a consequence of the rational attitude the Greeks had always adopted in this realm of knowledge, as we can see even in the *Iliad*, where the wounded are tended by surgeons and not magicians. Medical schools had been set up in the fifth century something like those to be met with in the Middle Ages in southwest Europe. Hippocrates (born about 460) belonged to the most important of these, on the island of Cos, and his name has been attached to a collection of medical treatises actually composed by a variety of authors. The works in this collection are unequal in value, but we can find in them an attentive observation of pathological facts, as advanced a knowledge of anatomy as could be expected at a period when dissection was not practised, and finally an effort to define the scope of medical science. In the treatise *Of airs, waters, and places* the rudiments of human geography are explained.

The scholars of the fifth century studied man, not only in his physical but also in his mental attributes, his modes of thought and their expression. Prodicus of Ceos and Protagoras wrote treatises which were intermediate between grammar-books, studies in vocabulary, and in the philosophy of language. These theoretical studies were accompanied by practical teaching, for these grammarians taught rhetoric. Gorgias was typical of these teachers of oratory.

Philosophers who specialised in this way were henceforth called sophists, a word which had had a number of very different meanings. At first it denoted any man experienced in his trade, and then one having general intellectual competence. Only towards the end of the fifth century does the word acquire a restricted and pejorative significance. This degeneration in meaning did not merely reflect that vague distrust of intellectuals felt by the masses, for the sophists themselves deliberately adopted an arrogant and condescending manner. If their pride had been due only to a feeling for the dignity of knowledge no one could have objected, but they swaggered around Greece dressed in purple, and grew wealthy by charging dearly for their teaching. Such a mercenary spirit was obnoxious to anyone with any distinction of mind. Still more serious were the misapprehensions due to some of their declarations. The study of the forms of logical reasoning had led them to assert that every affirmation contained a part of truth. 'In everything there are two arguments, the one opposed to the other', said Protagoras. The sophists applied themselves with great subtlety to the task of disentangling this element of truth, and their efforts could well be interpreted as attempts to make the less worthy argument triumph over the better, which in the eyes of the public amounted to an affront to reason.

On the fringe of this intellectual movement was a man whose influence on the development of Greek thought – indeed of European thought – has been immense. Socrates, unlike the sophists, was no rich lord of cosmopolitan science but an Athenian of modest means who never left his native city except to take part in the early campaigns of the Peloponnesian War. In his common sense, his love of clarity, his good humour he was doubtless very much akin to the craftsmen of the market-place whose shops he was so fond of visiting; but to these national qualities he added the peculiarities of a remarkable temperament. The image we get of Socrates, like that of all great men who have left no writings of their own, has undoubtedly been distorted by his disciples, who have given us a variety of portraits of him. We can picture him to ourselves as a man with an intense inner life, attentive to the precepts of his conscience (which he more or less ironically called his 'genius') and endowed with an intellectual daring superior even to the physical courage of which he had given proof on the battle-field.

His main purpose seems to have been the achievement of a moral perfection, which he proposed to attain by submitting false and obscure ideas to critical discussion. To this task he devoted himself as passionately as if he had been appointed its holy apostle, interrogating his fellow citizens as he chanced to meet them, and forcing them by a subtle use of questions to realise how ill-founded their beliefs were. In these inquiries he was not afraid to use the analytical methods of the sophists, with whom he nevertheless found fault for their pride and their greed. Yet the crowd failed to distinguish him either from the sophists or from the physicists, whose theories had so much attracted him in his youth; and even before circumstances had involved him in a tragic conflict with his fellow citizens, the mocking dislike which many Athenians felt for intellectuals seems to have been concentrated against Socrates.

All these labourers in the fields of thought and language had a great influence on their contemporaries. By teaching their hearers to take their ideas to pieces, to regroup them, and to utilise a vocabulary which could be adjusted to the finer shades of thought, the sophists induced their disciples to make considerable progress in the art of words. Their efforts, abetted by a fortunate conjunction of political circumstances, took the Athenian dialect, which until then had been an archaic *patois* spoken only in Attica, and made of it the language which imposed itself first on the Athenian Empire, and finally on the whole of Greece. During the last quarter of the fifth century it is possible to measure the advance it made in flexibility and precision, thanks to the work of the sophists. We cannot tell if they had much influence on the orators of Pericles's time. Their real speeches we may be sure had little in common with the subtle analyses we find in Thucydides, but the effects of the sophists' teaching can be clearly seen in the first examples of the oratory of the law-courts that have come down to us, the *Tetralogies* attributed to Antiphon of Rhamnus, who died in 411. These are school exercises on fictitious cases; but the same Antiphon composed genuine pleas in real cases in which the skilful reasoning and the clever establishing of probabilities may recall the arts of the sophists, but where the plain directness with which the facts are related shows what a distinguished mastery of rhetoric could be developed by such exercises.

The whole of literature was fertilised by these new disciplines. Under the influence of tragedy, history became a form of art, and under the influence of philosophy it became a purveyor of thoughtful reflexion. The first of these tendencies is chiefly noticeable in the work of Herodotus of Halicarnassus, born about 484. In his nine books we can see a real effort to compose a work of art. The results of his inquiries (*historia*) into the peoples of the Orient served as a vast preface to his tale of the Persian wars, in which his art as a story-teller was exquisitely displayed. But his critical powers were slight, his information was of unequal value, and his accounts of recent events are very disconcerting to modern historians: the causes he suggests for these happenings are often childishly absurd, and he attempts to account for events by the idea, almost a commonplace even in his own day, that excessive prosperity is bound to lead to catastrophe.

Although the Athenian Thucydides (*c.* 460–*c.* 400) was younger than Herodotus by only a quarter of a century, the two might be several generations apart. Thucydides came of a family connected with Miltiades but with some foreign blood, and he had been profoundly influenced by the philosophers. He has left an account of the Peloponnesian War, and a most valuable one, since he himself took an active part in it as *strategos* in 424. No other period of Greek history, perhaps even of ancient history, is more clearly and more accurately known to us. His exposition is plain and sober enough, and contains all that is essential. This bare narrative of tragic events is the more moving for its simplicity. The influence of philosophy can be recognised in his sustained effort at impartiality, and in his careful investigation into fundamental causes. From this came a detailed study of the hearts and minds of individuals and of the masses, which he expounded in a language possessed of a subtle and expressive vocabulary, which he had learned from the sophists, and included attempts to reproduce the oratorical eloquence which had swayed public opinion.

Even the theatre felt the influence of philosophy. Euripides (480–406), one of the most cultured minds of his time, introduced new elements into his tragedies. He treated human feelings with much greater subtlety. Love, to which Aeschylus and Sophocles had made only discreet allusions, was depicted by Euripides with a deep understanding which later delighted the expert Racine. In the *Bacchae* we have a remarkable study of the frenzy of mysticism. These psychological analyses are combined not only with the moral reflections that were normally to be looked for in tragedy, but with generalisations about man and the universe which might indicate a reader, perhaps a hearer, of Anaxagoras and Protagoras. But all these innovations detract from the artistic value of tragedy, however much they may otherwise improve it. The characters in Euripides are often insufferably argumentative, and his lyric passages are frequently as commonplace as an opera *libretto*.

The general public did not always receive these novelties favourably. In circles where a taste for the things of the mind already existed, the *savants* and sophists might be welcomed with acclaim. We know (from Plato and Xenophon) with what hospitality Protagoras, Hippias, and Prodicus were received in the house of the Athenian Callias. Thinkers of all kinds could even aspire to play a part in politics. After the tyrant Meton of Agrigentum was expelled, Empedocles was called in to reform the constitution in a democratic direction; Hippias of Elis, Gorgias of Leontini, became ambassadors for their cities; at Athens, Anaxagoras had great influence over a circle of cultivated men of which Pericles was the centre. But intimacy with these thinkers encouraged much freedom of mind in their associates, and a propensity to criticise the ideas underlying religion and civic institutions; the common people felt their discussions to be dangerous. This mistrust, even in a city as liberal as Athens, soon showed itself in action. Anaxagoras was accused of impiety and forced to leave in *c.* 432-1, as was Pythagoras in *c.* 415.

Aristophanes, the writer of comedies, is a characteristic representative of this turn of mind. He does not seem to have effected any real change in the structure of the old comedy, which gave no scope either for the development of a properly constructed plot or for the study of character. His comedies were merely put together for the occasion like an end-of-year revue, in which jesting allusions to recent events were hung around some sketchy plot or some central personage who was being burlesqued. But he brought to this task the temperament of a true artist who could combine the traditional vulgarities with a most graceful realism and a charming fantasy. His own ideas, however, were of the most elementary. He was a strong conservative who looked back to 'the good old times' as to a marvellous wonderland. He mocked at everything new: at the growth of democratic institutions; at the philosophic ideas of the day, which he put together quite fantastically into the caricature of Socrates in *The Clouds* (423); and at the changes in the theatre, of which he made Euripides the clownish representative. All this inevitably produced obvious self-contradictions, and the same writer who exalts the glories of the *Knights* (424) and of the aristocratic youth of Athens, cannot be sufficiently scathing about the theories which were fashionable in precisely that section of society. The extent of his influence on political and social attitudes cannot be assessed, but he certainly mirrored current tendencies, reflecting the popular misunderstanding of Socrates and the Sophists and the dis-content of certain groups at the policies of the popular leaders, and the conduct of the war.

In spite of the opposition exemplified by Aristophanes, Athens had become the intellectual capital of Greece just as she was its artistic capital. Even before a truly Athenian school of philosophy had been built up, a kind of tradition was created that scholars and thinkers must go to Athens to receive the sort of consecration of their talents that philosophers and writers of the eighth century A.D. went to seek in Paris. This sovereignty of the mind, which was to some extent due to Athenian political supremacy, was destined to survive it. The disasters of the Peloponnesian War did not prevent Athens from remaining, in Thucydides's proud words, 'The School of Hellas'.

XX

THE PELOPONNESIAN WAR UNTIL THE PEACE OF NICIAS

Fourteen years after the truce of 445 a war broke out more devastating than any previous conflict between Greeks. The importance of what was at stake, its relentlessness, the dramatic nature of some of its episodes, and also the fact that its story was recorded by a Thucydides, have made it one of the best known events of antiquity. It has sometimes been regarded as the last outburst of a long conflict between Ionians and Dorians.

This theory, which appears to have been in circulation even in Thucydides's time, is hardly in accordance with the facts. Actually, in the fifth century there was no Ionian 'bloc' and no Dorian 'bloc'. Between a town of soldier-land-owners like Sparta, a port with a mixed population like Corinth, and a political and intellectual centre like Syracuse, there was no link other than a similarity of dialect and a temporary community of interest. It must not be overlooked that on the one hand it was the alliance between Dorian Corcyra and Ionian Athens that was one of the pretexts for war, and that the Boeotians, who had nothing Dorian about them, and later even the Aeolian and Ionian cities of the Confederacy of Delos were among the allies of Sparta, while on the other hand Athens benefited by the benevolent neutrality and finally the effective alliance of Dorian Argos.

The real underlying cause of the war, Thucydides tells us, was the extension of Athenian power and the fear this inspired in the Lacedaemonians. The war was certainly not one between rival imperialisms. Before the Peloponnesian War no one could have called Sparta imperialistic. In the Peloponnesian Confederation the freedom of member cities was respected. On the Athenian side things were very different. We know how her empire was built up (*cf.* p. 113), though some Athenians may well have wished for a wider and more flexible organisation. About 447 Pericles had invited the Greek cities to send representatives to Athens to discuss certain religious questions as well as the freedom of the seas and the maintenance of peace. This conference, which might well have been the beginning of a Panhellenic confederation, failed owing to Sparta's ill-will. Henceforward Athenian statesmen, and Pericles foremost among them, thought only of developing and centralising the power of their own city.

In the year 454 the treasury of the Delian League was moved from Delos to the Acropolis; in 446 we find the inhabitants of Chalcis having to conduct their criminal trials at Athens, a practice which spread to other subject or allied towns; in 442 the Delian League was divided into five districts to reassess the tribute which bore so heavily on the subjects of Athens. Some towns, e.g. Aegina and Thasos, had to pay no less than thirty talents each. A whole organisation was required to ensure its collection, and the inscribed 'Quota Lists' were issued annually in Athens. Power at the centre was reinforced by the allotment of lands (cleruchies) in the territories of subject states (often as a form of punishment) for the benefit of Athenian citizens who, unlike the earlier colonists, retained citizenship of their town of origin. Finally, Athens interfered in the internal affairs of cities which had joined the Delian League, using her power to establish in some of them democratic constitutions like her own.

This system aroused resentment, which was clearly demonstrated in 440. At Samos, one of the few cities which had so far retained its status as an ally, the aristocratic party, annoyed that Athens should attempt to impose a democratic constitution on their state, incited the city to rebel. Byzantium joined in the movement; the insurgents tried in vain to find further support in the Greek world, but only the Satrap of Lydia promised to send a Phoenician fleet to their aid. Pericles acted vigorously. A fleet of sixty vessels with himself in command sailed for Samos, and, reinforced by Athenians and allies to a total of very nearly two hundred ships, he laid siege to Samos and sent detachments to cruise along the coasts of Caria to meet the Phoenician squadron, which, as it happened, did not put in an appearance. After being beleaguered for nine months and after a series of battles with varying fortunes, Samos was forced to surrender, to decline in rank to a subject town, and to accept a garrison. Byzantium also submitted. This crisis showed both the continuing interest which the Persian government took in what happened in the Aegean Sea, but also the state of mind that existed in the Athenian Empire.

Still more serious was the mistrust which the spread of the Athenian Empire was causing throughout Greece. When they were having to make up their minds whether to support the Samians in their rebellion, a majority of members of the Peloponnesian Confederation had decided to refrain from interference: but less from any friendship for Athens than from respect for the Thirty Years' Truce, and a feeling that the time for action was not yet ripe. In point of fact everyone realised the danger of further extension of Athenian power. The Delian League no longer satisfied her ambitions. Pericles, renewing the policy initiated by the Peisistratids, was marking the route to the Black Sea with Athenian possessions. Settlers were sent to Chalcis, to the mouth of the Strymon where Amphipolis, the outlet for the mineral resources of Mount Pan-

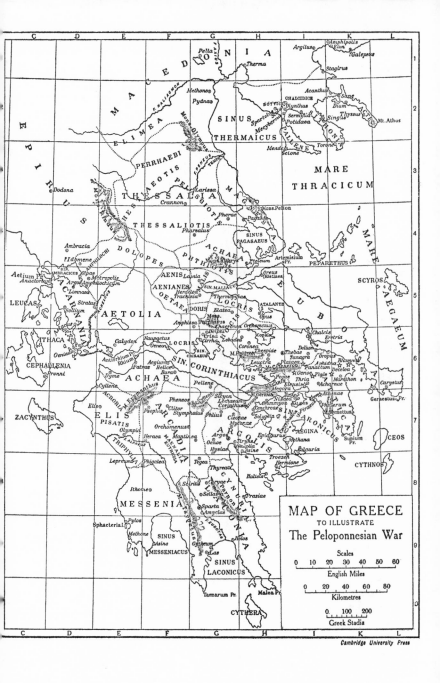

MAP OF GREECE
TO ILLUSTRATE
The Peloponnesian War

Scales

0   10   20   30   40   50   60
English Miles

0   20   40   60   80
Kilometres

0   100   200
Greek Stadia

gaeus, was founded in 437, to the Thracian Chersonese, to Sinope, and Amisos.

On the other side of the Hellenic world Athens was entering into relations with such Sicilian towns as were still independent of Syracuse; in Greece she took the lead in a Panhellenic enterprise which founded the new town of Thurii alongside the site of the former Sybaris, and peopled it with former inhabitants of the destroyed city and colonists coming from all parts of Greece (444-3). The maritime cities such as Syracuse, Corinth, and Megara were particularly concerned about these advances. Megara was with difficulty defending its independence, and a most iniquitous law had excluded her merchants in 432 from all the markets of the Athenian Empire. Sparta was slower to rouse herself and the war actually began as a result of quarrels between Athens on the one side and Corinth and Megara on the other.

The first of these conflicts certainly did not appear likely in its early stages to set off a general conflagration. The town of Epidamnus, a colony of Corcyra (modern Corfu) whose lands were being overrun by the Illyrians, asked its mother-city for help, and when this was refused, turned to Corinth (435) the mother-city of Corcyra itself. There was an old score still unsettled between Corcyra and Corinth, the latter holding that her colony had shown too much independence of its mother-city and had become altogether too active a competitor in the Adriatic. The opportunity seemed a good one to the Corinthians, who sent a colony to Epidamnus and a garrison, supported by a fleet of seventy-five ships. The Corcyraeans defeated this squadron and seized the garrison, whereupon the Corinthians made considerable preparations for a punitive expedition. At this juncture the Corcyraeans, in alarm, asked Athens for aid, and the Athenian Assembly decided to conclude a defensive alliance with Corcyra and to send reinforcements.

It was a serious move: Pericles, who must have foreseen its consequences, evidently considered that a major conflict was inevitable and did not wish to make the enemy a gift of the Corcyraean fleet and unimpeded navigation of the Ionian Sea. In the summer of 433, off the isles of Sybota near the southern tip of Corcyra, the fleets of Corinth and Corcyra clashed with each other. The Corcyraeans were helped by ten Athenian triremes which had been given instructions not to attack, but to prevent any Corinthian landing on the island of Corcyra. In spite of the fact that the Athenian crews disobeyed their orders and became involved in the battle, the Corcyraean fleet was defeated, but the arrival of a further twenty Athenian triremes halted the Corinthians and saved Corcyra from invasion.

After this indecisive encounter the fleets drew apart, but the Corinthians considered that the Athenians had broken the Thirty Years' Truce. Before this legal question could be settled, a new incident set the two cities by the ears. Not long after the battle of Sybota an Athenian decree ordered Potidaea in Chalcidice, one of the towns in the League but an old Corinthian colony which had remained in touch with its mother-city, to raze its walls, give hostages, and refuse to admit the officials whom Corinth sent there each year. At the same time Athens decided to send a squadron with a landing-force of one thousand men, both to subdue Potidaea and to keep watch over Perdiccas, King of Macedon, who was intriguing with the towns of Chalcidice and the Peloponnesians. The Athenian forces arrived in Chalcidice to find Potidaea and the neighbouring cities in revolt and Perdiccas openly at war with Athens (432). Corinth sent two thousand men to help the Potidaeans. Athens for her part sent a further two thousand, who with the earlier contingent won their first engagement and then settled down to fortify the isthmus behind Potidaea while the squadron blockaded the port.

This time hostilities were direct. At a Congress of the Peloponnesian League in Sparta, the Corinthians lodged a strong complaint against the conduct of Athens, and Megara denounced the iniquity of the decree restricting her trade. The Spartan Assembly, in private session, decided that the truce had been broken, and a few weeks later a new Congress voted for war. Both sides now prepared for the hostilities, which could not begin until the coming spring. The Spartan government, headed by the prudent old King Archidamus, entered into the adventure without enthusiasm, and only the failure of a last embassy to Athens persuaded him to accept the inevitable. For he realised that the outcome of the struggle would be very doubtful. Athens could count on her empire, her financial resources, a thousand talents in reserve on the Acropolis, her fleet which consisted at this time of three hundred triremes, their well-trained crews, and the productive capacity of her arsenals. She had also, besides a reserve of sixteen thousand older men and foreigners, an army of thirteen thousand hoplites and a thousand cavalry – if not the best *disciplined* troops in all Greece, at any rate the most experienced in every kind of warfare, troops who had given proof of their quality from Thrace to Egypt.

To oppose the whole Athenian Empire the Peloponnesian League had a less closely knit organisation. Sparta had never previously threatened the freedom and autonomy of any allied city. Nevertheless, some improvements in cohesion had been made during the fifth century. The contingents to be provided for each campaign by the allied states were decided upon and allocated by Sparta, and put under Spartan officers for the whole duration of hostilities. The League could mobilise thirty-five thousand hoplites, of whom the hard core consisted of four thousand Lacedaemonians armed with old-fashioned weapons but splendidly disciplined. Boeotia could supply an additional seven thousand hoplites, ten thousand lightly armed infantry, and a strong contingent of cavalry. The towns along the Gulf of Corinth could furnish a hundred triremes. In a conflict where the opposing forces were so evenly balanced, with Athens preponderating by sea and Sparta by land, 'imponderables' were bound to play a great part, as well as what might happen within the belligerent states.

Early in the spring of 431 one of Sparta's allies put her side irretrievably in the wrong. Thebes had long been aggrieved that Plataea had remained outside the Boeotian confederation since 519, and had kept up the alliance with Athens which had been sealed with the blood they had shed in common at Marathon and at Plataea itself. In case of war, Plataea might well serve as a base for Athenian operations in Boeotia. One night in March a Theban detachment occupied Plataea, without any provocation. After a momentary astonishment, the population recovered its courage, defeated the invaders in bitter street fighting, put to death the one hundred and eighty Thebans who were unable to escape, and applied for help to Athens, who at once sent a protective garrison. This treacherous action by the Thebans, and the slaughterous night that followed, provoked reprisals and gave the war an unusually ferocious character from the start.

A few weeks later, twenty-five thousand Peloponnesians and Boeotians invaded Attica, camped at Eleusis and then at Acharnae, laid waste the crops and orchards, and after a month withdrew. This feeble plan of campaign was all that the old king, Archidamus, could devise, and it was repeated the next year, though obviously unlikely to obtain a quick decision. With the siege-material available in those days an assault on the city was out of the question, and Athens in the shelter of her walls could always reprovision herself by sea. Pericles contented himself with bringing all the inhabitants of Attica inside the walls, avoiding any serious pitched battle, trying to create a diversion along the coasts of the Peloponnese, and ravaging the territory of Megara. His tactics were based on the idea that a people with a strong navy is invincible, and this seems to have brought about a dangerous lethargy. He does not seem to have foreseen that Sparta would one day have a powerful and well-trained fleet at her disposal.

Nor does he seem to have weighed up the effects of his military dispositions on morale. In the army thus cooped up within the walls, among country folk condemned to watch their harvests being burnt, and among restless and easily influenced townsfolk, signs of nervous irritation were soon manifest. An occurrence for which Pericles was not responsible, but which was greatly aggravated by the tactics he had adopted, increased the general demoralisation. In the spring of 430, just after the Peloponnesians had again invaded Attica, a malady (considered by Thucydides to have spread over the sea from Ethiopia and Egypt) broke out in the Piraeus and then at Athens. In the two towns, in which many thousands of refugees were crowded together in most unhygienic conditions, frightful havoc was caused by the plague, which raged for three years with occasional intermissions. The army alone lost more than five thousand men.

Passions ran high; a ridiculous lawsuit for misappropriation was rigged against Pericles, who had to pay an enormous fine and relinquish the office of *strategos*, which he had held for fifteen years. The following spring he was re-elected, by a queer twist of fortune, which may perhaps be explained by the capture of Potidaea in the winter of 430-29 – followed it is true by an Athenian defeat in Chalcidice. It was for a very brief spell, however, for he caught the plague and died during the summer. He left behind him an Athens splendid in its pride, conscious of its power, but engaged in a conflict for which he must bear the chief responsibility.

With his disappearance there was no slackening in the conduct of the war. The man whose influence replaced his was Cleon, not at first in the College of *Strategoi* which he did not join until 424, but immediately in the Popular Assembly. Cleon was very far from being the ridiculous brute which Aristophanes represented him to be. He belonged to the merchant class who wanted a radically democratic government, and he had the uncompromising patriotism of a Jacobin. Backed up by public opinion he wished to push on more vigorously with the war. In Sparta the same sort of thing was happening under the influence of Brasidas, a daring soldier with a mind open to new ideas. Both sides now realised that there was no chance of deciding their quarrel under the walls of Athens. The springtime invasion of Attica no longer took place except intermittently (428, 427, 425), and both sides looked around for other theatres of operations.

In 429 the Peloponnesians laid siege to Plataea, which actually held out for two more years. In 429 also an Athenian squadron, which had sailed the previous autumn under the command of Phormio into the Gulf of Corinth to blockade its ports, won two successive victories off Naupactus (Lepanto) which were largely due to the unskilful handling of their ships by the Peloponnesian crews. On the other hand a raid by Brasidas on the Piraeus almost succeeded.

In 428 a serious set-back put the Athenian Empire in jeopardy. The little isle of Lesbos, one of the few states of the Delian League which had retained full status as an ally, revolted, was immediately admitted into the Peloponnesian League and was promised help at once. Cleon reacted energetically. By autumn a fleet and landing force were blockading Mytilene, the centre of the rebellion: one squadron made a demonstration against the coasts of Laconia, and another off the Isthmus where the main Peloponnesian army was concentrated. The following summer the democratic party in Mytilene compelled the government to capitulate before the relieving fleet could arrive. A terrible vengeance ensued: the first vote of the Athenian Assembly that every male in Mytilene should be put to death came within an ace of being carried out before the countermanding instructions to execute only those responsible for the rebellion could reach the city.

The war took on an ever more savage character. In that same summer of 427, after a siege during which the Peloponnesians had made laborious attempts with battering-rams and other siege methods, the remnants of Plataea's garrison had to surrender. They were all butchered, the town razed to the ground, and the territory handed over to the Thebans. The same year troubles broke out at Corcyra between democrats and aristo-crats. Both Athens and the Peloponnesians sent a naval division, and in the end the arrival of sixty Athenian triremes assured the victory of the democratic party. For several days the most terrible reprisals were taken, and these had their repercussions throughout Greece, which was now divided into two camps.

Even the nations on the frontiers of the Hellenic world were drawn into the struggle. In the autumn of 429 Sitalces, king of the Odrysae in Thrace, had invaded Macedon at the instigation of Athens, with a huge horde. His expedition, which the winter halted, was a warning to the traitor Perdiccas and the states of central Greece. In 426 the *strategoi*, who now included an enterprising man named Demosthenes, devised a plan for a large-scale campaign from the west, to force the tribes of Acarnania and Aetolia into submission and then to drive through Phocis into Boeotia. The Athenian heavy infantry was at first bewildered by the unfamiliar tactics of the Aetolian archers and suffered a severe defeat in the spring, but in the autumn a brilliant victory gave Demosthenes control of Acarnania and Ambracia. It seemed more and more probable that a decisive result must be sought in the west. In Sicily the democratic state of Syracuse, having captured Agrigentum about 446, was trying to rebuild for itself the former empire of Hieron. But the towns which were unwilling to accept Syracusan domination sent an embassy in 427 under the direction of Gorgias to ask help from Athens, which sent a small naval division into the neighbourhood.

In 425, while the Peloponnesians were carrying out a last futile invasion of Attica, the Athenians sent a further squadron to Sicily. Commanded by Demosthenes, it put in on the western coast of Messenia to land a body of hoplites on the steep slopes of the peninsula which commanded the roadstead of Pylos. The spot was well chosen as a base of operations. The Spartan army, returning from Attica, met the Peloponnesian fleet close to Pylos, and when an attack from the sea had failed to carry the fortifi-cations built by the Athenian soldiers, the Lacedaemonians made the mistake of landing four hundred and twenty hoplites (one tenth of the Spartan infantry) on the island of Sphacteria at the mouth of the bay. There followed what could have been foreseen: an Athenian squadron drove off the Peloponnesian ships, entered the bay, and blockaded the island. The siege was a long one, so that at the end of the summer Cleon impatiently persuaded the Assembly to vote him an extraordinary commission and appeared at Pylos with reinforcements of light troops. A vigorous attack, in which Demosthenes made great use of archers and slingers, carried the enemy positions. Three hundred surviving Spartans were made prisoners, an unprecedented humiliation for an army whose motto had been 'never surrender'.

This success strengthened Cleon's influence, and that of the war-party at Athens. He was elected a *strategos*. But the year 424, apart from a naval expedition which ended in the seizure of Cythera, failed to answer the expectations aroused by the victory at Sphacteria. The Sicilian expedition had met opposition, had provoked mistrust, and had finally united all the towns in a peace-convention concluded at Gela, so that the Athenian fleet had had to retire. An attack on Megara, made in great strength, was unsuccessful, but the Athenians gained by it the port of Nisaea.

That same summer the Spartans at last realised that Athens was most vulnerable through her external possessions. Having just saved Megara, Brasidas left the city with a small army of Helot freedmen and Arcadian mercenaries, crossed friendly Boeotia, then Thessaly which was politically hostile but astounded by the audacity of the little force, then Macedon where Perdiccas was quite willing to turn traitor once again, and finally captured Amphipolis, before Thucydides (the historian), who was in command of the Thracian squadron, could relieve the city. Brasidas vigorously increased his forces with contingents of barbarian tribesmen, and all the towns of the region made their submission to him. Thus Athens lost the forests of Chalcidice and the mines of Pangaeus, though she was able to keep the port of Eion. At the same time she suffered a cruel blow in Boeotia, where her generals had planned a three-pronged invasion which was to have been supported by an internal rising of the democratic party. The revolt failed; the three armies could not act in concert, and the one which succeeded in entering Boeotia from the southeast was crushed at Delium, leaving a thousand hoplites dead on the field.

The war had now lasted eight years and there were still no decisive results. The Athenian Empire remained almost intact, her fleet invincible and continually renewed. The Peloponnesian Confederation was not shaken, and her victory at Delium showed that the infantry of other states could make good any wastage suffered by the Spartan hoplites. At Sparta, those in favour of peace pointed out the shrinking numbers of citizens (few enough to start with) and the risks of a revolt of the helots, many of whom had been enrolled in the army and had acquired a taste for freedom. They also pointed out that the truce concluded with Argos in 451 was about to expire, and that Sparta's ancient rival was not disguising her sympathy with Athens. And so, in 426 the old King Pleistoanax, who had been in exile for twenty years because he had outraged his nationalistic opponents by arranging the Peace Convention of 446, was recalled to Sparta.

At Athens, a considerable clique of aristocrats, admirers of the Spartan constitution, had never ceased to deplore the war. By a swing of party fortunes, easy to understand in the circumstances, they were joined by the rural class, who until then had been the firmest supporters of democratic governments: they had grown tired of seeing their Attic fields ravaged while they stood by powerless to prevent it, and tired, too, of paying more than their share of its price in blood, in this as in other wars. Many city-dwellers felt that all this commotion was not worth while, and regretted the good old days when Megara pork and eels from Lake Copais could be bought in the market. In the spring of 425 Aristophanes gave vent to this materialistic brand of pacifism in the *Acharnians*.

The man who embodied all these tendencies was Nicias, who was one of the richest Athenians of his day, and as *strategos* he had been lucky in several skirmishes. He had earned the people's confidence by his proved attachment to the democratic cause, a confidence which his opposition to Cleon had not undermined. After the disaster at Delium, peace negotiations (begun once before after Sphacteria) were resumed, and an armistice was concluded.

Affairs in Thrace had still to be settled, however. Brasidas wished to follow up his victory, but Cleon had arrived there with a thousand hoplites to restore the Athenian position. In the autumn of 422, as the Athenian army was returning from a reconnaissance under the walls of Amphipolis, Brasidas made a sudden sortie and fell upon their infantry, who had neglected to detail a proper rear-guard. A rout followed, in which the Athenians lost six hundred men, Cleon among them, but Brasidas was mortally wounded during the pursuit. With both these leaders out of the way peace negotiations were less difficult. In the spring of 421, Nicias and Pleistoanax persuaded their respective Assemblies to ratify a fifty-year truce, which was designed to restore the situation as it had been before 431. By its terms, which could not be fully implemented, Athens was to recover almost all her possessions, and in place of the territory of Plataea obtained the port of Nisaea in Megara. On the other hand she gave back all the places she had occupied during the hostilities and returned the prisoners captured on Sphacteria. To arrive at this unprofitable peace Athens and the towns of the Peloponnese had poured out blood and treasure like water. That such terrible sacrifices had produced so ludicrous a result should have given hope that the treaty of Nicias was to be the prelude to a long period of peace.

XXI

THE SICILIAN EXPEDITION AND THE FALL OF ATHENS

The value of the peace of 421 was bound to depend, as with all such treaties, on the goodwill of those who had concluded it; during the following two years, concord did indeed seem to reign between Sparta and Athens, and the treaty was even extended into a defensive alliance for fifty years.

Unfortunately there were states and individuals who were dissatisfied with this situation: Corinth, which had lost Corcyra and Potidaea; Boeotia still breathing hatred; and Megara refused to ratify the treaty of 421. In Sparta and Athens too there were people who thought peace had been made too soon. At Sparta new ephors had been elected since 421, who disapproved of the treaty and who promptly concluded an alliance with the Boeotians. In Thrace, Clearidas (who had succeeded Brasidas) refused to hand over Amphipolis to the Athenians, whereupon the latter retained Pylos. A party in favour of resuming hostilities was formed in Athens, and obtained unexpected support from a man destined to play a notable part in the events of the next few years.

This was Alcibiades, related through his mother to Pericles and the Alcmaeonids, and through his father to a family which had long and loyally served the democracy. He had all the qualities that win the favour of the crowd, and moreover had boundless personal ambition; to gain his own ends he was quite prepared to launch his country into hazardous enterprises. His dream was of an Athenian Empire in which he should have the first place. To realise this project he would have to change the city's constitution, in order to bring power into his own hands; as a first step he upset the state of equilibrium brought about by the treaty of Nicias. As soon as he was elected *strategos* in 420, Alcibiades negotiated a treaty between Athens and Argos, since he saw that Argos wished to group around itself all the Peloponnesian cities which were dissatisfied with the results of recent events, and would thus be likely to draw Athens into new quarrels.

In 419 Argos invaded the territory of Epidaurus, and Sparta sent help to the latter and in turn prepared to invade Argolis. Athens hastened to reinforce her new ally. King Agis, who commanded the Spartans, disposed his troops so as to cut off Argos from the Argive forces; when an Argive general appealed to him he agreed to a four-months' truce in hope of a political settlement. This was by no means what Alcibiades wanted, so he went in person to Argos with the intention of breaking the agreement. Hostilities began again, resulting in August 418 in the battle of Mantinea, in which about twenty thousand hoplites in addition to lightly armed troops were engaged. In this battle the triumph of Sparta was assured, and then followed by an oligarchic revolution at Argos which drove out the partisans of Athens. Sparta and Argos entered into a treaty of alliance, but the return of the democratic party to power in Argos soon put an end to it. Sparta was thus still threatened from the north. To the south she had to watch an Athenian garrison being established, contrary to accepted custom, in the island of Melos – a Lacedaemonian colony – while to the west the army of occupation in Pylos still kept guard over Messenia.

This seemed to Alcibiades the appropriate moment to propose to the Athenians the realisation of a vast project. His suggestion was to renew the attempt made in 425 at intervention in Sicily; but this time he had in mind an expedition on the grand scale which should subdue first Syracuse and then the whole of Sicily and southern Italy, whose corn and timber supplies would reassure Athens, anxious as always about her revictualling problem, and no longer able since the loss of Amphipolis to exploit the forests of Mount Pangaeus. Alcibiades perhaps had even longer and larger views, envisaging finally the conquest of Carthage and access to Spain; a reservoir of men and wealth which would have enabled Athens to subdue, once and for all, the Peloponnesian Confederation and to become mistress of the whole Mediterranean.

In a stormy session of the Assembly, and in spite of opposition by Nicias, Alcibiades managed to have the scheme for an expedition to Sicily accepted. The Assembly also voted the measures that so long-range a campaign would necessitate. At the beginning of the summer of 415 a hundred triremes were launched from the shipyards of the Piraeus, and the elaborate equipment of the fleet was evidence of the lofty confidence prevalent in Athens at the time. The generals Nicias, Alcibiades, and Lamachus were about to take charge of the expedition when one morning the busts of Hermes (which were placed as guardians at the entrances of houses and sanctuaries) were discovered to have been mutilated. Everyone was in so excited a frame of mind at the time that this impiety seemed not only to forebode disaster, but also to prove the existence of some political conspiracy. An inquiry was opened which at first brought to light only more facts of the same order, among others a bout of debauchery at which the Mysteries of Eleusis had been parodied; and in this affair Alcibiades himself was compromised.

The Athenian fleet finally left the Piraeus by mid-summer and sailed for Corcyra, where the allied forces were to concentrate. One hundred and thirty-four triremes were assembled there, more than six thousand soldiers, including fifteen hundred Athenian hoplites, and in addition the supply services and material for siege warfare. Expectations ran high as to the results of so huge and so well organised an expedition, but difficulties arose as soon as it reached its destination. The towns of southern Italy refused to open their gates or to provision the fleet, and in Sicily the allies of Athens turned out not to have the resources of which they had boasted. Nicias was already proposing that they should return to Athens. He had not the moral courage to refuse command of the expedition, though he saw nothing but its dangers. At this juncture Alcibiades was peremptorily recalled. Inquiries had led to the discovery of those guilty of mutilating the Hermae, but the scandal about the Mysteries was now coupled (in the case of Alcibiades) with an accusation of high treason. What the truth was about both these charges, neither contemporaries nor modern historians have been able to find out, but certainly Alcibiades behaved as if he were guilty. At Thurii he slipped away from the trireme which was taking him back to Athens, and fled into the Peloponnese.

The reputation of Nicias now made it certain that he would be put in charge of the expedition. Against the advice of Lamachus, who would have preferred an immediate sudden assault on Syracuse, the fleet wasted the end of the season in useless demonstrations. A landing under the walls of Syracuse, followed by a battle which the Athenians won, was not turned to advantage; for the winter was approaching, and the Athenian fleet had to sail away to Naxos and Catana to go into winter quarters. The Syracusans made good use of this respite to take defensive measures. They reorganised the command of their army; the town, its suburbs and harbour were made ready for defence, and they sent ambassadors to Sparta and Corinth to ask for help.

However, when the Athenian army reappeared under the walls of Syracuse in the spring of 414, reinforced by contingents of cavalry from Athens and Sicily, it began by winning a victory which should have been decisive, for it gave them possession of the steeply scarped plateau of Epipolae which commanded the city. The Athenian infantry established their position there and began building a double rampart with the intention of cutting off the town completely from the mainland. A strange kind of siege warfare ensued, the Athenians pushing on in haste with their wall of timber and stones, the Syracusans endeavouring, without much success, to hinder the work by building counter-walls at right angles to the enemy's.

There was already talk in Syracuse of surrender when help arrived. At the instigation of Alcibiades, who had taken refuge in Laconia and was now hoping to re-enter his defeated fatherland in the guise of a conqueror, Sparta had decided to join vigorously in the struggle. She sent an enterprising leader named Gylippus with instructions to raise a relieving army on the spot, and thanks to Nicias's lack of energy he was able, with three thousand Sicilians, to drive a wedge between the coast and the end of the wall on which the Athenians were working. This changed the whole complexion of the struggle. A successful raid enabled Gylippus to seize the summit of Epipolae, to establish a post there, and finally to link this garrison to the city walls by a rampart at right angles to that of the Athenians, who thus lost all hopes of surrounding the city. Nicias, in poor health, could only reply with ineffective displays of strength and ask Athens to send more troops.

At the same time Sparta struck in Attica, and this time it was no half-hearted invasion as had been those of the aged Archidamus. In the spring of 413 a Peloponnesian army led by King Agis occupied Decelea, a township on the slopes of Mount Parnes which commanded the road to Euboea. This really took Athens by the throat. Raids by the Peloponnesian cavalry made it impossible to grow any crops in the neighbourhood of Athens, and even disorganised the working of the silver mines at Laurium. Her supply-line from Euboea was cut and Athens could be fed only by sea. Yet the best part of her fleet was in Sicily and was destined to remain there useless.

The Syracusans had received reinforcements which brought the number of their ships to eighty. The superior handiness of the Athenian triremes was offset by the bad state into which their hulls and tackle had fallen in winter quarters and during a whole year away from their refitting yards. Thus, after a series of stubborn engagements, they were forced to give way under the pressure of the enemy squadrons; and the situation of this Athenian fleet, cooped-up in the Great Harbour of Syracuse, became critical. Fortunately the Athenians had been stirred by the reports from Nicias. Early in the summer seventy-three triremes and fifteen hundred Athenian hoplites, with the support of a strong allied contingent, appeared before Syracuse. This was an unprecedented effort for a city which had experienced twenty years of continuous warfare and was actually be-leaguered. The leader of this relieving force was Demosthenes, victor of Pylos. He realised at once that a quick decision must be sought, and that if the attempt failed the siege must be raised. At the head of his heavy infantry, one moonlit night, he attempted to take the summit of Epipolae by assault. The attack at first almost succeeded, but was finally repulsed in disorder and panic. Further precious time was then wasted in persuading Nicias (who was caught up in a mesh of scruples, fantastic projects, and deplorable superstitions) that a withdrawal was inevitable; and the Syracusans made use of this delay to drive the Athenian fleet into the recess of the Great Harbour and to block the entry. To release the blockaded fleet an attack with boarding-parties was the only chance, and Demosthenes decided to attempt it. But in spite of their numerical superiority the Athenian triremes, weighed down with fighting-men, hurled themselves in vain against the Syracusan vessels, and after a desperate fight had to withdraw.

Now the Athenian generals had no alternative but to abandon the fleet, which they could not even burn, and retreat with their army overland to Catana, the nearest allied town. After heart-rending scenes at their departure, for they had to leave behind thousands of sick and wounded, they began a terrible retreat made much worse by the great heat and late summer storms. Demosthenes, in charge of the rear-guard, lost touch with Nicias who had gone ahead with the main body without troubling to make sure that communications were being maintained. Unprovided with cavalry or missile-weapons, and hampered by a mass of non-combatants, the two parties were overtaken by the Syracusan army, and after a devastating massacre the remnants were obliged to surrender.

This unprecedented disaster put Athens in a desperate situation. She had lost the greater part of her fleet, two thousand hoplites had been killed in battle or imprisoned in the stone-quarries of Syracuse, her best general Demosthenes had been executed, as had Nicias too, in contravention of international custom: and all the while the Spartans were encamped at Decelea. But everything was not yet lost. Athens still kept part of her maritime empire and the alliance of Argos, while a reserve of a thousand talents lay untouched in the temple of Athena.

The winter of 413-12 was used in building a new fleet and in carrying through some important financial and political reforms, in particular the setting up of what amounted to a Committee of Public Safety of ten members, the *Probouloi*. But the spring of 412 was to bring further cause for alarm. Ever since they had heard of the disaster in Sicily, the allied and subject cities were in a ferment. In vain had Athens cancelled the hated tribute early in 413, and substituted for it an import duty. This wise move, which if taken earlier might have reorientated the whole organisation of the Athenian Empire towards a much more federal constitution, came too late. Euboea, Chios, and various Asiatic towns were preparing to revolt, and were negotiating with Agis. Sparta was also acquiring a navy: five Laconian ships appeared at Chios, and this was enough to provoke the town to change sides, an action which immediately put some sixty vessels at the Spartan admiral's disposal. In face of this small squadron several towns of Ionia surrendered, Miletus among them.

In Miletus the Spartans also gained the support of a new ally. Since the beginning of the war the Court at Susa had followed the course of operations with interest. In 412 it seemed to Tissaphernes and Pharnabazus, the satraps of Lydia and of Phrygia, that the moment had come to conclude an alliance with Sparta, with the object of destroying the Athenian Empire and restoring to Darius, who had come to the throne twelve years earlier, the Greek towns in Asia Minor which his grandfather had once possessed. A scandalous treaty was signed which put in hazard once more all that had been gained by the Persian wars. From this time forward the kings of Persia and their gold were to intervene continually in Greek affairs, but for the moment Sparta could see only the advantages of an arrangement which freed her from all financial cares, for one article of the treaty of Miletus laid it down that the king of Persia should accept full responsibility for the pay of all allied crews.

Nevertheless, Athens tried desperately to rebuild her fleet. Some twenty ships managed to blockade a Peloponnesian division for several weeks in the Gulf of Corinth as it was on its way to Ionia. From the shipyards of the Piraeus there emerged eight, then twelve, sixteen, ten, forty-eight, and then thirty-five triremes, which were dispatched immediately to Chios and Miletus, where they were able to besiege these two towns and to relieve the threatened Mytilene; but when a Peloponnesian and Syracusan squadron of fifty-five ships came in sight the Athenian Phryni-chus refused battle. Defections continued in Ionia, in Caria, and then at Rhodes, where the Peloponnesian fleet – now almost a hundred strong – took up its winter quarters, while seventy-four Athenian triremes established theirs at Samos and thirty others maintained the siege of Chios. It looked as if the year 411 must bring a decision: Athens was making inroads into the last of her financial resources, half her empire had already seceded, and since the end of 412 Argos appeared to have deserted her.

These conditions created in the city an atmosphere favourable to revolutionary enterprises. For a long time a number of the richer and better educated men had been most discontented with the existing régime, pledged as it was to all-out war and responsible also for the Sicilian expedition. Among these some, like the orator Antiphon, dreamt of arranging peace with Sparta at any price, and then establishing a radical oligarchy. Others, such as Theramenes, a skilful and wily politician, wanted a wide-based democracy with a property qualification. Their theories won them adherents among the young aristocrats; the secret societies (hetairiai) were soon involved in taking direct action, and by a series of assassinations instituted a reign of terror in Athens.

A queer piece of chicanery gave them their triumph. In Ionia, where he had helped to foment the rebellion against Athens, Alcibiades had got into touch with Tissaphernes. He persuaded the satrap that he ought not to work with the Peloponnesians to crush Athens, but rather should hold the balance between the two belligerents. In such a policy Alcibiades saw a possibility of making himself the arbiter of Greek destinies when both combatants were exhausted. Tissaphernes for his part hoped the more surely to be able to restore the Greek towns of Asia to the king his master; so he held back on the coast of Caria a Phoenician fleet which was to have sailed for Ionia, and handed over the pay of the Greek crews so irregularly as to provoke spasmodic mutinies. During this period Alcibiades was carrying on clandestine negotiations with the commanders of the Greek fleet at Samos, to whom he boasted that he could gain for them the friendship of Tissaphernes.

A small group of officers made a plot, intending both to suppress the democracy which a revolutionary movement had just re-established in Samos, and at the same time to support the recall to Athens of Alcibiades, as the only man capable of bringing the war to an honourable conclusion. Alcibiades declared himself ready to re-enter his fatherland, but only on condition that the régime which had banished him should not still be in power. The Athenian people, intimidated and war-weary, allowed themselves to be outmanoeuvred. In a meeting-extraordinary of the Assembly they were prepared to decree the annulment of all magistracies conferred under the old system; to suppress indemnities; and finally to set up a body of four hundred citizens with full powers of government, from among whom all the city magistrates were to be recruited. These 'Four Hundred' were to draw up a list of five thousand citizens to be summoned to meet when occasion arose, and to take the place of the Assembly. The Council, which had always been the symbol of democratic institutions, was of course abolished in 411. For the first time for a century the constitutional framework devised by Cleisthenes was seriously modified.

Once in power, the Four Hundred took good care not to send for Alcibiades, and continued their reign of terror. In Athenian territory overseas the conspirators in Samos had already succeeded in suppressing democracy in several of the subject cities, a proceeding which merely resulted in throwing these states into the arms of the Peloponnesian Confederation. But the oligarchic movement broke down in the place where it had begun. The ships' crews, recruited among the populace of the Piraeus and faithful to democratic principles, refused to obey the conspirators. Under the leadership of a handful of officers, and in alliance with the Samian democrats, they deposed the traitor-chiefs and replaced them with men they could trust. The situation was a strange one: at Athens there was an oligarchic and reactionary usurping government; at Samos a democratic army which proclaimed its allegiance to the regular government and in any case was the only viable force that Athens still possessed. This was a splendid opportunity for her enemies: yet Tissaphernes, who probably did not want too speedy a conclusion, and the Spartan Admiral Astyochus, who was a dullard, let the chance slip.

But Alcibiades skilfully turned the situation to good account. To the crews at Samos he represented himself as the friend of Tissaphernes, able to bring the Persians over to the Athenian side and at the same time to reconcile the fleet with Athens, where the events at Samos had caused consternation among the Four Hundred. Many of the latter now regretted the brutal excesses of the new government, which was already negotiating with Sparta and had begun to fortify the Eetionean peninsula which commands the Piraeus – obvious preludes to treachery. With the secret support of moderate leaders such as Theramenes, the hoplites who had been set to work on these fortifications mutinied. At this juncture a Peloponnesian fleet appeared in the Saronic Gulf, and sailed towards Euboea which was known to be ripe for revolt. The Four Hundred hastily fitted out a fleet, which was defeated in the Euripus: Euboea rebelled. At the same time the towns on the Dardanelles went over to the enemy. Famine stared Athens in the face.

This new disaster, which created panic in Athens, dealt a death blow to the prestige of the Four Hundred. Theramenes had no difficulty in persuading a meeting-extraordinary of the Assembly, gathered according to ancient tradition on the Pnyx, to vote for a constitution which would restore their legislative powers to all Athenians of the first three property-classes. This was an ingenious middle-of-the-road scheme, which also won over the fleet at Samos. In the autumn of 411 the fleet defeated the Peloponnesian squadron in the Hellespont, and Alcibiades completed its annihilation the following spring near the port of Cyzicus. The whole region, apart from Byzantium and Chalcedon which submitted later in 408, now came once more under Athenian influence; and Athens, for the time being at any rate, was saved from starvation since her enemies no longer had a fleet. At this time Sparta also lost the support of Syracuse, for that city was threatened in Sicily itself and from 410 onwards could take no part in the affairs of the eastern Mediterranean.

It looked as if Athens was saved. The radical democratic party raised its head once more, abolished Theramenes's constitution, and restored the Council of Five Hundred and the indemnities, although these had to be for reduced amounts because the treasury was almost empty. In the Assembly, the merchants and industrial classes again played a notable part. Most of them were in favour of all-out warfare, like the lyre-maker Cleophon, who forced the rejection of Spartan peace proposals.

The year 409-8, however, brought serious reverses: the *strategos* Thrasyllus, in command of fifty triremes, was unable to bring the revolted cities of Ionia into submission; Corcyra abandoned the Athenian alliance: Pylos was at last retaken by the Lacedaemonians; and in the Saronic Gulf itself Athens lost Nisaea, the port of Megara. The political situation, too, remained an absurd one. The fleet at Samos would take orders from no one but Alcibiades, who was still legally a banished man with a capital charge hanging over him. But in the elections of 407 he was voted a *strategos*. He was able to return in triumph to his fatherland, and supreme command was conferred on him. In the spring his colleague Thrasybulus had reconquered Thasos and Abdera, and in the autumn Alcibiades himself set out for Ionia in command of a hundred triremes. The Athenians could already see themselves at the head of a rejuvenated empire!

Meanwhile, however, Sparta had found in the admiral Lysander the versatile and energetic man that she needed, but had never had since the death of Brasidas. Lysander realised that no decisive result could be looked for so long as Tissaphernes continued his seesaw policy, playing off one side against the other. A Spartan embassy was sent to Susa, and secured the recall of Tissaphernes, who was replaced in Sardis by Cyrus, the younger son of the king, whose ambition it was to reassemble under his own rule the various possessions of the great Darius. Henceforward the Peloponnesian crews were paid regularly.

In the spring of 406 a lieutenant of Alcibiades was defeated at Notium. The disappointment of the Athenians showed itself at that year's elections, in which Alcibiades failed to secure re-election. He left the fleet and refused to return to Athens. His successor Conon, though a good sailor, had taken over command of a disorganised fleet, and after losing a battle was blockaded in the harbour of Mytilene. Once again Athens seemed to be doomed. She made a last frantic effort. In only a few weeks a new fleet of one hundred and fifty triremes was fitted out, and improvised crews were made up out of the free men not engaged in defending the walls – foreign 'metics' and enfranchised slaves. Near Arginusae, to the south of Mytilene, the enemy squadron was defeated, seventy of its ships captured or sunk, and the Spartan Admiral Callicratidas killed.

This totally unexpected success was not, however, exploited. The Athenian commanders allowed 100 enemy ships to escape and were not even able to save the crews of twenty-five Athenian triremes which had been wrecked during the battle, admittedly a very hazardous task because of an autumn gale which sprang up after the fight. On their return they were put on trial, accused of indecision, and charged with responsibility for the deaths of several hundred sailors, many of them Athenian citizens, and this at a time when as a result of twenty-five years of warfare Athens was suffering a severe shortage of man-power. Exactly what happened at the trial, which was carried on in an atmosphere of near-hysteria, is still obscure. It is far from certain that the popular frenzy was not deliberately inflamed by agents of Alcibiades or of the aristocratic party. The *strategoi* were condemned and six of them were executed, among them Thrasyllus, the son of Pericles, and Diomedon, all loyal servants of the democracy.

For the Peloponnesians, on the other hand, the defeat at Arginusae was none the less a heavy blow. It seemed quite impossible ever to be rid of this Athenian fleet which rose up again after every apparent knock-out blow. The army occupying Decelea was becoming demoralised by the long and weary siege, of which the tedium was relieved only by costly attempts to take the defences by storm. King Agis offered the Athenians a peace on the basis of the *status quo*, but it was refused.

Meanwhile Lysander was constructing a new fleet of two hundred vessels with the subsidies given him by Cyrus, and with this he took possession of Lampsacus in the spring of 405. The neighbourhood of the Hellespont was always of vital concern to Athens, and she promptly sent one hundred and eighty triremes there. The two squadrons faced one another for five days, and then the Athenian crews went ashore in the bay of Aegospotami to forage for supplies. At this moment Lysander launched a sudden attack, and caught the Athenians just as they were hastily preparing to re-embark. Only nine triremes escaped: the rest were captured almost without a fight.

This was in August 405. When one of the fugitive vessels brought news of the disaster to the Piraeus by night, a wave of deep and justifiable consternation swept over Athens. This time it really was the end. What remained of the Athenian Empire surrendered without striking a blow, except for Samos which held out until the following year. A few weeks after the disaster at Aegospotami, Lysander's fleet appeared in the Saronic Gulf, and a Spartan army arrived to reinforce the garrison occupying Decelea. Nevertheless, it required several months of siege and consequent famine to convince the Athenians that they were at the mercy of their foes. At the beginning of 404 Theramenes was sent to Lysander's camp, and thence as a plenipotentiary to Sparta. He brought back conditions which the Assembly had no choice but to ratify. Athens was allowed to keep her independence; together with Attica and Salamis. These were very considerable concessions, for the Boeotians had demanded the complete destruction of the city. But she had to join the Peloponnesian Confederation, to restrict her fleet to a dozen ships, and to demolish the fortifications of the Piraeus as well as the Long Walls.

Thus, at the end of twenty-seven years' fighting, the greatest maritime power in Greece was vanquished, and at sea! The demagogic imperialism of her politicians had first provoked and then prolonged the war. The obstinate determination to stake everything on the navy, which they inherited from Pericles, had been one of the reasons for their defeat. With the Athenian Empire there disappeared the first attempt, perhaps a rough and clumsy attempt, to unify Hellenism in one common organisation. Would Sparta be able to rebuild such a unity more skilfully – Sparta which was now, to the music of flutes, tearing down the Long Walls, those symbols to the Greeks of the restoration of their liberty? This was the vital question, for without a unifying agent Hellenism would remain a scattered dust of cities.

XXII

PERSIA AND THE SPARTAN HEGEMONY:
SYRACUSE AND CARTHAGE

A Spartan Empire was now about to succeed to the Athenian. Except in the towns of Asia Minor, which fell once more under Persian domination, Spartan governors (harmosts) were installed in place of the 'phrourarchs' of Athens and levied tribute in their place. Sparta did nothing to change an organisation which events had proved to be ineffective. She did make a great effort to replace democracies by oligarchies, however, and at Athens in particular. Very soon after the capitulation, and under pressure from Lysander himself, a provisional government was set up consisting of thirty persons chosen from the aristocratic party, and given the task of devising a new constitution. Of the twenty thousand citizens and metics (resident aliens) who so recently had mounted guard on the walls or fought on the ships, only three thousand privileged men were allowed to keep their military accoutrements and to retain full political rights. On the Acropolis seven hundred Lacedaemonian soldiers guaranteed the maintenance of the new order, and there ensued a period of arbitrary arrests, proscriptions, and confiscations. Critias, one of the intellectuals whom the preceding régime had distrusted and whom his banishment had made a bitter enemy of democracy, led the oppression together with a few friends.

The government made itself most unpopular by this policy of terror. Many of the Greek states not directly subservient to Sparta were willing to shelter Athenian exiles – particularly in Boeotia, which a few months earlier had been so bitterly hostile to Athens. It was in Boeotia that some dozens of exiles gathered around the former *strategos*, Thrasybulus. He was a reliable democrat, in spite of his immense personal fortune, and a good general, and he formed a bold plan to invade Attica at the head of the exiles. In the winter of 404-3 he seized the fortress of Phyle on the frontier between Boeotia and Attica, and made it a rallying point for proscribed and discontented partisans. Soon he had an army a thousand strong, with which he occupied the Piraeus, after some street-fighting in which Critias was killed.

The Thirty, no longer feeling safe in Athens, took refuge in Eleusis where a provisional government was appointed, and implored help from

Sparta. Lysander's fleet blockaded the Piraeus, and a Peloponnesian army marched into Attica under the command of King Pausanias, who was a member of the Agid family which had always been inclined to favour Athens, and he was jealous of the preponderant part which Lysander had been playing. Pausanias imposed a peace convention which both sides accepted. Thrasybulus and the exiles were allowed to return to Athens (which had now been evacuated by its Lacedaemonian garrison) and the Thirty were to stay in Eleusis. A general amnesty was voted, from which only the Thirty were excluded. The democracy was thus re-established in its entirety. Two years later Eleusis was taken by the government of Athens and the generals of the oligarchy were put to death (401).

At the price of this execution civil peace was restored in Attica. The amnesty was scrupulously respected, and this permitted the return, with the full restoration of their property, of a large number of aristocrats who would continue to enjoy individual access to the Assembly, to the Council, and the Offices of State. But the oligarchic party, which for forty years had been nothing more than a barren and unpatriotic opposition, had completely discredited itself during its few months in power by acts of violence which had disgusted the whole of Greece.

The Spartans let matters take their course. Many of them were afraid of the responsibility of this great empire that had devolved upon them, in which their harmosts were unable to win the sympathies of the populations they had to govern, and where many cities rejected the oligarchic institutions imposed upon them. Nor could Sparta feel happy about Lysander's wide-ranging projects. Peloponnesian affairs, as of old, were more closely their concern, and in 401 an expedition was sent under King Agis against Elis (for many years an ally of Athens and a thorn in Sparta's side) which compelled her to rejoin the Peloponnesian League.

But Sparta was soon to be driven by sheer force of events, whether she liked it or not, to play a part in the east. On the death of King Darius in 404 the customary rebellions had broken out in various parts of his empire. While Egypt was still in turmoil the young Cyrus, who was master of Lydia, quarrelled openly with Tissaphernes, the satrap of re-conquered Ionia, and recruited more than ten thousand mercenaries in that Hellenic world where warfare had been the normal condition for the past thirty years. His plan was nothing less than to march on Susa and dethrone his brother Artaxerxes. Sparta could not but be conscious of the debt she owed to Cyrus for his services to her towards the end of the Peloponnesian war, and sent him seven hundred hoplites and a fleet of thirty-five triremes. His army inflicted a defeat on the royal troops at Cunaxa near Babylon, but Cyrus himself was killed in the battle. The Greek generals were lured to Artaxerxes's camp on the pretext of negotiations and all murdered, so that the Greek detachment now found itself leaderless, in the face of a vastly superior hostile army, deep in enemy territory and over five hundred miles from the nearest sea. New *strategoi* were nominated, among them the Athenian Xenophon, who regrouped the demoralised Greeks, organised a body of archers and slingers and a small squadron of cavalry, and led a heroic retreat across Armenia. In spite of the rigours of the winter and attacks by hostile natives they eventually brought them to Trapezus (Trebizond) on the Black Sea. A small army, thanks to its discipline and the initiative of the Greek foot-soldier, had thus shown itself able to traverse the Persian Empire. The lesson was not lost!

Following the death of Cyrus, Tissaphernes tried to reconquer Ionia, but the Greek cities there refused to admit his garrisons and asked Sparta for aid. No doubt it was against their will that the Lacedaemonians allowed themselves to be drawn into an adventure so far from home, but on this occasion they could not ignore the fact that their good fame was at stake, and in the general view Sparta had replaced Athens in order to continue, wherever necessary, the defence of Greek liberty.

In 397 Tissaphernes proposed a peace treaty: the Greek forces were to depart from Asia Minor, and the recent Spartan garrisons in the Greek cities were to be withdrawn. During the negotiations the Spartans discovered that Tissaphernes was preparing large forces. So they had to send heavy reinforcements to Asia – eight thousand men under the command of King Agesilaus, who had just succeeded Agis. Agesilaus was soon to prove himself one of the best captains of the age, but the means at his disposal lacked two essential elements: he had no cavalry beyond what he could improvise on the spot, and no siege material. The years 396 and 395 were occupied in brilliant campaigns, firstly in Phrygia and then in Lydia, in which he defeated the army of Tissaphernes in the region of Sardis, in Phrygia, and yet again in Paphlagonia.

These remarkable successes confirmed the lesson of the retreat after Cunaxa – that Persia had no infantry who could stand up to the Greeks, and that a well-disciplined Hellenic army could live on the country and find for itself both food and pay for its soldiers. But the final results of these campaigns were negligible, for the Persian garrisons remained intact in the shelter of their fortresses; Agesilaus had no cavalry capable of following up the successes he had won, and after each campaign the satraps of Lydia and Phrygia had concluded an armistice which they used to rebuild their armies. Now events in Europe were to require the recall of Agesilaus.

The coalition which had joined forces against Athens did not long survive their victory. Boeotia, who next to Sparta had the best infantry in Greece, and Corinth whose fleet had made a powerful contribution to the common victory, regretted that the sole result of their efforts had been to substitute a Spartan for an Athenian hegemony. At Athens itself the democratic party, now back in power, was hampered by the weakness of a city deprived of its overseas empire and worse still of the fleet, which had assured its food supplies, its prosperity, and its strength for the last eighty years. It looked as if a chance to rebuild the fleet might present itself, for Agesilaus's campaigns had made it clear to the Persian government that it did not possess the resources needed to defeat Sparta on land. But Sparta had held control of the Aegean Sea for only ten years, and this it was which had enabled her to transport great armies to Asia without loss.

The Phoenician shipyards were ordered to build a fleet: all that was needed was a leader. Now since 405 Conon, the Athenian *strategos* who had not dared return to his country after the disaster of Aegospotami, had been living at the court of Evagoras, King of Salamis in Cyprus. Evagoras was keen to win the favour of King Artaxerxes, so he displayed a great zeal for the expedition that was in preparation, supplied a number of ships, and nominated Conon as admiral for the projected flotilla. So an Athenian, commanding a squadron comparable to those which had sailed from Athens in the days of her splendour, appeared before Rhodes with fifty triremes in 396. He drove out the Lacedaemonian garrison, re-established the democratic government, and provided himself with an excellent base for further operations.

In the winter of 396-5 Athens was visited by deputies from Rhodes, sent by the king and furnished with supplies of the Persian gold which had played so large a part in the affairs of Greece since 412. These deputies also visited Argos (Sparta's old rival), Thebes (where an anti-Spartan group had recently come into power), and Corinth (whose discontent they were able to exploit). Sparta was not ignorant of what was going on, and had equipped a fleet of about a hundred vessels. But she hesitated to bring matters to a head in Greece so long as Agesilaus was away in Asia. In 395, however, when Thebes intervened against the Phocians, who were allies of Sparta in their conflict with Locris, Sparta sent two armies into Boeotia, one commanded by Pausanias the other by Lysander himself. This latter army suffered a serious defeat under the walls of Haliartus and Lysander was killed. Pausanias saw that the Boeotians had just been joined by a contingent from Athens, so that his was the only force confronting them, and was only too pleased to conclude an armistice which enabled him to retreat from Boeotia.

A coalition was formed against Sparta, who saw the whole of central Greece banded together with Corinth and Argos in arms against her. Agesilaus was recalled from Asia, where he left only four thousand men. Even before his return Sparta was able to assemble on the isthmus a Peloponnesian army of about fifteen thousand men, who defeated the Confederates between Corinth and Sicyon. A few weeks later Agesilaus, having raced through Thrace, Macedon, and Thessaly, reached Boeotia where he inflicted a second defeat on the allies in the plain of Coronea (394). But Agesilaus had been wounded in the battle and his army had to withdraw from Boeotia without exploiting the victory.

During this time the Spartan fleet clashed with the Phoenician and Cyprian fleets near Cnidus, and lost fifty triremes and its admiral Pisander. At the head of his victorious fleet and with the support of the Satrap Pharnabazus, Conon led an expedition during 394, as a result of which all the towns of Asia Minor and the Cyclades, except those on the Hellespont, expelled their Lacedaemonian garrisons. He then sailed around the Peloponnese, made a landing on the shores of Laconia, and finally returned in triumph to Athens where he contributed to rebuilding the Long Walls with the King's gold – a further infraction of the treaty of 404. The Athenian League was already coming together again, and Athens made treaties with some of the towns which had formerly been part of her empire.

Sparta was in a difficult situation. On the isthmus of Corinth her troops were in conflict with detachments under the Athenian Iphicrates, who was baffling the Spartan hoplites with his lightly-armed troops and with his raids deep into Arcadia. Corinth, in spite of the treachery of her oligarchic party which nearly cost her the port of Lechaeum, remained faithful to the enemies of Sparta and accepted federation with Argos. On the sea Sparta no longer had a fleet and was in no position to build herself another. She had to see the ships and gold of Persia, whose help she herself had sought twenty years earlier, now being used against her. Her only hope was to negotiate direct with the court at Susa, whose official policy had been hesitant and vacillating because of the personal quarrels between the provincial satraps in Asia Minor, especially between Tissaphernes and Pharnabazus.

During the campaigns of Agesilaus, Tissaphernes was accused of slackness in his conduct of operations and was executed. In 392 Sparta sent her ambassador Antalcidas to Tiribazus at Sardis; he found that the representatives of the Greek cities were also at Sardis. Thus a satrap became the arbiter of Greek destinies! Sparta proposed peace, offering the king the towns of Asia Minor, but demanding freedom and independence for those of the archipelago and European Greece. This would have meant that Athens would have to renounce her attempts to rebuild her empire, Argos to separate herself again from Corinth, and Thebes to give up her supremacy over Boeotia. The three cities refused. Yet by these negotiations the Spartans had at least succeeded in discrediting Conon, who died shortly afterwards.

Encouraged by the feeling of security she derived from having rebuilt her Long Walls, Athens set about restoring her navy. In 389 she sent out, under the command of Thrasybulus, a squadron of forty triremes which cruised triumphantly over the northern Aegean, and re-established the

Athenian control in that region, gaining control of the straits where the toll of ten per cent was reimposed. Once again free access to the Black Sea and the wheat-growing lands had been secured. In continental Greece wily generals like Iphicrates and Chabrias were employing their new tactical methods with success. In 390 Iphicrates wiped out a Spartan battalion near Corinth, and in 388 he defeated the Spartan Anaxibius in the Chersonese.

Athens now felt herself strong enough to resume her traditional policy, to free herself from the protection of the Persians, and defend the rights of Hellenism against the barbarians. An opportunity soon presented itself. Evagoras found an expedition headed by the Satrap of Lydia landing in Cyprus, and asked for help from Athens, who sent Chabrias with a force of light infantry. This was an open breach with Persia. In consequence the Spartan Admiral Antalcidas obtained energetic support from Tiribazus, and at the same time received reinforcements from Syracuse where, now that the city was free from the Carthaginian peril, the services of Sparta in 413 were remembered and could now be repaid. The Lacedaemonian fleet was guarding the Hellespont with eighty ships, and once again Athens was threatened in a vital spot; so when Tiribazus summoned representatives from Greece in the winter of 387-6, the Athenians and Lacedaemonians responded to his call, and the Thebans and Argives followed suit.

This time the war-worn Greek cities accepted the peace proposals. The treaty confirmed the humiliation of Argos and dissolved the federation with Corinth. Thebes became a small town isolated in Boeotia; Athens, on the other hand, with her Long Walls reconstructed, her rejuvenated fleet, and with the three islands of Imbros, Lemnos, and Scyros reconquered, could look forward to better days. The principle of 'autonomy' – that is to say the right of even the smallest city to control its own affairs – was especially favourable to Sparta, who gained by the disappearance of every coalition capable of opposing her will. But her reputation had not improved during the last fifteen years. Not only had she proved unable to promote Greek unity, but her generals had worn themselves out in brilliant campaigns which were sterile of results, and accompanied by devastation that recalled the worst days of the Peloponnesian War. Finally she had for the second time abandoned to the king the cities of Asia Minor, thus revealing the retreat of Hellenism in the face of Persian diplomacy. She had also imposed tribute and supported oligarchies.

A similar withdrawal had nearly occurred in the central Mediterranean too. Syracuse, in spite of her final victory, had been left devoid of manpower and money by her struggle against Athens, and was torn by internal dissensions between democrats and oligarchs. Carthage thought this a splendid opportunity to avenge the defeat of eighty years earlier. A quarrel between Segesta and Selinus provided an excuse for her intervention. In 409 a huge army with contingents of Libyans and Iberian mercenaries, and equipped with powerful siege material, disembarked at Lilybaeum. Selinus was captured, then Himera, and the fall of these two prosperous towns – bulwarks of Hellenism to the south and north of Sicily – made all the greater impression on the Greeks of Sicily and Italy because the Carthaginians spared neither men nor cities. Sixteen thousand inhabitants of Selinus were massacred, a disaster from which the city never recovered; Himera was razed to the ground.

In 406 a new expedition came to lay siege to Agrigentum (Acragas), but this time the Syracusan generals had a confederate army of thirty thousand with which to oppose the Carthaginians. Even so they were not strong enough to raise the siege, and only succeeded in evacuating all the inhabitants before the city was taken. The approach of the enemy threw the people of Syracuse into a state of excitement which was favourable to revolution. A young officer, Dionysius, convinced them that the *strategoi* were traitors, and that he should be given extraordinary powers to meet the situation. He also staged an attempted assassination, as Peisistratus had done so successfully at Athens a hundred and fifty years earlier, and was voted a bodyguard under whose protection he installed himself in the arsenal. Syracuse was again ruled by a tyrant.

The new régime did not immediately demonstrate its effectiveness. When the Carthaginians reappeared in Sicily in 405 Dionysius was unable to save the town of Gela, which suffered the same fate as Agrigentum. The plague which had been raging in the Carthaginian army since the previous year saved Syracuse from a siege which might well have been disastrous, and Dionysius was only too pleased to conclude an armistice which forfeited to the Carthaginians all they had won, gave independence to the other Sicilian towns, and left Dionysius with only the territory of Syracuse itself as the remnant of his empire.

It took the tyrant seven years to recover from this blow. During this time he consolidated his position. In 405 he repressed an aristocratic revolt which began among his cavalry. In 404 another attempted military *coup* nearly succeeded. On both occasions Dionysius acted energetically and with tact, and in the end his authority was strengthened. At the same time he prepared for war, pushing on with the manufacture of armaments and building two hundred vessels in the shipyards of his port. Profiting by the experience of the siege of 414 he had the Epipolae plateau connected to the city by two continuous walls, which made a siege of Syracuse very difficult. He broke the truce by seizing quite a number of towns in eastern Sicily. In 398 he persuaded the Assembly to vote for war, a decision that was followed by a kind of Sicilian Vespers in which large numbers of Carthaginian merchants were murdered. But Dionysius was soon forced to evacuate all western Sicily; a naval battle off Catana cost the Greek fleet a hundred vessels, and the Carthaginian army advanced to encamp under the walls of Syracuse while their fleet seized the Great Harbour.

The strength of the new fortifications made a siege more difficult than in 415, however, and the Carthaginians could not force a decision before winter set in. In the spring of 396 the towns of the Peloponnese sent a relieving fleet. The Carthaginian army in the marshes of Anapos was decimated by fever and plague, which spread to the ships' crews, and a surprise attack on the Great Harbour enabled Dionysius to destroy most of the enemy fleet. The Carthaginian general Himilco hastily embarked the remnants of his army and sailed away to Africa. Syracuse was saved and again became mistress of eastern Sicily. In 393 Carthage sent another expedition, but its fleet was defeated, and on land its general, Mago, was forced to accept an agreement which restricted the Carthaginian occupation to the north-west corner of Sicily.

Dionysius seized the opportunity to carve out an empire for himself in the western Mediterranean. Already master of three-quarters of Sicily, he wanted to make certain that no danger should threaten him from the Greeks in southern Italy. Under threats themselves from the Samnites and Lucanians, they had formed a league to ensure their independence both from the surrounding natives and from the tyrant of Syracuse. Two campaigns, those of 390 and 388, the second terminating in the victory of Elleporus, gave him possession of the southern extremity of the Abruzzi; and Rhegium, thus cut off, had to surrender. In this way Dionysius became master of the straits of Messina. He founded colonies on the Illyrian coast and possibly as far north as the Po. The Syracusan fleet raided the Etruscan coast and even established a naval base in Corsica, but the Carthaginian threat still hung over him so long as Carthage remained mistress of western Sicily. In 383 Dionysius felt strong enough to drive her out of the island.

When the Carthaginians learned that the towns ceded to them by the treaty of 393 had joined their enemy, they sent one expedition to Italy and another to Sicily. After five years of campaigning Dionysius won a great victory in 375 at Cabala in western Sicily, and tried to insist that the Carthaginians should leave the island altogether. But while the negotiations were still going on they assembled a new army, and in their turn defeated Dionysius at Cronion. Once more peace talks began, and once more Dionysius had to give up control of western Sicily from Thermae to the river Halycus. In 368 he made a last effort and advanced as far as Mount Eryx; but he failed to take Lilybaeum, the pivot of enemy resistance, and had to content himself with renewing the peace conditions of 393.

A few months later the old Tyrant died. If he had not succeeded in freeing the whole island he had at least re-established the position almost as it had been after Gelo's victories, and in this he was more fortunate than the Spartan generals had been in Asia Minor. Three-quarters of Sicily, its richest agricultural areas, its best ports, its largest towns, had been won back for Hellenism, and Dionysius had been able to weld the Greeks of the western Mediterranean into an empire which was at least as considerable in cohesion, if not in extent, as the league created a century earlier at the eastern end by the Athenian *strategoi*.

XXIII

THE SECOND ATHENIAN NAVAL
CONFEDERACY AND THEBAN HEGEMONY

The peace of 386, the 'King's Peace' as it was called even by contemporaries, had been imposed on the Greek world by a foreign
potentate who knew little about conditions there, and could not in
the nature of things last long. It was based, too, on the absurd misappre-
hension that supremacy could be vested in a declining state. The number
of Spartans who could claim full citizenship grew ever smaller. Even
Xenophon, who was favourably disposed towards Spartan institutions,
noted that she was 'poor in men'. At Leuctra she could not put more than
seven hundred full citizens into the line. The number of these 'citizens'
(ὅμοιοί) continued to diminish because economic laws, stronger in their
effect than an outdated legal system, forced many of them to dispose of
lands which could no longer maintain them. From the fourth century,
ownership of the land was concentrated in the hands of a few great proprietors – the prelude to the agrarian socialism of the next century.

The Spartans who had been dispossessed of their holdings became a
new category of 'inferiors', and soon were as rancorous as the Helots and
Perioikoi. In 398 a conspiracy organised by the young Cinadon was discovered by sheer chance, and shocked the Spartan magistrates by the
ferocity of the hatreds which they found underlying it. Quarrels between
the ephors and the kings, and misunderstandings which too often arose
between the kings personally, led to indiscipline on the part of the
generals who, since they were sure of protection from one party or the
other, initiated action – frequently with deplorable results. So far, the
fact that the Spartans had had good generals had masked this weakness,
but by 380 Brasidas, Gylippus, and Lysander were all dead, and Agesilaus
was old, and had no new ideas on tactics or the art of warfare. He held
firmly to the old principle of frontal attacks by massed infantry, whose
only manoeuvre was an outflanking movement to the right, as was
natural with troops who carried shields on their left arms. Yet we have
already seen how, at Athens in particular, generals accessible to fresh ideas
had begun to use more lively and more flexible tactical schemes with
considerable success.

The material strength of Sparta was thus illusory, and at the same time her moral reputation was declining, but she showed no signs of changing her policy. Not long after the peace of 386 a Lacedaemonian army marched into Arcadia to prevent the defection of Mantinea, seized the town, and forced its inhabitants to disperse into the five outlying townships which had united at an earlier date to constitute the city. On the frontier of Argolis the Spartans decided to intervene at Phlius. To the north of Greece Sparta assisted King Amyntas of Macedon against the Greek towns of Chalcidice, and, after capturing the town of Olynthus, forcibly dissolved their League. The policy of 'autonomy' served as a pretext for this process of disintegration. In 382 a Spartan detachment seized the Theban citadel of Cadmea without warning; Ismenias, the leader of the party opposed to Sparta, was executed and three hundred other Thebans fled to Athens where memories of the events of 403 ensured for them a cordial welcome. Three years later seven banished men crept back into Thebes one winter's night, assassinated the members of the government and drove out the Lacedaemonian garrison.

Thus far Athens had remained neutral. It is not at all certain that she gave any official support to the successful insurrection, but in 378 Sphodrias led his Spartans to attack the Piraeus; although he was halted near Eleusis, this provocation decided Athens to make a defensive alliance with Thebes. Two expeditions led by Agesilaus in 378 and 377 hurled themselves in vain against the improvised fortifications around Thebes.

Athens took advantage of her breach with Sparta to embark once more on the naval policy which had been checked by Sparta and Persia since 386. The fleet was increased, and in the spring of 377 a league was constituted which was openly aimed against Sparta, and had Athens as its centre.

Those in control of the new policy at Athens had, however, learned by bitter experience, and avoided the mistaken imperialist system of Pericles. An acceptable system of financial contributions was instituted. Allied cities were to keep their autonomy. Athens undertook not to establish any cleruchies there. The Council of the Allies, in which Athens no longer had representatives, was set up again, and negotiated on an equal footing with the Athenian State all questions affecting the League. No tribute was to be imposed. At Athens itself important financial reforms accompanied this revival. The imposition of direct taxation, which in theory had always been an exceptional measure but in practice had been found more and more necessary now that tribute from her allies had ceased, was reorganised under new regulations thanks to a complete assessment of all private fortunes in Attica.

Many cities of the old League joined the new one, except those which the Peace of 386 had handed over to the king of Persia. In 376 the *strategos* Chabrias consolidated the League by defeating the Spartan fleet off Naxos. Then in 375 an expedition into the Aegean, and another into the

Ionian Sea, brought the towns of Chalcidice and Thrace (except Amphipolis) and Corcyra back into the Athenian alliance. Affairs seemed to stand much as they had done a century earlier. Sparta was overwhelmed, and asked for peace; Athens was very ready to grant it since the new organisation of the League required her to find most of the financial cost of the war from her own resources; but the treaty signed between Athens and Sparta in 374, which included recognition of the new Athenian League, did not last very long. Sparta could not easily resign herself to loss of control of the Ionian Sea since this endangered her communications with her Syracusan ally, so she sent a fleet and an expeditionary force to Corcyra and Zacynthus (Zante). Her infantry were beaten by the Corcyraeans, and the fleet was forced to retire before the threat of an Athenian squadron commanded by Iphicrates.

Sparta's weakness had become obvious to all, and it was clear that Athens need fear her obstruction no longer. Politicians like the orator Callistratus, who had been the most resolute advocates of the fight against Sparta, now realised that the real danger lay elsewhere. Thebes, ever since she drove out the Lacedaemonian garrison, had been reimposing her authority little by little on her neighbouring cities. Out of the former Boeotian League she was building up a federal state with its centre in Thebes. Its executive body composed of seven 'Boeotarchs' had its sessions there, and the Assembly of all Boeotian citizens met in the city. A vigorous state was thus created whose population was almost as numerous as that of Attica; they were mostly country-dwellers, and provided a tough, hard-fighting infantry.

Atrocities signalised the new Theban policy. The unfortunate town of Plataea, restored by the goodwill of Sparta only five years earlier, was again destroyed and its population for the second time had to take refuge in Attica. It became clear that the struggle between Athens and Sparta could profit no one but Thebes, so when in 371 a Panhellenic congress met at Sparta, Athens showed a desire to participate. Her representatives, led by Callistratus, soon reached agreement with the Spartan government: Sparta was to remain head of the Peloponnesian Confederation and Athens of the Second Athenian Naval Confederacy. But when they came to the ceremony, Epaminondas (the Theban Boeotarch) would only take an oath in the name of all the Boeotians. To allow this would have been tantamount to acknowledging the existence of the Boeotian League, which both Athens and Sparta refused to do, so Thebes was excluded from the treaty.

Epaminondas, who had just taken so grave a decision on behalf of his country, had not hitherto played any great part in public affairs, but from this moment he seems to have been vividly aware of the material strength of the Boeotian League – not to mention the great possibilities of Boeotian infantry. When Cleombrotus, King of Sparta, invaded Boeotia in July

371, ten thousand Peloponnesians found themselves face to face with seven thousand Boeotians in the little plain of Leuctra. Epaminondas, whose novel tactics were at first screened by a cavalry engagement, stationed his best troops (his Theban infantry) on the left flank (not as usual on the right), massing them there in depth while refusing battle with his right wing. The Theban phalanx broke through the Spartans opposed to them, and a thousand Peloponnesians, including four hundred Spartans, King Cleombrotus among them, were left dead on the field.

For the first time in history a Spartan army had been beaten in battle in open country. The rout at Leuctra was a more terrible blow to Spartan prestige even than the defeat at Sphacteria. Scarcely had Archidamus the son of Agesilaus brought home the vanquished army from Boeotia than Athens invited the Peloponnesian cities to join her alliance. News of the Theban victory had been received in Athens without any great enthusiasm, but for Sparta it was the end of the great league over which she had ruled for at least two hundred years. Shortly afterwards Epaminondas invaded Laconia, and for the first time the Spartan women saw the smoke of enemy camp-fires. What his reasons were is unknown, but Epaminondas would not risk an attempt to take the little unwalled city which only thirty years earlier had been supreme over all Greece. He did not cross the Eurotas but marched down to the sea ravaging the countryside as he went, then returned through Arcadia and so into Messenia. Here memories of their ancient independence still lived on, and the whole population (except the small coastal towns) rose in revolt against Sparta. In the spring of 368 Epaminondas crossed the isthmus a second time, and captured Sicyon in spite of resistance from the Spartan and Athenian armies. But he failed to take Corinth, and was not elected as boeotarch at the next elections.

Besides being tired of war, the Boeotians could not very well be unaware of the alarm which their policy was causing throughout Greece. Athens had already made an alliance with Sparta, which Syracuse had also joined. To the north of Greece, on the other hand, the Boeotians found states with a more friendly attitude towards their ambitions. In Macedon the Queen-mother Eurydice had appealed to Iphicrates, an Athenian general, for help to suppress a revolt; but Thebes imposed an alliance on Eurydice, not wishing this rich and important region to fall under the influence of Athens. In Thessaly, on the other hand, under the influence of Jason, an elective monarchy had been set up in place of the aristocratic federation, in spite of opposition from the 'squirearchy'. With the support of Sparta, his father Lycophron had extended his power over several towns of Thessaly, and by 372 Jason was master of the whole countryside which, with its numerous population, its agricultural wealth, and its cavalry

THE SECOND ATHENIAN
NAVAL CONFEDERACY:
The names of the principal states which
were members are underlined.

0 10 20 30 40 50
English Miles
0 100 200 300 400 500
Greek Stadia

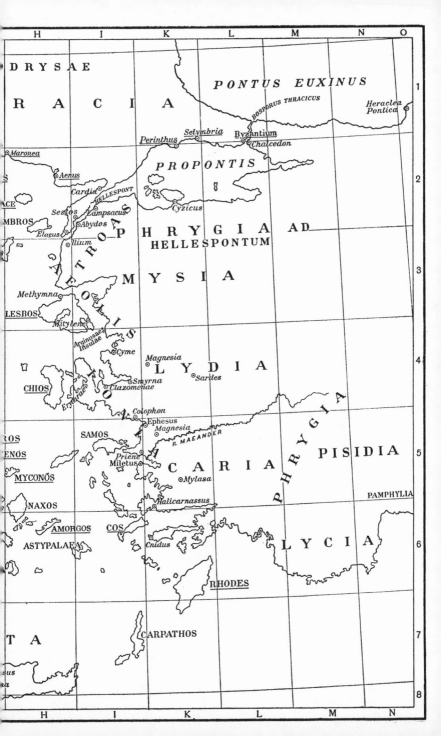

might well have become one of the most powerful of Greek states. But in 370 Jason was assassinated, and his nephew and successor Alexander of Pherae made himself thoroughly hated. The aristocracy rebelled, and asked Thebes for help both against the Tyrant and against Alexander of Macedon, who had intervened by seizing Larissa. An expedition was sent into Thessaly, as a result of which Epaminondas, who had distinguished himself even though he was serving only in a subordinate capacity, was re-elected boeotarch.

The following year (367) a further campaign limited the authority of Alexander to Pherae and southern Thessaly, restored the Thessalian federal system, and made it possible for Epaminondas to intervene once again in Greek affairs. In 366 he pushed into Achaea, reduced it to submission, and replaced many oligarchies by democracies closely allied to Thebes. But these changes proved ephemeral, for as soon as the Boeotians withdrew the aristocrats returned, and put the country once more under Spartan influence.

Sparta decided that it would be opportune to return to the former policy which had for half a century past worked to her advantage, and to ask the Persian king for aid. But other states sent envoys to Susa and the king was inclined to conditions favourable to the Thebans; that Messenia should have her independence; that the territory of the Arcadian League should be reduced; that Amphipolis should be a free city; and the Athenian fleet disarmed (366). But the days when the sight of the king's seal overawed the assembled Greeks had gone for ever. Events of the last twenty years had shown how weak his empire was. Asia Minor was in rebellion. The satraps of Cappadocia and Pontus, Datames, and Ariobarzanes, had risen against the king, and the loyal satraps of Lydia and Caria were trying in vain to suppress the revolt (366). The Greek representatives, who had traversed half the empire to reach Susa, obviously knew all about these happenings, and they were also able to estimate at its true value the king's wealth, of which such fabulous tales were circulated in Greece. So they announced that they were not empowered to accept the king's terms without prior reference to their own governments. A few weeks later a congress which met at Thebes could reach no conclusion, thanks to the intransigence of the Arcadians who would accept no reduction of their territory, and who demanded that the congress should be convened in the Peloponnese. Several towns, with Corinth at their head, refused to accept the proposals put forward by the Persian king. The attempt by Thebes in her turn to impose a second 'King's Peace' on Greece was a total failure.

Thebes was nevertheless anxious to retain the reputation which she had won throughout Greece on the battle-field of Leuctra. One city alone could dispute her claims, and that was no longer Sparta but Athens. From 366 onwards Thebes had planted a garrison at Oropus, and almost cut

Athenian communications with Euboea. No ally of Athens, not even Sparta, made any move to intervene. This brutal stroke, and the lack of reaction to it, drove Athens back into alliance with the Arcadian League, but here again Thebes was able to disrupt the communications through the isthmus which united the new allies. She forced Corinth to dismantle the Athenian posts which Iphicrates had established in that region after 390, and to enter into an alliance with her. But Epaminondas realised that only on the sea could Athens be defeated, for she had energetically resumed her old maritime policy and made no secret of her intention to rebuild the old League in due course. So Epaminondas resolved to provide Thebes also with a fleet. Euboea had been recently won over from the Athenian League, and its forests would certainly furnish the timber, but it was no easy task to make sailors out of the agricultural rustics of Boeotia. Nevertheless in 364 Epaminondas was able to sail at the head of a squadron bound for the Hellespont. He succeeded in persuading Byzantium to change her allegiance, which was no light blow for Athens, but hesitated to make a direct attack on the Athenian fleet, and we hear no more of a Boeotian navy.

Thebes was determined on the other hand to maintain her authority on land. Yet just at this time some of her allies were showing signs of weariness. In Boeotia itself Orchomenus threatened to withdraw from the confederation. The town was besieged and destroyed, all the male population executed, and the women and children sold into slavery (363). In the Peloponnese the situation remained most confused. Sparta, with the help of Syracusan reinforcements, had again laid hands on northern Laconia, which was so threatening a base of operations against the Arcadians; the people of Elis allied themselves again with Sparta; and so the Arcadians saw themselves ringed round on three sides with enemies. In 365 the Eleans thought themselves strong enough to invade their territory, but were soon repulsed. The army of the Arcadian League then drove right into the heart of Elis, and left a permanent outpost on the hill which dominated the shrine of Olympia, whose administration thus fell into the hands of the Arcadian League.

Olympia was one of the richest sanctuaries in Greece. The leaders of the Arcadian army could not resist the temptation to pay the federal army out of this wealth, a sacrilege which provoked the liveliest indignation even in Arcadia itself. To mitigate their offence the Arcadians offered to restore Olympia to Elis and make peace. Meanwhile the magistrates who had been responsible for pillaging the temple treasury appealed for help to Thebes, and Epaminondas promptly seized upon this excuse for intervention. In 362 the negotiators from Elis and Arcadia, who had come to arrange terms for the peace-treaty, were arrested and this high-handed action had the effect of uniting against Thebes all those opposed to her policy. Some of the towns from the shattered Arcadian League, with Elis and Achaea, made a defensive alliance which Sparta and Athens later joined. This became practically a reconstitution of the old Peloponnesian League, except that Sparta claimed no overlordship.

The alliance was, however, unable to prevent Epaminondas from crossing the Isthmus early in the summer of 362. He penetrated deep into the Peloponnese, and would have taken Sparta by assault but for the arrival of Agesilaus. This blow having missed its mark, Epaminondas turned northward again and sent on his cavalry against Mantinea. They were encountered by the Athenian cavalry, and this gave the allied infantry time to come up with them. The two armies, each of over twenty thousand men, were now face to face before Mantinea. The tactics which had triumphed at Leuctra were again successful: after a cavalry engagement the Boeotian infantry, massed in deep formation, broke through the Spartan troops, but Epaminondas fell mortally wounded in the onslaught. The moral effect of his loss altered the course of the battle, and its outcome was indecisive. Deprived of their chief, terribly reduced in man-power, the Boeotian League had to accept a profitless peace.

All Theban hopes thus came to an end. Faced with the opposition of Athens, still mistress of the Aegean Sea, and of the reunited Peloponnesians who had driven their army out of the peninsula, the Boeotian League was reduced once more to the position of a small land-locked confederation. The man who had made it the predominant Greek power for ten years was indubitably a great soldier. His scheme of mass attack directed against the enemy's strongest point and his clever use of cavalry foreshadowed the tactics of Alexander the Great. Nor are we in a position to discount his reputation, elaborated though it was by Plutarch and other historians of a later date, who have treated Epaminondas as a philosopher-statesman of first-rate quality. But it is unrealistic to regard him as the greatest politician in all Greek history, as some writers have done. No doubt he finally laid the ghost of Spartan supremacy and freed the peoples of the Peloponnese from the yoke of the declining city; but the states which owed him their existence or their rejuvenation were intended only to serve the selfish interests of Thebes who wanted to establish her hegemony over Greece by the same oppressive methods that had already disgraced the names of Sparta and Athens. This she had proved by her destruction for the second time of Plataea, by that of Orchomenus, by her inept conduct in diplomacy, and by the laying waste of the Laconian countryside. The idea of a Hellenic federation seems never to have crossed the mind of Epaminondas, and so his work was doomed to perish with him. Even his contemporaries realised that the Boeotian domination had merely increased the disarray of Greece. Where Athens, Sparta, and Thebes had failed, could another power succeed?

XXIV

MATERIAL AND MORAL CHANGES AFTER
THE PELOPONNESIAN WAR

Seventy years had passed from the outbreak of the Peloponnesian War to the battle of Mantinea, seventy years of almost continuous and ruinous hostilities. Towns had been destroyed, rich agricultural lands – Thessaly, Boeotia, Laconia – had been devastated, some of them (for instance Attica) again and again. Wealthy cities like Athens and Syracuse had completely exhausted their monetary reserves, large private fortunes had been demolished or greatly reduced by pillage, confiscations, and war-time taxes. Consider, for example, the effects of the 'ship money' to fit out triremes, which some Athenian citizens had had to find several years in succession towards the end of the Peloponnesian War. What is surprising is that the prosperity of Greece was not irretrievably ruined during these disastrous years. It must be remembered, of course, that ancient wars did not involve so much slaughter as modern conflicts. The fighting around Syracuse and the subsequent retreat cost Athens and her allies twenty thousand men, and in the battle of Arginusae the two fleets between them probably lost ten thousand; but apart from these two catastrophes, the number of those killed in any one battle never exceeded four thousand and was usually much below that figure. A high birthrate and considerable immigration into the large towns rapidly made good these losses. Attica, for example, so grievously depleted by war and plague, seems to have attained once more by the middle of the fourth century her population figures of 431, though with a lower proportion of full citizens.

Great fortunes were again accumulated – that of the Athenian banker Pasion amounted to fifty talents, almost as much as those of the fifth century capitalists. Nor had the purchasing power of money declined as much as one might have expected in so many years of war. Between the middle of the fifth century and the first quarter of the fourth century, prices only went up by about fifty per cent. The reserves in city treasuries, however, did not recover with the same ease as those of private persons. For many towns there began a period of mediocrity, if not of poverty, which was destined to last as long as Hellenic history. Athens herself, in spite of the vitality she displayed, was no longer the depot for all the capital of the Aegean. As soon as her maritime empire was re-established her citizens had to resign themselves to heavy and frequent capital levies, and the financial problem was henceforth one of the chief preoccupations of her statesmen. One significant fact was that the plunder taken away by Lysander after the fall of Athens, which for a time made Sparta the wealthiest town for precious metals in all Greece, did not have the slightest effect on the economic apathy of the victorious city. The only result of this great influx of money was that it probably hastened the process by which ownership of what had been the state-lands of Sparta was concentrated into a very few hands.

The moral effects of these long wars were probably of more consequence than their economic results. It was only natural that attempts should be made to think out afresh the principles for which men had fought so long. Wars between cities, internal revolutions like those at Corcyra, at Athens, and more recently at Argos where twelve hundred citizens had perished (370), had shown the evils of political ideas which were too narrow or too radical. At the same time these upheavals had inevitably widened the outlook of many people. Thousands of citizens had been away in exile. Others, especially from such agricultural districts as the Peloponnese, Achaea, and Arcadia, whose out-of-date legal systems continued to encourage emigration, had gone to enrol themselves in the armies of kings and tyrants where they were well paid – in Thessaly, in Asia Minor, in Egypt (where the aged Agesilaus was to bring his military career to an unhappy end as a captain of mercenaries) or in Sicily. Banded around chieftains for whom war had become a trade, they provided armies for sale. And as banished men or as mercenaries, in forced or in voluntary exile, they could not but compare the laws of other states and nations with those of their home towns, which hitherto had seemed admirable and eternal.

Ideas to which previous generations had been passionately attached were subjected to critical examination by philosophers, historians, and writers of all kinds: a process not without its dangers. When in 399 Socrates was accused by an obscure minor poet – but really at the instigation of the influential democrat Anytus – of having proposed to replace the gods of the city by strange divinities and of corrupting the youth of Athens, he was condemned by the Court of the Heliastae. This was not because the philosopher had been the friend of Alcibiades and Critias – for the amnesty law had forbidden such raking up of old grievances – but was designed to silence a man who, at a moment when every effort was being made to restore the prosperity and patriotic enthusiasm of the devastated city, insisted on proclaiming everywhere that one thing only was needed – the self-improvement of the individual.

But the condemnation of Socrates to death did not discourage other thinkers. His disciple Antisthenes, in affirming that Greek and barbarian, free man and slave, were all equal was undermining the accepted standards of social and political life. Others, less radical, advocated at least a Hellenism into which all municipal separatism should be absorbed. At the Olympic Games in 392, the aged Gorgias had preached union among all the Greeks. In 388 the orator Lysias, and then in 380 Isocrates, made use of the same concourse of people (*panegyris*) the former to pronounce, the latter to publish, discourses (panegyrics) on the same topic. No doubt Isocrates was largely reviving ideas developed during the previous century when he proposed that Athens, his fatherland, should resume the control and guidance of all Greek affairs. But he himself soon came to envisage a Greece united not under the hegemony of a single city but under the control of a man who would lead her in a profitable crusade against that hereditary enemy, whose interference and whose gold had for more than half a century perverted the policies of Greek city-states – against Persia.

Since Syracuse had found in the tyrant Dionysius a saviour who, while continuing to respect certain democratic formulae, had successfully united the western Greeks under his leadership against the barbarians, tyranny had ceased in the eyes of many men to be that hated *régime* against which it had formerly been the most sacred of duties to rebel. Isocrates devoted much of his long career to the search for a leader worthy to unite all Greece. He addressed himself to the children of Jason of Pherae, the elder Dionysius, to Archidamus, the son of Agesilaus. It was only at the very end of his life that he met the man who was destined to unite all Greece under his authority. In thus conceiving the notion of the whole Hellenic world submissive to a single ruler it was also necessary to imagine a ruler endowed with all the qualities which would make him worthy to command free men. A series of curious treatises dating from the first half of the fourth century elaborated the portrait of the 'good monarch'. Models for these edifying pictures were supplied by various leaders – Hiero of Syracuse, Evagoras of Cyprus, Agesilaus of Sparta – whose idealised characteristics were reproduced by Xenophon and Isocrates. In his political tale *The Cyropaedeia* Xenophon showed how a good king should be educated. These books were not without influence. As the writings of the eighteenth century philosophers paved the way for the French Revolution, they prepared public opinion for the upheavals which were to change the appearance of the Hellenic world in the second half of the fourth century.

The decline of the city-state ideal, the impoverishment of the towns, naturally slowed down that kind of artistic activity which had been a reflection of a prosperous financial situation combined with vigorous municipal pride. From 410 to 375 not a single building comparable to the great temples of the preceding century was erected in Greece. The only new well-designed constructions were small sanctuaries, such as the shrines of Delphi, the Temple of the Athenians at Delos, and especially that of Athena Nike, built perhaps as a memorial to the battle of Cyzicus on a headland of the Acropolis (where incidentally the Athenians had not yet managed to complete either the Propylaea or even the Erectheum). Only after 375 were any sites of importance developed – at Epidaurus in the shrine of the hero Asclepius, and above all at Delphi, where inter-state subscription made possible the reconstruction of the temple of Apollo burnt down in 373. At Tegea, too, a fine new building arose as a symbol of liberties re-won, in place of an ancient temple of Athena.

New movements were likewise developing in sculpture, in accord with this temporary eclipse of large-scale architecture. For works of more modest scope, intended to be seen close at hand and sometimes in isolation, sculptors were less interested in stylisation and composition and more in portraying movement and life. At Olympia and at Athens, 'Victories' – symbols of an era of strife – momentarily poised, palpitated with life under their transparent tunics. In the cemetery of Ceramicus at the gates of Athens, unknown artists ventured to express a restrained emotion in some admirable funerary *bas-reliefs*; in Tegea, Scopas was producing his highly emotive carvings.

The arts of the theatre, which had been essentially of municipal inspiration, were so far as we can judge completely decadent. We do not know the names of Euripides's successors, but their tragedies, of which a number were composed to be read rather than represented on the stage, seem to have been regarded by their contemporaries as unsatisfactory. Instead, the people demanded the production of plays from the repertory of the fifth century masters, as officially 'revived' for the Dionysiac competitions from 386 onwards. Aristophanes, now grown old and grievously affected by the catastrophes of the end of the last century, no longer dared, after fifteen years of silence, to resuscitate the old quarrels which the amnesty law demanded should be forgotten. Making no attempt at broad caricature, he tried in a rather feeble style to give a new look to the old framework of comedy, and his last compositions (e.g. the *Plutus* of 388) bear the marks of his doubts and difficulties.

On the other hand, the fourth century from its very beginning was the century of Attic prose. Its imperial language survived the fall of the Athenian Empire. Thanks to the work of the sophists it had become an exact and flexible instrument, which to this day is the delight of men of letters and the despair of translators. Carried everywhere by officials, soldiers, cleruchs, merchants, provided from 403 with a new alphabet, it imposed itself on the whole Hellenic world. Only the physician Ctesias, who had spent seventeen years at the court of Susa, persisted in writing his *History of Persia* in Ionian about 390 – and proved himself equally out-of-date in his dialect and in his critical quality.

It was not from patriotism that Xenophon wrote in the language of

Athens, but because he could not imagine how anyone could use any other. This soldier-author was a characteristic figure of his age. He felt frustrated in his fatherland, whose democratic organisation was repugnant to his aristocratic nature, and went to Asia Minor in search of heroic adventures. After his return he was banished from Athens, and it was in Elis, on an estate granted to him by the Spartan government, that he led the life of a landed proprietor which he so clearly evoked in his *Economicus*. His wandering life, and no doubt a certain instability of character, were responsible for his attempting so many different types of authorship: history, historical romances, philosophy, and essays on the most varied topics. An old pupil of Socrates, he drew a perhaps rather limited picture of his master in his *Memorabilia*, but he certainly had the gift of recounting vividly things he had seen. If his *Hellenica* is, in general, merely an unsatisfactory sequel to Thucydides's history, his story of the retreat of the Ten Thousand mercenaries is a masterpiece.

The misfortunes of the end of the fifth century had the effect of calming political passions; one has to come down to the middle of the fourth century to hear the Athenian Assembly resounding to the voices of the truly great orators. But the disturbances of recent years had created an atmosphere in which lawsuits flourished and legal talents could be displayed. Lysias, a metic, was the best representative of this forensic eloquence with his sober expositions, so nicely flavoured with emotion or malice and providing the perfect examples of the rather austere form of art known as 'Atticism'.

Isocrates (436-338) worked in an entirely different spirit. An Athenian of good family, but prevented from 'practising regularly at the bar' by physical weakness, he specialised in teaching rhetoric and in the composition of speeches intended merely as models and as propaganda for his own cherished notions. They are artfully polished in every detail, each sentence impeccably balanced. This gives the modern reader an impression of monotony, but these short treatises had considerable stylistic influence.

Little information is available about the progress of science during the early part of the fourth century. The great fame of Hippocrates and the reputation of his pupils seems to have had a somewhat depressing effect on the development of medicine. In mathematics, from one end of the Hellenic world to the other, learned men such as Archytas of Tarentum and Eudoxus of Cnidus were carrying forward the great task of analysis which was to culminate at the end of the fourth century in the work of Euclid. As the realm of knowledge widens there has to be some specialisation; hence the older type of 'physicist' who was at one and the same time mathematician, astronomer, and chemist (using all these as the basis for a general theory of the universe) had disappeared. The philosopher, in the modern sense of the term (the word seems to have been an invention of this epoch), makes his appearance constructing an ethics or a metaphysics on psychological or logical data. It was towards such a goal that Socrates had directed his efforts: his disciples Antisthenes and Aristippus founded genuine systems of moral philosophy by exercising their critical faculties on the ideas of virtue and happiness.

It was a theory of morals, too, that Plato was attempting to establish. A member of Socrates's regular audience, he had during his master's life-time tried to draw a portrait of Socrates and outline his methods of dis-cussion in his first dialogues, at that time a new literary form. The trial of 399 seem to have produced in him a radical change of attitude. Hence-forward one thing only seemed to him to be necessary – the moral reformation of the individual, based on a rational conception of the universe. This is not the place to attempt even a brief account of his complex and supple philosophy, in which bold personal speculations mingle with a variety of extraneous influences; nor to dilate on the charms of his style. No one has ever given more attractive expression to the superiority of the ideal world, of the world of ideas over that of the senses; and to the moral consequences of this conclusion. A kind of emotion in the search for truth, an alliance of logic and compassion, make of Plato's work a unique moment in the history of Greek – indeed of human thought.

Plato belonged to the aristocracy which, after 401, played only a minor part in public affairs. Though he may have been present at the defeat and then at the renaissance of Athens, he seems to have taken no part in political life. He allowed himself to be persuaded by Dionysius and his successors to visit Syracuse three times, but his attempts at social reform there almost cost him his liberty and his life. His *Republic* and his *Laws* were not drawn up for the guidance of his fellow citizens, nor even for that of any particular Greek city. He simply wished to show, in the abstract, what kind of political organisation would allow individuals to devote themselves to living the good life. It is none the less true that it was to Athens that he returned after a wandering existence, and it was in a suburb of Athens that he founded the Academy, an institution for advanced teaching which filled a serious gap in the organisation of education in Greece, and which was to last as long as Hellenism. Even for those who disapproved of her institutions, and in spite of all her tribulations, Athens remained the intellectual and moral centre of the Hellenic world.

XXV

CITIES, CONFEDERATIONS, MONARCHIES

Events seemed to shape themselves in accordance with the ideas which were 'in the air' about half way through the fourth century, and which writers of that time were beginning to put forward. All over the Greek world political combinations were emerging which went far beyond the limits of the city-states of earlier days. It is true that there were still some towns which could neither act as nucleus to a confederation of their own nor were willing to join any neighbouring alliance. Argos is an example; she clung to a selfish policy of which the chief aim was to prevent any recrudescence of a league like that formerly centred on Sparta. At Mantinea she had sent reinforcements to fight against the Arcadians; yet her own territory was very small in area. Similarly the ports in the region around the Isthmus, Sicyon, Corinth, and Megara – becoming detached little by little from Sparta – continued to exist in isolation. But alongside these few towns, which still represented the old-fashioned principle of the small autonomous city, more important and more complex political systems were being organised or maintained which foreshadowed the great states of the Hellenistic period.

The league of which Sparta was the centre, very greatly disrupted since Leuctra, occupied only a quarter of the Peloponnese. But alongside her, Arcadia – split into two parts at the time of the battle of Mantinea – and Achaea and the reborn Messenia, constituted federations each with its own political, financial, and military organisation. It was the same in central Greece where the Boeotian League, in spite of the death of Epaminondas, was still defended by the finest infantry in all Greece, and where in the mountain-state of Phocis energetic rulers were soon to emerge. Thessaly, apart from the small area that remained in the hands of the tyrants of Pherae, was a huge aristocratic federation which, if better led, could have played a much greater part in Greek affairs, since she had a large population – probably half a million inhabitants – and good cavalry. But she was paralysed by the quarrels between the old family of the Aleuadae and the tyrants of Pherae, the ambitious and bloodthirsty heirs of Jason.

Of all these confederations the most powerful was that which Athens had so tenaciously begun to reassemble round her from the beginning of the fourth century. Shortly after the battle of Mantinea it comprised many of the Aegean isles, together with Euboea, which was later recovered in 357; it had bases in Chalcidice, Thrace, and Propontis, and in the west such important islands as Cephallenia and Corcyra. It was, in fact, the old Athenian Empire, but without Byzantium and Amphipolis and the Asiatic towns. But even if Athens seemed reconciled to leaving the cities of Asia Minor in the grip of the Persian satraps, she obviously felt that she could not do without the ports on the Bosphorus, nor the town which commanded the region of Mount Pangaeus. Her notable lack of success in fulfilling most of her ambitions annoyed the public so much that a number of law-suits were instituted against top-ranking soldiers and politicians such as Callistratus, the leader of the anti-Theban policy in the last few years, and they were condemned in the courts. On the other hand signs of discontent manifested themselves within the Confederacy itself. The lessons of the final year of the Peloponnesian War were being forgotten in Athens, and the Athenians tended to act independently of the Confederacy, without any consultation. Suspicions were aroused by Athenian activities elsewhere; cleruchies reappeared in Samos and at Potidaea; the inhabitants of some islands were once again made to submit to the jurisdiction of Athenian courts; and in some cities even the constitution was not respected. The effects of this policy were soon to become evident.

On the outskirts of Hellenism political combinations took a different form. The close neighbourhood of the barbarians, and sometimes a diminution of civic sense in populations that were only half Greek, led to the maintenance or establishment of military monarchies. In Sicily the domination which the Carthaginian peril had given Dionysius passed at his death, without implying any dynastic system, to his son Dionysius 'the Younger', who had neither the qualities nor the faults which go to make a leader. Under the influence of his uncle Dion he would have liked to experiment in Syracuse with the political notions of Plato whom he had recalled to Sicily, but he suspected that his uncle was merely working for his own ends and in the secret hope of supplanting him. So Dion and Plato were sent back to Athens, where a queer conspiracy of intellectuals was organised, with the Academy as its focus, which enabled Dion to disembark in Sicily at the head of three thousand mercenaries in 357. With the active help of the Carthaginian garrisons of the west and the support of the republican opposition in the Greek towns, he entered Syracuse in triumph. Dionysius was besieged in the fortress which his father had built on the island of Ortygia. In 356 Dion's victory in the port of Syracuse itself made the position of Dionysius still more precarious, and he was fortunate to succeed in breaking through the blockade and escaping to Locris. But when it was seen that Dion was establishing his authority by the same cruel means that the elder Dionysius had used, the opposition parties which had helped to overthrow his nephew now rallied against Dion. A period of confused struggles ensued, which was to end in the assassination of Dion (354) and the return of Dionysius the Younger to Syracuse. In the course of these upheavals the confederation built up by the elder Dionysius was broken apart, and the Carthaginians prepared to take advantage once more of this disturbed situation.

At the other end of the Hellenic world, in Asia Minor, a monarchy had been set up under the domination of Hecatomnus, the lord of Mylasa, who had reduced almost the whole of Caria to submission and had been appointed satrap of that region by the king. The authority of the Susa government was growing more and more precarious in the eastern Mediterranean. Artaxerxes, in spite of his armies of mercenaries commanded by a man who was one of the best Greek generals of the day (Iphicrates) could not effectively subdue the Egyptian insurrection, and it was only with the greatest difficulty that he was able to put an end to a revolt of the satraps of Asia Minor who were supported by Sparta (366-59). Taking advantage of this situation, Mausolus the son of Hecatomnus, who had for a time taken part in the satraps' rebellion, but had made his submission at a moment when he could still earn the king's gratitude by so doing, had been able to extend his authority in the directions of Ionia and Lycia. Thoroughly hellenised in spite of his Carian name and that strange half-barbarian appearance preserved for us in an admirable statue, he aimed to make Caria a really civilised country. He made use of the discontent which was rankling in the Second Athenian League to detach from it the Carian off-shore islands – Chios, Rhodes, and Cos. Meanwhile he converted Halicarnassus into a great modern port. The new king, Artaxerxes Ochus, who had ascended the throne in 359-8, naturally approved the policy of his enterprising satrap, just as Darius, a century and a half earlier, had done with Aristagoras of Miletus.

Athens sent two large fleets into the Aegean against Chios and Byzantium, which had also joined the rebels. When Iphicrates and Timotheus were defeated near Chios (356), public opinion in Athens was furious; Timotheus was put on trial and condemned to pay the enormous fine of a hundred talents, but Chares, who took over command from the two older generals, was no more successful. Chares then tried to attack Persia directly by supporting the revolt of Artabazus, the satrap of Phrygia. The new king, however, was an energetic ruler who had affirmed his authority in his kingdom in the usual Asiatic manner by having a number of relatives and obstructive noblemen executed; and scarcely had Chares landed in Asia Minor than the Greeks heard of a great concentration of land and sea forces in Cilicia. Athens had no wish to engage in a full-scale war against Persia, and Chares was recalled. At the same time the struggle against Mausolus was abandoned and the independence of the three islands recognised in 355. Soon afterwards they accepted Carian garrisons. Not only had Corcyra broken away, but also Perinthus, Selymbria, and Byzantium, and by 353-2 Mytilene. The confederacy was shrinking alarmingly and now had to reckon with Caria which had developed into a great maritime power.

A state friendly towards Athens, on the other hand, was establishing itself at the outlet from the corn-lands of Scythia on the Tauric Chersonese (the Crimea). Indeed, its essential basis consisted of cities which had left the Athenian League at the time of its downfall at the end of the fifth century and had never rejoined. A series of astute tyrants had renewed good relations with Athens by means of a liberal policy about grain exports, since she was their chief customer. The Bosphoran monarchy, as much a military as a trading state, extended during the fourth century under the kingship of Leucon and his sons Spartocus and Paeris from the Caucasus to the Don, and formed a bastion for Hellenism on its northern flank.

The most extensive of the states which surrounded the Greek world just after the battle of Mantinea was Macedon, with an area of about eleven thousand five hundred square miles and a population of some half a million. The Greeks considered the Macedonians to be barbarians, partly because they were unable to understand their dialect, which although apparently related to Greek differed widely from it. Moreover their uncivilised manners, their heavy drinking bouts, their political organisation as a monarchy ruling uneasily over a turbulent aristocracy of great land-owners, shocked both the refined taste and the democratic ideals of the Greeks. However, efforts had been made from the fifth century onwards to civilise and Hellenise the country. At the end of the Peloponnesian War an intelligent king, Archelaus, had built roads and fortresses, had attracted philosophers and poets such as Euripides to his court, and had encouraged the spread of Greek in its Attic form, which by this time had become the recognised language of civilisation. King Perdiccas (365-59) developed an effective fiscal system. Later, though we do not know at what precise date, he introduced the phalanx – that formidable formation of serried ranks of foot-soldiers armed with long pikes – which was soon to prove itself invincible on the battle-field.

Nevertheless, the part played by Macedon in Greek affairs had thus far been a very restricted one. Only those states which had vital interest in the north (Athens before 403, Sparta after Aegospotami, Thebes after Leuctra) had entered into relations with the Macedonian kings. About 400 an attempt by Archelaus to occupy Larissa in Thessaly indicated an inclination to establish direct communication with the Hellenic world, but Macedon's activity was paralysed by repeated palace revolutions. During the forty years from the death of Archelaus in 399 to 359, no fewer than nine kings followed one another on the throne. During these reigns, cut short in most cases by assassination, not only was any territorial expansion impossible but Macedon seemed defenceless against her neighbours. The Illyrians exercised overlordship over part of the kingdom from 384, and Perdiccas fell in 359 in an attempt to free the northern provinces from their yoke. (This was the region of lakes and the river Tscherna, whose strategic importance was again shown by the events of A.D. 1918.)

On the death of Perdiccas his son Amyntas was still a child, and three pretenders – all more or less related to the royal family – rose in opposition to the prince's guardian, the legitimate regent. All three of them relied on foreign help: Argaeus on the Athenians; Archelaus, elder brother of Perdiccas, on the Paeonians; and Pausanias on the Thracians. There was little sign that the period of Macedonian anarchy and helplessness would soon be over.

Of the various types of political organisation to be found in the Hellenic world about 360 it was very difficult to guess which had the best chance of imposing its pattern on the whole of Greece. Organisation in the form of a confederation, of which the Second Athenian League remained the most conspicuous example, was open to two alternative dangers: either the central power lacked authority (like the Arcadian League), or else it tried to impose its rule too forcibly and fell into the errors of a demagogic imperialism. Monarchies, on the other hand, whether they were based on hereditary royal families or were merely tyrannies, showed all the evils which go with personal power. The examples of Thessaly with its detestable petty tyrants from Pherae, of Sicily disgraced by open warfare between uncle and nephew, and of Macedon where, under attack from turbulent vassals and from pretenders supported by foreign armies, the legitimate principle was represented by an infant in the hands of a twenty-three-year-old guardian, could hardly give rise to any expectation that Greece, a mere quarter of a century after the battle of Mantinea, would recognise the authority of a single ruler.

XXVI

PHILIP OF MACEDON

It happened, however, that the king of Macedon's guardian, his uncle Philip, was one of those men who change the course of events. His physical courage and his boundless energy made him one of the finest soldiers of his day; his supple tenacity and personal charm, which even his enemies could not altogether resist, made him also the best diplomat of the period. He is the outstanding representative of a series of sovereigns who combined the qualities of the barbarian with those of the civilised Greek, and from Mausolus to Mithridates played so prominent a rôle in a decaying Hellenism. But whatever, from the outset, may have been the ambitions of this astonishing man, his first efforts were directed to restoring the domains of the young king entrusted to his care. He persevered doggedly in this task, but without attempting any startling or heroic solutions to the problem. It is true that he defeated the army of Argaeus, but he bribed the Paeonians and Thracians to withdraw from his territory and abandon their respective pretenders. On the other hand again, it was in a pitched battle that he drove the Illyrians from Upper Macedon, and immediately the great vassals of that area returned to their former obedience. Thus, little by little, Macedon recovered the frontiers it had had in the reign of Archelaus, and about this time (whether voluntarily or not) the young King Amyntas effaced himself, and Philip took the title of king in 357.

Philip knew his Greece. He had been a hostage in Thebes for several years, had seen the Boeotian infantry at close quarters, and had been able to judge the strength and weakness of the federal system. Yet it is most unlikely that he conceived the idea of uniting all Greece under his power as soon as he became king. It would have been a fantastic ambition for a young man of twenty-five, who had only just succeeded with considerable difficulty in rebuilding a dilapidated kingdom. During his first years of power he was fully occupied in rounding off his kingdom towards the sea and in the directions of Mount Pangaeus, Thrace, and eventually of Chalcidice. But Pangaeus, Thrace, and Chalcidice – so necessary for Macedon's maritime expansion – were of vital interest to Athens, yet Philip was not at all anxious to provoke a direct conflict with a power that had considerable resources of ships in its naval bases. This was the reason for the complicated and tortuous diplomacy of the king over a period of years, now aggressive against Athens, now ready for concessions and compromises.

In 357 Philip seized Amphipolis, the town from whose loss the Athenians had suffered ever since 424. He had done so, he announced, in order to restore it to the Athenians in return for Pydna – which would give him access to the region of Olympia. Confused discussions took place, and the outcome was that Pydna was not handed over to him. So he seized it, and kept both towns together with Crenides, right in the middle of the Strymon mining area, whereupon Athens retaliated. Hostilities were carried on without much enthusiasm on either side, and some arrangement might have been patched up, had not Philip been drawn into more direct intervention in Greek affairs.

In the last few years another military power had arisen. Phocis had always been annoyed that the shrine of Delphi, though it was situated in her territory, was nevertheless administered by the Amphictyonic Council. Some Phocian notables had been condemned by the League, at the instigation of Thebes, to pay a heavy fine to the temple. They refused to submit; their fellow citizens took up their cause, and under the leadership of Philomelus seized Delphi in 356. The moral authority of this sanctuary had greatly declined; for a hundred and fifty years it had successively given support to the victors of today who were destined to be the vanquished of tomorrow – the Persians, the Athenians, then the Spartans, and now the Boeotians. Demosthenes might well speak of 'the ghost which is at Delphi', but under the protection of that ghost enormous riches had been accumulated. The Phocians, imitating the action of the Arcadians at Olympia eight years earlier, had no hesitation in appropriating the treasure.

At this period, when mercenaries were the backbone of every army, those who had gold had military strength, and this became very clear when Philomelus was able to put an army of ten thousand men into the field. At the same time he negotiated with all the enemies of Thebes throughout Greece and secured alliances with Sparta, Corinth, and Athens. He was, however, defeated and killed in a battle in which his half-trained troops had had to meet the Theban infantry supported by auxiliary forces, but his successors Onomarchus and Phayllus continued the struggle and strengthened their army. Onomarchus marched into Boeotia and re-established the inhabitants of Orchomenus, a direct blow against Thebes which was then engaged in an unlucky expedition in Asia Minor. In Thessaly he helped Lycophron, the tyrant of Pherae, against the rest of the Amphictyonic Council.

So long as this new 'Sacred War' had been merely the concern of central Greece Philip had not intervened, but kings of Macedon could never be indifferent to what was happening in Thessaly. In Thessaly there were reserves of man-power, of horses, of corn, that could not be left in the hands of the petty tyrants of Pherae, still less in those of the Phocian League. At the appeal of the aristocratic party therefore Philip marched into Thessaly. In 354 he was twice defeated, for the Phocian army was now the best in Greece. But Philip was not the man to accept defeat. In 353 he reappeared in Thessaly, and with the support of the League's cavalry he defeated the forces of Lycophron and Onomarchus near Pherae; Onomarchus was killed in the battle. This victory had considerable consequences: it not only put an end to the tyrants of Pherae, but it united Thessaly at last, under the hegemony of Macedon. At the same time Philip found himself committed to carrying on, as a main contestant, the 'Sacred War' in which he had joined for indirect motives; and since Phayllus was reorganising his army, Philip decided to forestall him and, advancing against Phocis, appeared at Thermopylae.

This menace brought to a head the disquiet that Macedonian policy had for some time been arousing. The Greeks were much more concerned about matters on the near side of Thermopylae than about anything beyond it. Philip found the army of Phayllus guarding the defile, with ten thousand Greeks as reinforcements, including five thousand Athenian hoplites. As in the time of the Persian wars, a coalition had been formed to oppose the invader approaching from the north, and once again Athens had taken the lead from the first. Naturally, Thebes was bound to be in favour of Philip's policy directed against the Phocians; while Sparta, which had only been able to contribute a thousand men, was entangled in unfortunate attempts to re-establish her hegemony over the Peloponnese, and could not even manage to retake Megalopolis.

Athens, on the contrary, after her unsuccessful war with Mausolus, was experiencing a period of retrenchment which had restored her fortunes. The *strategoi* were no longer in charge of her policy-making. Since they were more and more absorbed in the technicalities of warfare, which by reason of new tactics and up-to-date methods was becoming an increasingly difficult art, their place was taken by 'civilians', men whose administrative or oratorical talents marked them out for control of the city's affairs. A group of prudent men, with Eubulus at their head, reorganised the depleted municipal finances, began to build a great arsenal at the Piraeus, and re-equipped the fleet, which by 353-2 comprised three hundred and fifty triremes, a number never previously attained.

It was Eubulus and his party who persuaded the Assembly to send the Athenian contingent to Thermopylae. Before such a display of force, Philip withdrew and returned to Thessaly, but Eubulus made no attempt to follow up his success. He was opposed to an adventurous policy, and it had been his influence that persuaded the Athenians to accept the peace of 355. He had likewise approved the efforts of a young orator, Demosthenes, to restrain the ardour of those who wished to make Persian preparations to subdue the rebellious satraps an excuse for plunging Athens into a great maritime war. But in 351, when the same Demosthenes was asking for action to support the revolt at Rhodes against Artemisia, the sister and widow of Mausolus, who had succeeded to his kingdom, he felt bound to oppose him.

No doubt Eubulus hoped that Athens could co-exist on good terms with Philip, but equilibrium between the two powers was not feasible, for the King of Macedon proved to have ambitions which conflicted with Athenian interests in the northern Aegean – interests which no Athenian statesman dare forget. Besides Amphipolis, which Philip still declined to give up, there were other causes of renewed friction in Thrace which Eubulus was powerless to remove.

Philip, after his set-back at Thermopylae, had extended his power westward by making the kings of Epirus and Illyria his vassals; and then, in 352, returned to Thrace and forced King Cersobleptes of the Odrysae to agree to an alliance. This was a threat to Sestos which Athens had recently recaptured, and to the cleruchies which she had established in the Chersonese. Still more serious were events in Chalcidice, where a whole region on the frontiers of Macedon, rich in forests and with prosperous towns, was following with much anxiety the progress of the king's plans. Olynthus, the most powerful of these towns, now regretted having allied herself with Philip in 356, and even wished she had not seceded from the Second Athenian League in 371. In 349 she concluded a hasty defensive alliance with Athens which was intended to secure peace for herself and Amphipolis for Athens. In 349 Philip advanced into Chalcidice, and when Athens sent reinforcements, he was able to prevent her taking any more active part in the war by organising a revolt against her in Euboea. The result was that Athens was forced to recognise once again the independence of the great island, even though it was so vital for her food imports; nor could she prevent the fall of Olynthus, which was razed to the ground, nor the incorporation of all the towns of Chalcidice into Macedon (348).

These grave events were in themselves a condemnation of the policy that Athens had been following. Both foresight and decision had been lacking. Though at Thermopylae Athens had put five thousand men in the field, in Chalcidice she had indulged in a little-by-little policy, sending at first thirty triremes and two thousand men, then eighteen triremes and four thousand troops, and finally, when it was too late, another seventeen triremes and two thousand men. But worst of all she had failed to realise that things were fundamentally changed in Greece, and that if Athens wished to save the remnants of her League she must be on her guard not against Sparta, nor Thebes, but against this young northern power. To fight successfully against this new enemy she would have to forget old enmities and such memories as Aegospotami and Mantinea, and instead re-create against Philip the unity of Salamis and Plataea.

Athens, too, would herself need to awaken from the easy-going apathy of the last few years. The ever-increasing reliance on mercenary soldiers had caused the principle of the military service due from every citizen to be forgotten. The men who were fighting on Athens's behalf in Thrace or in the Archipelago were very largely foreigners – including the leaders, such as Charidemus, who was a Euboean. Nor did this costly practice prevent useless prodigality elsewhere; some men criticised the practice whereby surplus revenues were paid into the Theoric Fund to subsidise the attendance of the poor at state festivals, arguing that funds must be carefully conserved. The strictest economy, respect for military regulations, a policy of reconciliation and alliance with the other Greek cities, were now vital necessities for Athens.

Such home-truths as these were unpleasant hearing for men still obsessed with the old prejudices against Thebes and Sparta, who liked their ease and pleasure, and had no desire whatever, once they had done with their youthful military duties, to gird on their armour again and go to fight outside Attica. Yet there was in Athens a small group of men who were not afraid to preach this energetic doctrine. Their numerical weakness was compensated for by the oratorical skill possessed by some of them such as Hyperides, and above all, Demosthenes. The latter, like so many great Athenians, belonged to the industrial middle-class. His father, a large-scale manufacturer of armaments, had left him a fortune which was badly administered by his guardians. The law-suit which he brought against them on his majority, followed by several famous legal cases, had already drawn attention to him, before his energetic intervention in the matter of Olynthus made him one of the leading politicians of Athens. Some have poured scorn on this 'orators' party', this 'republic of lawyers'; but in fact these men, by their culture, their critical acumen, and their civic courage, should rather be considered a party of intellectuals, whose patriotism and far-sightedness no one could deny.

For the moment, since she was unprepared both materially and morally, Athens needed to put an end to the state of undeclared hostilities, which existed between herself and Philip, and which had already cost her as much as open warfare would have done. She was almost isolated in Greece; in Phocis the treasure of Delphi was almost exhausted, and with it the hope of raising more mercenaries; and the policy of the Phocians was unstable and contradictory. For example, after offering to hand over the forts at Thermopylae to the Athenians, they occupied them on their own account.

Philip, for his part, wanted peace, for Athens was still the strongest maritime power in the Greek world. Hence the Athenian Assembly gladly accepted the proposition that an embassy be sent to Philip consisting of Demosthenes, Philocrates, and another orator named Aeschines. He was a man whose family had formerly been wealthy but had fallen on hard times, and who had consequently had to try various professions. This had given him pliability, charm, and self-confidence. We need not accept all the charges of vice and venality brought against him by Demosthenes, who as a result of this embassy became his lifelong enemy, but we can at least feel sure that he was not as intractable as Demosthenes, for he was sent as envoy to Philip after Philip's great victory at Chaeronea. But once it was established, he deplored the Macedonian hegemony which he had not prevented, just as much as others did. But in 346 he seems still to have been obsessed, as were so many other Athenians, with the Theban danger. It was with these mistaken ideas in mind that he came to deal with King Philip, and his fluency made him the chief personality among the ambassadors, since Demosthenes's behaviour before the king was most inept.

A protocol was drawn up by Philocrates in which both sides, in mutual alliance, guaranteed the maintenance of the existing state of affairs. For Athens, this meant renouncing all ideas of obtaining Amphipolis and Chalcidice. Her best hope now was to hasten the matter to a definite conclusion before anything irreparable happened in either Thrace (where Cersobleptes was holding out with great difficulty against fresh Macedonian attacks) or Phocis. But after the Athenian Assembly had ratified Philocrates's draft treaty, not without misgivings, the same ambassadors returned with it to Pella in a deplorably dilatory manner, to obtain Philip's necessary oath of agreement. By the time they arrived three weeks later, the last fortresses in Thrace had been captured and the kingdom of Cersobleptes had become a vassal state. The cordial welcome they received, together with some illusory promises about Euboea, Oropus, and Plataea, led Aeschines and Philocrates to overlook these disastrous events (as did the Athenian Assembly a few weeks later) and caused them likewise to neglect what was happening in Phocis, where Phalaecus, the son of Onomarchus, realising that his situation was hopeless, capitulated a few days after the conclusion of the 'Peace of Philocrates' in 346.

The 'Sacred War' thus ended sadly with Phocis depopulated by wholesale banishments, its towns razed to the ground, and enormous reparations imposed on the country. Philip remained master of Thermopylae and obtained two votes in the Amphictyonic Council, to whose administration the sanctuary at Delphi was once more restored, and which now had the support of Philip's army in enforcing its decisions throughout Greece. Between Athens and the most advanced Macedonian positions there stood now only Boeotia, a state with whom she had endured long periods of indifferent relations.

There is little doubt that it was from this moment that Philip began to dream of extending his hegemony over the whole of Greece. He was conscious of his material strength, of the prestige conferred on him by his victories and by his position in the Delphic Amphictyony. Was not Macedon henceforth the most powerful continental state in the Hellenic world? Besides the wide territories under the direct rule of her king, she was surrounded by a belt of vassal states – Thrace; Epirus, where Alexander, the young brother-in-law of Philip, was installed; Thessaly, now reorganised into four provinces (tetrarchies) under Macedon's protection, and enjoying under this new régime an internal peace that she had not experienced for sixty years past. This situation was soon to be rounded off with a series of well-planned alliances.

Through the submission of Cersobleptes, Philip had come very close indeed to the possessions of Artaxerxes Ochus. The Persian king was not a neighbour whom it was safe to despise. After nationalist revolts had robbed him of Phoenicia and Cyprus and had deprived him of his best sailors, he had reconquered Cyprus with the support of King Idrieus, and then, thanks to reinforcements sent by Thebes and Argos, he had retaken Sidon and the whole of Phoenicia, and at last reconquered Egypt, which had been independent for sixty years, and thus the kingdom of the great Darius was re-established in its integrity. Whatever Asiatic projects Philip might then have had in mind, he realised that it would be most foolish to antagonise so powerful a neighbour, and about 343 the two kings concluded a treaty of alliance.

At the same time Philip did not neglect Greek affairs. In the Peloponnese, fears inspired by Sparta's spirit of revenge secured for Macedon a close alliance with Messenia and Megalopolis. The oligarchs of Elis, and tyrants who had come to power in Oreus and Eretria in Euboea since the island had seceded from the Second Athenian League, all maintained a pro-Macedonian policy. Finally, Thebes could scarcely have other than good relations with the man who had subdued the Phocians and had helped her to re-establish in Boeotia itself the position which had been shaken by the Sacred War, though she was nervous of his influence.

Athens alone repulsed Philip's repeated advances. Immediately after the Peace of Philocrates, Philip persuaded the Amphictyonic Council to discountenance an attempt by Delos to claim independence from Athens. In 343 he sent an unsuccessful embassy to ask Athens to negotiate a revision of the peace-treaty of 346. In 342 he offered to return to Athens the islet of Halonnesus in the Aegean, a pirates' stronghold which he himself had recently cleaned up. He suggested a peaceful solution by arbitration to a quarrel which had broken out between the cleruchies of the Chersonese and the town of Cardia, which was under his authority.

All these efforts came to nothing in face of the unshakeable opposition of the patriotic party inspired by Demosthenes. The great orator thought that the balance-of-power policy advocated by Eubulus was impracticable, and urged Athens to prepare for battle. Like all those who, rightly or wrongly, believe that their fatherland is in danger, he demanded energetic measures, and first of all against those in Athens itself who did not share his views. Prosecutions were instituted against the men who had been responsible for the peace of 346. Philocrates fled from Athens without waiting to be condemned, and Aeschines was only acquitted by a very small majority. Disquiet began to spread throughout the peace party, and among the Athenian populace. Spy-fever and a witch-hunt for traitors began to rage. At the same time Demosthenes unceasingly demanded effective regulations for military service, an improved fleet, and a reduction in luxury-spending.

These measures, it must be admitted, were useless by themselves. They needed to be supplemented by an energetic and well-calculated foreign policy. In a thoroughly realistic spirit, and refusing to be hypnotised either by sentiment or tradition, Demosthenes proposed to carry out a complete reversal of alliances. He urged that not only ought the seesaw policy in the Peloponnese to be abandoned with its alternating support now for Sparta, now for her adversaries, but that Athens should seek reconciliation with Boeotia; and however repugnant such a move might seem to public opinion, she should ask for an alliance with the Persian king! Active and enterprising as Ochus might be, he was not the present threat to Greek liberties. A diplomatic circuit of the Peloponnese by Demosthenes obtained for Athens the alliance of all the chief states of the peninsula, but an embassy sent to Persia returned empty-handed, and Demosthenes's adversaries were not slow to brand him as an agent of the king. As for Thebes, although Demosthenes was *proxenos* for that city, the alliance of the two states was only concluded under a direct threat of Philip's actions, and too late at that.

In these conditions, and so long as Boeotia's attitude remained uncertain, any hostilities against Philip which the Athenians might be persuaded to begin would need to be staged in distant territories. War in central Greece was bound to lead in a very short time to the invasion of Attica, and the people of Athens knew only too well what that meant. In 342 an Athenian detachment sent to Ambracia prevented Philip from seizing that town for the benefit of his brother-in-law, the king of Epirus. By the same action Corcyra and Corinth, the mother-city of Ambracia, were won over to the Athenian alliance. At the northern end of the Aegean the vital needs of Athens, cutting right across Philip's ambitions, naturally provided many causes of conflict. In 342, Cersobleptes, who had shown too much independence of mind, was dethroned and his kingdom became a Macedonian province. This was a direct threat to Byzantium, which began to regret ever having left the Athenian League, as Olynthus had done eight years earlier.

In the Chersonese the force protecting Athenian settlements was commanded by Diopeithes, an active and resourceful soldier, whose army was living off Philip's lands and who had no hesitation in attacking towns which were subject to Philip's authority. The years 341-40 were signalised for the Athenians by great military successes. In Euboea, the petty tyrants who had been Philip's friends were driven out of their various towns, or else offered submission, and the whole island again became accessible to Athens. An energetic intervention by the Athenian fleet, supported by contingents from the isles, forced Philip to abandon his siege of Byzantium. From one end of Greece to the other the success of Demosthenes's policy, as expounded in the persuasive sentences of his third *Philippic*, was now obvious.

After the affair at Byzantium, war was officially declared against the king of Macedon, and Athens found herself leading a vast coalition. Demosthenes now had a great reputation among his fellow citizens. He was inspector-general of the navy, and could thus impose reforms on the system of naval command without discussion; and he even arranged that funds previously used for the festivals should be diverted to war purposes.

From one quarter, however, danger still threatened – from Thebes; and it was indeed this city which was to provoke, at the Delphic shrine (always a hotbed of political intrigues) an incident involving serious consequences. In 340 a rumour was circulated at the Amphictyonic Assembly that the men of Amphissa, surreptitiously instigated by Thebes, intended to put forward a proposition to the detriment of Athens. In the interests of Greece as a whole this quarrel ought to have been settled peacefully, but Aeschines, the Athenian delegate at the Assembly, thought it was a clever move to denounce the encroachments of the people of Amphissa, who were cultivating for their own profit certain lands reserved for the god. He whipped up the excitement of the Assembly, and after an expedition organised by the men of Delphi themselves had ended in ridiculous failure, the Amphictyons decided to launch a campaign the following season. A new 'Sacred War' was in preparation.

As should have been foreseen, Philip, newly returned from an expedition to the Danubian region, assumed command in the summer of 339. His previous advance had taken him as far as Thermopylae, and to forestall a similar happening the Thebans, already becoming alarmed, occupied Nicaea, the main fortress in the defile. Hence everyone felt at ease until November 339, when it was suddenly learned that Philip had by-passed the Theban garrison and occupied Elatea, situated where the passes of Mount Oeta come out, and hence commanding the road to the Boeotian plain. This news, as devastating for Athens as for Thebes, had at least one result which for ten years past had seemed impossible – an alliance between the two cities. Demosthenes's policy was crowned with success, but very late in the day, for war in central Greece was now inevitable.

The confederate states of the League were able to put an army of forty thousand men into the field, one division of which was sent to cover

Amphissa while the main body guarded the Boeotian frontier before Elatea. The winter campaign turned out unfavourably for Philip, but in the spring of 338 a Macedonian force marched into Locris, annihilated the allied troops there, and took Amphissa. In the autumn Philip's main army forced an entry into Boeotia and met the Greek army near Chaeronea. Facing the Boeotians was the strongest contingent of Macedonians under the command of Alexander, the king's son. He thrust aside the Theban phalanx and took the Athenians in the rear just as they had driven back Philip's wing and thought the battle was already won. Instead it ended in a rout, and Thebes opened its gates.

Athens still had her fleet intact, however, and immediately took all necessary measures to sustain a siege. But the older citizens could still remember what the last years of the Peloponnesian War had been like, and the Long Walls, which had never been properly rebuilt since the hasty repairs of 394, were in no condition to resist Philip's modern siege machinery. The *strategos* Phocion, one of the good Athenian generals, had long been resigned to the idea of a truce and urged the opening of negotiations. For these Philip also smoothed the way since he was probably not anxious, in view of his failure at Byzantium, to begin another long blockade. He sent one of the prisoners from Chaeronea as his spokesman to Athens; this was Demades, a gifted orator who was convinced that further resistance was useless. That view could of course not be seriously or effectively challenged in any way, and so Demades was able to persuade the Assembly to accept peace conditions which on the whole were quite favourable. Athens was to keep her freedom and her territory, together with Salamis, her cleruchies at Samos, Imbros, and Lemnos, and the administration of the sanctuary at Delos. But the Second Athenian League was dissolved, and this time for ever. Athens also lost for ever the vital strong-points on the Dardanelles and the Bosphorus which had ensured her economic independence.

The Athenian League could have no place in the grandiose plan which Philip was at last in a position to realise, now that the Boeotian army had been destroyed and the Athenian fleet neutralised. Welcomed in triumph into the Peloponnese, he met no resistance except from the Spartans, who now proved as obstinate as they had been short-sighted. They had been unwilling to fight alongside a Theban army in the Chaeronea campaign; now they were forced to submit. Sparta had her territory strictly reduced to within the frontiers of Laconia.

Towards the end of 338 Philip called together delegates from the whole of Greece to Corinth, and made clear to them the new order which he proposed to establish. All the cities and states of Greece were to retain their freedom and their autonomy, and special measures were taken to prevent any political or social revolutions. Reconciled to each other in a universal peace, they were to form a vast League with a council meeting at Corinth. This new League concluded a defensive and offensive alliance with Macedon whose king, in time of war, was to take command of combined operations in which each city would participate according to its means. This seemed to be an improvement on the forms of political organisation formerly imposed by Athens, Sparta, and Thebes in turn. The internal stability of states was assured, their independence appeared to be respected, no tribute was specified, and by admitting the new young states of the Peloponnese (such as Arcadia and Messenia) the new League seemed to foreshadow a more flexible federal system. The patriotic party at Athens is often reproached with having delayed the advent of this inevitable and desirable régime.

That such a régime was inevitable can now easily and conveniently be affirmed, but we should nevertheless try to understand how monstrous it must have seemed to fourth-century Greeks that their many cities should be united under a feudal and semi-barbarian monarchy. The immediate conseqence of Chaeronea was not so much to inaugurate an era of peace and prosperity for Greece as to impose a Macedonian hegemony by clever moves and in easy stages. This was made quite clear by the suppression of the Athenian League and the Boeotian Confederation, and the planting of Macedonian garrisons at key points such as Chalcis, Thebes, Corinth, Ambracia, and eventually even in Athens. Such rare resolutions as were passed by the Council of Corinth never did anything more than register the decisions of the kings of Macedon.

Certainly Philip's policy had far-reaching and unexpected results, but these were due in great measure to the unforeseeable contingency that two soldier-administrators of genius succeeded one another on the Macedonian throne. These exceptional consequences affected mainly Macedon on the one hand and the East on the other, but Greece proper, the Greece on the hither side of Thermopylae, never obtained from them more than slight and mediocre benefits. The forms of federalism imposed from above by Philip's rule were to prove somewhat precarious. After Alexander's death, separatism and disputes were destined to reappear, with the added complications and conflicts due to the rivalries and intrigues of kings.

Worst of all, Macedonian domination weakened the springs of action, the youthful vigour of the little Greek cities, which had made them powerful moral forces for two centuries. Overshadowed by the huge states which were growing up, they were destined to decline into small, ordinary towns whose political, economic and (except for Athens) intellectual life was to pulse ever more slowly. The battle of Chaeronea marked the end of an epoch, and the extraordinary diffusion of Greek civilisation which was to be its main consequence ought not to blind us to the fact that Hellenism in its earliest form, restricted perhaps, but oh so perfect, was thereby doomed to disappear, since its basis had lain in the free and prosperous city-states.

XXVII

ALEXANDER. THE CONQUEST OF ASIA

Everyone knew that, now that Greece was subjugated, Philip was preparing a great expedition against Persia. Among the decrees promulgated by the Council of Corinth in the autumn of 338, on Philip's instructions, was one forbidding any citizen of a town in the League to accept service under a foreign power. This regulation was obviously aimed against Persia, where mercenaries from every quarter of Greece had provided the best part of the infantry both of the king and his satraps for the past half century.

In the spring of 336 Philip had despatched a body of ten thousand men beyond the Hellespont under the command of his best general, Parmenio. The events which were to follow are so well-known that one comes to regard them as having been inevitable, and no longer asks oneself what motives Philip could have had, the moment that Greece was pacified, for attacking an empire which still remained, in financial and maritime resources, the greatest power in the Mediterranean world. There is much talk of the satisfaction that could be given to Greek 'national feeling' by attacking the hereditary enemy. The importance of this feeling must not be exaggerated. No doubt it had found expression in some of Isocrates's propaganda pamphlets, and it may have been shared by a minority of intellectuals; but the idea of a holy war against Persia was no longer popular among the Hellenes. We shall see how little enthusiasm the Greek towns showed for participating in Alexander's expedition.

Still more characteristic was the resistance put up by some of the 'enslaved' cities of Asia Minor against the man whom theoretically they ought to have regarded as their liberator.

The fact is that Persia was an inconvenient and dangerous neighbour for Philip. The defeat of Cersobleptes, and that of Athens which had resulted in the submission of Byzantium, had secured for Philip the European shores of the Bosphorus and the Hellespont. But so long as the further shore obeyed a Persian satrap the possession of the straits, which would have given Macedon the mastery of the Aegean Sea as formerly it had given it to Athens, remained illusory. Furthermore, for the past eighty years, thanks to its gold and the reputation of its navy, Persia had played a part, sometimes secret but at times decisive, in the affairs of Greece. Philip could forget neither the relieving army sent by the satrap of Phrygia to raise the siege of Perinthus, which he had blockaded in 340 prior to an attack on Byzantium, nor the approaches made to the king by the Athenians. It was evident that Macedon's hegemony would not be solidly established until the day when Persia no longer had access to the Hellenic world. It was to cut the bridge made by the Anatolian peninsula between central Asia and Greece that Philip had planned his expedition into Asia Minor. We cannot be sure how far he had hoped to carry this enterprise or if he foresaw its extraordinary developments under his son's inspiration.

In any case he was destined not to witness even its beginnings. Scarcely had Greece accepted his overlordship than he was to demonstrate the evils of personal rule. Serious quarrels broke out within the royal family, and the main cause was Philip's own misconduct. His wife, the ambitious and violent Olympias, found it hard to tolerate his secondary wives and illegitimate sons, and was even less disposed meekly to accept Philip's marriage in 337 to a high-born Macedonian beauty. She withdrew from the kingdom, accompanied by her son Alexander, whose rights to the succession seemed to be compromised, but in 336 she returned for the wedding, adroitly planned by Philip, of their daughter with Olympias's brother the king of Epirus. During the marriage festivities Philip was assassinated by a young nobleman, Pausanias. It is not by any means impossible that Olympias herself may have been implicated in the murder. Whoever was responsible for the deed, the disappearance of the victor of Chaeronea appeared to throw everything back into the melting pot.

In Macedon itself Alexander promptly repressed all tendencies to rebellion by a series of executions, but in Greece various districts – Thessaly, Boeotia, and the Peloponnese – showed signs of unrest. The centre of this movement was, of course, Athens. There the events of 338 had scarcely shaken the prestige of the patriotic party, and once again defeat had been followed by a great effort at restoration, directed by Demosthenes and his friends. The Long Walls were put into a state of repair, and rebuilt to withstand the new up-to-date siege-machinery. The exhausted city finances were reorganised by Lycurgus, a strict and prudent administrator. Work on a great arsenal at the Piraeus went ahead. All this activity had one aim only – to prepare for the revenge which Philip's death now seemed to make possible.

Little did they know the young king, in spite of his brilliant showing at Chaeronea, and in spite of the renown of his teacher, Aristotle. Demosthenes spoke of the 'simpleton' of Pella: he was soon to be undeceived! Before the end of 336 Alexander marched into Thessaly, made the Amphictyonic Council confirm his inheritance of the two votes which his father had controlled therein, then went on into Boeotia and thence to

Corinth, where the League without any discussion conferred on him the functions of its General-in-Chief.

It is not at all certain that Alexander, to begin with, had planned to carry out his father's great Asiatic scheme. For the moment it seemed to him that the chief danger threatened from the northern barbarians, and he devoted the first part of the year 335 to a military expedition which pushed through to the Danube and was followed by a campaign against rebellious Illyria. During this time a rumour spread throughout Greece that Alexander was dead, and immediately disturbances began again. Thebes rose in revolt and beleaguered its Macedonian garrison in the citadel. For a second time, the Greek world was taught to fear the young king's lightning strategy. While he was thought to be still in Illyria he suddenly appeared in Boeotia. The Thebans, trapped between the relieving army and the citadel, were cut to pieces in terrible street-fighting; their town was utterly destroyed and its inhabitants dispersed and sold into slavery.

The destruction of this ancient city, one of the most important in the Hellenic world, which had been its chief military power only twenty years earlier, struck terror into all Greece. Every trace of resistance disappeared. Athens was only too pleased to submit, at the sacrifice of one of her generals, Charidemus, who had to leave the city.

Persia's influence could be seen in this second rising. She had sent envoys and subsidies into Greece, and it is alleged that Demosthenes at Athens received three hundred talents to be used 'in the king's best interests'. Greece would never remain tranquil as long as she could communicate freely with Persia; recourse must be had to Philip's plan. The army of occupation, sent two years before into Asia Minor, had been driven back into the Troad and was maintaining itself there with difficulty against superior forces. But it did at least facilitate the opening phase of Alexander's new campaign which he prepared during the winter of 335. In the spring of 334 he placed Macedon under the regency of Antipater, one of Philip's generals who was completely devoted to the royal family, crossed the Hellespont, and landed his troops in Troas.

The empire which he was about to attack was still the same kind of patchwork as in the days of Xerxes. Its central authority was not always able to make its influence felt; and the satraps, freed from supervision by the royal agents, showed a disposition to independence that sometimes developed into open revolt. Obviously it would be useless to look for anything that could be called patriotism in this vast conglomeration, except in the mountain provinces where the monarchy had been cradled some three centuries earlier. From the coastal cities of Asia Minor, which fought for independence rather than from loyalty to Persia, all the way to Iran, Alexander met with no resistance from the indigenous populations; and it should be noted that after his death no revolt broke out in any of his newly conquered territories. But the mineral wealth available and the tribute paid by tens of millions of men had naturally resulted in enormous reserves of coin and precious metal being amassed.

The Phoenician fleet still retained its centuries-old renown, and the Empire possessed military forces in great numerical strength, including some of high quality – for example, good cavalry very useful in the wide plains of Asia, and infantry whose best units were composed of Greek mercenaries, professional soldiers, well commanded and very well paid. But like the Empire at large, its army lacked leadership. The Greek commanders, some of whom were first-class soldiers such as Memnon of Rhodes, who had recently pushed Parmenio's army back to the sea, found their authority confined to the command of their own Hellenic units and subordinated to that of the satraps who were usually devoid of military talent. There was no idea of fusing the troops of different nationalities into the kind of amalgam which Alexander later on endeavoured to create. At the head of this heterogeneous army was the king. Artaxerxes Ochus had died soon after the battle of Chaeronea, assassinated by his minister, the eunuch Bagoas, who subsequently inflicted the same fate on the king's son and heir, Arses, and put on the throne in his place an officer who was very slightly, if at all, related to the royal family. This was Darius, whose first care was to rid himself of the sinister Bagoas in 336.

The picture of Darius III has been embellished by benevolent historians with many of those endearing traits which are often bestowed on sovereigns who meet with misfortune. He was probably a brave soldier, not without some knowledge of military lore, as Alexander must have realised just before the battle of Issus, but he was without persistent energy or foresight. One of his faults was that he underestimated the adversary whom it was his fate to encounter.

It is difficult to form an overall judgment of Alexander. A legend had already grown up around him in his lifetime. This depicts a man of unstable temperament in whom brutal rages alternated with the most generous impulses. The facts seem to show a better-balanced but decidedly complicated personality. Even today historians picture him according to their own inclinations, sometimes as the 'thunderbolt of war' with intuitions of genius; sometimes as the deep politician, who compounded out of the nations of Europe and Asia a fertile combination from which a new world emerged. At all events he most certainly possessed the qualities of a great military leader. There is no serious basis for attempts to attribute his successes to this or that general, for example Parmenio. His personal reputation, based on his courage, endurance, and seductive charm, which neither individuals nor crowds could resist, cannot be gainsaid. Nor can he be denied, when in the field, that power to choose at a glance the right spot for one of those sudden assaults which have been compared with the 'body-blows' of Napoleon's tactics.

His flair for choosing subordinates was based on sound judgment, and they served him intelligently and with devotion. Several of them, for example Antigonus, Seleucus, Eumenes, and Ptolemy, when thrown on their own resources proved themselves to be good generals and sound politicians.

Alexander took with him about forty thousand men, a small force compared with what Persia had at her disposal. Yet never before had a Greek army of this size crossed into Asia. An ingenious system of reinforcements brought periodically from Greece maintained a practically constant number of effectives throughout a period of eleven years, in spite of the gaps caused by sickness, 'home leave', and garrisons set up at key points in the new empire. Twelve thousand Macedonians provided the main body of infantry, with the addition of seven thousand men contributed by the cities and states of the League of Corinth, five thousand mercenaries, and eight thousand archers and slingers from Thrace. But beyond this Alexander had what Agesilaus had formerly so sorely missed: firstly, cavalry – five thousand troopers of whom one thousand eight hundred were the flower of the Macedonian nobility; and then an engineering corps capable of improvising siege methods which no fortress could withstand.

The morale of this army stood high, for the officers lived on close terms with their men. The one weak spot of the expedition was its fleet, which comprised no more than a hundred and sixty vessels of unequal value. Athens, still sulking, had sent only twenty triremes. It was a very small force compared with what could sail from the Syrian shipyards, and in the early part of the campaign Alexander had constantly to bear this inferiority in mind.

At news of his disembarkation the satraps of Asia Minor, at the head of their contingents, had joined Memnon in the Troad. The Greek *strategos* advised that they should refuse battle and retire, leaving a wilderness in the invader's path. But the satraps were confident in their cavalry, and decided to stand firm and await the enemy in prepared positions on the right bank of the river Granicus. Alexander marched straight for the enemy, forced a passage of the river and routed his opponents. For the first time the Persian cavalry had been beaten in fair fight, and in spite of a brave resistance. Hence the battle of Granicus, although the mass of the king's armies had never been engaged and the Persian losses were very small, had enormous repercussions in Europe and Asia Minor. Several Greek cities opened their gates and democratic governments were set up. Alexander still met with some resistance, however, notably at Miletus and Halicarnassus, which was defended by Memnon. One after the other these

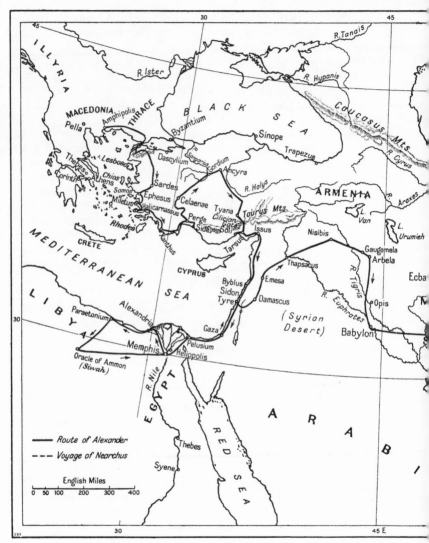

THE CONQUESTS

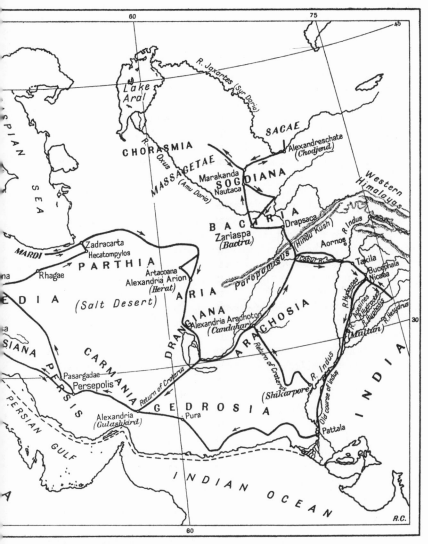

OF ALEXANDER

two cities were taken by assault, except the citadel of Halicarnassus which remained in enemy hands.

At sea the situation was less favourable. The Persian king's fleet which had helped in the defence of Miletus and Halicarnassus, and especially at the latter had made the besiegers' task very difficult, was entrusted in the spring of 333 to Memnon, who was as experienced a naval as an army commander. A sea-borne expedition forced the island of Chios to return to the Persian obedience, and Mytilene was blockaded and about to surrender when Memnon died. His successors, Autophradates and Pharnabazus, though unable to annihilate the Greek fleet, recaptured Mytilene, Tenedos, descended upon Miletus and Halicarnassus, and sent a squadron into the Archipelago.

Alexander had turned northwards again to pick up reinforcements at Gordium, where he passed the winter. In the spring of 333 he set out once more to meet the new Persian army, which Darius had concentrated in Mesopotamia and had then himself led into northern Syria. At the end of the summer, although he had been delayed at Tarsus by a serious illness, Alexander had managed to force the passage of the Cilician and Syrian 'Gates', at the base of the Gulf of Alexandretta – another defile like Thermopylae through which for twenty-five centuries invaders, whether from north or south, have passed. He then learned with surprise that Darius, whose movements had been hidden behind a cavalry screen, was in position behind him.

This manoeuvre put Alexander in a critical situation. He led back his army by forced marches to face Darius, who did not expect him so soon and was compelled to accept battle in the plain of Issus. The battle-field, hemmed in between the cliffs of Mount Amanus and the sea, did not allow Darius to make use of his superior numbers. Here again the furious cavalry charge led by Alexander on the right wing decided the victory, in spite of the stout resistance put up on the left against Parmenio's men. The battle ended in a rout. Darius, abandoning his camp and his family, fled as far as Babylonia, whence he thought he would be able to offer Alexander terms for partition and alliance. It was too late. Alexander already considered himself to be henceforth the sole 'king of Asia'.

Yet after his victory at Issus he did not march eastward. He knew that the Persian fleet was still a menace, and that its presence in the archipelago was sustaining the hopes of all Greek patriots. Although he could not destroy it at sea, he was now able to wipe out its land-base in Phoenicia, the very territory which lay open before him after his victory at Issus. One after another its seaports surrendered. Only Tyre and Gaza needed to be reduced by sieges in which both sides displayed a great deal of courage and much ingenuity in the construction of siege-engines.

The result was not long delayed. His Syrian and Cypriot contingents deserted Admiral Autophradates, whose fleet shrank to a tiny squadron, and the Greek fleet retook all the towns which the Persian admiral had captured the year before. Meanwhile an attempt by Darius to create a diversion in Asia Minor, in the rear of the Greek army, failed owing to the energy of Antigonus, whom Alexander had left behind in Phrygia at the head of a small detachment. The eastern Mediterranean was rapidly becoming a Macedonian lake; only Egypt was lacking to complete its encirclement, and Alexander was now welcomed there as a liberator from the reign of terror instituted by Artaxerxes Ochus.

He was fully aware that Darius would be unable to get a new army together for many long months, and his own passionate curiosity – a characteristic of Alexander's which must always be taken into account – kept him all that winter in this realm of ancient civilisation where there was so much for him to learn. Then in the spring of 332 he marched once more to meet Darius, who planned to entice him far from his Mediterranean bases and awaited his attack in distant Babylonia. The two armies encountered one another near the village of Gaugamela, a day's march from the town of Arbela where Darius had established his supply services. They met in a wide plain where this time Darius would be able to profit from his numerical superiority, which ancient historians no doubt exaggerated but which must have been considerable.

This was really a battle of Europe against Asia. Face to face with the Greeks were contingents from the oriental provinces of the empire, using chariots armed with scythes, a legacy from Assyria, and Indian elephants which the Greeks saw for the first time. By a clever use of reserves, and thanks to the fury of the Macedonian cavalry-charges together with the well-drilled precision of the phalanx, and in spite of a critical moment when a gap appeared in the Greek line, the battle ended in the rout and massacre of the Persian army on the 1st October 331. For Alexander it opened the road to Babylon and to Susa, which he entered without having to strike another blow.

He judged quite correctly that his victory would not be complete in the eyes of Asiatic peoples until he made himself master of the heart of the empire and of the person of Darius himself. In spite of the mountaineers' resistance he forced the passes, still-so difficult for modern travellers, which lead to the Iranian plateau from the plains of Mesopotamia. He could now enter without let or hindrance the royal palaces of the Achaemenid family at Persepolis, which were burnt down – a symbol of the downfall of the dynasty; and at Ecbatana, the ancient capital of the Medes.

A headlong pursuit enabled him to come up with Darius, just beyond the defile of the Caspian Gates, as he was fleeing eastwards. He was assassinated by his own men just as Alexander was about to make him prisoner. This murder, for which Alexander was certainly in no way responsible, nevertheless simplified the situation and made him the only legitimate master of the Empire.

One can indeed imagine what must have been the effect of these un-precedented events when news of them was spread abroad in Greece on the return of the troops supplied by the Corinthian League, whom Alexander had sent home after his entry into Ecbatana. Only Sparta, once again, failed to understand the scope and importance of Alexander's conquest. She had not joined the League of Corinth and was satisfied with the illusory autonomy which Philip had benevolently allowed her. This had made it possible for her to avoid any participation in Alexander's expedition. When the Persian ships under Pharnabazus and Auto-phradates put to sea from Chios, King Agis now thought the time oppor-tune, since Alexander was deep in Asia, to plan the annexation of Crete and the destruction of the Macedonian force of occupation which was stationed in the Peloponnese. But he had reckoned without Alexander's fleet and the regent Antipater, who arrived in the Peloponnese with four thousand men. Agis was defeated and killed outside Megalopolis (331). There was no further movement of revolt in Greece until after the death of Alexander, who was now unchallenged master of an empire which stretched from Corcyra to the Caspian.

The oriental provinces of the Persian kingdom remained to be dealt with. The best of Darius's soldiers had come from these mountainous regions where a number of satraps still refused to surrender, among them Bessus, the murderer of Darius, who had made himself king under the name of Artaxerxes and was trying to organise effective resistance. So having pacified Hyrcania, south of the Caspian, Alexander proceeded eastwards. Soon, however, he changed direction towards the south, for he naturally needed to remove all threats to his right flank before marching into Bactria, and in the southern provinces the satrap Barsaentes was fomenting a rebellion. He easily subdued Aria and Drangiana and could then turn northwards; in the depths of winter he penetrated into Bactria (Afghanistan).

Bessus had fled further north, so in the spring of 329, crossing the formidable passes of the Hindu Kush, Alexander entered Bactria (Balkh) without having to strike a blow. Not far from there he made Bessus prisoner, and then, still advancing northwards, passed through Marakanda (Samarkand). He does not seem ever to have intended going beyond the limits of the empire of Cyrus in this direction, and was satisfied to teach the nomads of Turkestan to respect his frontiers by a mere raid beyond the river Jaxartes (the Syr-Daria). The years 329 and 328 were disagreeably spent in repressing insurrections by Afghan mountain-tribes and in subduing Sogdiana and Bactria. He appeared to attach great importance to the pacification of these territories, since they ensured the safety of the oriental provinces and command of the main routes of central Asia, for which conquerors in every age have fought.

About the end of the sixth century Darius the Great had annexed the basin of the Upper Indus, which made a rampart for his eastern frontier. Alexander already held the high valleys and tributaries of the great river. The conquest of the land of elephants must also have been facilitated by the chronic political fragmentation and racial rivalry in which India lived. This state of affairs had allowed him, months beforehand, to establish relations with some of the rajahs of the Punjab. His descent towards the Indus, undertaken in 327 through the valley of the Kabul (across that north-west frontier so long jealously guarded by British and Indian soldiers) was made dangerous by the hostility of the mountain tribes on the northern bank, whose chief fortresses he had first to reduce.

In the spring of 326 Alexander marched into the Punjab. The Rajah Taxiles gave him a warm welcome, but on the other hand his passage of the river Hydaspes (Jhelum), swollen by the seasonal rains and defended by the army of elephants of the Rajah Porus, was one of the most difficult and most notable feats of arms of the campaign. After the submission of Porus and the conquest of the 'Free Indies' (the land of the Sikhs who later put up so tenacious a resistance against the British) the whole of the Punjab was pacified. But Alexander could go no further. It is by no means certain that he was prevented from so doing, as tradition asserts, by the protestations of his exhausted veterans. Indeed, what motive could he have had for undertaking the desperate journey across the Thar desert which would have taken him to the Ganges? It appears, on the contrary, that immediately on his arrival in the Indus valley he had made preparations for his return journey.

This return was planned by way of the Indus and the Persian Gulf. He wished both to display the might of the Macedonian army to the riverside peoples, and also to explore the possibilities of communication by water between his newly conquered territories and the central provinces of the empire. At the end of the sixth century a flotilla under a Greek captain, Scylax, had made the same journey at the command of Darius the Great. His descent of the Indus was delayed by the resistance of some tribes living in the valley, and indeed Alexander himself was seriously wounded in an attack on the fortress of the Mallians. In addition, when the fleet had reached the Indus delta it was almost involved in disaster by the monsoon tides. Hence, although he left the Punjab before the end of 326 he did not reach the sea until the summer of 325. From the mouth of the Indus the fleet, commanded by Nearchus, reached the Persian Gulf by keeping along the coast while Alexander marched through Gedrosia and Carmania, traversing desert regions whose passages involved some of the most trying episodes of the whole campaign. In the spring of 324 Alexander was back in Susa.

It was almost seven years since he had set out on this extraordinary expedition, whose chief objective we are now perhaps in a position to understand. Undoubtedly one has to make allowances for Alexander's taste for exploration, for pioneering, which drew him along the roads of central Asia leading him on to the fabled lands of griffins, of gold, silver, and silk. But it may well have been that his mind was haunted by the notion of an 'Empire of the Earth' as extensive as the known world. Above all we must take account of his determination to conquer the whole Persian Empire in its integrity, to crush every last remnant of resistance and lay down plans for its future. It will be noted that he made no serious attempt to exceed the limits reached by the Achaemenids either to north or east, apart from an extension of the Punjab *glacis*.

This empire, which even in its most remote and forbidding regions had witnessed the march of Alexander's great army, was reconstituted as nearly as possible on the old model, and the administration of its districts was entrusted partly to Macedonians and partly to native rulers, often the very same men who had held sway there under the former régime. Only the Rajah Porus retained the sovereignty of his kingdom as a Macedonian protectorate. Military and financial agents were attached to the satraps to represent the central power, which Alexander professed to exercise as lawful successor to the Achaemenids. His behaviour towards Bessus, who was condemned to death as a traitor to Darius, by a court-martial over which Alexander himself presided, is indicative of this; as were the oriental dress which he took to wearing and the Persian Court etiquette which he now required his followers to adopt.

Alexander could not forget, however, that he was first and foremost king of Macedon, and that it was at the head of a Graeco-Macedonian army that he had conquered his Asiatic Empire. This expedition had proved not only the genius of its leader, but also Hellenism's continued powers of expansion. In the course of his conquests Alexander seems to have been imbued with the idea of making this gifted race, so rich in vitality, work as a kind of leaven to rejuvenate the ancient lands of the east. He tried to put this notion into practice in two ways – by military and administrative collaboration. Not only were Persian contingents enlisted in his army, but he even hammered out a plan to incorporate them in the phalanx, where in future Macedonian veterans would provide a stiffening for a dozen ranks of lightly armed Asiatics. This kind of reform was also symbolised by the marriages between Greek soldiers and oriental women encouraged by Alexander, who set an example himself by marrying Roxana, the daughter of a high-ranking Afghan chieftain.

In the administrative realm the corresponding institution was a string of colonies which staked out the new empire, and especially the eastern provinces, with outposts of Hellenism. Perhaps the cleruchies of the old Athenian Empire inspired the idea. Many of these 'colonies' must at first have resembled the posts set up in regions newly subdued by our own early colonial administrators. There would be a Hellenic garrison to guard some strategically important point, and at the same time to protect a native market; but a number of them, by their subsequent development, show how sure was the judgment of their founder. In the heart of Asia two Alexandrias – now Herat and Kandahar – are to this day great caravan cross-roads. The famous Alexandria in Egypt had become within half a century of its foundation a major trading centre in the eastern Mediterranean. It may well be true that these vast projects were not without their weak spots, their uncertainties and self-contradictions, and modern historians have an easy task in denouncing their errors. But they should be considered merely as grandiose schemes, sketched out in the course of an unprecedented expedition by a young man who died at thirty-three, and of which nevertheless enough survived to change the fate of the ancient world.

Not unnaturally his policy of interfusion met with a good deal of opposition. The Macedonian soldiers, whether nobles or peasants, conscious of the great part they had played in the conquest, were naturally jealous at seeing Persians in the army treated on exactly the same footing as themselves, and their king aping the manners of the vanquished prince. Hence there were a number of conspiracies and mutinies. While in hot pursuit of Bessus, Alexander had to execute several of his high officers, including his best general, Parmenio. In 328 there was the dispute which cost his best friend, Cleitus, his life, and in 327 there was a plot by some young nobles, made famous in intellectual circles by the courageous attitude of the philosopher Callisthenes. Finally, in 324, after his return to Mesopotamia, there was a veritable rebellion which broke out when Alexander announced his intention of sending the senior age-groups of his army back home to Macedon. All these events show what opposition Alexander's plans had to face even among his nearest supporters.

Nevertheless if tradition can be trusted he had formed other plans on a still vaster scale; and from Babylon, which he seems to have taken as the centre of his new empire, he ordered preparations to be made for an expedition into Arabia. But his constitution had been weakened and overtaxed in a deadly climate and he was carried off suddenly, in June 323, by an infectious illness.

XXVIII

THE PARTITIONS

Alexander's enormous empire was more heterogeneous even than that of the Achaemenid kings, and the efforts made by Alexander to weld together the disparate elements had not yet had time to produce firm results. Only the prestige of its master had until now ensured the cohesion of this huge mass, and even he had not been able to prevent military rebellions and palace conspiracies. On his return from India Alexander had been disappointed at finding, and having to reprove, a number of cases of negligence and indiscipline among his officials, especially the native officials whom he had himself installed in office. It can be imagined, therefore, what would happen when he was no longer there. Moreover, among his nearest associates there was a small group of men, mostly in the prime of life and almost all of that vigorous Macedonian race which seemed destined to rule the world, who had been too closely concerned with his activities ever again to be satisfied with subordinate posts. In addition to their abilities as soldiers and administrators they had great material resources at their disposal: firstly, Alexander's army, of which the Macedonian and Greek elements at least were animated by a strong corporate spirit which a clever leader could turn to his own advantage; and next a huge monetary reserve which had passed from the Persian royal treasury into the coffers of the new empire.

Alexander had not been able to nominate his successor, so that dynastic problems immediately arose and from the first emphasised the seriousness of the situation. His family consisted, besides his mother Olympias who had stayed on in Epirus, of a half-witted brother Philip Arrhidaeus, the son of King Philip and a dancing-girl. He was chosen as heir to the throne by the Macedonian infantrymen, recruited among a peasantry who were blindly loyal to the dynasty. But the high officials were able to persuade the lordlings of the cavalry to accept a successor who would leave the future more open. Queen Roxana was with child; and while awaiting the infant's birth – a son as was hoped for, who was given the name of Alexander – it was proposed to set up a Regency Council to administer the empire. Thus arose one source of conflict, between foot-soldiers and cavalry, which was settled by a compromise. Philip Arrhidaeus was provisionally recognised as being under the guardianship of Craterus. Perdiccas was appointed 'Chiliarch', a title borrowed by Alexander from the Persian hierarchy, which gave its holder the absolute power of a Grand-Vizier; Antipater was left in charge of Macedon and Greece; and a fresh distribution of the provinces completed the reorganisation. Thus the unity of the Empire was respected – but not for long: there soon developed a contest between those who wished to maintain this unity on behalf of the legitimate heirs, those who would have liked to get control of it on their own account, and those who wished to carve kingdoms to their own measure out of this over-vast empire.

The first difficulties which the new masters had to face came from the Hellenic element. An insurrection of the Greek veterans who had been settled by Alexander along the eastern borderlands was easily repressed, but in the west things were more difficult. During Alexander's reign Athens, more or less resigned to her fate, had nevertheless been able to make once more a great effort at recovery under the financial administration of Lycurgus. Military service for the young men had been reorganised, the fortifications rebuilt and three hundred triremes made ready in the arsenals of the Piraeus. These measures enabled Athens to keep a certain freedom of action: and even though she did agree, after discussion, to accord to Alexander the divine honours which he had required in 324 of the Greek cities, she felt able to protest and bargain, if not to refuse outright, when the king wished that same year to force all Greek states to take back all their banished citizens. This proposal was intended to get rid of the bands of pitiable stateless wanderers and mercenaries who for a century past had been roaming all over the Greek world, but was nevertheless contrary to one of the fundamental principles of the League of Corinth. Aetolia was the only other state which objected, and during the discussions news came of Alexander's death.

At this particular moment the great inspirer of revolt, Demosthenes, was not present. In 324 Harpalus, Alexander's treasurer, had fled from Babylon taking with him five thousand talents and six thousand mercenaries, with whom he hoped to raise a rebellion in Greece. He was only allowed to enter Athens on condition that he came without troops and placed in deposit the money that he held. The disappearance from the treasury of part of this sum, together with the unexplained flight of Harpalus, led to a prosecution, details of which are still obscure, in which both Demades and Demosthenes himself – although he had been the instigator of the precautions taken when Harpalus came – were accused of having allowed themselves to be bribed and were condemned to banishment. But in the year after the death of Alexander the great orator was recalled in triumph.

Around Athens a strong coalition was formed of Aetolians, Illyrians, even Thessalians, with various states of central Greece and eventually of the Peloponnese, except Sparta. In the winter of 323-2 the Athenian general, Leosthenes, occupied Thermopylae, and Antipater only managed to disengage himself with difficulty from Lamia, in which he had been blockaded by the allied army. But in the spring of 322 their fleet was defeated near Amorgos, the last battle in which any large Athenian squadron took part. Since Aegospotami the Athenians had known that they could not carry on a war without control of the sea, and so, after an unsuccessful but indecisive engagement at Crannon in Thessaly, in which in spite of Thessalian support they were defeated by Antipater, the Athenians asked for peace.

The terms were harsh: a plutocratic system of government which deprived more than half the citizens of all political rights; a Macedonian garrison at Munychia, and the handing over of the leaders of the resistance. Demosthenes poisoned himself before falling into the hands of Antipater's soldiers. He had fought to the end for his limited ideal of the city-state – fought passionately, courageously, and clearsightedly: and when all has been said, the most serious complaint that has ever been brought against him was that he did not succeed.

The submission of Athens ended the war. All Greece fell once more under Macedonian domination – but without the safeguards which Philip had instituted and Alexander had respected. There was no longer any question of a League of Corinth – Antipater had no interest whatever in encouraging coalitions of Greek cities. On the contrary it suited him better to disunite them, and amid the dust of states to support those factions which favoured Macedon. The Aetolians alone kept up a resistance. Antipater was engaged in suppressing them when disquieting news reached him from Asia. Perdiccas, at the head of the 'Grand Army', had made his intentions very clear. He proposed to marry a sister of Alexander's, and was making pronouncements as if he were master of the Empire. Had he not already ordered Antigonus, the Governor of Phrygia, to put his troops at the disposition of Eumenes, who was to take possession of the province of Cappadocia – a region through which Alexander's march had not led and which was only half-subdued?

Eumenes, born at Cardia, had never been liked by Alexander's other close associates on account of his un-Macedonian origins, his supple reserve, and his scandalously large fortune. Antigonus refused, left Phrygia and took refuge in Macedon. Perdiccas and Eumenes now found the three best generals of the day – Antipater, Craterus, and Antigonus – united against them, together with Lysimachus, Governor of Thrace, and Ptolemy, Governor of Egypt.

Ptolemy, to whose portion had fallen the richest and most homogeneous province in the Empire, dreamed of making it an independent principality for himself. He had already succeeded in annexing Cyrene, and by a bold stroke had diverted into Egypt the mortal remains of

Alexander which Perdiccas wished to send to Macedon for burial there. Ptolemy brought to the coalition very considerable military, financial, and moral contributions, and it is no wonder that Perdiccas decided to deal with him first. While Eumenes in Cappadocia was defeating one of the coalition armies in a battle in which Craterus was killed, Perdiccas set out through Syria for Egypt. But he could not penetrate beyond the Delta, and after a series of failures which sapped the morale of his army he was assassinated in his tent by a group of disaffected officers.

A few weeks later at Triparadeisus (Upper Syria), Ptolemy, Antigonus, and Antipater, disengaging themselves as best they could from the war in Aetolia, organised the Empire anew. Antipater became regent in the name of the two kings, but the command of the army in Asia fell to Antigonus, with Cassander the son of Antipater as his adjutant. In spite of this scheme for a balance of power, the ambitions of these three personalities, together with those of the other governors – Ptolemy, Lysimachus, and Seleucus the Satrap of Babylonia – foreshadowed further conflicts.

Antigonus received the lion's share. He had control of the army, with which he counted on being able not only to subdue Eumenes but to secure the overlordship of Asia, where from 320 he began behaving like lord and master, giving orders and handing out offices and commissions. So when Antipater died in 319, his successor Polyperchon (one of Alexander's most senior generals, a good soldier but a poor politician) sought by every means in his power to consolidate his own position in face of so dangerous an opponent. First of all it was essential to avoid a repetition of the events of 322 in Europe. In 319, therefore, a proclamation in the name of King Philip Arrhidaeus reaffirmed for all Greek towns the conditions and liberties enjoyed in the times of Philip and Alexander and recalled all exiles from banishment.

The application of this edict, however, caused further troubles. At Athens, the restored democracy promptly brought to trial the leaders of the government set up by Antipater, in particular Phocion, who during a quarter of a century had continually preached abject surrender to the Macedonian hegemony, and who now (in 318) paid with his life for this poor-spirited policy. But in general the sympathies of the Greek cities were won over for the regent and the royal family. In addition Polyperchon renewed relations with Eumenes, whose position in Asia was somewhat peculiar. The partition at Triparadeisus had dispossessed him of his satrapy, but he claimed to be defending the unity of the Empire in the name of the dead but deified Alexander, and on behalf of his legitimate heirs, against the rapacious generals and governors solely concerned with their selfish interests. This attitude, dictated perhaps by the fact that he was not

Macedonian by birth, won a great reputation for him among Alexander's veterans in Asia, reinforced by his own personal qualities and the immense wealth at his disposal. Hence his support was by no means to be despised. Antigonus, who had beaten him in Cappadocia in 320-19 and then shut him up in the fortress of Nora, had offered him an alliance which Eumenes had refused. But he quite naturally accepted an alliance offered him in the name of the royal family by Polyperchon.

To disrupt this confederation between Polyperchon, locally elected as regent of Macedon, and Eumenes with his army in Asia, the best means would be to gain control of the seas. Antigonus did just this, by defeating Polyperchon's fleet near Byzantium. Henceforward communications between the two allies were severed, and Antigonus now turned against the more formidable of the two. From Syria Eumenes was forced to retreat into the provinces of central Asia which were more loyal to Alexander's memory. There he found reinforcements of men, horses, and elephants. A series of operations began in 318 on the grand scale, to end, after various changes of fortune, in the defection of Eumenes's forces and his betrayal to Antigonus, who had him executed in 317.

In Europe, Polyperchon's position had not improved meantime. Cassander, whom his dying father Antipater had recommended to the regent, had no wish to put his ambitious energy at the service of a worn-out general and an imbecile king; so he had joined hands with Antigonus, who had sent him into Greece in the summer of 318. With thirty-five ships he appeared in the Saronic Gulf and came to the support of the garrison set up by Antipater in 322, which was still holding Munychia in spite of Polyperchon's edict. In the winter of 318-17 Athens made submission and agreed to the re-establishment of a plutocratic constitution, though less exclusive than that of 322. But the direction of the city's affairs was entrusted to a single person – something which had never happened since the days of the Peisistratids – called, it is true a president (*epistates*) but who really had the power of a tyrant backed by the Macedonian garrison at Munychia.

Demetrius of Phalerum was an Athenian and an educated man, a writer and philosopher. He is usually credited with a broad range of ideas based on the theories of Aristotle, but this does too much honour to this dilettante opportunist. During his rule of ten years his great merit was that, taking advantage of peace, he restored Athens's financial strength; and his chief objective seems to have been to protect the large and medium-sized fortunes of the citizens with full political rights, by means of sumptuary laws and the suppression of the 'liturgies' (the taxes on capital). In foreign affairs it was clear that Athens, deprived of her empire, was at the mercy of the great Powers who controlled her food supply-lines. Demetrius did nothing to improve this situation: on the contrary by diverting his fellow citizens from any kind of military or naval activity he brought nearer the end of Athenian political prestige. She must now merely endure the repercussion of great events of which she was no longer the centre.

But it was not merely in Athens but throughout Greece that Polyperchon was losing ground. By the end of 315 his son Alexander held only a few places in the Peloponnese and in central Greece. In Macedon itself the position of the aged regent was severely shaken when Olympias, whom he had allowed to return from Epirus, had Philip Arrhidaeus and his wife Eurydice put to death, thus paying off old scores against her former detested rivals and those who were now her grandson's competitors for the succession. At this news Cassander marched into Macedonia, where Polyperchon dared not stand and face him, and captured Pydna along with the old queen who had taken refuge there. She was executed. It was obvious that since the death of Eumenes no one cared in the least for the interests of the royal family, now reduced to Roxana and her son Alexander – both kept under strict guard by Cassander at Amphipolis. He intended to rule Macedonia for his own benefit, and Greece into the bargain, since his rebuilding of Thebes in 316 had won him golden opinions which he meant to exploit.

For Cassander, however, as for Lysimachus in Thrace and Ptolemy in Egypt, the great might of Antigonus in Asia was henceforward the main threat. How far would the old general's ambition stretch, commanding as he did the finest army in the Hellenic world, with the treasures and the revenues of Asia, and aided and incited by his son the bold Demetrius? The same motives which had united the generals four years earlier against Perdiccas now brought Ptolemy, Lysimachus, and Cassander into a coalition against Antigonus. Seleucus, since he no longer felt safe in Babylon, also joined with them and had already taken refuge with Ptolemy.

Against this coalition Antigonus, like the great leader he was, organised the struggle on a wide front from the Ionian Sea to the Indus. In Europe he allied himself with all Cassander's enemies – the Aetolians, with cities in the Peloponnese and in central Greece, and with Polyperchon, whom he appointed *strategos* of the Peloponnese. At the same time he proclaimed himself throughout all Greece and in the archipelago – where he had set up a Confederation of the Islands under his patronage – to be the restorer of the liberties taken away by Cassander and Lysimachus. In Syria he took from Ptolemy the ports of Phoenicia as bases for the fleet which he still had to build. And he put men of his own at the head of the chief satrapies of Asia. During the years 314 and 313 war was general throughout Greece and Asia. There is little definite information about this lamentable period, but it seems that by the end of 313, although Antigonus had sent into Greece only mercenary soldiers commanded by generals of a sometimes doubtful loyalty, Cassander had lost part of central Greece, part of the

Peloponnese, and was with difficulty holding his own in the north-west against the Aetolians and Illyrians.

Now Antigonus planned a great expedition into Europe. He had already assembled an army near the Hellespont, but the resolute attitude of Lysimachus and the clearly declared determination of Byzantium to remain neutral prevented his crossing the straits. Then in the spring of 312 he learned that an Egyptian army under Ptolemy and Seleucus had entered Syria. Against them he sent his son Demetrius, who met the enemy near Gaza. Demetrius thought that he had inherited the military genius of Alexander, but the old campaigners who were his opponents had the advantage of numbers and experience. Demetrius, soundly beaten, rejoined his father with the remnants of his army, but there could be no further thoughts of crossing into Europe.

Seleucus, for his part, took immediate advantage of the victory to return to Babylon. His presence in that province, in the rear of Antigonus, changed the situation entirely, and although Demetrius in 311 had regained possession of Syria there was no longer a possibility of crushing the coalition. So Antigonus began negotiations, first with Lysimachus and then with Ptolemy, and reached agreement. Cassander was nominated *strategos* of Macedon until the young Alexander should reach his majority; Lysimachus remained master of Thrace; Ptolemy of Egypt, with Libya and Arabia; and Antigonus of Asia. All the Greek cities obtained their freedom and autonomy.

Of course none of the signatories of the treaty of 311 had any intention of respecting it. Cassander was unlikely to be satisfied with provisional power; moreover the freedom granted to the Greek cities would limit his authority and that of Lysimachus in an intolerable manner. Ptolemy for his part could not resign himself to the loss of Syria, which he regarded (as have all those who have ruled Egypt before and since his time) as an indispensable outpost covering the isthmus of Pelusium. The overlordship of Asia by Antigonus, with the sympathies which he had been able to retain in Greece, were a danger to all. Hence Cassander, Ptolemy, and Antigonus were soon once again disputing the possession of Greece where none of them was willing to allow the others to gain a firm foothold. Ptolemy had managed in 309 to seduce from his allegiance Polemaeus, one of Antigonus's generals, at Chalcis – a place of strategic importance. At the same time he was trying to get a grip on the southern coast of Asia Minor, or in the Cyclades, and even in Greece, where he appeared in 308 and attempted to revive the League of Corinth for his own benefit.

Then Antigonus took a bold step. In the summer of 307 Demetrius suddenly appeared off the Piraeus with a strong fleet of 250 ships. The garrison imposed on Athens by Cassander and Demetrius of Phalerum was driven out, and the city received with tremendous enthusiasm the young general who had come to re-establish democracy, and restore some shreds of her former empire – Lemnos and Imbros – and who announced that a Panhellenic assembly was to be summoned, at which the interests of all the Greek cities would be considered. Demetrius intended that the city should serve as his naval base, and wished to rebuild its walls and furnish its arsenals with timber and shipbuilding materials. From the Piraeus he set out in 306 with one hundred and sixty-three warships to make a direct attack on the ruler of Egypt.

Ptolemy had always considered Cyprus to be a necessary adjunct to his province, all the more essential to him because it kept watch over Syria to which he would not renounce his claim. In 310 he had finally succeeded, not without difficulty, in suppressing the last of the petty tyrants of the island. It was here that Demetrius, under instructions from Antigonus, launched his attack. He laid siege to the town of Salamis, which Ptolemy tried to relieve at the head of a fleet of one hundred and forty vessels. Though he was a successful diplomat and administrator Ptolemy was a far from brilliant general; he was thoroughly beaten and most of his ships taken or sunk. This disaster gave Antigonus complete mastery of the Aegean. Shortly afterwards he assumed the title of king, as did Demetrius also, thus signifying his assumption of absolute authority and personal rule, which he meant to exercise himself and hand down to his descendants.

Ptolemy, Lysimachus, and Seleucus all followed his example; so did Cassander, who in 310 had cleared away the last obstacles barring his way to the Macedonian throne by executing Roxana and her son and persuading Polyperchon to assassinate the pretended son of Alexander. In point of fact, however, it was Antigonus, with his vast Asiatic empire, his control of the sea, and the fame he enjoyed in Greece, who could really consider himself to be Alexander's successor. But now the great warrior was growing old. He relied a good deal upon his son Demetrius. This harum-scarum fellow, who himself founded nothing and organised nothing, was not even a very good soldier. History, which shows a remarkable partiality for rascals, has preserved for him the name of Poliorcetes – 'Taker of towns'. In reality he never took any towns unless they were poorly defended, nor vanquished other generals except very mediocre ones. In 306, he and Antigonus failed in a combined land and sea expedition against Egypt, just as Perdiccas had done sixteen years earlier. In 305, Demetrius laid siege to Rhodes. That great commercial city had wished not to take part in the war against Egypt, for she intended to make use of her insular position to avoid being drawn into the conflicts which were ravaging the Hellenic world, and thus had initiated the policy of neutrality to which she adhered, and with advantage, for the next hundred and fifty years. The military operations, conducted with great energy on both sides and with extraordinary technical devices, ended in a convention greatly to the advantage of the Rhodians, confirming their freedom and authorising them to maintain friendly relations with Ptolemy.

In Greece, on the other hand, where Cassander had been regaining ground, Demetrius arrived in time to prevent his recapturing Athens. He was pleased to take up his quarters in the city, where he could lead a wild life. In 303 a successful campaign re-established his authority in the Peloponnese, where Polyperchon retained only a few strong-points. In 302 the revived League of Corinth nominated him General-in-Chief of the confederate Greek armies.

Cassander was more alarmed than anyone by these successes of Demetrius in Greece. He strongly emphasised the need to reinvigorate the coalition against Antigonus, and urged his allies to take action. In 302 Lysimachus marched into Asia Minor, and before the news had reached Antigonus, installed in his Syrian capital of Antigoneia since 306, he had conquered the greater part of the Anatolian plateau, and more serious still, the Greek towns along the Ionian coast. The old king advanced to meet him, at the same time ordering his son Demetrius (who was then in Thessaly facing Cassander) to rejoin him. But Lysimachus avoided a pitched battle, for he was counting on a reinforcement from the orient which he felt would be decisive.

Our scanty knowledge of these troubled years does not inform us as to the doings of Seleucus since his return to Babylon, indeed we are by no means sure that he was a party to the convention of 311. We can only guess at a great campaign in India during those ten years, taking him as far as the Ganges; and then a treaty with King Chandra-Gupta – whom the Greeks called Sandrakottos – by which Seleucus had to give up all claim to the Punjab and the valley of the Indus – a sacrifice made necessary perhaps so that he could turn all his strength westwards. In any case, in 301 he was able to bring Lysimachus large reinforcements, including the whole apparatus of Asiatic wars – elephants and chariots armed with scythes. In the plain of Ipsus in Phrygia some hundred and fifty thousand men confronted one another. The confederates won: by the end of the day Demetrius and his broken army were in flight and Antigonus lay dead.

So ended, at the age of eighty-one, the greatest soldier of the epoch and the last exponent of a policy founded on maintaining the unity of Alexander's empire. This policy, as can now be seen, was beyond realisation. Around the Aegean Sea during the past ten years it could be discerned that the lines of great territorial divisions were being sketched in. The partition decided upon by the conquerors of 301 made these divisions clearer in outline. Cassander kept Macedon and Greece; Lysimachus took Thrace and Asia Minor as far as the Taurus range; and Seleucus all the eastern provinces with the addition of Syria. Ptolemy had prudently abstained from taking any part in the fighting in 301, and so obtained none of the spoils except a somewhat precarious title to southern

Syria (Coele Syria) which Seleucus abandoned to him but without formally ceding the territory. Thus upon the ruins of Alexander's Empire were built the four kingdoms of Macedon, Asia Minor, Syria, and Egypt, with whose wars all the next century was to resound.

XXIX

THE GREAT MONARCHIES

There is no gainsaying that the partition of Ipsus had contained within itself the seeds of future wars. It could be foreseen that a long conflict between the Seleucids and the Lagids (the descendants of Ptolemy, who was himself the son of Lagus) was bound to arise from the unsettled question of Coele Syria, and would last almost as long as the two dynasties themselves. From another direction Seleucus was threatened by the sweep of territory given to Lysimachus, stretching as it did from the Hellespont to the Taurus. He was menaced, too, by the union of his two neighbours in an alliance confirmed by the marriages of Lysimachus and, later, his son Agathocles to daughters of Ptolemy. This exemplifies the diplomatic tradition, revived later in western Europe, which associated the policies of great states with the interfamily relationships of their rulers.

Seleucus, for his part, naturally looked round for an ally, but could find no better than the son of his recently vanquished enemy. After the battle of Ipsus, Demetrius was in a very singular situation. The Asiatic empire built up by his father had been taken over by Lysimachus and Seleucus, but in addition to the garrisons which Demetrius still kept at various points in Asia Minor and Syria, his fleet gave him the continuing mastery of the seas. This state of affairs was well suited to his pirate's temperament, but could not easily be prolonged, for a fleet could only continue to operate if it had land-bases, dockyards, and supplies of timber. Demetrius hoped to find all these somewhere in Europe. Athens, when he put in an appearance there, politely closed its gates against him. He now retained in Greece only Corinth and a few garrisons in the archipelago and the Peloponnese. His expedition along the coasts of Thrace was merely an excuse for pillage. At this point, in 298 to be exact, Seleucus asked him for an alliance and the hand of his daughter, Stratonice.

The relationship between father and son-in-law soon deteriorated, however. Seleucus made no difficulties about Demetrius establishing his pirate's lair in Cilicia, but was uneasy at his maintaining garrisons in Tyre and Sidon, and seeking to ally himself with Ptolemy. Exact details as to what happened are not known, but it is clear that about the year 296 the coalition of 301 had been revived in opposition to Demetrius, who was soon to be deprived of his last footholds in Asia.

Demetrius now turned his attack against Greece, where the death of Cassander seemed to favour his enterprises. He reappeared before Athens, which had to open its gates after a two years' siege and allow a Macedonian garrison to be installed at Munychia. He next marched into the Peloponnese and was threatening Sparta when he was recalled northwards by events in Macedon. There the two sons of Cassander were in dispute about their father's inheritance and asking for help, the one from Lysimachus, the other from Pyrrhus, King of Epirus, and from Demetrius. Once in Macedon, Demetrius put to death the man who had invited his help and took his place. This summary proceeding seems not to have offended the Macedonians. They disliked Cassander whom they had never forgiven for his liquidation of Alexander's family. Demetrius, on the other hand, came with the prestige of his father's military prowess and his own reputation.

Although the new king met with no difficulties from the Macedonians, his position was nevertheless precarious. Macedon was exhausted. For fifty years it had served as the great reservoir of men from which Philip, Alexander, Antipater, and Cassander had in turn drawn off their armies, as had also various oriental rulers by the voluntary emigration of mercenaries. The sovereign of a kingdom thus bled white was sure to have difficulty in maintaining his authority over the Greek towns, where there still existed a party unreconciled to the consequences of the battle of Chaeronea. In 293 Boeotia rebelled. After this revolt had been put down, she rose again in 291, when Demetrius captured Thebes only after a long siege. At Athens, those who had supported Demetrius when he had posed as the defender of Greek liberties naturally turned against him now that he was merely Cassander's successor, and it was no easy task for Phaedrus, a man of the moderate party, to dissuade the city from an open breach with Demetrius.

Still more difficult was his position with his royal neighbours. Macedon was no longer the only powerful state in northern Greece. Lysimachus had made Thrace into a great military power, which also possessed a good fleet. Since Ipsus, he owned (at least in theory) the whole of Asia Minor, and there existed between him and Demetrius a lasting hatred, the cause of which is unknown but of which the effects were obvious. In 291 Lysimachus had been made prisoner by the Getae, in the course of an unfortunate expedition in the north. Immediately Demetrius invaded his kingdom, but hearing that Lysimachus had been set free he left Thrace in a great hurry. Lysimachus, naturally, did not forget this attack.

To the west Demetrius had very little security either. The Aetolian Confederation was chiefly concerned to defend the independence which it had been able to maintain against Philip, Alexander, and Antipater in turn, but had already shown in 322 what might be its attitude towards a Macedon which was either too weak or too aggressive.

From Epirus the threat was even clearer. This federal monarchy had subsisted for a century, under the overlordship first of Thessalian chieftains and then of the Macedonian rulers who made and unmade its kings. In 302 Pyrrhus, son of King Aeacides, had been driven from his inheritance by a revolution in which Cassander no doubt played a part. He took refuge with Antigonus and fought valiantly at the battle of Ipsus. At the time of the dubious reconciliation of 298, Demetrius, who had married his sister, sent the young king as his hostage to Alexandria, where the exile became a favourite at the Egyptian court. Ptolemy, who all his life had been seeking in Greece for some counter-weight to Macedon, supplied him with troops and money with which he reconquered his kingdom of Epirus, where he became a dangerous neighbour for Demetrius. Restless and of an adventurous temperament Pyrrhus was hesitating – and this was eventually his ruin – between the temptation to conquer an oriental empire and that of a warlike policy against Italy, so close to his own shores. He turned out to be a better general than Demetrius, and his contemporaries said that he could take in a situation with the swift perception of a second Alexander.

With surprising lack of foresight Demetrius, instead of consolidating his position in Macedon, thought mainly of rebuilding Alexander's empire for his own aggrandisement. The Syrian shipyards built for him an enormous fleet – as many as five hundred ships it is said. At the same time his marriage – his fourth – with the divorced wife of Pyrrhus gave him possession of Corcyra, on the way to Italy. In 289, expeditions by Demetrius into Epirus and by Pyrrhus into Macedon were indecisive and ended in a compromise. But in 288 Pyrrus joined the partly revived Grand Coalition, and together with Lysimachus invaded Macedon. Deserted by most of his soldiers, whose affections he had failed to win and who were tired of his endless adventures, Demetrius had to fly from his kingdom. He turned first of all towards Greece with an army recruited as he went. Athens was about to open her gates to him, but Pyrrhus was in Attica close upon his heels; and Demetrius, after accepting a truce by which he ceded Macedon to the king of Epirus, set sail for Asia in 287. For two years he wandered about with his motley army, raiding the territories of Lysimachus to begin with, and then those of Seleucus, until the latter tracked him down and forced him to surrender. The luxurious but strict captivity which Demetrius was forced to accept continued until his death in 283-2.

The disappearance of this adventurer failed to bring general peace. To begin with the relations between Pyrrhus and Lysimachus, who had hastily divided Macedon between them, could scarcely remain cordial –

nor those between Lysimachus and Seleucus. Furthermore, Demetrius had left behind him in Greece his son Antigonus (called for some unknown reason Gonatas), whose earnest tenacity of purpose inherited from his grandfathers – Antigonus and Antipater – was in complete contrast with his father's restlessness. He had decided to reconquer the kingdom of which his father had proclaimed him to be the heir. In fact he still held several firm footholds in Greece: Demetrias, Chalcis, Corinth, and even the Piraeus, where he maintained a garrison right alongside free Athens. He had lost the League of Islands which went over to Ptolemy, and a squadron under the command of the Syrian Philocles which likewise joined the Egyptian king; but he retained a considerable fleet, and hence in the struggle for which preparations were being made he could bring useful support to any power which secured his alliance.

In 285 Pyrrhus, becoming anxious at the growing understanding between his eastern and his western neighbours, Lysimachus and the Aetolians, concluded a secret treaty with Antigonus. The results, however, were far from fortunate. In spite of the help received from Greece, Pyrrhus was driven out of Macedon by Lysimachus and forced to abandon the whole kingdom. So now it was Lysimachus who stood at the head of an enormous empire comprising Macedon and Thessaly, Thrace, and almost all Asia Minor. He extended his protectorate over Paeonia northwards; to the south west he freed Acarnania from the Epirot yoke; he annexed the islands of the Aegean and established friendly relations with Athens and the sanctuary of Delos.

Pyrrhus, now full of his western projects, let him proceed unhindered. Antigonus was trying to re-establish his position in Greece. Nothing from those quarters seemed to threaten Lysimachus; it was dynastic problems and palace intrigues which were again to provoke a great conflict. In Egypt, about the year 290, Ptolemy had designated his son by his second wife as his successor, the future Ptolemy II, setting aside Ptolemy Ceraunus the child of his first marriage, who left his father's kingdom and went sulkily to the court of his brother-in-law, Lysimachus. There he found a situation very like the one which had just driven him from Egypt. Arsinoë, the second wife of the old king, to ensure the succession to the throne of her own children, had persuaded Lysimachus to have his rightful heir Agathocles executed. The latter's family, and Ptolemy Ceraunus himself, found refuge with Seleucus who, taking advantage of the discontent caused by Agathocles's fate, marched into Asia Minor. The armies of these two veteran generals of Alexander's campaigns met in the 'Plain of Corus' (Corupedion), where Lysimachus was defeated and slain.

Perhaps without deliberately intending to do so, Seleucus had reunited under his rule almost the whole of Alexander's empire. Only Egypt and a few garrisons in Greece were lacking. In particular he found himself once more king of Macedon, which he had not revisited for half a century. Leaving the regency of Asia to his son Antiochus, he returned to his native shore. On landing in Europe in 280 he was assassinated by Ptolemy Ceraunus, who now despaired of ever regaining Egypt but thought the inheritance of Lysimachus to be within his grasp and worth the taking. Ptolemy I had died in 283: and so with Lysimachus there disappeared the last of those companions of Alexander who, as great captains and the founders of empires, had proved themselves worthy of their former leader. A less brilliant generation was to replace them.

In the royal families of Macedon assassination has, in all periods, been one of the normal instruments of government. After the murder of Seleucus, Ptolemy Ceraunus married Arsinoë, the widow of Lysimachus and his own half-sister, and then put her children to death. This series of crimes seems in no way to have offended the army, which recognised him as its leader, nor the Macedonians, who accepted him as king. His authority was not challenged by Antiochus, who was busy surmounting the difficulties of establishing himself in Asia, nor by Pyrrhus who was more and more absorbed by affairs in Italy (cf. Chapter XXX). The fleet of Antigonus, which headed towards Macedon, was heavily defeated by the navy which Ptolemy had inherited from Lysimachus. Nor was the new king of Macedon seriously threatened from the south.

In the north, however, trouble was brewing. Great movements of peoples, perhaps begun in northern Europe in the fourth century, had ended by setting in motion the Celtic tribes settled at that time in central Europe. The Greeks were rather ignorant about these barbarians whom they called Galatae, and had failed to realise what a service Lysimachus was rendering by maintaining along that frontier a strong barrier against them. The crumbling of his empire had swift results. In 279 three bands of Celts pushed southwards, one towards Thrace, and the other two by the valley of the Axius (Vardar) and through Illyria towards Macedon. Ptolemy, who thought he could easily repulse these savages, was defeated and killed, and Macedon was pillaged. In the autumn the horde, under a chieftain named Brennus, entered Thessaly.

After a lapse of two centuries this seemed like the Persian terror over again, and Greece was weaker and more divided than ever. Athens no longer had a navy, the towns of the Peloponnese once again reckoned on being able to defend themselves behind the isthmus. Antigonus held only the garrisons of Demetrias, Chalcis, the Piraeus, and Corinth. Moreover he was engaged in some senseless war with Antiochus, the objective of which seems to have been a Macedon which neither of them possessed, which the Galatae had just ravaged, and for which various short-lived pretenders were disputing among themselves. However, the approach of the common enemy seems once more to have induced a temporary unity: at the pass of Thermopylae contingents assembled from Antigonus and Antiochus (now reconciled) the cities of central Greece, Athens, Aetolia.

Again as in 480 the position was outflanked, and while one division of Celts made a demonstration westwards which resulted in the Aetolians being recalled home, the remainder reached Delphi. But the barbarians found the sanctuary defended by the Phocians, with whom an Aetolian contingent had combined, and the lateness of the season forced them to make a rapid and difficult retreat, which legend soon embellished with miraculous episodes. Swiftly they crossed Thessaly and Macedon, devastated by their own recent passage, and turned off, some towards the Danube, others towards Thrace. There they met Antigonus, who inflicted a crushing defeat on them (277).

This great disturbance had the effect of modifying the whole aspect of Greek politics. The Aetolians and Antigonus had deserved well of Hellenism, and their success against the Celts earned them a great reputation. Later we shall note what use the Aetolians made of this. As for Antigonus, one consequence of the invasion was to leave Macedon without a master, so that he no longer had any competitor. The treaty which had reconciled him with Antiochus had abandoned Macedon to him. Pyrrhus was busy in Italy. In 276 Antigonus was again established in the kingdom which his father had ruled for so short a time. Thessaly remained obedient to him. For the moment Greece accepted the event. Athens resigned herself to the fact of a Macedonian garrison stationed in the Piraeus. Even Sparta seemed to have renounced her hostility, which in any case had been in vain but which she had maintained against the kings of Macedon ever since Chaeronea. Antigonus is really to be considered the founder of a new Macedonian dynasty. He and his successors were able to rebuild out of this exhausted kingdom the chief military power in the Hellenic world. A kind of equilibrium was to be established between the three portions of Alexander's empire: a regenerated Macedon; Egypt; and that enormous, chaotic empire of Asia whose integrity the descendants of Seleucus were setting themselves to maintain against great odds.

XXX

SICILY BETWEEN CARTHAGE AND ROME

The two parts of the Greek world which are separated by the Ionian Sea had remained in close political and intellectual communion until the end of the fifth century. At the time of the Persian wars Gelo of Syracuse had very nearly been put in supreme command of the Greek forces, while during the Peloponnesian War Ionian foot-soldiers had fought under the walls of Syracuse, and Syracusan triremes in the Hellespont. In the fourth century their relationship became less close. European Greece turned its attention more and more to the orient, where an empire in dissolution offered prizes for its soldiers; and the fertile turmoil caused in Asia by Alexander's conquests strengthened the movement. In the west, Carthage on the one hand, the peoples of central Italy on the other, were demanding more and more attention by their threats to the safety of the cities of Sicily and southern Italy.

Yet these western cities never forgot their origins: in fact it was precisely the external danger, and sometimes internal troubles too, that drove them several times to beg for help from the mother-country, at first from the older mother-states and later from the new young states of northern Greece. For some months it looked as if Pyrrhus, King of Epirus, was destined to enact in the west a magnificent sequel to the oriental achievements of the Macedonian monarchs. But the vigorous growth of the Roman Republic gave events an unexpected turn, and soon halted all progress of Hellenism in the western Mediterranean.

In 345 Syracuse addressed an appeal to Corinth. The return of Dionysius had not brought peace. A whole party which was hostile to the tyrant had left the town and taken refuge at Leontini with Hiketas, an old friend of Dion's, and was hoping to re-enter Syracuse by force. Carthage was waiting for the moment when these quarrels should give her a chance to take possession, not only of the city she had coveted so earnestly for a century and a half, but of all Sicily with it.

At this juncture the enemies of Dionysius appealed to Corinth, the mother-city of Syracuse, who in response sent a small squadron under Timoleon. He was one of the most notable citizens of Corinth, and had proved his respect for her democratic constitution by overthrowing his own brother in 365, when he tried to set up a tyranny there. He found on

arrival that the situation in Sicily had altered: Hiketas had beaten Dionysius, held him beleaguered in Syracuse, and had made peace with the
Carthaginians. Timoleon defeated Hiketas, forced him to conclude a
pact and to hand over command of his army. Timoleon was then received
as a liberator by the towns of eastern Sicily, and with reinforcements from
Corinth was able to capture Syracuse and with it Dionysius, who was sent
to end his days as a private citizen in Corinth.

Timoleon then inflicted a decisive defeat on the Carthaginians in 341,
on the banks of the river Crimisus in eastern Sicily. A further treacherous
move by Hiketas was nipped in the bud by a revolt of his troops, and he
was handed over to Timoleon and executed. The Carthaginians were
pushed right back into the western corner of the island; the confederation
of Greek cities was revived – it seemed as if the good old days of Dionysius
the Elder, or even of Hiero, had returned. Indeed the city was endowed
with a constitution based on 'wise moderation' – something that neither
Dionysius nor Hiero had done for it – and Timoleon was able to watch
it functioning normally, for after the victory he gave up his dictatorial
functions, and ended his days as a private citizen in the town he had saved.

But the equilibrium which Timoleon had hoped to establish, by
balancing the Popular Assembly with the coterie of 'the six hundred'
drawn from wealthy citizens, did not long survive him. For a whole
decade control of the government was in dispute between democrats and
oligarchs, until the day when a soldier from Rhegium named Agathocles,
who had been serving in the Syracusan army since 343, recruited a small
army with which the People's Party could resist the oligarchs. In 317 the
Carthaginians intervened to give him military command if he would
swear to respect the laws. He had no hesitation in complying – nor in
using force at the first opportunity, and after two days of street-fighting
he was master of Syracuse.

The oligarchs who had fled to other cities continued their opposition.
They asked Sparta for help, and in response Acrotatus was sent with a
small squadron; the Spartans and Tarentines, who supplied twenty
ships, failed to deploy their forces effectively; by 313 the authority of
Agathocles was recognised throughout the eastern part of the island, except by Messana and Agrigentum. At this Carthage became dissatisfied
with the behaviour of the new master of Syracuse, and abandoned the
policy of neutrality which she had adopted after the battle of Crimisus.
In 311 a powerful expedition landed on the promontory of Ecnomos
under Hamilcar, and defeated Agathocles with the aid of contingents from
Agrigentum and the oligarchic party, which brought its strength up to
about forty-five thousand men. Agathocles lost all his territory except
Syracuse itself.

At this point he conceived the bold plan – adopted by Scipio a century
later – of forcing the Carthaginians to return home by carrying the war

into Africa. Outwitting the blockading fleet which Hamilcar had stationed around Syracuse, Agathocles crossed into Libya with an army of fourteen thousand men, captured Tunis and laid siege to Carthage itself. Part of the Carthaginian army was recalled from Sicily only to be defeated near Tunis. Agathocles overran the incredibly rich lands around Carthage, took great quantities of booty, and provoked various revolts. But he was exhausting his resources. In 309 the tyrant of Cyrene, Ophellas, who seems to have made himself independent of Ptolemy about this time, brought him reinforcements of ten thousand men. Agathocles had him assassinated and kept his troops, and with an army thus augmented he was able to make himself master of almost all Carthaginian Libya. But to reduce Carthage he needed command of the sea and hence a fleet.

While one was being built he handed over command of the army in Africa to his son Archagathus, and returned to Sicily where the situation had changed for the better. What remained of the Carthaginian army under the walls of Syracuse had been beaten, Hamilcar captured and put to death, and the troops of the oligarchic party, who still had Agrigentum as their base of operations, were waging the war on their own account. A series of successes gained almost all western Sicily for Agathocles, and led to the dissolution of the coalition centred on Agrigentum. But bad news recalled him to Africa, where he found his army so diminished by desertion and a series of defeats that he did not feel at all safe there and returned hastily to Syracuse, leaving the remnant of his troops to make their submission to the Carthaginians in 307.

From the material point of view the expedition thus ended in complete failure, but its moral effect had been considerable. For three years Carthage had had the unprecedented humiliation of having a Greek army camped under its walls. Hence she accepted the peace that Agathocles offered her together with the restoration of western Sicily. Agathocles now had his hands free to deal with the forces of the oligarchic party, who soon had to submit. Apart from Agrigentum which persisted in its opposition, the eastern half of the island once more belonged to the master of Syracuse, who followed the example of the great captains of the orient, and called himself king.

The new sovereign was soon to have a chance to exercise his powers outside Sicily. In Italy the Greek cities had realised for some time that they were endangered by the local populations, who had shown themselves to be endued with great powers of expansion; and though their civilisation was not of a high order they made up for it by military prowess. In 343 Tarentum, hard pressed by the Lucanians and Messapians, had imitated Syracuse and appealed to Sparta, as their mother-state, for help. In response King Archidamus had been sent at the head of an army of mercenaries. He was defeated and killed in 338. Tarentum then turned to the peoples of northern Greece, whose vitality had been demonstrated by recent events.

Macedon was at this time engaged in a great struggle against Persia. But Alexander, King of Epirus (the uncle of Alexander the Great) asked no better than to have a chance to imitate in the west his nephew's great deeds in the east. He landed in Greater Greece in 334-3, and in his first campaigns conquered the whole of south Italy as far as Campania. But the Tarentines now realised that, through fear of an enemy, they were handing themselves over to a tyrant. Tarentum and then other cities dissociated themselves from Alexander, who was finally defeated and killed by the Lucanians in 331. His intervention had nevertheless relieved the pressure on Tarentum and freed her from Lucanian threats, but twenty-five years after his death she found herself being menaced by a much more redoubtable foe.

Little by little, Rome had established her authority over the whole of southern Italy. In 327 Naples had joined her alliance, the first Greek city to acknowledge the Roman hegemony. The Second Samnite War, concluded in 304, extended her sphere of influence almost to the gates of Tarentum, which the Lucanians, encouraged by the Romans, were again threatening. For the second time Tarentum appealed to Sparta, who sent Cleonymus, the brother of Acrotatus. He compelled the Lucians to accept peace, but soon quarrelled with the Tarentines. Thrown again on their own resources the latter now appealed to Agathocles, who crossed into Italy, defeated the Italici in a series of campaigns, and forced them to join him in an alliance which, for the moment, freed south Italy from Roman influence.

At the same time Agathocles was tempted to take a hand in oriental affairs. Cleonymus proved to be merely another of those adventurers who were so numerous in the Hellenic world after the death of Alexander, and his Italian expedition had been a pretext in his search for lands to conquer. He seized Corcyra, as a good vantage point from which to keep an eye on both shores of the Adriatic, and from this base his fleet made several raids along the Italian coast. But Cassander could not tolerate a Spartan installed so near the shores of Illyria, which all the successors of Philip had regarded as a dependency of Macedon, and drove him out. Agathocles intervened, expelled the Macedonian garrison in its turn, and gave the island as a dowry to his daughter Lanassa, who married first Pyrrhus and then Demetrius Poliorcetes.

And so the affairs of east and west seemed about to be interwoven by one of those diplomatic marriages whose object was clearly to secure for Agathocles the alliance of one of the great Greek powers. He obviously needed support in the east at a time when he was projecting a revival of the grandiose schemes of Dionysius the Elder and the expulsion of the

Carthaginians from the whole of Sicily. A fleet of two hundred ships had been prepared, when in 289 the old king died. One of the boldest of his generation of great captains, he had little by little rebuilt the empire of Gelo and Dionysius and had countered first the Carthaginian menace and then that of Rome.

But he, too, had built upon sand. No sooner was he dead than his empire disintegrated. The Sicilian towns were divided among themselves and fell into the hands of petty tyrants – Hiketas at Syracuse, Phintias at Agrigentum, while the Italic mercenaries of his army seized Messana. This seemed to the Carthaginians an excellent opportunity to make an end of the Sicilian quarrel. In 278 they blockaded Syracuse by land and sea so that all seemed lost. Meanwhile the Lucanians in Italy were again advancing against the local Greek community of Thurii, which threw in their lot with Rome as the only power in the peninsula which was strong enough to protect them. Roman garrisons were set up forthwith in Rhegium and Thurii; in 282 a Roman flotilla had the audacity to sail into the Gulf of Tarentum. The great city reacted violently: her ships sank four of the Roman raiders, while her infantry drove the Roman garrison from Thurii. This meant war before long, with a power which was certainly not strong at sea, but whose large army had already displayed its firm discipline and fine organisation.

Once more Tarentum looked to Greece for help, and once more the only power in a position to give it was Epirus. Pyrrhus seized with alacrity this chance to take a major part in Italian affairs. In 281 a body of three thousand Epirots arrived in Tarentum and a Roman army which was pillaging the neighbourhood retired; in 280 Pyrrhus, at the head of at least 25,000 Epirots and Greeks, disembarked in Italy; and near Heraclea a Greek and a Roman army met for the first time. The Roman legion was a more flexible weapon than the cumbersome phalanx, but the tactics of Pyrrhus and his elephants won him the victory – but a costly one. This success gave Pyrrhus control of southern Italy, but Rome was not so easily beaten. A raid by Pyrrhus into Latium was without result, while the victory at Asculum, as dearly bought as that of Heraclea, brought a decision no nearer.

During this time the Tarentines had grown weary of the military obligations imposed on them by the king, to whom they had accorded full powers for the duration of the war. Moreover, Pyrrhus received disquieting news from Greece, where the Celtic invasion might any day become a direct danger to Epirus. The Roman Senate opened negotiations with Pyrrhus, and a settlement was in sight when a Carthaginian embassy reached Rome. The presence of Pyrrhus in Greater Greece was a threat to all the powers of the western Mediterranean. Hence Carthage, fearing for her Sicilian possessions, offered the Romans an alliance, and what they needed above all, a fleet. The negotiations with Pyrrhus were promptly broken off, and Pyrrhus decided to turn against his new enemy and attack them in Sicily, where Syracuse after long months of siege was pleading for help. Leaving his son Alexander in Italy in command of an army of occupation, he landed at Tauromenium and relieved Syracuse.

In four years Sicily, united under his rule, was almost entirely cleared of Carthaginian garrisons except for the impregnable Lilybaeum. But the Hellenes of the island, like those of Greater Greece, and for the same reasons, grew tired of their new master and his demands for men and money. Pyrrhus was recalled to Italy by news that the Romans had defeated his Lucanian and Samnite allies, and as soon as he had quitted the island, Syracuse made peace with the Carthaginians, who again handed eastern Sicily over to her. Pyrrhus was left alone to face the Romans in Italy. He knew that Epirus was threatened by the Celts (Galatae); the Carthaginians were masters of the sea; his army was dwindling; and operations in Samnia and Lucania, where the Roman army was encamped, had ended in failure. The expedition so brilliantly begun was degenerating into disaster, so in 275 he recrossed the Adriatic to seek his fortune in Greece, where the throne of Macedon had been vacant for four years.

Apart from its fear of the oriental monarchies, which the Roman Senate could not shake off for many years to come, no trace of this exploit was to endure. The garrison which Pyrrhus left at Tarentum, to keep a foothold there for the future, was recalled in 272 by his successor Alexander. Tarentum had to make peace with Rome and declined to the rank of a confederate city with a Roman garrison. In 266 the surrender of the Messapians assured Rome's rule over the whole of Greater Greece. Between the great Italian state and Carthage the position of Sicily became precarious, especially as the Campanian mercenaries, calling themselves Mamertini (Sons of Mars) kept their hold upon Messana and its surrounding territory.

Once more a bold stroke of military policy altered events. The Syracusan army proclaimed as its commander an officer named Hiero who had distinguished himself under Pyrrhus. He had his election ratified by the people of Syracuse after he had defeated the Mamertini and shut them up in the town of Messana. The Mamertini appealed to Carthage, which established a garrison in Messana, and then appealed to Rome to oust the Carthaginians. The Romans of course felt that they could not allow so great a power to occupy the other side of the narrow strait. The Carthaginian garrison was driven out and a Roman army crossed into Sicily. Hiero seems to have understood the serious nature of this event, for he allied himself with the Carthaginians and his troops came to reinforce the Carthaginian army besieging Messana. But in the summer of 264 the consul Appius Claudius raised the siege of Messana, brought the town into the Roman alliance, and separated Hiero's troops from the Carthaginian army. Hiero decided to make peace, though on terms that reduced his empire to Syracuse, Leontini, and Tauromenium. Henceforth the Romans had control of the strait, and a base on the island.

For the next twenty-two years Sicily was to be a battle-ground for the Romans and Carthaginians. We know that this first Punic War, in which Hiero was careful to take no part, was brought to an end, after the Senate had decided to seek victory afloat, by a treaty in 241 which ceded the whole of Sicily to Rome. The dream of Gelo, of Hiero, of Dionysius, of Timoleon, of Agathocles, and of Pyrrhus at last was realised: Sicily was cleared of the barbarians from Africa; but it was for the benefit of Rome, whose first overseas province the island now became. The small Syracusan state, administered with prudence and fidelity by Hiero under Roman protection, survived after the beginning of the Second Punic War until the Romans entered the town in 212. But from 264 onwards the Greeks of the west were no longer masters of their own destiny, and the ultimate fate of the Greek cities of Greater Greece and of Sicily was closely linked with that of the great military republic which, by its possession of Italy and Sicily, and soon afterwards of Sardinia and Corsica, developed into the chief power of the western Mediterranean.

XXXI

EXTENSION AND TRANSFORMATION OF
THE HELLENIC WORLD

At the time when Alexander crossed the Hellespont it could be said that Hellenism had made no territorial progress for at least two centuries past. This is a fact to which the brilliance of Greek civilisation in the fifth and fourth centuries should not blind us. The great colonising movement of ancient Greece had stopped at the end of the sixth century, after which date the territories won over for Greek influence and language amount to very little. The Sicilian tyrants had founded a few colonies in the Adriatic. Dionysius the Elder had perhaps tried to civilise the natives of western Sicily; in Asia Minor circumstances – especially after the fall of the Athenian Empire – were not propitious for Hellenism, and it could make only modest and precarious progress – the tiny Hellenised kingdom of Mausolus and Artemisia being merely a curious exception.

From 338 to 323 Graeco-Macedonian armies marched through the northern Balkans, through Egypt, and half of Asia. In these vast regions they left behind them, as a kind of sediment, numerous colonies some of which were destined to develop prodigiously. In this respect Alexander's successors continued his policy, and most of them were great founders of cities – above all the Seleucids, who deserved well of Hellenism for their part in the matter. In Egypt, it is true, since it was an agricultural country whose inhabitants had long been accustomed to absolute obedience, the Ptolemies concentrated on developing Alexandria their capital. In Europe, neither Cassandria nor Demetrias (cities founded by Cassander and Demetrius Poliorcetes) contributed to the spread of Hellenism, for they were both in essentially Greek districts – the former in Chalcidice, the latter at the foot of Mount Pelion. Thessalonica, Philippopolis, and Lysimachia were cities inside Greek regions – built respectively by Cassander in the Thermaic Gulf, by Philip in Thrace, and by Lysimachus in the Chersonese.

Above all it was in Asia that this kind of activity was displayed by Alexander's successors. In Asia Minor Lysimachus rebuilt Ephesus on a more favourable site; on the main road from the river Maeander there arose Laodicea and Apamea; while Pergamum, still an insignificant fortress in Xenophon's day, became in the second century a magnificent capital city. In Syria, the favourite country of the Seleucids, Antioch and its port Seleucia were founded at the outlet of the road joining the upper course of the Euphrates to the sea. In Mesopotamia another Seleucia was to take the place of Babylon; and building went on as far as Persia or even in Turkestan, where another Antioch became important in the Merv oasis. On the other hand, in the west the growth of Carthage and then of Rome definitely put an end to the progress of Hellenism, and the expeditions by Agathocles into Africa and by Pyrrhus in central Italy proved to have no future.

It must not be thought, however, that the immense territories of the orient were wholly won for Hellenism in the way that Greater Greece or Sicily had been in the seventh and sixth centuries. To begin with, many of these colonies had an essentially military character, and their civilising influence can only have been a very slight one. Furthermore, in spite of the efforts of Alexander and his successors to plant the veterans of their armies on the newly conquered soil, they were not able to give to agricultural settlement (except perhaps in Egypt and particularly in the Fayum basin) the development which it was to attain later on in some regions of the Roman Empire. Greek colonisation at the end of the fourth and beginning of the third centuries was essentially urban, and even the most flourishing of these new towns did not extend far over its surrounding countryside.

The Aramaic dialect perpetuated itself, until the end of the Roman Empire, in the very suburbs of Syrian Antioch, which nevertheless was one of the chief centres of Hellenism in the Ancient World. All the efforts of the Ptolemies could not prevent the Egyptian tongue from successfully resisting Greek their official language in the rural areas. On the other hand, even in the great urban centres the population was a very mixed one. It comprised, as was natural, a strong native element; for instance, the inhabitants of the Egyptian town of Canopus became the core of Alexandria's population. Even the Greeks were of very diverse origin, though it is true that among them were people from Greece proper. Some Athenians had settled in the capital which Antigonus founded in Syria, and whose population was soon transferred to Antioch. But Macedonians formed the main part of the new cities' Greek population, at least to begin with.

The conquest of the orient, so often and so mistakenly presented as a new effort to find living-space by an over-populated Greece, was in reality an entirely Macedonian affair. Macedonians were the squirearchy – and they never forgot the fact – who founded the dynasties of the Antigonids, the Seleucids, and the Ptolemies; and Macedonians, to begin with, supplied their high officials. Macedonians, too, were the peasants who made up the bulk of Alexander's armies, and who peopled his colonies and those of Lysimachus and Seleucus. Nor must it be overlooked that Greek civilisation had spread into Macedon a bare century earlier, and only among the upper classes. Alongside these Macedonians, a great many of the mercenaries came from the poorest parts of the Peloponnese or of Crete; or from the most barbarous regions of the Balkans, from Illyria, Epirus, and Thrace. Here we have the essential difference between this expansion and that of the seventh and sixth centuries, when the majority of colonists, whatever their social status may have been, came from the very heart of Greek civilisation – from Chalcis, Corinth, or Miletus. And so the Greek element in the new domains did not possess the power of resistance to outside influences which its forbears had shown in Sicily or in southern Italy; since it was now coming into conflict with very tenacious ancient civilisations, it allowed itself to be contaminated by its local environment.

In Egypt, where an abundance of documents enables us to follow this transformation better than elsewhere, we can see (especially in the agricultural colonies which had been settled with veterans) how the interplay of mixed marriages and naturalisations little by little created a Graeco-Egyptian population which spoke Greek, as modern Levantines speak French or Italian, but whose manners, tastes, and religious tendencies were powerfully affected by their native environment. The result was that complex type of civilisation which modern historians call 'Hellenistic', in which Greek and indigenous elements combined so curiously and often so fruitfully. By this transformation Hellenism certainly gained in extent, and sometimes in richness, what it lost in purity.

This transformed civilisation was the kind which eventually imposed itself not only upon Egypt and the near east, but to some extent and in the long run on European Greece too. This was owing to the fact that its main supporters were the powerful states which henceforward became the economic and political centre of gravity of the Greek world. The empires which rose on the ruins of Alexander's empire greatly surpassed, in population and area, anything that Greece had previously known. Macedon, the most compact of them all, had between 27,000 and 30,000 square miles at the time of Antigonus Gonatas, which was about four times the size of the Peloponnesian Confederation of the fifth and fourth centuries at the zenith of its power. Egypt had more than 38,000 square miles; and what is to be said of the vast and vague empire of the Seleucids, whose area must have been measured in millions of square miles? Sparse as its population may have been in some regions, it is difficult to assess that of the Seleucid empire at less than thirty millions, Egypt's at fewer than seven or eight millions, Macedon's at four millions. Enormous towns rapidly grew up in them: the populations of Antioch and of Seleucia were counted in hundreds of thousands; that of Alexandria reached the half million mark by the end of the third century, a figure which only Imperial Rome was later destined to exceed.

Naturally, the masters of these new states had vast resources at their disposal. Without claiming to give any precise valuation it may be estimated that their taxes provided the kings of Egypt and of Syria with huge sources of income for that period in world history. Such revenues, incomparably greater than those Athens could amass even at her most powerful, enabled them to raise and equip armies larger than any Greece had previously known. At Ipsus, Seleucus and Lysimachus had been able to get together some seventy-five thousand men, while their opponent Antigonus had about as many. These figures compare with those engaged in Napoleon's early battles. Even in times of peace the vast extent of their dominions, and the complete absence of loyalty among their populations, compelled the rulers to maintain very large contingents under arms, great standing armies which were reinforced in times of war from reserve establishments.

More noticeable even than this increase in the number of troops was the improvement in equipment. Since the days of Philip, the use at sieges of enormous machines, more complicated it is true than scientific, had become general. The siege-engine called *Helepolis* (Destroyer of Cities) of Demetrius Poliorcetes has remained famous in spite of its mediocre results. In pitched battles elephants were used, sometimes in considerable numbers. Antigonus had seventy-five at Ipsus, Pyrrhus transported twenty into Italy. At sea, although no new techniques were evolved, a similar increase in the dimensions of warships took place. Ships with oars in units of four or five (quadriremes or quinqueremes), their decks often protected with a kind of armour, replaced the triremes of the Athenian epoch. Recent discoveries show how the rowers were disposed on these great vessels, and we do know that some ships were really enormous for those days.

As compared with these powerful empires the weakness of the Greek states was all the more striking. Their population, which continual wars and the restraints imposed by fears of famine had always kept at a moderate density, now remained stationary or even declined. At the census conducted by Demetrius of Phalerum during a period of peace and comparative prosperity, Athens proved to have no more than twenty-one thousand citizens, perhaps half the number she had had at the beginning of the Peloponnesian War. This decline in population was even more noticeable in the agricultural regions. Sparta was no more than a petty township. In these shrunken cities patriotism, too, had diminished. No more citizen-armies, no more fleets fitted out and maintained by rich individuals, but only parade troops, mercenary police, and weak flotillas, to act merely as frontier guards and to protect the coasts from pirates.

The political independence of the Greek towns, too, was really no more than a name. The liberty which the successive masters of Greece, from Philip to the Roman consuls, had loudly promised to the Greek towns was nothing more than a limited and precarious autonomy. Only the Republic of Rhodes, like Venice in the sixteenth and seventeenth centuries A.D., thanks to its island situation, the wealth of its commerce and its very great naval skill, preserved an independence which had been hallowed by its defeat of Demetrius Poliorcetes and reinforced by an international influence to which Rome alone proved able to put an end. Everywhere else political life was more and more confined to the administration of municipal affairs. Its poverty is made obvious by the decrees promulgated in the third and second centuries, whose verbose nullity appears in the abundant documents of the period. Thus there disappeared, little by little, what had for three centuries provided the framework of Greek political life: the city, with its restricted territory, its intense life, its jealously guarded sovereignty. Henceforward the story of Hellenism is that of three or four great states.

Most of these were kingdoms. It is true that the principle of a federal republic which had had such interesting applications in Boeotia and in fourth century Arcadia and in Aetolia had not been forgotten. In the Peloponnese there developed during the third century (*cf.* Chapter XXXIII) confederations whose extent and influence finally became considerable. But the Aetolian Confederation was never a great civilising influence, and the Achaean League never had more than scanty material resources at its disposal. In the other great states of the Greek world monarchy assumed a variety of aspects. In Sicily it remained a 'tyranny' in the old sense of the term, that is to say an entirely personal government, based on one individual's prestige, but paying at least formal respect to democratic institutions. Only Agathocles and Hiero, the last sovereigns of Syracuse, took the title of king.

In Macedonia, royalty was hereditary in principle; but it was founded on the free consent of the people, citizens and army alike. The reason that the Antigonid dynasty, which in the end replaced the descendants of Alexander, continued to rule there until the Roman conquest was because the rare qualities of its princes justified the loyalty of their subjects. The same was not true in Asia or Egypt. There was nothing there, either in customs or political organisation, to limit the authority of the monarch. This had always been so in Egypt and Mesopotamia, and from the end of the sixth century the Achaemenid Empire had tended more and more towards despotic forms of government in which institutions, customs, and court ceremonial placed an impassable barrier between the sovereign and his subjects. The new rulers easily accommodated themselves to this state of affairs. After all, were they not members of a superior race, and did not the right of conquest give them absolute power over these new territories and their inhabitants? It was understood, of course, that Greeks (and particularly Macedonians) should receive most favoured treatment. In the armies they formed special corps. In the military colonies they enjoyed a more favourable status than the natives. And above all the Greek cities in these states enjoyed special privileges. Like those in Greece itself they kept their own magistrates, their own law-courts and democratic institutions – although here too their powers were circumscribed to municipal matters, and they had to be careful never to interfere in the general conduct of affairs of the state in which they were incorporated. They had no voice as to the amount of tax they had to pay, which under the collective and polite name of 'contribution' ($\sigma\acute{u}\nu\tau\alpha\xi\iota\varsigma$) was just as compulsory as the tribute ($\phi\acute{o}\rho\acute{o}\varsigma$) imposed on the natives; they frequently had to put up with the presence of a garrison, and sometimes even of an agent of the central power.

The absolute power of the monarchy found its symbol in the worship of the kings. This institution has a complexity of origin which makes it typical of the Hellenistic period, for in it are mingled, in proportions not easy to define, the Greek custom of hero-worship, the idea of a god-king long familiar to the populations of Egypt and Mesopotamia, and the effect of the express wishes of Alexander and his successors. It is not quite certain that the starting-point of this institution was to be found in a visit paid by Alexander in the winter of 332-1 to the shrine of Ammon Ra in Libya, where he had himself hailed by the priests as the son of this god whom the Greeks identified with Zeus; but it is at least sure that he accepted the divine honours accorded to him by those close to him, and demanded that they should be officially paid him by the towns of Greece. After his death, Eumenes (by appealing in the course of political deliberations to Alexander's real presence), and Ptolemy (by conveying his mortal remains to Alexandria as sort of a holy relic) contributed to the continuance and spread of the belief in Alexander's divine nature, which finally developed into a formal cult. The Seleucids and Ptolemies, inheritors of his authority, also shared in his essence and became gods in their turn. This principle first expressed itself in a somewhat timid way: the reigning king gave divine honours to his dead father. But from the middle of the third century the living king received adoration and was identified with one of the great gods of the Hellenic pantheon. In the second century, he became a visible and incarnate god in the persons of Ptolemy V and Antiochus IV.

Yet it must be said that this institution did not develop with the same success everywhere. It is not surprising that it never flourished in Macedonia, whose people would not have accepted either the religious ideas on which it was based or the despotism to which it was complementary. In Greece the title 'Saviour-God' given to Demetrius Poliorcetes at Athens, and to Ptolemy I at Rhodes, was merely the expression of a temporary gratitude. But in Egypt it was a different matter, since there the worship of kings was founded in national tradition; so, too, in the Seleucid Empire, where this institution served to give concrete form to the royal authority, both among native populations and in the Greek cities, and where it became part of the machinery of government, through detailed organisation of the priesthood and their division into dioceses, just as the worship of the Roman Emperors did in later times.

The machinery of government naturally developed a complicated structure in these vast empires. The king was surrounded by a council (συνέδριον) of friends (φίλοι) recruited as in the days of Philip and Alexander from the aristocratic ranks and the royal pages (βασιλικοὶ παῖδες). These high functionaries, almost always Greek by birth after the unfortunate attempt made by Alexander to include some of native origin, shared between them the various ministries: general control (ὁ ἐπὶ τῶν πραγμάτων), war, finance, home affairs. This central organisation – both Macedonian and Greek in style – was superimposed on a provincial administration based on the régimes of the ancient kingdoms, although it was staffed by Greek personnel, at least in the case of the higher officials. In Asia the departments allotted to governors (*strategoi*) usually coincided with the satrapies of the Achaemenid rulers. In Egypt, the Ptolemies retained the old territorial divisions (nomes) of the Pharaohs, and developed even further the expert bureaucracy which had been built up there in the course of centuries, and was so well suited to the niggling, litigious nature of the people. The financial administration of Egypt is well-known to us in all its details, thanks to the papyri, and was as complicated and encumbered with paper-work as that of any great modern state. But of course the officials who controlled this administration were not chosen by the votes of the peoples concerned, but nominated by the central authority. In this way the Hellenic world became well acquainted with a bureaucratic régime, a system superimposed on the local magistracy of the Greek cities by an administrative evolution not unlike that which three centuries later was to develop throughout the Roman world as reorganised by Augustus.

The Macedonian hegemony and the conquest of Egypt and Asia were also destined to have serious economic consequences. In European Greece, where the decline in population was most marked in rural areas, the great estate reappeared, which democratic institutions had formerly helped to portion out among small proprietors. This tendency was noticeable not only in Sparta or Thessaly (where it merely accentuated a long-standing state of affairs) but throughout the Peloponnese, in Boeotia, in Euboea, perhaps even in Attica. The system was accompanied by various evils, as always in ancient times when the primitive state of agrarian implements had made the intensive exploitation of large domains impossible. The problem of food supplies became more and more difficult; yet by a contradiction which made itself only too obvious, the situation of the farmers and land-owners became ever more wretched. An agricultural proletariat was being recreated, and latter-day Greece, as in the early times of Solon, was distraught by the claims of these landless tenants and by demands for land-reform and the abolition of debts.

In Sicily, the wise policy of Hiero annulled any such movement, and the western part of the island continued throughout the third century to supply wheat to all parts of the Mediterranean. Agrarian troubles only broke out there after the Roman occupation.

In Egypt and in Asia the conquest produced conditions of labour previously unknown to Greek civilisation. It conferred on the kings a dominant right to the land, since it had been 'won by the spear' ($\delta o\rho i\kappa\tau\eta\tau os$). In Egypt it seems quite certain that the Ptolemies, as inheritors of the Pharaohs, were owners at least in theory of all the soil – except of course the territories of the Greek cities: at all events it is certain that they exploited directly the agricultural and mineral wealth of vast domains.

The Seleucids and the Attalids were also great land-owners, though perhaps to a lesser degree. The large numbers of slaves, detailed supervision by the royal authority, the institution of leasehold crop-sharing in Egypt, and the continuance of serfdom on royal estates in Asia, all permitted an active farming policy in spite of the miserable conditions in which the labourers often had to live. On the other hand, by an ever-increasing number of concessions to Macedonian veterans, to officials, to immigrants coming from Greece, the sovereigns did maintain in their dominions quite a numerous class of small and middling land-owners.

Industry too, like agriculture, underwent changes due to the new political and social conditions. Not that material progress had been very marked. It is easy to see that the existence of a large slave-population, which encouraged the laziest solutions of technical problems, also to some extent explained the spirit of routine in practical matters, which contrasted so strongly with the vigour of disinterested philosophical speculation. Practical applications of science remained mere objects of curiosity except in Egypt, the typical land of irrigation, where the use of the Archimedes' screw became general. On the other hand, in European Greece the population of free men declined without any increase in the number of slaves, and hence industry stagnated in the great towns, except perhaps Corinth. The large factories which had been founded in the fourth century showed no further development.

In the countries newly won for Hellenism, however, things were different owing to the dense population, both free and enslaved, from which labour could be recruited. Alongside small-scale businesses, always so lively in the Orient, large workshops now grew up, in Alexandria, in the great cities of Asia Minor, Syria and Mesopotamia, and also on the

Crown lands where the serfs provided a ready-made labour-force and where monopolies – at least in Egypt and perhaps under the Attalids – increased the prosperity of royal manufactories. In them were made not so much luxury articles as mass-produced goods. This was particularly obvious in ceramics, where the use of moulds for casting, practised discreetly from the end of the fifth century by the Athenian potters, now led to the manufacture in commercial quantities of pretty vases ornamented with designs borrowed from metalware, and at low prices – but which killed the painted vase on which the personal talent of the artist could express itself. Artistic decadence was the price to be paid, in this as in other spheres, for a productivity greatly surpassing anything previously known in the Greek world.

A busy commercial life went with this thriving industry. Its scope had been vastly extended by Alexander's conquests. The fall of the Persian Empire allowed the Hellenic world to communicate directly with the Upper Nile Valley, Arabia, and India; and with central Asia and China, through Afghanistan, whose importance in Alexander's eyes we can well appreciate. Greek merchants exchanged the products of Egyptian and Syrian manufactures for silk and spices. The Greek dynasts brought craftsmen from their own country, and the stone-carvers of the Gandhara region drew inspiration from the methods of Greek sculptors.

In the West the Etruscan Empire, which had been a faithful customer for Greek industry, was overwhelmed by Rome at the beginning of the third century, but her disappearance was outweighed by the growth of Carthage, and the political and economic progress of the peoples of central Italy, where new outlets were being created for Greek products.

In this enlarged market the means of communication had to be improved. Navigation grew bolder. New methods of construction first used for warships were then applied to trading vessels, and very large ships were now laid down such as the *Syracuse*, built by Hiero for the Sicily to Alexandria trade, whose displacement must have been about five thousand tons. These larger vessels in no way limited themselves to coasting, but launched out boldly across the Mediterranean in all weathers, sometimes even in winter, by night as well as day. The tower built at the beginning of the third century on the island of Pharos at the entrance to the port of Alexandria was intended to serve as a sea-mark by day and a lighthouse by night, and was imitated at several points on the Mediterranean coast.

Land routes, too, were improved. Though roads in Greece itself remained poor, the Seleucids inherited a good road network from the Persian kings and perfected it. Along the great land and sea routes the commercial cities of the Hellenistic world prospered: to the west, Syracuse and Tarentum, which until Roman times, were still the main markets of Sicily and southern Italy; between the Ionian Sea and Asia stood Corinth, which took advantage of the decline of Athens; Delos, which from the

middle of the second century became a grain depot and a great commercial centre; Rhodes; and at the gateway to the Black Sea, Byzantium.
In Asia there were Ephesus, the terminus of the most important route in
Asia Minor; Antioch and Seleucia-on-the-Tigris; and finally, Alexandria
in Egypt, where were brought together the products of the Aegean area,
of Egypt and Arabia. Merchants, warehousemen, ship-owners of all
nations met in these towns and set up powerful corporations there, an
image of these new times in which, owing to cosmopolitan sentiments and
the division of labour, men were classed according to their professional
activity quite as much as by their country of origin.

A large monetary circulation was necessary to sustain all this economic
activity. Its provision was greatly facilitated by the enormous quantities
of precious metals disgorged on to the Hellenic markets at the end of the
fourth century. The treasures hoarded in the palaces of Susa, Persepolis,
and Ecbatana, and put into circulation by Alexander's victories, have been
estimated at amounts which seem truly enormous. Even this influx of
coin scarcely met the new needs of the Hellenic world. It certainly did not
flow to all parts. Many regions retained the old-fashioned system of barter.
In Epirus, in rural parts of Asia, and most curious of all even in Egypt,
where, then as now, there existed side by side very ancient and very
advanced economic institutions, transactions in the country districts took
place in the form of goods, taxes were paid in kind, and petty officials
drew their state salaries in the form of goods. In each Egyptian township
the presence of both a bank and a public granary evidences this paradoxical
state of affairs.

It is noticeable, on the other hand – and this is one of the most extraordinary facts of the period – that throughout the Greek world, in the
years following Alexander's conquests, although prices at first experienced
a violent rise (clearly explicable by the great increase in the quantity of
gold) they then fell during the course of the third century almost to the
level at which they had been about a hundred years earlier. In this way a
new equilibrium was established between the increased quantity of money
and the much intensified production of goods. The more abundant coinage also carried the imprint of the new political organisation. Small local
mints disappeared; even that at Athens, which for a century and a half had
set the standard for all Greece, had its output reduced. Coinage and its
regulation were chiefly a matter for the great states. This, of course,
simplified the whole monetary system, but nevertheless, in this as in
everything else, the Greek world was never able to achieve unity. The
old rivalry continued between the Attic drachma (which served as the
basis for the system adopted by Macedon and the Asian kings) and the
drachma of Aegina (which, through the mediation of Rhodes, passed into

Egypt, was imposed with some slight modification on the Cyclades, and was adopted by Syracuse).

The organisation of credit became more sophisticated in response to this more intense circulation of money. It is well known that from the end of the fifth century the money-changers had developed into genuine bankers. Their business in the course of the fourth century became very prosperous. At Athens, the banker Pasion possessed a capital of fifty talents (some 12,500 gold sovereigns). The Hellenistic civilisation inherited this credit organisation and improved upon it. Alongside the private banks there developed banks attached to sanctuaries and to towns, and (especially in Egypt) numbers of actual state banks. These establishments paid out their customers on presentation of what virtually amounted to cheques, and their normal rate of interest sometimes fell below ten per cent – an extremely low figure for the Ancient World. True, the Roman conquest forced it up again, but it remains proof of a very advanced state of economic development. Indeed, of the Greek world after Alexander, as of Italy in the sixteenth century or Britain in the eighteenth century, it can be said that social and financial organisation outstripped the progress of industrial technique.

Owing to the conquest of both Greece and the Persian Empire by the kings of Macedon, the political and economic centre of gravity of the Greek world had shifted towards the east. Alexandria and Antioch now became its real capitals. Although European Greece had lost a little of its glory, merchandise and capital circulated with a freedom and in quantities not previously experienced in the countries newly acquired for Hellenism. Other consequences of this fusion of the two worlds were no less important.

XXXII

INTELLECTUAL AND ARTISTIC EVOLUTION

The narrow but vigorous patriotism which had been the mainspring of Greek moral and intellectual life until the middle of the fourth century no longer activated either the cities of old Greece, or the new towns which were founded in the lands recently opened to the influence of Hellenism. Nor could any comparable sentiment be aroused by the new states. How could the empires of the Ptolemies or the Seleucids, with their formal codes requiring that the king should be worshipped, inspire in their subjects any genuine regard for the empire of which they formed part? Only in rural Macedon did the peasant population retain a personal loyalty to their sovereign, which was to last as long as the kingdom itself. But what was lost in local sentiment was gained by the strengthening of that long-standing feeling of Panhellenic solidarity which had existed since the beginnings of Greek history, and which was now reinforced and encouraged by recent events. Men from every corner of Greece had fought shoulder to shoulder in the armies of Alexander and his successors: in the colonies and towns of the new empires they naturally united in the face of native populations; they continually met one another at court, and in the royal service in which the highest offices were reserved for Greeks. And so in the Hellenistic States old enmities and local differences melted away and counted for less.

One striking illustration of this tendency is to be found in the evolution of the Greek language. The kings of Macedon had from the fifth century onwards adopted Attic Greek as their official language, and this had important consequences, for it was through them and Alexander's successors that the Attic dialect spread right across the new countries which they conquered. But when it thus became the language of millions of men it was naturally modified, and lost some of its individual flavour and artistic qualities. Under the influence of Ionian and barbaric tongues it gradually evolved into the 'common language' (κοινή) which, because it was relatively easy to speak, spread throughout the Greek world east of the Adriatic as both a spoken and a literary language. In Sicily, however, there developed a Dorian κοινή, which Archimedes used and Theocritus conventionalised. These common languages displaced dialects, and are a

258

good example of that tendency towards uniformity which had taken the place of earlier separatism.

Moreover, the same events which were smoothing out differences between Greeks were also bringing the Greeks closer to other nations. It is true that Alexander's wonderful scheme, which had aimed at promoting a union between Greeks and Asiatics, was officially regarded as a failure. On the other hand a small minority of choice spirits continued to affirm the notion of Antisthenes and the Stoic philosophers that all men are born equal, and enriched the vocabulary with that splendid word κοσμοπολίτης, (cosmopolitan, or 'citizen of the universe'). It is also no less true that in the new Hellenistic world Greeks and barbarians were close neighbours, and from their contacts various mixtures and compounds were bound to arise.

These combinations developed from below. The celebrated savants of the Hellenistic epoch were not in general acquainted with non-Greek peoples and civilisations except very indirectly. It is curious to note that not one of them took the trouble to learn Persian or Aramaic, or Egyptian! But in the poorer quarters of Antioch, Alexandria, and Seleucia, and before long of Delos too, the 'melting-pot' was steadily at work, with consequences which from the moral and religious points of view were remarkable. The lower-class Greeks were able to take a close look at the gods of Asia Minor, Syria, and Egypt. Most remarkable of all was the growth of the new cult of Osiris (as vitalised by Ptolemy I) during the third century. In the name of Osiris-Apis or Serapis it spread throughout the Hellenic world. Devotees of the great goddesses of Syria and Phrygia also became numerous, and their worship was associated with that of the male gods with whom they were united or for whom they mourned in violent and symbolic rites. An emotional and mystical element crept into religious thought at its basic level and brought back into it notions of decay and renewal, of death and resurrection, which three centuries of intellectualism had almost succeeded in eliminating. These oriental religions, with their universal appeal and their acceptance of all kinds of worshippers whatever their origin, also helped considerably in loosening the ties which bound men to the city-state.

No doubt this religious evolution was a slow process. In the scientific sphere, however, the effects of changes due to the new state of affairs were felt more rapidly. Internationalism, the disappearance of local dialects, increasing ease of communication, all helped the development of the exact sciences. From this point of view, the Ancient World had no period more brilliant than the third century, when Ptolemy I founded the Museum at Alexandria, really an institute of scientific research. There Euclid gave shape and definite coherence to the geometric discoveries of previous centuries, and made of them the orderly structure which still serves as a basis for instruction. There Apollonius of Perga studied conic sections; and Archimedes, the greatest mathematician of antiquity, published his resounding discoveries in geometry – the approximate measurement of spherical surfaces and circumferences – in physics and in mechanics. Dissection was now authorised and practised in the medical schools – an important landmark in the history of anatomy.

In astronomy, not only was the roundness of the earth admitted to be a fact by most thinkers, but the calculations of Eratosthenes (and also of Dicaearchus) gave a reasonably exact figure for its circumference. Aristarchus of Samos boldly declared that this small earth rotates around an enormous sun, a declaration which, it must be admitted, caused almost as great a scandal as that of Galileo. Knowledge of the earth's shape, together with the discoveries and explorations resulting from Alexander's expedition, gave a great impetus to the study of geography, and enabled Eratosthenes to draw the first useful map of the known world.

Great historical events do not always call forth historians of genius to record them. In the slight fragments which have come down to us of the *Hellenica* in which Theopompus tried to continue Thucydides, and of his *Philippica* which he devoted to the reign of Philip of Macedonia, there is more bombast than sense of history, and a great deal of partiality. What is far more regrettable is that the memoirs written by Alexander's generals and officials such as Ptolemy, Callisthenes, Aristobulus, and Nearchus have largely disappeared, as well as those of Timaeus, which were concerned with the history of the western regions of Hellenism about which so little is known. Henceforward, history concerned itself with the whole field of human endeavour. Under the heading 'science of things written' it included the study of the literary output of the past.

Learned men of all nations found a marvellous instrument for this kind of work at Alexandria, where Ptolemy I had founded, early in the third century, a library which soon contained four hundred thousand scrolls representing, with duplicates, several thousand original works. Such a collection required, and at the same time facilitated, a vast output of editions and commentaries, in the production of which the directors of the library seem to have excelled. They had come from all quarters of the Hellenic world – Zenodotus of Ephesus, Aristophanes of Byzantium, Aristarchus of Samothrace, and others. Guided by their very acute literary sense, which was based on an astonishing erudition, they cleared up dubious renderings and established the texts of the great classics for a long period to come; what has survived of their notes has made a good starting-point for the work of modern criticism.

Generally speaking, progress in the sciences leads to increased specialisation. Yet at the opening of the Hellenistic period there appeared, for the last time in the history of Greek thought, a scholar who took all knowledge for his province. Aristotle (384-22), the child of a family of medical doctors at Stagira (one of the towns of Chalcidice where memories of the great Ionian tradition were still cherished) wrote a veritable 'Summa' of all the knowledge of his time. The works attributed to him, some of which seem merely notes taken at his lectures or collections of material for his courses, deal with physics, natural history, psychology, and moral philosophy, in addition to logic and what would today be called metaphysics. They bear witness to astonishingly wide reading and to well-organised effort, both individual and collective. But Aristotle's work is not so much a progress in thought as the end-product of the scientific labours of several generations. It demonstrates no new methods of investigation, but as so often in Greece, flashes of insight occur, side by side with errors which have weighed heavily upon the thought of the western world for many centuries.

The son of one of King Philip's doctors, Aristotle himself was Alexander's tutor and spent much of his life at Athens, first as one of Plato's disciples and then as director of a teaching establishment, the Lyceum, which was in competition with Plato's Academy. Yet this sagacious thinker quite failed to understand the meaning of events which were happening before his eyes. At a time when the framework of the Hellenic world was being burst asunder he still considered Greek and barbarian as two separate universes which could never communicate one with another. Nor could he imagine a Greece other than the old, out-of-date jumble of small city-states.

His disciples, inheriting the methods of the master, continued to give a scientific basis to their own teaching. Theophrastus, who directed the Lyceum from 322 to 287, was a naturalist and a psychologist. Elsewhere the separation between philosophy and science, which was first noticeable towards the end of the fifth century, grew wider. The Platonic Academy provided only the traditional abstract instruction, and in the third century came, to its detriment, under the influence of the Sceptics, who reconsidered the problems concerning the nature of knowledge, which had been investigated by the sixth century philosophers, only to arrive at a complete intellectual nihilism. All the subtleties of the Megarian school are mere word-play, and as philosophy lost touch with science it concerned itself more and more with moral questions. This was a change something like that which occurred at the beginning of the present century in favour of pragmatism. The chief aim henceforward seems to have been to determine man's 'chief good'. A return to nature (advocated by the Cynics) produced merely an inverted snobbery: while the School of Cyrene, cultivating ultimate and true pleasure through the exercise of intelligence and self-control, arrived only at the deepest pessimism.

At the end of the fourth century, however, two powerful personalities founded two schools of thought whose influence was to last as long as the ancient world itself. Epicurus was but a moderately good metaphysician, and such changes as he proposed in Democritus's atomic theory were not really improvements. But his lofty conception of what constitutes happiness, his freedom of thought as to the indifferent gods, and the quiet optimism he distilled from these notions assured the lasting success of his doctrine. Zeno began his speculations from a different angle, to reach very similar practical conclusions. Since the world is controlled by an intelligent will, enlightened conformity with its behests is man's chief good and is what constitutes virtue. These simple but noble doctrines, amid the moral confusion which accompanied the decline of the city-state, must have carried conviction to all those cultivated minds who felt the need for moral discipline, but were repelled by the mysticism of oriental religions. They remained the finest expression of the moral law of antiquity in the Graeco-Roman world until the end of paganism.

Theophrastus came from Lesbos; Zeno was only half-Greek, having been born in Cyprus to a Semitic father; Epicurus alone among the philosophers of the fourth and third centuries was of Athenian origin, and even he was born in the cleruchy of Samos. But every head of a school wished to teach at Athens. It was at Athens that both the Academy and the Lyceum remained, in spite of some difficulties caused for Aristotle and Theophrastus by their Macedonian allegiance. And it was at Athens, in his own garden, that Epicurus assembled his disciples; whilst Zeno met his under a porch (stoa) in the Agora – hence their name of Stoics. Thus took place its evolution from an imperial city and commercial centre to an admirable museum and a university town, to which generations of students flocked to follow courses not in the exact sciences or in philology, as at Alexandria, but in metaphysics and moral philosophy.

The arts, which formerly had a free, prosperous and proud city to nurture them, now atrophied. But before their final disappearance, one art at least shone with remarkable radiance. Nowhere else in the world perhaps, has a political crisis in a free country produced such brilliant orators as at Athens during the forty years preceding the Lamian war against Antipater. Trained in the school of forensic oratory by the lawyers of the previous generation, they had learned to adopt a realistic outlook, to use the arts of presentation and close argument, and a style that was flexible yet precise, all enlivened by such original temperaments as those of Hyperides, Aeschines, Demades, and Lycurgus. With Demosthenes his strong feelings, confused but always well-intended, disrupted the rules of the formal sentence as laid down by Isocrates, and made of it an oratorical wave that swells and then breaks, sweeping away all resistance and carrying all hearts along with it.

The Macedonian conquest cut off this race of great orators or reduced them to silence. Tragedy, already decadent at the beginning of the fourth century, continued its decline during the Hellenistic period and the public turned its back on an art-form which instead of renewing itself was content to produce frigid imitations. Comedy, on the other hand, took a new lease of life, and the process which had been begun in the fourth century now resulted in the so-called 'new comedy' for which Philemon and particularly Menander became renowned. Menander's romantic plots, his realistic characters sketched from everyday life and neatly differentiated, his sentimental conclusions, would not have been out of place in eighteenth century Europe. They were the product of an age of refinement which at this time still found its most perfect expression at Athens. It should be noted that it was at Athens and not in Alexandria that all the comic poets of the end of the fourth and of the third century lived and had their plays performed. Elsewhere, however, various other styles developed, more vulgar and to the point – parodies in Sicily and southern Italy (countries where special types of farce had previously existed) and miming displays in Sicily and at Alexandria, and short realistic sketches which had great comic verve.

The great choral lyric had disappeared. Attempts to revive the long epic poem produced only feeble and artificial effusions, but the new political and social conditions favoured the birth of new literary styles. In a great city like Alexandria, a royal residence and centre of scientific learning, an official and erudite poetry naturally developed. Most of its representative authors were learned men – librarians or scholars. Their productions – whether they were didactic poems, epigrams, hymns written to order, or brief epic extracts – all had the common characteristics, mythological and scientific erudition, wit, refinement, and cultivated artistry, which taken together comprise what is known as 'Alexandrianism'. However artificial the most celebrated productions of this period may seem to us today – the hymns of Callimachus for example – their success cannot be denied, nor the influence they were to have on the future development of poetry in the Graeco-Roman world.

Among a number of authors of somewhat similar and mediocre talent one original genius stands out: in the Idylls (or *Bucolics*) of Theocritus we hear a distant echo of the passionate lyric of the close of the fourth century; and amid his graceful and meretricious pastoral tales can be glimpsed a pleasant vision, not of nature's grandeur as seen by the lightning flashes of Homer or the old tragic authors, but at least of the rich countryside just outside Cos or Syracuse such as the refined town-dweller might be expected to enjoy.

In continental Greece the great municipal and Panhellenic sanctuaries were in decline. Delphi and Olympia were recovering with difficulty from the effects of the earthquakes and pillages of the fourth and third centuries. Only the shrine of Asclepius at Epidaurus showed, by the costliness and beauty of its buildings, the favour enjoyed by the gods of healing among the general public – a curious phenomenon in a period of great scientific progress! In the archipelago the kings of Macedon, Egypt, and Pergamum outrivalled each other in generosity to Delos which, for religious and commercial reasons, had now become a centre of influence of the greatest importance, and on which the Attalids and the Antigonids built and dedicated several beautiful porticoes in the latter part of the third century.

Above all, however, it was in the new Greek territories, in Asia Minor and Syria, that the great building enterprises around the temples of Apollo at Didyma and of Artemis at Ephesus were set up from the middle of the fourth century onwards, and equalled or surpassed the most colossal undertakings of the fifth century. Alongside these vast constructions, however, new outlets were being found for further activity. Everywhere a taste for comfort was finding expression, both private and public comfort, such as previous ages had never known. The new towns were built on regular plans: their colonnades and perspectives were the forerunners of the monotonous splendour of Graeco-Roman town-planning. Places of amusement became more numerous and better adapted to their purpose. Theatres in stone replaced the old wooden amphitheatres – the oldest perhaps being that at Athens, which Lycurgus did not complete until about 330 – stadia were built, palaestra and gymnasia for physical exercise, hydrotherapy, and elegant idling. Private luxury matched this public luxury: the finest Athenian houses of the fifth century would have seemed modest buildings beside those which were to be found in small provincial towns of Asia Minor such as Priene, or later on in the commercial quarter at Delos. With their interior peristyle around which rooms were cleverly planned, with all kinds of conveniences, and decorated with paintings and mosaics, these dwellings were forerunners of the Roman villa.

It is not surprising that in the prevailing conditions sculpture should have taken a new direction. Decorative sculpture on the grand scale was by no means dead in the fourth century. It showed its vitality – at Ephesus, at Magnesia-on-the-Maeander, at Tralles, and in the magnificent monument which Artemisia had erected to the memory of Mausolus – in works that were full of expression, true to nature, flexible in style, and which displayed the talents of Scopas and his school. Yet the plastic arts tended more and more towards the individual item, towards the isolated statue, in which a Praxiteles could exemplify his elegant exactitude. Some admirable anonymous works (such as the Victory of Samothrace or the Venus de Milo) were undoubtedly made in the late fourth or early third century, and it seems that they were always intended to be admired by themselves and at close quarters. Many statues of this period, moreover, were no longer idealised types but faithful and characteristic images of particular individuals. Lysippus was the official portraitist of the Macedonian court, and it is to the third century that several of the finest busts, formerly credited to Roman sculpture, must really be attributed. A similar change also took place in painting, where the easel-picture – genre-painting or portrait – replaced the mural.

The complexity and novelty of many aspects of the Hellenistic civilisation are obvious. From the strictly artistic point of view it is inferior to that of the fifth or the first half of the fourth century, and the exquisite flower then nurtured on the free soil of Attica, which was never to bloom again, may indeed be regretted. But the Hellenistic period marks the highest point reached in ancient times in the development of exact sciences and literary studies. Nor should it be forgotten that it was in the third century that the most estimable systems of morals known to antiquity were elaborated. The political disturbances which had so deeply shaken the foundations of the Greek world, far from bringing intellectual activity to a halt, had renewed it by giving to it forms that may have been less perfect but were certainly more varied, and every whit as fertile and fruitful.

XXXIII

QUARRELS BETWEEN KINGS:
QUARRELS BETWEEN LEAGUES OF CITIES

All the wisdom and skill of Antigonus, the philosopher-king, the pupil and friend of Zeno, were needed to restore Macedon to its former prosperity. It must be admitted that he had one trump card in his hand – the loyalty of the Macedonian people, who were accustomed to monarchy, and – once Alexander's family had been removed – could not do otherwise than accept the authority of the man who was both the son of Demetrius and (on his mother's side) the grandson of Antipater. Hence he had no need to fear internal difficulties. By enlisting into his army the Gauls who had stayed in Macedon he strengthened his forces, and so was able to remove some not very dangerous rivals and reconquer Thessaly. An agreement with Antiochus I guaranteed the tranquillity of his eastern frontier, but in 274 a serious happening almost brought ruin to the rejuvenated kingdom.

Pyrrhus had returned from the west bitterly incensed against the Greek rulers who had given him no help. Although he had failed in Italy, at least Macedon, which had once been in his possession, seemed to be his for the taking. The wise Antigonus was not a particularly good general, and in spite of his Gauls was completely defeated on two separate occasions and on his own ground. By the end of 274 he held only a few coastal towns, and the Greek cities in which he had maintained or re-established Macedonian garrisons deserted his cause. Several of them had even appealed to the king of Epirus, and considering that the conquest of Macedonia was as good as achieved, Pyrrhus crossed Aetolia and entered the Peloponnese, where Cleonymus, competing against his nephew Areus for the throne of Sparta, was promising Pyrrhus an enthusiastic welcome. But where Epaminondas had failed a century earlier Pyrrhus was not likely to succeed, especially as Sparta had been strongly fortified in 285. So after a useless and costly assault he had to retreat northwards, where Antigonus had marched to meet him.

Pyrrhus found the Macedonian troops near Argos, where they had been joined by a Spartan army, and when Antigonus avoided battle Pyrrhus tried to storm the town. Antigonus's son and Areus came to the rescue, and in the street fighting that ensued Pyrrhus was killed. This event entirely changed the situation. The Epirot army quitted the Peloponnese; Antigonus had no difficulty in retaking Macedon, and was then able to re-establish his authority in continental Greece. For this he had no need to reoccupy the whole country but merely to establish garrisons at a number of key points: Demetrias, Chalcis, the Piraeus, and Corinth. Elsewhere he was content to rely, whenever he could find one, on any government which was well-disposed towards Macedon. And as always happened when a foreign power tried to exercise authority over part of the Hellenic world, there sprang up all over the Peloponnese a number of petty local tyrants all devoted to Antigonus. A happy combination of circumstances and the persistence of its king seemed to have restored Macedon once again to the position that Philip II had won for it seventy years before.

There was, however, an important difference: Macedon was no longer the only powerful Hellenic state in the eastern Mediterranean, and although the Seleucids were inclined to direct their activities towards the south and east of their empire, the Ptolemies were clearly interested in what was happening in Europe. For a hundred and fifty years the main principle of their policy had been not to get too deeply involved themselves in Greek affairs but to prevent any other power obtaining a preponderant influence over them. This is the reason why they supported any city or state capable of opposing Macedon – Sparta especially, but also Athens and possibly Pyrrhus. No doubt the death of the king of Epirus had been a severe blow to Ptolemy II, and if he had not reacted immediately it was because his hands were fully occupied at the moment with difficulties nearer home. His half-brother, Magas, governor of Cyrene, had recently rebelled against him in 274, had come within two days' march of Alexandria, and had only been halted by rioting and great disorder in Cyrenaica. Moreover, Antiochus was still resentful at seeing the Egyptians masters of Cilicia and southern Syria (Coele Syria or Hollow Syria) not to mention other territories in Asia Minor – Lycia, Halicarnassus, Samos – which had become possessions of the Lagids by the marriage of Arsinoë, widow of Lysimachus, to her brother Ptolemy II according to the custom of the country. In 274 war broke out between the kings of Egypt and Syria.

Antiochus was, however, in no position to wage a war of conquest. His vast amorphous empire seemed to be on the verge of disintegration. On its borders various dynasties were setting themselves up in Cappadocia, in Pontus, in Bithynia, and Armenia, and acknowledging only the nominal overlordship of the Seleucids. Even deep in Asia Minor he was having trouble. One of the hordes of Galatae, who had invaded Greece in 279, had crossed the Hellespont and ravaged the coasts of Aeolis and Ionia. About 275 Antiochus defeated them in a battle which earned him the title of 'Soter' (Saviour), but whose results were by no means final. The Gauls installed themselves in Upper Phrygia, a region which was to take the name of Galatia, set up a federal state there which the Seleucids had to tolerate right in the midst of their empire, and continued for nearly half a century to terrorise the Greek towns and exact tribute from them. In these conditions, then, it is easy to understand why hostilities between Ptolemy II and Antiochus did not last very long. In 272 Antiochus agreed to recognise Egyptian suzerainty over Coele Syria.

This freed Ptolemy to take a hand in Greek affairs. He incited Alexander, king of Epirus (the son of Pyrrhus) to attack Macedon with the aid of Sparta, where King Areus felt himself called upon to become one of the great monarchs of the age, and was trying to revive the Peloponnesian League for his own benefit – and of Athens where the patriot party, with the stoic Chremonides at its head, thought they could put back the clock a hundred years, and were still not resigned to the presence of a Macedonian garrison in the Piraeus. Once again the old rival cities found themselves united in defence of Greek liberties.

Antigonus made a swift riposte, however. In 265 he laid siege to Athens. The following year he defeated the Spartans near Corinth, in which battle Areus was killed. Demetrius the son of Antigonus inflicted a severe defeat on Alexander of Epirus, who was even expelled for several months from his own kingdom in consequence. In 262 the Spartan army was again beaten, this time by Aristodemus, tyrant of Megalopolis and the ally of Antigonus. The inaction of the Egyptian fleet must be noted, though it is hard to understand, for in spite of being moored in the Saronic Gulf it was not able even to relieve Athens, which was forced to capitulate in 262-1. Reprisals were not exacted, but the full weight of Macedonian authority fell henceforth on the city, and garrisons were installed not only in the Piraeus, but in Athens itself and on Cape Sunium. Her democratic constitution was revised, and Athens lost even the right to mint her own coins – a symbol of the economic decline which threatened to follow her political downfall.

This war, wrongly named after Chremonides, for the Athenian patriot had been merely a tool of Ptolemaic diplomacy, thus ended in the collapse of the anti-Macedonian coalition. Now a new combination was contrived against Egypt. Antiochus had held aloof from these latest events in Europe since his position in Asia continued to deteriorate. In Mysia, Philetaerus, who had formerly been appointed by Lysimachus to take charge of the citadel at Pergamum and the large monetary reserves accumulated there, had quietly succeeded in making this strong-point the centre of a small principality, nominally subject to the Seleucids but really independent. After his death his nephew Eumenes continued the same policy of discreet expansion, and by the time Antiochus had decided to limit the encroachments of this troublesome vassal it was too late. In 262 Antiochus I was beaten near Sardis by the

Pergamene dynasty and died either in the battle or soon afterwards.

His son, Antiochus II, inherited a kingdom in decomposition. Wisdom would have advised him to conclude an alliance with the most militarily powerful state in the Hellenic world – Macedon – and this he seems to have done in 259. Strengthened by this support, he was able to retake the Ionian coast towns – Ephesus and Miletus – where Ptolemy had installed governors of his own, and perhaps also Samos for a time, and to threaten Coele Syria once more.

During this time diplomatic and matrimonial negotiations had placed Demetrius (the Handsome), half-brother of Antigonus, on the throne of Cyrene. In this coalition aimed at encircling Ptolemy, the weak spot was still the Seleucid, whose military resources were decidedly inadequate. His pressure upon Syria seems to have been unavailing. At the same time Demetrius was assassinated at Cyrene as the result of a harem intrigue.

Matters in Europe also made Antigonus anxious. In Epirus, Alexander had regained his throne, while in Greece itself the discontent in the con-quered cities – particularly in Athens – was liable to cause trouble. He was also very conscious of what had all along been his chief weakness. His conflict with Ptolemy (as has been said of a modern struggle) was that of a bear with a whale: Egypt had a rather poor army, but Macedon, since the disappearance of Demetrius Poliorcetes, had no fleet at all. Antigonus decided to alter this state of affairs, and it appears that in 258 a Macedonian squadron was cruising in the Aegean, and defeated the Egyptian fleet at Cos.

Nevertheless, the dissolution of the Asiatic Empire went on apace. About 255 Diodotus the satrap of Bactria turned his province into an inde-pendent princedom. To the south-east of the Caspian Sea, the land of the Parthians, which was to become so great a threat to successive masters of the Euphrates line whether Seleucid or Romans, detached itself from the Empire. To preserve what was left to him of his oriental provinces, Antiochus bowed to the necessity of making peace with Ptolemy, and according to diplomatic usage this had to be confirmed by a marriage; so in 252 Antiochus took to wife Berenice, the much-disputed daughter of Ptolemy. But Antiochus II was already married to Laodice, his half-sister. There ensued one of those harem quarrels so frequent in Macedon-ian families which had adopted oriental customs. The result was that after the death of Antiochus, Berenice and her son were assassinated in 246. The son of Antiochus II and Laodice, who thus became Seleucus II, was only a young man.

The same year old Ptolemy II Philadelphus died in Egypt. His son, Ptolemy III, the most energetic of the Lagid dynasty, was not the man to leave his sister's murderer unpunished. Syria was invaded and Ptolemy penetrated as far as Antioch, and perhaps much further towards the east, so that the Seleucid kingdom seemed to be doomed. But apart from some obscure internal difficulties which recalled Ptolemy to Egypt, the Macedonian alliance served Seleucus well, for there is little doubt that about 245, in a second naval battle, Antigonus defeated the Egyptian fleet at Andros. In the end a new treaty, concluded in 241, returned northern Syria to Seleucus but gave Ptolemy, with possession of Ephesus and Seleucia-Pieria at the Gates of Antioch, a ready-made opening for some future attack. Antigonus was in a dominant position, and had become the arbiter of Greek destinies. At Delos, from 258 onwards, noble buildings – the pious foundations of the King of Macedon and of his wife Stratonice – bear witness to his fame in the Cyclades, from which Ptolemaic influence had been ousted.

Against all expectation it was in European Greece that the main obstacles to his authority soon appeared. For several years the spirit of federalism, which had previously demonstrated its existence but always in a provisional manner, had reasserted itself. This time the lead was to come from the least civilised regions of Greece. The mountain tribes of Aetolia, who had hitherto played only a modest part, had during the fourth century grouped themselves into a community whose independence Alexander and his successors had been obliged to respect. Its resistance to the Celtic invasion in 278 had won it great popularity in Greece, and an ever-growing influence on the Amphictyonic Council of Delphi, in which the kings of Macedon since Philip had always had the ruling voice, but which now became an instrument of Aetolian policy. By the middle of the third century a series of additions had made this League an important power, and had extended its authority over most of central Greece from the Malian Gulf to the Gulf of Corinth.

The inception of the Achaean League was rather more modest. Several small towns on the north coast of the Peloponnese had reconstituted an ancient federation which had always been self-effacing, and their new coalition seemed likely to vegetate too. But in 251 Aratus freed his native state Sicyon from its tyrant, and affiliated the city to this League, which thereupon became the centre of all Peloponnesian aspirations towards liberty.

In each of these leagues, finance and the army were common concerns. They also contrived to avoid what had formerly been the besetting sin of both the Athenian and Boeotian Leagues – the supremacy claimed by one of the participating cities. Each city was given a certain number of votes in the Council and Assembly, which met once a year and decided all questions whether of external policy or disputes between member-cities. A *strategos* was head of the executive body and led the army in time of war. Never since the beginning of Greek history had the federal principle been better applied: and so, since about the middle of the third century, the great powers had been obliged to reckon with the Aetolian and Achaean Leagues.

At first Antigonus does not seem to have realised the importance of these Leagues. He thought he had nothing to fear from the Aetolians since he was their ally, and when their confederation spread across central Greece he put no obstacle in its way. In the Peloponnese, too, he felt quite secure, for he had recently retaken possession of the citadel of Acro-Corinth, which a revolt of its governor had for several years withdrawn from his control. Antigonus therefore left Sicyon in the hands of the Achaeans, who soon entrusted the direction of their League to Aratus. Indeed the new state might well prove useful to him. Together with the Arcadian League which had been provisionally regrouped, had they not just inflicted a severe defeat on Sparta, the determined enemy of Macedon? No doubt Antigonus was unaware that Aratus was negotiating with Ptolemy, from whom he had received subsidies, but in 243 another bold stroke by Aratus left him with no illusions. Thanks to the treachery of part of its Macedonian garrison, Aratus seized the Acro-Corinth. This had a very considerable moral effect: the towns of the isthmus joined the League and Antigonus lost the key to the Peloponnese.

This was the moment to make use of his Aetolian allies. In 241 their army crossed the isthmus, but was defeated near Corinth. A second expedition two or three years later, against Sparta, also came to nothing. The authority and reputation of Aratus south of the isthmus remained intact. When he died in 239 the aged Antigonus left to his son, Demetrius, a position much less splendid for Macedon than that which he thought he had in 250. Cyrene and some of the Cyclades had fallen once more into Egyptian hands; the Peloponnese was slipping from his grasp; in 235 a part of Arcadia joined the Achaean League, while another part with Megalopolis went to the Aetolian League. Finally, by a diplomatic manoeuvre which would have changed the fate of Greece had it led to a durable result, Aratus concluded a treaty of alliance with the Aetolians. Central Greece and the major part of the Peloponnese thus formed a vast group of federations all inimical to Macedon. A serious defeat which Demetrius inflicted on the Achaeans had no conclusive results.

In 234 a revolution changed Epirus, one of the oldest monarchies in the Greek world, into a republic. Its unity was not proof against such a shock and it broke into two, the northern half forming a federation which then made a treaty of alliance with the pirate-state of Illyria, while the southern and more civilised half entered the Aetolian League.

In 229 Demetrius died after a battle against his warlike northern neighbours the Dardanians, leaving a son aged nine years. The regency was entrusted to the late king's nearest relative – Antigonus the son of that Demetrius (the Handsome) who had been assassinated at Cyrene. But no one could deflect the course of events, which had now become inevitable.

In 230-29 Argos joined the Achaean League. The following year the commander of the Macedonian garrison at the Piraeus handed the place over to the Athenians, who, however, refused to enter the League even though Aratus had collaborated in freeing the Piraeus. Antigonus now no longer held any territory south of Olympus except part of Euboea.

For different reasons the great Asiatic monarchy, too, seemed to be in absolute decline. Scarcely had the peace of 241 safeguarded its tranquillity on the Egyptian side than a quarrel broke out between Seleucus II and his brother Antiochus Hierax – after their unhappy attempt at a joint regency – which was to last for a decade. The petty kings of the adjacent countries – Pontus, Cappadocia, and Bithynia – seem to have added fuel to the fire of conflict. Seleucus II of Pergamum took part against Antiochus, who defeated his brother at Ancyra and went on to devastate Asia Minor, and several times defeated his brother's bands of Galatae (229-8). Antiochus finally surrendered himself to Ptolemy III. Although kept under close watch at Alexandria he escaped and went to fight in Thrace in 227, where he was killed.

Seleucus II died the following year. The war which he had been forced to wage against his brother had prevented his having any chance to consolidate his tottering empire. An expedition he had undertaken in 235 in the east had failed to retake either Bactria or Parthia for him. In Asia Minor Attalus I, the heir of Eumenes of Pergamum, had beaten the Gauls first by themselves and afterwards in association with Antiochus Hierax in a series of victories between 240 and 228, which definitely freed him from all obligation to pay tribute to the barbarians, authorised him to take for himself the title of king, and extended his rule over the greater part of Asia Minor. With the intention of retaking this province the son of Seleucus II crossed the Taurus mountains but was assassinated there, leaving the throne to his brother Antiochus III, a young man of eighteen.

The Seleucid Empire, shorn of its finest provinces and reduced to Syria and Mesopotamia, was now, like Macedon, in the hands of an extremely young man. While Egypt remained intact, thanks to its special situation, its homogeneous population, and the prudent policies of its kings, in Greece the republican ideal revived in a federal form, and in Asia quite other causes of disintegration seemed to threaten the two greatest monarchies of the Hellenic world with speedy collapse.

XXXIV

THE REBUILDING OF THE GREAT
MONARCHIES: FIRST CONTACTS WITH ROME

The situation in Greece to the south of Thermopylae had not been so favourable for many a year. Large groups of states had been built up, and this might well have been the first step towards a general federation. As to foreign affairs, Egypt showed no desire for conquests in Europe; the Seleucid Empire was falling to pieces; Macedonia had been driven back inside her old frontiers of the year 350. But separatist tendencies were again setting the Greek cities one against another, and the result of their quarrels proved to be the restoration of the Macedonian hegemony until such time as there appeared a power altogether more redoubtable than Macedon.

It was Sparta that disturbed the peace of the Peloponnese. This city was suffering from an internal malaise which grew steadily worse. The fall in the number of citizens with full rights, and the concentration of landed property in a few hands, caused a condition of instability from which the great land-owners, weighed down with mortgages, themselves suffered. With wide domains poorly cultivated, with a complicated network of debts, with a sluggish commerce and monetary circulation, Sparta was in the same sort of situation that Athens had experienced three centuries earlier, and the reforms which had been beneficial for Athens in Solon's day began to appear opportune to Sparta in the year 250 – all the more so since great moral distress accompanied this social disequilibrium, in a city where the old social framework based on discipline and public spirit had long ago broken down.

The young king Agis, indoctrinated by his cousin Agesilaus and their friend the ephor Lysander, persuaded the Council to approve a scheme by which mortgages were to be cancelled, the land-owners being bound in return to share out a part of their estates among the dispossessed. At the same time the number of citizens with full rights was to be increased. The second king, Leonidas, was opposed to reform and was banished; re-calcitrant ephors were removed from office, and at least the first part of the programme – the cancellation of mortgages – was carried out in 242. But the landless labourers waited in vain for the promised redistribution of land, and this was the first cause of discontent.

Moreover, Agis forfeited popular esteem: his foreign policy, based on an understanding with the Achaeans, was unpopular and became much more so in 241 when an army, led by the young king to help the League's troops to repulse the Aetolians, was very unceremoniously dismissed by Aratus, who mistrusted the spirit then animating the Spartans. On his return Agis was overwhelmed by violent opposition; Leonidas was recalled from exile, Agesilaus had to fly the country, and Agis was imprisoned, tried, and executed.

But the idea of reform was in the air. Ten years later Cleomenes, who had been king since 235, took up the scheme again and carried it through. He realised, however, that reform at Sparta could only be accomplished by someone who had already acquired considerable prestige by his foreign policy, so he decided to accompany reform by the re-establishment of Spartan authority in the Peloponnese. From 229 he began making skirmishes against the Achaeans, and this soon developed into open war. A serious defect was then revealed in the League's constitution. The *strategos*, the political head of the state, was also supreme commander of the armed forces in time of war. But this arrangement, which had been abandoned by all the great Greek cities in the fourth century, was incompatible with the complexity of modern warfare. Moreover Aratus was only a mediocre general. A first repulse in the spring of 227 was followed in the autumn of the same year by his defeat under the walls of Megalopolis. Although the main cause of this disaster was the undisciplined conduct during the battle of Lydiades, who was a rival of Aratus for leadership of the League, Aratus's reputation was tarnished.

Cleomenes could now risk carrying out his reform. On his return from Arcadia he had the ephors in office executed, banished eighty citizens who opposed his plan, and announced to the Assembly the re-establishment of the 'Constitution of Lycurgus'. The sharing out of lands was really accomplished, four thousand *Perioikoi* became citizens with full rights, and even the system of common meals, with the frugal menu which tradition attributed to Lycurgus, was brought back into use.

The repercussions of such events throughout the Peloponnese can be imagined. The revolutionary enthusiasm which was inspiring the old city made it redoubtable once again, and when its army had been reinforced by the influx of the new citizens Cleomenes reorganised it on up-to-date lines, that is to say after the Macedonian model. And since Egypt's traditional policy was not to interfere directly in Greek affairs, but to support all enemies of Macedon, Cleomenes benefitted by valuable subsidies from Ptolemy III.

The Achaeans were naturally perturbed, and a fresh defeat decided them to open negotiations. But Cleomenes demanded nothing less than complete control of the League, which would soon have meant the virtual restoration of the old Peloponnesian League under heavy Spartan domination. Nevertheless a majority was prepared to accept this. Aratus, however, had devoted his whole life to building up the League, and rather than see it disappear in this way he preferred to ask for help from the very power at whose expense the League had been formed – from Macedon! This was the only source of help on which he could count. Naturally it would be of no use to appeal to Ptolemy; relations with the Aetolians had been strained for several years; the sovereigns of Asia had no interest whatever in the Peloponnese. Aratus has been reproached for having brought the barbarians back into Greece, but the Macedon of the end of the third century was a much more civilised state than Sparta, which had so abruptly passed from a backward régime to a revolutionary one. Aratus hoped that under the hegemony of a distant Macedon the League would have the chance to reform itself in the expectation of better days to come.

It so happened that Antigonus Doson was a remarkably intelligent and energetic ruler. He had recently cleared all northern Macedon of the Dardanians, and he had made sure of peace with the Aetolians, though at the price of part of Thessaly. He listened without recriminations to the proposals which Aratus made to him, and asked one thing only in return for his help – Corinth and its citadel. It would have been a hard bargain for the League to give up such an important position if Cleomenes, with whom negotiations had meanwhile been broken off, had not captured first Argos and then Corinth itself between 226 and 224. The Achaeans agreed therefore to accept Antigonus Doson's terms, and he immediately put an army of twenty thousand men into the field. Cleomenes held the isthmus, but since he was threatened in the rear by the Achaean army he had to abandon Corinth (where Antigonus promptly re-established a garrison) and retreated into the Peloponnese. Antigonus pursued him through Argolis and Arcadia.

The lateness of the season put an end to military operations, but not to the diplomatic activity of Antigonus, who persuaded the League at their Assembly in the autumn of 224 to participate in a vast 'General Alliance' which, along with Macedon, included several Greek federations: the Boeotians, Phocians, Thessalians, Epirots, and Acarnanians. It was a re-construction – minus Athens – of the old League of Corinth, but with the difference that Macedon was now confronted, not with a dust of cities, but with imposing Leagues of whose wishes her king was compelled to take notice. In three years Antigonus Doson had reorganised for himself a position in Greece scarcely inferior from a material point of view, and morally superior to that of Antigonus Gonatas.

From now on, Cleomenes was isolated in the Peloponnese. Egyptian policy did not usually support the vanquished, and Ptolemy cut off his subsidies. In the spring of 222 Antigonus marched into Laconia. There

Cleomenes and his twenty thousand men, who were barring the road in the Œnas valley, were crushingly defeated by the combined armies of Macedon and the Achaeans, under the command of Antigonus, in spite of the advantage of their prepared position at Sellasia. For Cleomenes the game was up, and after crossing Sparta closely pursued by Antigonus he fled to Egypt. His reforms were annulled. Sparta was compelled to join the new League organised by Antigonus. In this adventure Sparta had lost what little reputation she still possessed, and the battle of Sellasia marked the last turning point in her history. With Cleomenes, royalty as Sparta had known it ever since her origin disappeared. Lycurgus who took the place of the unlucky reformer was not even related to the royal family. He was able to dispose of his colleague Agesipolis, and in future Sparta was governed by a series of tyrants: Lycurgus, Machanidas, and Nabis who seem to have been not devoid of military talent, but who could not provide the Peloponnese with any policy more advanced than that of bandit chieftains. Under their rule Sparta, with the small territory to which she was reduced, now represented nothing more than yet another element of confusion and discord.

But Antigonus was destined not to see the results of his victory. Setting out northward to check another invasion by the Dardanians he fell ill and died after the campaign. His death was the signal for another great conflict. The Aetolians had not wished to join the General Alliance of Antigonus. Their warlike and domineering nature was ill-suited to a peaceful Greece in which Macedon held first place and the Achaeans the second. And so in 220 an Aetolian detachment entered the Peloponnese and invaded Messenia. Having for many years stayed aloof from all quarrels and alliances, Messenia now had to abandon her isolation and ask the Achaeans for help. Aratus marched to intercept the Aetolians, who had completed their raid and were returning through the isthmus. He was soundly beaten. A second invasion by the Aetolians was left unpunished, and caused an open breach between the two Leagues. Sparta joined the Aetolians. For some months everyone expected the return of Cleomenes, but the ex-king had not been an altogether satisfactory guest of the Egyptians. Ptolemy III had welcomed him, but Ptolemy IV had him closely guarded, and after an unsuccessful attempt to escape Cleomenes committed suicide. His death did not prevent a revival of the anti-Macedonian party in Sparta. The monarchy, suppressed after the battle of Sellasia, was re-established, and in 219 Lycurgus invaded Argolis.

Until then the authority of Macedon had remained ineffective. The young King Philip, only seventeen years old, and the counsellors whom the dying Antigonus had appointed to protect him, were not anxious to intervene in a war in Greece at a time when the Romans were establishing themselves in Illyria, and when the great struggle which was imminent between Rome and Carthage was presenting the west with such serious problems. A Macedonian expedition into the Peloponnese in 220 had failed to achieve results. In 219 Philip had marched into Aetolia, but had quickly been recalled home by an Aetolian and Dardanian invasion of Macedon.

But Philip was soon to display military qualities that no one had suspected. In the depths of the winter of 219-18, he appeared in the Peloponnese at the head of an army of six thousand men and defeated Aetolian contingents. In the spring of 218 he crossed the Gulf of Corinth and penetrated into Aetolia as far as Thermum, the League's sanctuary. A few days later, to everyone's astonishment, he was back in the Peloponnese and had advanced on Sparta. Returning to Macedon in the following year he cleared the north of his country of Dardanians, and then marched once more against the Aetolians and took Phthiotis from them. The Aetolians had opposed these lightning campaigns with nothing but vain marching, so when the men of Rhodes and Chios, who needed a peaceful Greece in which to carry on their trading and who had already begun to play the part of mediators which they were to continue for the next half-century, proposed their good offices in agreement with Ptolemy, the Aetolians agreed to enter into negotiations with Philip.

He, for his part, had every reason to come to an arrangement of affairs in Greece so that he would be free to attend to events in the war which had now broken out between Rome and Carthage. The Assembly of the Aetolian League, meeting at Naupactus in 217, agreed with Philip and Aratus to return to the *status quo*. In short, they agreed to the Macedonian hegemony, strengthened by additional footholds in Phthiotis and the Peloponnese, from which the Aetolians were completely excluded. The power of Macedon was extended even beyond continental Greece. In Crete, which for so long had kept clear of Hellenic affairs, several towns, growing tired of the continual quarrels in which they had worn themselves out for so many years, had asked for a Macedonian force to be sent there and had entered the Grand Alliance. The organisation devised by Antigonus Doson had come victoriously through the tests of a change of sovereign and a great war.

It was a young man, too, who had restored the authority of the Seleucids in the east. At the accession of Antiochus III, Asia Minor was in the hands of Attalus of Pergamum; at the very heart of the kingdom the Egyptian enclave, Seleucia Pieria, offered a direct threat to Antioch the capital; in the east the empire was crumbling away, for the Satrap of Media, Molon, had rebelled and was making the borderland provinces into an independent kingdom. Achaeus, the king's cousin and a good soldier, had been able early in the reign to recapture the territories in Asia Minor taken by Attalus; but Antiochus, ill advised by his guardian Hermeias, had undertaken an expedition into Coele Syria which produced no results, while his lieutenants were being beaten in Media and had allowed Molon to advance into Mesopotamia.

In 221 the young king took charge of operations himself and marched against Molon, who was defeated and killed. But difficulties now supervened in the west, where Achaeus had suddenly declared himself king of Asia Minor. The influence of Egyptian diplomacy was obvious in this unexpected rebellion, and not without good reason Antiochus decided to turn against Egypt. Circumstances favoured his plan: Ptolemy III had just died, and palace intrigues, which cost the Queen-Mother her life, had followed the accession of Ptolemy IV. Moreover, after capturing Seleucia, at the moment when he was about to invade Coele Syria, Antiochus received offers of service from its governor, the Aetolian Theodotus who had just revolted against the government at Alexandria. By the end of 219 Antiochus was master of the whole country. Ptolemy and his minister, Sosibius, began negotiations and dragged them out while they prepared great contingents, half native troops, half Greeks, armed in the Macedonian fashion and organised by the best mercenary chieftains of the day. In 217 the armies of Ptolemy and Antiochus met at Raphia, south of Gaza. In spite of a brilliant cavalry charge by Antiochus, the Egyptian infantry, which was more numerous, much more effective, and more homogeneous, crushed the motley Asian battalions. Coele Syria once again was lost to Antiochus, and from this tremendous effort his only gain was Seleucia, which was granted to him by a peace treaty now hastily concluded with Ptolemy.

At least he could now turn his attention to Achaeus, who had been held in check during these last two years by Attalus and by Prusias, king of Bithynia. Besieged in the citadel of Sardis, the rebel prince was betrayed and tortured to death. Asia Minor was reconquered, the kingdom of Pergamum was considerably reduced in 213, in spite of territorial concessions to which Antiochus agreed as payment for the help Attalus had given.

The time had now come to make the royal power felt once again in those provinces to the north and east, which half a century of internal dissensions and apathy had allowed to detach themselves from the empire. In 211 Antiochus compelled the king of Armenia to acknowledge his authority. From 210 to 205 a great expedition, details of which are not well known but which recalled by its duration and line of march that which Alexander had undertaken a hundred and twenty years earlier, enabled him to impose his overlordship on the kings of Parthia and on the Bactrian dynasty whose kingdom proved to be an outpost of Hellenism for the next century and a half, and extended its influence and incursions as far as the Ganges basin. It is true that each of these kings kept his crown and his royal status, but at last the most distant provinces of the Empire of

Seleucus had seen the victorious passage of the armies of his great-grand-son. The Rajahs of the Punjab had renewed relations with him, and Antiochus could henceforth consider himself truly the successor of Alexander and of the great Achaemenid kings whose title he now assumed. Greece had followed sympathetically the course of this triumphant expedition by a sovereign whose courage, youthful energy, and vast territories seemed such as to qualify him soon to become master of the fate of the Mediterranean world.

But a new power was about to intervene in Greek affairs. Rome had hitherto shown little curiosity about events in the orient. No doubt the incursions of Pyrrhus had made plain to the Senate the power of Hellenistic monarchs, the bravery and organisation of their troops, and the daring and initiative of their rulers. But Rome was chiefly preoccupied with what was happening in the western Mediterranean, and was neither well-informed about Greek events nor disposed to meddle with them. No text worth serious consideration, no authentic document, supports a belief in any political or diplomatic activity by Rome to the east of the Adriatic before the late third century. A series of events and their consequences were now, however, to bring about her intervention in eastern affairs almost against her will.

The decline of Greek naval strength, as always in the Mediterranean when the coastal states were no longer in a position to police her shores, had encouraged the growth of piracy almost everywhere, and nowhere more than in the Adriatic, where the kingdom of Illyria – much enlarged since the decadence of Epirus – was practically living on pillage. Her light craft appeared as far away as Laconia, and the towns of the Italian shore, whose commerce was naturally directed towards the east, found their trade being completely disrupted by the Illyrian corsairs. They appealed for help to Rome.

Mistress of the whole of southern Italy since 266, a great maritime power ever since the Carthaginian menace had compelled her to build herself a battle-fleet, Rome could not afford to ignore these complaints. She decided in 230 to send an embassy to Illyria, but Queen Teuta had a legate assassinated, and the piracies continued worse than ever. Corcyra was taken, Epidamnus besieged, and when the Aetolian and Achaean fleets went to its rescue they were beaten at Paxos. Finally an energetic intervention replied effectively to all these provocations. In 229 a naval expedition, commanded by the consuls in office, relieved Epidamnus and recaptured Corcyra; the Illyrian barques were no match for Roman quinqueremes, and Teuta sued for peace. Illyria had to give up all her possessions in the southern Adriatic and agree never again to send ships there. A small rival state was set up on her flank with Demetrius of

Pharos in charge, and Rome extended her protection over all the Greek cities of the eastern coast from Issa down to Corcyra.

There is no indication that in imposing these conditions the Senate had any intention of introducing a policy of conquest in the east; the sole object was to put down piracy on the high seas; but beyond Illyria there lay Greece, disturbed by the notion that western barbarians should be extending their protectorate across the Adriatic. Macedon in particular was much displeased at seeing a foreign influence becoming paramount over Illyria, a country which Philip, Alexander, and the early Antigonids had always considered a dependency of their own kingdom. Antigonus Doson, and then Philip, succeeded in inducing Demetrius of Pharos to join their alliance, and when in 219 he renewed Queen Teuta's piratical activities and the Romans in a short, brilliant campaign suppressed his kingdom, it was with Philip that he took refuge. Subsequently in 216 Philip made his attitude quite plain by invading Illyria, whence he was only dislodged by the appearance of a Roman flotilla. Finally, when in 216 the battle of Cannae seemed to put the very existence of Rome in jeopardy, he hastened to conclude with Hannibal an offensive and defensive alliance which was intended to ensure the eradication of Roman influence east of the Adriatic.

Before coming really to grips with Rome, however, Philip needed to secure his rear. He had an uneasy feeling that Aetolia and Sparta were still unresigned to the terms of the Peace of Naupactus, and would be ready to take advantage of his absence to disturb Greece once more. This was why in 215 and in 214 he invaded the Peloponnese, his objective being to seize Mount Ithome, which he thought would give him command over all the south-west of the peninsula. These expeditions, which were disgraced by frightful ravages, failed in their object and merely served to anger the Achaeans and to unite against him the Aetolians, Spartiates, Messenians, and Eleans. This coalition received an unexpected addition. Attalus of Pergamum, seeing his Asiatic ambitions ruined by the activities of Antiochus, turned hopefully towards the west, to Thrace and the archipelago. In this direction he had everything to gain from weakening Macedon, so he became an ally of the Aetolians.

The Romans at first had no thought of profiting by this situation. By a lucky chance they came to know of the existence of the treaty arranged between Philip and Hannibal. They also knew that in 214 Philip and his fleet had been expecting the arrival of a Carthaginian fleet in Illyria, and with it the chance to cross over into Italy, and that only the arrival of a Roman naval division had foiled these plans. But it was not until 212 that a clever general, the praetor Marcus Laevinus, took it upon himself to conclude a treaty with the Aetolians which secured for the confederates the support of the Roman fleet. Thus the war between Rome and Carthage developed into a 'World War', in which states in Africa, Italy,

Greece, and Asia all took part; and so the Romans found themselves directly engaged in an oriental conflict.

The confederates made no direct attack on Macedon. The Aetolian troops, whose discipline and organisation were certainly not first-rate, could scarcely hope to defeat on its own ground an army which had lost none of its old reputation and whose victories at Sellasia and in Philip's recent campaigns had shown again and again its bravery and tactical skill. Nor did the Romans wish to become too deeply engaged or to deprive Philip of his kingdom, but merely to distract his attention from Italy. Hence it was in Illyria, in the Adriatic islands, and in Acarnania that the Aetolians and the Roman fleet proceeded to harass Philip's subjects. From 210 the war was extended to central Greece, where the Roman squadron captured Aegina, and into the Peloponnese where the Achaeans, in spite of everything, were still faithful to their Macedonian ally. Philip was indefatigable, parrying blows from whatever direction they came, in Illyria, in Euboea, or in Achaea. But his army was being worn down, and his encumbered finances were insufficient to allow him to build anything but a poor fleet compared with those of Rome or of Attalus, which retained command of the seas and made his movements difficult. At the instigation of the confederates, too, the ever-present threat from the northern barbarians (Dardanians and others), brought renewed pressure to bear on Macedon, and recalled Philip home when he should have been busy in the south.

But the whole situation was about to change again. In the autumn of 208 Attalus had to return to Asia to meet an invasion by Prusias, king of Bithynia: and in 207 the threat of Hasdrubal's army, which had come to join his brother Hannibal's in Italy, after marching through Spain and Gaul, decided the Senate to recall their raiding-parties and the Roman fleet from Greece.

The Aetolians and their allies thus found themselves thrown entirely on their own resources to face Philip and the Achaeans. This was also the moment when an energetic leader was at last to give the Achaean League that military organisation which hitherto it had lacked. Aratus had died in 213, a disappointed man, since he had seen Philip treating the League as a subject rather than an ally, and his own family dishonoured by the king's caprices. In 208 the Achaeans chose as their *strategos* Philopoemen of Megalopolis, who had distinguished himself at Sellasia by his courage and his tactical skill. Like Aratus, he intended to remain faithful to the Macedonian alliance, but he had the independent and complementary idea of creating an Achaean army which everyone, including Philip, would have to reckon with. By arousing in his fellow citizens an enthusiasm for military matters, by inspiring the soldiery with a truly national spirit and by arming them with better weapons, he raised for the League a splendid army of fifteen to twenty thousand men which was soon to prove its mettle.

The Spartans had seized Tegea and ravaged the district around Megalopolis. Philopoemen defeated them convincingly and advanced as far as Sparta. This victory cut off the Aetolians from their allies in the Peloponnese, and isolated them. They were tired of war and particularly disgusted by the way in which the Romans had abandoned them, and they hastened to conclude a separate peace with Philip and the Achaeans, which turned out to be the prelude to a general settlement. Ever since 206 various neutrals, especially the Rhodians, had been trying to reconcile the belligerents. In 205 the Epirots arranged on their own territory at Phoenice a conference at which the Roman proconsul Sempronius Tuditanus met Philip. The Romans were inclined to come to an agreement. They had retaken Tarentum, which could otherwise have been a port of disembarkation for an invading Macedonian army. They had defeated Hasdrubal at the battle of the river Metaurus. Henceforth it was impossible for Philip to join forces with Hannibal, and the Romans considered that they no longer needed to have any anxiety about Macedonian and Greek affairs. While retaining most of what they had won in Illyria, they agreed (in the Peace Treaty of Phoenice) that Philip should be allowed to retain his outlets to the Adriatic, and they confirmed his possessions in Greece.

Thus ended the conflict which is mistakenly called the 'First Macedonian War', for in it Rome and Macedon had encountered one another only indirectly. The Romans had made themselves known to the Greeks in a very unfavourable light. Their alliance with the Aetolians whom they afterwards so outrageously left in the lurch – the brutal conduct of their landing-parties – Aegina, one of the oldest and most glorious of Greek cities, sacked by the proconsul Sulpicius Galba, then handed to the Aetolians, and by them sold (supreme humiliation!) to Attalus for thirty talents – all this had certainly not improved the reputation of the western barbarians. As opposed to all this, Philip's activity, his constant initiative and his brave little army – so mobile and always ready to face any new threat – had made him seem to be the real defender of Hellenic civilisation and liberty. His standing in Greece was excellent, and since he had no anxieties in that direction he felt able to enlarge the scope of his ambitions elsewhere. The defeat of the Carthaginians had certainly made nonsense of his aspirations about Italy, but he could still look eastwards where grave events appeared to be impending.

XXXV

ROME AND THE MONARCHIES OF GREECE
AND THE NEAR EAST

There has always been an Eastern Question whenever a great empire to the east of the Mediterranean has begun to disintegrate and has become a prey for its covetous neighbours. At the end of the third century it was Egypt, which by its wealth, its geographical position, and its deplorably weak government was attracting the attention of the other Mediterranean states. Of the Macedonian families established on oriental thrones, none had succumbed so rapidly to the enervating effects of climate and environment as the Ptolemies, and to the consequences also of their consanguineous marriages of which Ptolemy II had set the example. Ptolemy III had been the last of this dynasty to show any energy. After him, even the fame of the victory at Raphia (won possibly by means of mercenaries) could not for long disguise the scandals of Ptolemy IV's reign: the worthless favourites, the palace quarrels and harem intrigues, the popular risings in Alexandria, the mystery surrounding the king's death, or the troubles of the regency during the infancy of Ptolemy V, who was only five years old at his accession.

Under Ptolemy IV, and perhaps even immediately after the battle of Raphia, there had also begun a long series of rebellions by native populations, due both to an oppressive system of taxation and to the unequal treatment instituted and maintained by the Ptolemies as between Greeks and Egyptians. In view of this situation those old rivals of the Ptolemies, the kings of Macedon and of Syria, came to an agreement to share between them Egypt's numerous and various outlying territories, from the islands and coastal towns of Thrace to Coele Syria, which by marriage or right of conquest had become dependencies of Egypt. Neither Macedon nor Syria would have dreamt of occupying the Nile valley, partly because it was a large indivisible unit, and partly because neither would have allowed the other to occupy it.

In 202 Philip, whose forces were the more easily mobilised, invaded Thrace and attacked and sacked Abydos. In 200 a fleet such as Macedon had not owned for many years seized on Samos. The Greek world was perturbed. The Egyptian government offered no resistance to Philip; two powers, however, were particularly annoyed by these onslaughts:

Attalus, for whom any attempt by Philip against the Asiatic coast was a threat; and Rhodes, which considered peace and security in the Aegean to be a necessity for her commerce. The combined fleets of Pergamum and Rhodes encountered Philip's fleet near Chios, and although the battle was indecisive almost half the Macedonian fleet was sunk. For this loss at sea Philip tried to compensate himself on land by a long and arduous campaign in Asia Minor, at first invading the territory of Pergamum, where Attalus avoided giving battle and allowed the countryside to be severely ravaged, and then Caria, where he soon captured Stratonicea and various Rhodian possessions. Having returned in haste to Greece, not without some difficulty, Philip incurred the anger of the Aetolians by an attack on Phthiotis; and of the Athenians, in spite of their determination to remain neutral, by attacking and ravaging Attica.

Philip was thus ruining the good reputation he had recently enjoyed in Greece by the impulsiveness of temperament, which was the bane of his life, and by his abominable appetite for rapine which had made his behaviour in 215 so notorious. He thought he could act in this way with impunity, for the states which he wronged had no armies capable of opposing his, and no one to whom they could appeal except the Seleucid who was his partner in crime! But now there was also Rome, whose recent victory over Carthage had given her an unbelievably high reputation. In 201-200, embassies sent from Egypt, Rhodes, and Pergamum all met one another in Italy. It may well be wondered if these states realised the possible consequences of their actions, but after all, though Rome's soldiers were brutal and her policy a tortuous one, there was no proof that she had the slightest wish to make conquests in the east. The imperialist schemes with which historians sometimes credit the Senate at this period were in fact very far from its thoughts. One fact and one alone could have induced the Senate, and did in fact induce it, to intervene in these eastern quarrels – and that was the alliance, which was reported to the Senate, between Philip and Antiochus.

At Rome the military strength of Macedon was fully realised; that of Antiochus the Romans were inclined to overestimate, since this astonishing king had rebuilt for himself an empire which, but for Macedon and Egypt, was as great as Alexander's. The Senate imagined, quite wrongly, that the agreement of the two kings was directed against Italy, which had been invaded thrice in less than a century. It decided to profit by the opportunity to strike at the weaker and nearer of the two allies. By the same stroke of policy it would both give satisfaction to the numerous Greek states who wished for an end of the Macedonian hegemony, and also erect against Macedon, and more important still against Antiochus, the barrier of a free Greece, loyally allied to Rome, which in case of danger from the east would give early warning and, at need, take the first enemy blows.

Such a decision amounted to a great change in the Senate's policy, a change which had far-reaching consequences and which was to lead the Senate much further than at first was intended. To realise their plan haste was needed, so as to profit by the fact that Antiochus was occupied in 201 in the conquest of Coele Syria. Circumstances were favourable: the prospect of an overseas campaign was nothing alarming for a country which had just carried through a successful war in Africa against Carthage. The Republic's army was 'in form' as it had perhaps never been before. Philip's fleet had been seriously reduced in size at Chios, and the low state of the royal treasury would not permit him to build another. This was a serious inferiority, for the combined fleets of Rome, Pergamum, and Rhodes could ensure command of the Aegean and were thus able to supply and support their land armies.

The Senate was not slow in finding good reasons for war: it pretended that Philip had attacked its ally Attalus; and while the Athenians declared war on Philip, a Roman army of thirty thousand crossed into Illyria. But the Romans soon found that they were not welcomed everywhere as liberators. The Achaean League decided to remain neutral. The Aetolians, remembering what happened in 207, wished to wait and see; and it required the invasion of Macedon by the proconsul Sulpicius Galba, and his victory over Philip in the region of the lakes in 199, to persuade the Aetolians to take an active part in operations.

Even so, the war was merely smouldering on until the arrival of the Consul, Titus Quinctius Flamininus – an ambitious official, a good soldier, and a wise diplomat – fanned it into flame. He forced the passes of the Pindus range and successfully made contact with the Aetolians in Thessaly. The presence of this army in mid-Greece, supported by the allied fleet which had recently captured Eretria and shortly afterwards appeared off Corinth, forced everyone and particularly the Achaeans to take notice, while Flamininus was able by his protestations of friendship for Greece to wipe out the painful memories of the years 211-08. Since 204 the League had been engaged in a tough struggle with Nabis, tyrant of Sparta, who had almost succeeded in retaking Megalopolis from them, and it certainly had no wish to try conclusions with the Roman army too. After a very stormy session the Assembly decided to break the alliance which had united Achaea with Macedon ever since 224, and to join the Romans.

Philip, now without allies in Greece, was inclined to negotiate, and Flamininus, who was not certain that his period of office would be extended the following year, wished to bring the war to a successful conclusion himself since he regarded it as his own particular business. But at the conferences at Nicaea in 198, where Philip met Flamininus together with delegates from Achaea, Aetolia, Rhodes, and Pergamum, the king again indulged his fantastic temperament and the Greeks showed the extent of their demands. They required that Philip should give up all his possessions in Greece itself and all his Asian conquests; and the Senate, to which Philip appealed, refused to treat unless the fortresses of Demetrias, Chalcis, and Corinth were evacuated. The war was resumed.

Flamininus, who had spent the winter in Phocis, invaded Thessaly in the spring of 197, and his army – strengthened by allied contingents – met Philip's near the hills called Dogs' Heads (Cynoscephalae). The two forces were about equal in strength, some twenty-five thousand on either side, and fought a grim battle before the massive phalanx, in difficulties on this broken ground, finally proved inferior to the legion. About the same time the Achaeans dealt the Macedonian garrison at Corinth a severe blow, and the royal troops were beaten by the men of Rhodes in Caria.

Philip now needed peace at any price, and Flamininus was not the man to refuse it. Philip signed a convention by which he gave up the three fortresses which had enabled the Antigonids to hold Greece for nearly a century, and almost all his possessions in Asia too. Macedon, shorn even of Thessaly, was reduced once again to her boundaries of the year 350.

There remained to be answered the question as to what was to be done with the territories formerly held by the Macedonian garrisons, and the Greeks were asking one another what was likely to be the Senate's decision. It surpassed all their expectations. At the Isthmian Games of 196 Flamininus proclaimed unrestricted freedom for all cities and states recently liberated. This amounted, as his audience at once understood, to a guarantee of freedom for all European Greece. No doubt for two centuries this freedom had been the subject over and over again of resounding declarations, promptly retracted, but this time the proclamation had been made in the name of a people foreign to the Hellenic world, who seemed to have no interests to serve there. Hence we can understand the displays of delirious enthusiasm with which Flamininus was greeted. And at first the promise was borne out by the event: the federations of Thessaly and of Euboea were revived, Demetrias was handed over to the one and Chalcis to the other, while Corinth was returned to the Achaean League. Rome kept no stepping-stone in Greece; the Macedonian domination was ended: a new era seemed to have begun.

Yet Roman policy was not without its drawbacks. First of all it could not immediately suppress all dissensions between the Greeks; secondly, the manner in which Rome had favoured the Achaeans was sure to annoy those old enemies of the League – the Aetolians and Spartans. The Aetolians who, after all, had joined in the war on the Roman side before the Achaeans, were furious at seeing Corinth given to their rivals, and with it the mastery of all that mattered in the Peloponnese; their discontent, which they expressed openly in the presence of Flamininus, would be translated into action as soon as opportunity offered. At Sparta, Nabis could not bring himself to surrender Argos, which Flamininus had adjudged to the League. To make the stubborn tyrant see reason, it required the presence in Laconia of Roman and Achaean contingents, the capitulation of the port of Gythion, and an assault during which the Romans were only prevented from entering Sparta because the defenders set fire to it.

Outside Greece the Senate's policy also had a weak spot. It left a free hand to one of the two allies of 203: indeed there was nothing to prevent Antiochus from marching into Syria in 201, and then, after an Egyptian counter-offensive, from returning there in 200 and completely defeating his adversary at Panion. Coele Syria was thus finally lost to Egypt. The following years were occupied in clearing Asia Minor of its last Egyptian garrisons and in conquering Cilicia. Thus the first result of Philip's defeat was to allow Antiochus to seize the territories in Asia Minor which until then had belonged to the king of Macedon; this in turn brought the king of Syria into direct conflict with Rhodes, with Eumenes of Pergamum (the son and successor of Attalus), and finally with the Greek cities of Smyrna and Lampsacus. States and cities which were injured turned of course to Rome for redress.

A new and serious step by Antiochus decided the hesitant Senate to intervene. Among the territories abandoned by Philip was Thrace. Antiochus invaded it just at the time when Flamininus was making his proclamation. The king had the intention no doubt of reconstituting in its entirety the empire of Seleucus, whose victory in 281 had temporarily given him possession of this region which served as a corridor to northern Asia Minor. But the Romans did not see it in that way. They regarded this expedition into Europe as a direct threat to Greece, and through Greece to themselves. Their fears were confirmed when they learned in 195 that Hannibal, driven from Carthage, had taken refuge with the king of Syria. It seemed as though they had to begin all over again. Had they beaten Philip only to further the progress of a new Alexander? Protracted negotiations in 196 and 192, first of all in Thrace, then in Greece where Flamininus with ten Commissioners had been established to regulate Hellenic affairs, finally at Rome when the ambassadors of Antiochus presented themselves before the Senate, merely served to make clearer the opposition between the two adversaries. Antiochus would not give up the towns in Thrace, nor allow his rights over those in Asia Minor to be questioned. The Senate would not allow him to bring an army into Europe, and, extending beyond the Aegean Sea the policy that had served them so well in Greece, took under their protection the free cities of Asia Minor – an intolerable affront to the sovereignty of Antiochus, and, as the Romans fully anticipated, an incitement to rebellion in his kingdom.

These four years were employed by the two enemies, and especially by Antiochus, in making sure of allies in the east. Before plunging into a war with Rome, Antiochus wished to settle the Egyptian question. He used current procedure. His daughter Cleopatra, with Coele Syria revenues as her dowry, was married to Ptolemy V. Another of his daughters married the king of Cappadocia: and if Eumenes had been willing he could have married the third, but the king of Pergamum remained loyal to the Roman alliance. In Greece, Antiochus hoped to obtain the support of states injured by the settlement of 196. The Aetolians were in fact eager for war, and seized Demetrias early in 192. They appealed to Antiochus with great enthusiasm, and promised him a general uprising in his favour. The greatest mistake which the king of Syria ever made was to believe them, and – avoiding the difficulties of a general mobilisation in his motley empire – he crossed into Greece in 192 with an army of only ten thousand men, and those not particularly good in quality and discipline. His arrival did not provoke the expected rising. Philip remained faithful to the Roman alliance. Sparta, after the death of Nabis, and in spite of the presence there of an Aetolian detachment, joined the Achaean League. The installation of an Achaean garrison in the Piraeus easily held Athens in check, although the intentions of her democratic party were uncertain. The only support for the Aetolians in all the north of Greece was Amyander, the petty king of the Athamanes, and Elis and Messenia in the Peloponnese.

In view of these dispositions, once he had disembarked at Demetrias Antiochus had to content himself with taking Chalcis to use as a base, and with making a demonstration in Thessaly which was speedily countered by the presence of a Roman detachment at Larissa. Then in the spring of 191 a Roman army of twenty-two thousand men, commanded by the consul Acilius Glabrio, landed in Epirus, joined the Macedonian army, entered Thessaly in its turn, and marched to meet Antiochus, who attempted to halt it at Thermopylae. Once again the weakness of this position was made plain when held by a force whose left flank was unguarded. The flank was turned, as it had been twice in three centuries, and a rout followed. Antiochus fled in haste to Chalcis, and thence to Asia, abandoning Greece and the Aetolians to their fate.

This was a severe blow to his reputation, though his material losses were insignificant, compared with the resources of his empire. The Romans were fully aware of this, and to ensure that never again should the Seleucid menace oppress Greece, the Senate realised that it must engage in operations on an entirely vaster scale which would enable them to defeat Antiochus on his own ground, as they had defeated Philip. It was decided at Rome to prepare an expedition for the invasion of Asia Minor, but first of all Antiochus must be made incapable of transporting another army into Europe. He had a fine fleet on the coasts of Asia Minor, and

Hannibal was preparing another for him in Syria. In 191 a Roman squadron reappeared in the Aegean, and working with those of Rhodes and Pergamum began a series of operations in which the Rhodians in particular played a most important part, the objective of which was to prevent the junction of the two royal fleets. As a result of these operations the Romans secured control of the Hellespont.

During this time in Italy, where they were under no illusions as to the difficulties of the enterprise, an expeditionary force of thirteen thousand men was being equipped under the command of L. Scipio, helped by his brother P. Scipio Africanus, the victor of Zama. This force crossed into Epirus in 190. It went first to Greece to receive the submission of the Aetolians who, under the combined pressure of the armies of Glabrio and Philip, in spite of energetic defences of their fortresses of Heraclea and Naupactus, had to ask the Scipios for a six-months armistice. The situation in Greece was now clear, and Scipio's army – augmented with that of Glabrio and Hellenic contingents – passed through Thrace without hindrance, since Antiochus in panic had withdrawn all his garrisons and depots, and crossed the Hellespont. This force was about thirty thousand strong, almost as large as the force which Alexander had taken across a century and a half earlier.

Once again the difficulties of mobilising and concentrating an army in this great oriental empire became obvious, as did the weakness of its motley bands when faced with homogeneous and well-led western troops. The battle of Magnesia in 190, despite the courage of Antiochus and the fighting-spirit of the phalanxes of soldiers of Macedonian descent, ended in the rout and massacre of the royal army. The seventy-two thousand men whom Antiochus had recruited were but a small part of what he could raise, but he realised that it was useless to prolong the struggle. Negotiations were begun. Meanwhile the military situation was made still more definite in Asia by the defeat of the Galatae, allies of Antiochus and intolerable neighbours for the kings of Pergamum; and in Greece by a campaign against the Aetolians, who had taken up the struggle again when their armistice ended, but whose stubborn determination broke down after the defeat of their Asiatic ally.

A series of treaties settled the fates of Asia Minor and northern Greece. In Asia it was understood that Antiochus, in addition to paying a heavy fine and handing over his elephants, would give up almost all his warships and the whole region north of the Taurus range. The real question was to whom these territories should be given. During the negotiations two ambitions and two policies confronted one another: those of Rhodes who wished the liberty of all Greek cities to be respected, hoping no doubt to group around herself a great political and commercial confederation; and those of Eumenes, who asked that the territories taken from Antiochus should be awarded to him if Rome did not wish to keep them herself.

The Romans took little interest in principles, but they had begun to feel annoyed by the Republic's attitude and its independent-minded and crafty merchants; so they favoured Eumenes King of Pergamum who, they felt, was more amenable. Apart from Caria and a few cities south of the Maeander, which were awarded to the Rhodians, all the western part of Asia Minor and the region around the straits were given to Eumenes, who thus assembled in his own hands once again the short-lived kingdom of Lysimachus.

The terms laid down for Aetolia were singularly mild: the League was merely required to relinquish the territories she had lost during the war, and the preponderant position on the Amphictyonic Council of Delphi, which she had held for nearly a century. It was to the interest of the Romans not to be too hard on their former allies, since they were also old rivals of Macedon, but the Aetolians, in acknowledging 'the majesty of the Roman people', undertook to treat her enemies as their own and so lost all control over their foreign policy.

It will be noted that the Romans, here again, did not take any territory for themselves, or any financial or commercial advantage. They were quite satisfied to have destroyed the dangerous alliance of 203, and to have interposed between Italy on the one hand and Macedon and the Seleucid Empire on the other, the rampart of a free and (they hoped) a grateful Greece, and of a Pergamene kingdom resolutely loyal to their alliance. It is not necessary to discover in such a policy a Machiavellian farsightedness, or a preparation for future conquests, nor yet a sentimental disinterestedness. The idea of annexing a Greece which was both poor and undisciplined, or of taking over the almost unknown territories of the orient, never entered the heads of the officials who framed the treaties of 188. On the other hand the sympathy already felt in a few cultured and aristocratic Roman families for Greece, with her marvellous past and her literary and artistic fame, was a sentiment not yet so widely diffused as to influence the policy of careful opportunism which for the past thirty years had been that of the Senate with regard to oriental affairs.

It is, however, very hard to determine the exact moment at which a robust people, made distrustful by repeated invasions and having decided to organise a powerful defensive system, changes – sometimes quite unconscious of the fact – to a policy of imperialist domination. No doubt the Senate hoped for a continuance of the situation created by the Conventions of 196 and 188. But this whole situation was based on a misunderstanding. It assumed that all the states concerned freely accepted the fact that Rome had them in her grip, that she should control their foreign policy, and even their domestic policy to the extent that it depended on their foreign policy. Now this involved a loss of sovereignty which neither Rome's old enemies nor even her allies could accept. Not long after the war in Asia, the will of Rome began to clash with that of states which until now had shown her the greatest devotion.

The Achaean League had reached the finest hour of its history. By the accession of Sparta, Elis and Messenia, its territory had been increased to include the whole of the Peloponnese. This growth, and the energy of Philopoemen, gave it the illusion that it was completely independent, and in 187 it accepted an alliance with Ptolemy V and refused the offer of one from Eumenes, whose generous advances could not erase from their memory the scandal of Aegina. But such an attitude was displeasing to Rome. In 192 there had been some ill-feeling between Flamininus and Philopoemen after he had forced Sparta to join the League after the death of Nabis, and soon there came a chance to make clear to the Achaeans that they were strong only because the Senate wished them to be so.

A quarrel broke out between Sparta and the League, since the latter proposed to regulate to its own satisfaction the return of the men banished by Nabis, to impose upon Sparta a constitution analogous to those in force in other Achaean cities, to eradicate the dreaded spirit of social reform which had been influential there since the days of Agis and Cleomenes, and finally to dismantle the city's defences. The League had its way, but soon afterwards Messenia seceded. Philopoemen, setting out at the head of a detachment to subdue the rebels, was captured and executed at Messenia, and it needed a second expedition led by Lycortas to put an end to the revolt. Rome intervened. Although the secession of Messenia may well have been at her instigation she took no action when she saw how promptly it was repressed: but in her support of Sparta she insisted, and found means in the course of the negotiations to play off one party of Achaeans against another. Hence, although the Achaeans tried stubbornly to defend the League's sovereignty, Sparta was finally authorised to recall her exiles, to restore the 'Constitution of Lycurgus', and to rebuild her walls.

At the other end of the Greek world Rhodes was astounded to find that Rome approved the revolt of the Lycians in 177, although the Convention of 189 had formally assigned Lycia to Rhodes! Rome's policy, her interference in the internal affairs of other states, the crude way in which the Senate conducted negotiations, all created a sense of uneasiness which a new Macedonian war was soon to bring to a head.

The Macedonian armies had fought loyally and effectively alongside the Roman armies against Antiochus, but their reward was meagre – Demetrias and a few townships in Phthiotis – and after toilsome negotiations Philip was refused the towns in Thessaly and Thrace which he expected to be allowed to occupy. More keenly perhaps even than after Cynoscephalae he felt the inferior position in which defeat had placed him. After all his dreams of a Hellenic Empire he was now no more than ruler of a petty kingdom held in leading-strings by Rome. He consecrated the last years of his reign to the reorganisation – sometimes rather brutally conducted – of a state which was exhausted both militarily and financially. When he died in 179 he left to his elder son, Perseus, a kingdom recovering its strength but still in a difficult situation. To be able to live at peace with Rome it was obviously necessary to renounce all hopes of overlordship and to show the docility of a Eumenes. This was scarcely a fitting policy for the heir to the great Antigonids. Moreover, Perseus, instructed by his father and taught by his own experience, knew only too well the strength of the Roman Republic and how thoroughly it had disorganised the Greek world by its diplomacy. Hence his reign was full of anguish and self-contradiction, for he was torn between the wish to resume the traditions of his family and fear of the Roman armies. He presented the tragic spectacle of a king drawn almost inevitably into a war which he knew in advance that he was sure to lose.

From the beginning of his reign he displayed a great deal of energy. Besides the restoration of his country's internal fortunes he busied himself with renewing, throughout the Greek world, the sympathies which his father's odd temperament and military defeat had compromised. He re-established the good relations with the Achaean League, interrupted twenty years before; he won partisans in Aetolia, Boeotia, Thrace, even at Rhodes; he married the daughter of Seleucus IV, grand-daughter of Antiochus III. But the time when the Senate took no interest in Greek affairs had gone by: now it had observers everywhere, and above all it could rely on the vigilance of Eumenes, who was of course an interested party. It was he who in 172 came to Rome to denounce the activities of Perseus.

From this date the Senate contemplated the suppression of the Macedonian kingdom, whose existence seemed quite incompatible with Rome's safety. But it wished first of all to counteract the effects of Macedonian diplomacy, and its legates did this so successfully that when the ambassadors of Perseus, after some half-hearted negotiations, were brusquely ordered to leave Italy within thirty days, Perseus could only count on effective aid from the Epirots, some Galatae on the Danube (Bastarnae), a few Thracian princelets, and some cities in Boeotia. A kingdom with inferior numbers was fated to have to sustain a war against a state which (with Spanish auxiliaries) had greater reserves, one well accustomed to overseas expeditions, and to whom Masinissa, king of the Numidians, was supplying elephants and Eumenes his fleet.

Nevertheless, Macedon held firm for more than three years. Her peasant-bred infantry did its duty to the last. At the beginning of the war, marching to meet the Romans who, as on the previous occasion, intended to invade Macedon by the easiest route (the southern one), Perseus scored a success at Sycurium in Thessaly which ought to have been better exploited. But he was discouraged to begin with, and discouragement became panic when the Senate decided to replace the mediocre P. Licinius Crassus. In 169 Q. Marcius Philippus, avoiding the vale of Tempe, boldly forced an entry to Macedon across the Olympus massif; subsequently L. Æmilius Paullus, an experienced soldier, hustled the Macedonian army out of its prepared position south of the town of Pydna, between the foothills of Olympus and the sea. For the Romans this victory opened the road to the ports of the Thermaic Gulf (Salonica) and to the ancient capitals of Macedon. Perseus surrendered unconditionally, and despite their loyalty the Macedonian population made no attempt at further resistance.

Greece had followed the vicissitudes of this struggle with anxiety. She knew that her future was at stake. It was true that the hundred and seventy years of almost unbroken Macedonian rule had not been without friction, but Rome was an unknown quantity, and they could not forget her past brutalities nor the more recent outrages of the praetor C. Lucretius in Boeotia in 171. Many of the states were hoping for a stalemate and were negotiating secretly with Perseus, especially after his victory at Sycurium. Faithful to her policy of a balance of power, Rhodes had taken advantage of a victory won by the small Macedonian fleet to offer to mediate. Eumenes himself, realising perhaps what would be the consequences for his own kingdom of the disappearance of Macedon, seems to have begun some obscure negotiations with Perseus. The Romans were informed about all these combinations and all these hopes, and drew the conclusion that a generous policy was wasted on the Greek states and that henceforth they must rely on force alone. Everyone was made aware of this at Amphipolis when the terrible decisions of the Senate were made known by the Roman commissioners.

The Macedonian monarchy was suppressed. In its place were set up four 'free' republics, carved out of the territory of the former kingdom. They were to pay modest tributes to Rome and were entrusted to aristocratic governments which the Senate thought could easily be held in check. In almost all the Greek states the leaders of the Macedonian party, listed by name, were ordered to go to Rome there to 'justify their conduct'. Most of them were doomed never to return. In Epirus the confederation was dissolved, seventy villages were destroyed, and a hundred and fifty thousand men taken into slavery: the Romans had never forgotten the expedition of Pyrrhus. As for Rhodes, its independent attitude and its stubborn pretensions to play the part of mediator had exasperated the Senate. Almost all her Asiatic possessions were taken from her, and an even harder blow was struck at her commerce. The Italian merchants, who had begun to frequent Aegean ports from the beginning of the second century, had noted the ever-increasing volume of the trade of Delos. In 166 the island was returned to the Athenians and declared a free port, a measure which was a real disaster for the trade of Rhodes.

Eumenes himself was not spared the effects of the Senate's wrath. A Galatian insurrection which broke out in 168 had been, if not provoked, at least encouraged by Rome. When the king of Pergamum, after a first unlucky campaign, had recruited another army and beaten his enemy, the Senate intervened and declared the Galatae to be self-governing. Having come to Italy in person to plead his cause, Eumenes was told when he landed at Brundisium to come no further, and had to re-embark forthwith.

Another of Rome's allies, the king of Syria, suffered as great a humiliation. Antiochus III died a few months after his defeat. His elder son Seleucus IV reigned only for a few years, and the younger son Antiochus IV, Epiphanes, having been detained for many years as a hostage at Rome and having seen her strength at close quarters, wished only to live at peace with the Romans. But in 169 the military preparations and provocations of Egypt, where the advisers of the young King Ptolemy IV had the idea of retaking Syria, decided Antiochus to invade the Delta. Two successful campaigns seemed to ensure his control over it; he was threatening Alexandria; his troops were victorious in Cyprus. But the Senate would not allow one and the same ruler to reign in Alexandria, in Antioch, and in Babylon, and as soon as the Macedonian question was settled at Pydna, a Roman embassy came to give Antiochus an order to evacuate Egypt at once!

In this policy of calculated brutality the will of the Republic was quite clear. Rome had no wish to make annexations; not for an instant did she think of exploiting the conquered countries of the orient. It is an anachronism to attribute to the Senate at this period a policy of economic expansion. On the contrary, in 167 it forbade the working of the gold and silver mines in Macedon. What Rome wanted was to put it beyond the power of any of these countries to harm her, or to become a threat to her safety by any coalition or alliance, secret or open. Generosity had not paid. In this orient, with which she was now better acquainted, she decided to try violence instead; though it must be admitted that, as at first practised, it gave her scarcely more durable results.

XXXVI

THE ROMAN CONQUEST.
THE END OF THE GREEK STATES

The effect produced in Greece by such measures can well be imagined. What depths of disillusionment had been plumbed in the last thirty years! Before then, there seemed still to be hope of a balance between Macedon and Rome, or at least for a mild Roman hegemony which would allow all viable states to preserve their independence. But the fearful treatment inflicted on Epirus, the carving up of Macedon, the Achaean League beheaded, the downfall of Rhodes, the humiliation of Eumenes and Antiochus IV, all showed how Rome intended to wield her authority. A keen feeling of sympathy for her victims soon demonstrated itself – for Perseus, condemned to die in a Latin prison; for those carried off from the Greek cities who, in spite of repeated appeals by their fellow-countrymen, had to wait seventeen years before they saw their homes again; even for Eumenes, formerly so much blamed for his servile devotion to the Roman cause. Disappointment, resentment, economic hardship, and the political disturbances provoked here and there by the insolence of the partisans of Rome, were soon to find expression in violence.

Macedon had at first accepted the new order without much difficulty. Among her predominantly rural population there had never been much genuine patriotism, but only a strong attachment to the person of their king and his family. Now the Antigonid dynasty had disappeared, or so it was believed, when an adventurer named Andriscus, who claimed to be a son of Perseus, appeared in Macedon at the head of a small make-shift army recruited in Thrace. The prestige of his supposed birth gave him some easy successes and Macedon recognised him as king. A first Roman army sent to deal with him was defeated, and soon he had advanced into Thessaly. It took two Roman legions, the arrival of a good general (Q. Metellus) and the fleet from Pergamum, to put down this pretender in the year 148.

The same year an anti-Roman movement developed in Greece. Poor economic conditions had caused a general increase in the number of malcontents almost everywhere, and had made the poorest classes a more important element. This change was very noticeable even in the Achaean League, which had formerly been led by well-to-do citizens; and it was accompanied, as often happened in Greece, by a nationalist movement which needed only a spark to set it ablaze. Once again this spark was struck by Sparta. The old city in its decline was unwilling to resign itself to incorporation in the League. It demanded to keep its own law-courts, settle its quarrels with neighbours in its own way, and send its own embassies to Rome. The League's rulers could not agree to such requests: a minor war broke out, Sparta's territory was invaded and pillaged.

The Roman Senate, to whom Sparta appealed as arbitrator, waited until the Macedonian uprising was quelled before sending an embassy to Corinth to announce its good pleasure – that the League must give up not only Sparta but Argos and Corinth too. The indignation which this decision aroused in a country already discontented, and which estimated moreover that Rome was too deeply engaged in war in Spain and Africa to have legions to spare for dealing with Greece, can be understood. Negotiations were broken off, the League's *strategos* Diaeus took very bold social and economic measures, raised an army as best he could, and found allies in Boeotia, Euboea, and Phocis. In 146 his successor Critolaus marched to meet the Roman army led by Metellus, which was advancing through Thessaly. He was defeated at Scarpheia in Locris; Diaeus was beaten at the Isthmus by L. Mummius, successor to Metellus; Corinth was sacked and completely destroyed, a terrible punishment for a movement whose revolutionary character the Senate had no doubt recognised.

These events showed that the stern measures taken in 167 were nevertheless ineffective. If Rome wanted lasting peace she must not allow even the ghost of independence to survive in Greece. The Senate was gradually growing accustomed to the idea of putting distant territories under the direct rule of its own officials. This system had in 206 already been applied to Spain. Carthage, conquered for the third time, was about to be subjected to the same régime; and after 146 it was adopted in Macedonia, which became a Roman province under a praetor and had to pay tribute. Some additions of Illyrian territory put Macedonia into direct communication with the Adriatic and Italy, and a road – the trade-mark of Roman civilisation – soon crossed it from Dyrrhachium (Durazzo) to Salonica. Quietly accepting the new arrangements, it was henceforth to become one of the most loyal provinces of the Roman Empire.

Macedonia had been a centralised state for three centuries, and the Roman officials who were put in charge of its people inherited the authority of their ancient kings. In Greece the situation was less easy to regulate. To begin with it was necessary to crush every semblance of political vitality. The Achaean League was dissolved, and probably the Aetolian League too, and whatever was left of the Confederations of Boeotia and Euboea. Once this had been done, the Senate was in some embarrassment as to how to deal with the resulting collection of hetero-geneous states, which the Romans themselves had no wish to reduce to a uniform political régime. Some of them – those who had taken part in the rising of 146 – were being required to pay tribute, while others were exempt from any such payment; others again had their relations with Rome laid down in definite conventions.

No general scheme therefore was enforced, no regulations drawn up, but in fact the states and cities of Greece were all put under the control of the governor of Macedonia. Few details of this system are known, for it was probably regarded as provisional by those who planned it; but it was destined to last a full century, and all in all it produced the results that might have been expected, since Greece – quite pleased to get off so lightly, and conscious of its own weakness – henceforth accepted Rome's authority, and roused herself again only for a brief moment at the call of Mithridates.

An unexpected event was to cause the Senate to practise outside Europe the policy of annexation which it had applied to Macedonia. Eumenes II died in 160 after a reign full of vicissitudes. All his life he had struggled with supple pertinacity, by sea, on land, in arms, by diplomacy, against Philip of Macedon, against Antiochus III, against the Galatae, and the petty kings of Armenia, Pontus, and Bithynia. Of the little country handed down to him by his father he had made a great Asiatic kingdom; and after all his labours the resentment of the Romans, whom he had so often and so loyally helped, had seemed to threaten his life's work and bring the whole matter in question again. To sum up, however, in spite of the losses sustained at the end of his reign, he left to his brother, Attalus II, a large and prosperous state which he, in turn, was able to maintain and organise successfully from 160 to 139. Of all the oriental Hellenic monarchies that of Pergamum seemed the most solidly established, the most prosperous and best administered, when it was learned in 133 that Attalus III, the son of Eumenes and successor to Attalus II, had died, leaving his kingdom by will as a heritage to the Roman people!

What can have been the motives of this king who is often stated on the strength of a few anecdotes to have been a madman? No one knows: but his legacy caused acute embarrassment at Rome. Who was to benefit by the king's wealth, in land and in chattels? The Senate or the citizens? In any case the gift had come at a very opportune moment, when a social and economic crisis had been emphasised by the reforms of Tiberius Gracchus. What method of government was to be adopted for the king's domains, for the Greek cities there, for the indigenous populations who were his subjects?

While all these matters were being discussed at Rome, a natural son of

Eumenes, named Aristonicus, who not unnaturally was unwilling to agree
to the terms of his half-brother's will, had recruited a small army in Asia
and little by little had conquered almost the whole country. The ease
with which he accomplished this is partly explained by the same reasons
which fifteen years earlier had given early success to Andriscus in Macedonia. In addition he made lavish promises of a better life for the disinherited classes, and particularly for the slaves. A few of the Greek towns
only offered resistance, although Pergamum itself organised a vigorous
defence against him. Nevertheless the uprising was a serious matter. The
consul first sent into the region was defeated, and his successor needed two
years to put down the rebellion. The war had, however, changed the
situation. Attalus's kingdom was no longer an embarrassing legacy but a
conquered country, and could be treated as such, that is to say reduced to
the condition of a Roman province. The Greek cities – at least those
which had not sided with Aristonicus – retained the theoretical liberty
which they had enjoyed under the Pergamene kings.

In this way the Republic began outside Europe a policy of annexations, without apparently having ever intended it. At that period the disadvantages of such a policy seemed to the Senate to outweigh any economic
benefits likely to accrue. The great impetus which was soon to direct the
merchants and bankers of Italy – the Roman 'publicans' – towards the
eastern Mediterranean had as yet scarcely begun, and had certainly not
given rise to any political repercussions. And so the Senate continued,
during the whole of the second century, to respect the integrity of other
oriental states, whatever their weakness. That of the Seleucids, for
instance, was in full decline. A dynastic quarrel, begun that day in 175
when Antiochus IV (the second son of Antiochus III) had supplanted, with
the aid of Eumenes of Pergamum, his nephew Demetrius (the son of
Seleucus IV) filled all the second century with strife, and by a series of
palace revolutions, and of usurpations frequently instigated by Rome or
Egypt, cut short the reigns and lives of one sovereign after another.

The energetic and combative spirit of their Macedonian ancestors
survived in a number of them, however, with surprising persistence.
Antiochus IV, whimsical and impulsive, tried hard to diffuse Greek civilisation throughout his kingdom in accordance with his dynastic traditions.
Demetrius I (162-50), who had been held as a hostage at Rome, escaped on
the death of his uncle, and in spite of Roman ill-will and a revolt by
favourites of the late King Antiochus IV, found means to impose his
authority on the kingdom. Demetrius II had to remove a usurper (Alexander Balas (150-45), the reputed son of Antiochus IV) and then to recapture Coele Syria which Egypt had stolen during the brief interregnum.
But the shortness of their reigns made it impossible for them to eradicate
the causes of the dissolution which threatened their motley empire. In
particular they could not solve the problem of military recruitment, a

difficulty which the Achaemenids had already encountered in their day; at moments of crisis they could never raise troops who were much more than mediocre and ill-assorted. Besides this, Rome kept a jealous eye on their armaments. Immediately after the death of Antiochus IV, for example, a Roman commissioner had supervised personally the burning of all warships in Syrian ports and had had the elephants in the royal stables hamstrung.

So the empire was visibly falling to pieces. In the east Antiochus III and Antiochus IV were killed in rapid succession by the rebellious mountain tribes in Persia. In 141 the Parthians penetrated as far as Babylonia. When Demetrius II went to meet them he was beaten and made prisoner in 139. Ten years later his brother Antiochus VII decided to renew the struggle, but he was defeated and killed, and from that time onwards the Euphrates became the limit of the Seleucid kingdom. In the west, from the middle of the second century, the Jewish revolt proved how feeble the central authority had become. As long as Coele Syria had belonged to the Ptolemies the Jews had led a peaceful existence, since from indifference or policy Egypt had allowed them to retain the *de facto* autonomy which they had enjoyed under the Achaemenids. But under the Seleucids things were different. The kings needed money, and their policy of assimilation could not be reconciled with the continued existence of this little state with its peculiar system of priest-kings.

Although it had been surrounded by Hellenic cities ever since Alexander's day, Jerusalem remained hostile in temper to the Greek spirit, and, on religious principles averse from king-worship. A revolt broke out under Antiochus IV, who was the first to impose a regular tribute on the Jews. He entered Jerusalem twice by force, and the second time in 167 the temple of Zion was violated and the worship of Olympian Zeus, or perhaps that of the King Antiochus himself, installed in place of that of Jehovah. A small rebel army was raised under the leadership of energetic chieftains belonging to the family of the Maccabees. For more than thirty years with varying fortunes it held the royal troops in check, and made serious difficulties for the kings by supporting every usurper against them: Alexander Balas against Demetrius I and II, Tryphon and Alexander Zabinas against Demetrius II. Finally the independence of Judaea, probably favoured by Rome, was in fact recognised at the end of the reign of Demetrius II.

The history of the Ptolemaic dynasty in the second century was as deplorable as that of the Seleucids: palace revolutions, quarrels between wives (for the feminine share in government became more and more considerable), rivalries between favourites, not to mention the riotings of the Alexandrian populace! After the invasion by Antiochus IV an attempt at sharing power between the two brothers Ptolemy VI and Ptolemy VII merely resulted in a long conflict fomented by the Romans (168-54). It required dogged persistence by Ptolemy VI to retain his authority intact, and to refuse even the government of Cyprus to his brother, who nevertheless reascended the throne on the death of the elder brother. In his person, all the vices of this degenerate family were again exemplified – yet this ill-governed empire maintained a certain stability. This was due first of all to its geographical and ethnic unity, which meant that there was never any question of partitioning Egypt; secondly, to a strong administrative organisation, resistant to revolution; and finally to a skilful diplomacy whose strength, like that of Turkey in the nineteenth century A.D., was based on the cleverly exploited divisions of its enemies. Earlier it had promoted family quarrels and revolts of the satraps in the Seleucid Empire, and had played off Macedonia against the Greek states. Now that Macedonia was no more, it opposed Rome to the Seleucids, encouraging in the latter's realms every usurper and every rebellion, in particular that of the Jews; at Rome it manoeuvred so skilfully between parties, that after a hundred and fifty years of decrepitude it still required the dangerous scandal of Anthony and Cleopatra to decide Augustus to turn Egypt into a Roman province.

XXXVII

THE STATE OF GREEK CIVILISATION AT THE TIME OF THE ROMAN CONQUEST. CONCLUSION

In the second century Greek civilisation was in retreat. Its physical range was becoming restricted. In the west the Roman conquest naturally put a stop to its expansion, and in some Sicilian cantons, for example, it was only with the greatest difficulty that the Greek language and Hellenic customs perpetuated themselves. In the east, the frontiers of the Seleucid Empire were forced back to the Euphrates, and about 130 the Bactrian kingdom collapsed under pressure from the nomads of Turkestan. The small kingdoms of the Punjab, which had been active centres of Hellenism, all disappeared about the beginning of the first century.

Even within the Greek states themselves weaknesses were becoming obvious: the failure of the Seleucids to Hellenise Judaea has already been noted. In Egypt, revolts followed one another constantly until the dynasty came to an end, and their violence forced the sovereigns to make concessions not only to the Egyptian priests but to the natives in general. After the battle of Raphia, the natives were made liable to mobilisation on the same terms as Greeks – about which they were rather proud and gave themselves airs. Soon Egyptians, by simply changing their names, were infiltrating into military formations for Greeks only, and into civil service employments. Eventually Hellenism disappeared from the rural areas of Egypt. The category of 'village-dwelling Greeks', artificially sponsored and maintained with difficulty by means of unfair legislation, tended to vanish. Only in the large towns could a Hellenic civilisation persist, and even there in a somewhat contaminated form. No doubt this retreat was in some measure the natural ebb which was bound to follow the too rapid flow of expansion in the fourth century, but it must be admitted that the vitality of Hellenism was declining. In European Greece, which for six centuries had been a considerable reservoir of man-power, the population now was so obviously falling that contemporary writers noticed and mentioned it. The importance of some commercial cities (such as Corinth before its destruction, and Rhodes) or the rapid growth of a cosmopolitan port such as Delos, must not be allowed to disguise the rapid depopulation of the smaller towns and the rural areas.

Nor did this reduction in quantity lead to an improvement in quality – its most obvious result was the demise of Hellenism as a political force. The history of Greece as a nation ceases with the second century: we have already noted the end of Macedon, of the Achaean and Aetolian Leagues, the Pergamene kingdom, the dissolution of the Seleucid Empire, and the decrepitude of Egypt. The latter two states only continued an independent existence because Rome had no wish to absorb them, but they were at the mercy of a conspiracy of politicians and financiers. True, there still existed a number of 'free cities', but the freedom they enjoyed under the authority of Rome or the Seleucids was reduced to a matter of municipal police control, perhaps also the regulation of minor local squabbles. The management of the city's affairs had become henceforth no better than a 'municipal plaything' as Renan called it, an amusement for the citizens, a mockery for the Roman statesmen. This plaything often worked irregularly and spasmodically: at Delos, the whole cosmopolitan population of the island would be assembled to greet some personage of note; at Alexandria, deprived at some indeterminate date of its Council, the feelings of the populace could find expression only in tumultuous riots.

Political decadence was accompanied by a slowing down of intellectual activity. Yet the institutions founded at Alexandria, and following the same pattern at Pergamum and Rhodes, worked in fruitful competition with one another and maintained high scientific standards in spite of the persecutions to which savants at the Museum were subjected in the reign of Ptolemy VII. In astronomy Hipparchus, in mechanics Hero, in medicine Asclepiades, in literary studies Didymus, were worthy inheritors of the learned men of the previous century. The great events which took place between 264 and 146 were recounted (without great literary skill but conscientiously and intelligently) by Polybius of Megalopolis, the son of Lycortas. Sent with other prisoners to Rome after the battle of Pydna, he had been able to judge events in Greece with a certain detachment, to disentangle the essential reasons for the decline of the Hellenic states, to distinguish the principles on which Roman power was based.

Nevertheless, the true creative faculty seemed to have been obliterated. Poetry was dead. Eloquence and philosophy no longer existed – only teachers of rhetoric. Not that the part played by these popularisers was by any means negligible: it was by them and, too often alas, through them that the Romans at the end of the second and beginning of the first centuries came to know the orators and thinkers of Greece. The lectures of the Academician Carneades, sent by the Athenians as their ambassador to Rome in 155, mark an important date in the history of Latin civilisation and literature.

In most Greek cities, lack of financial resources prevented more of the elaborate building of preceding centuries. Even in a town as prosperous as Delos one is struck by the perfunctory style of public buildings of the middle or end of the second century. Only the kings of Egypt and Asia could any longer afford the luxury of large-scale building. We shall never know what the palaces and temples of Alexandria, of Antioch and of Daphne (the Versailles of the Seleucids) were like. But in addition to the porticoes with which Eumenes II and Attalus II endowed Athens, we do know the terraces, temples, altars, theatres, and palaces, arranged according to a generous and grandiose plan on the Acropolis at Pergamum; and perhaps for the last time in the Greek world, sculptors established productive studios alongside those great building-sites. At Pergamum remarkable statues and bas-reliefs, whose pathos and splendour make us forget their bombast, commemorate the triumph of the Attalids over the Galatae.

Fortunately the decline of Hellenism was soon to be halted. From the first century onwards, thanks to the support given by Roman power and organisation, it held all its positions. For the next three centuries, from Marseilles to the Euphrates, and from Alexandria to the Black Sea, Greek was to remain the chief language for all cultural and commercial exchanges, and a genuine artistic and philosophic renaissance in the Hellenic world was one consequence of the Roman peace. True, the Greek states had disappeared, but Greek civilisation remained and all its essential features: a mildness of manners, a taste for the things of the mind, a critical spirit, and artistic sensibility. Everyone knows what Rome, and through Rome all modern Europe, owed to Greece, and it is not the purpose of this book to labour the point. Let us simply note the important consequences, from the political point of view, of one of the chief tendencies of Hellenism in the second century. Thanks to the decline of the idea of the city-state, to greater ease of communications, to the progress of certain philosophic doctrines, the idea of equality between men and the tendency towards a state of affairs such that everyone, without distinction of nationality, could enjoy the benefits of civilisation spread more and more widely. This cosmopolitan ideal was realised in the great commercial cities which welcomed foreigners, and conferred full civic rights very freely; an excellent example was Delos where a Greek population, itself of very varied origin, lived alongside communities of Italians, Syrians, and Egyptians – all on good terms one with another and even sharing to some extent in public affairs.

The same tendency manifested itself in intellectual realms: philosophers addressed themselves to an ever wider public. Polybius showed quite clearly that in his opinion the great events which had taken place in the Mediterranean region during the past century were all interconnected.

Such an outlook was bound to have its effect on Roman mentality and policy. The Greeks had dreamed about and foreseen a great world community, and this the Romans were soon able to adopt as a gigantic but practical goal within their reach. More and more the minds of Roman statesmen were haunted by the idea of a world-empire under the direction of the Senate. Not that this notion, as is often mistakenly affirmed, was the motive for the Roman conquest of the Greek states: much rather was it the consequence of that conquest and of the contacts between Greece and Rome which it permanently established.

In yet another direction the cosmopolitanism of the second century was to have most surprising results. We have seen the relationships which existed between the Seleucids and Judaism: they were, and could only be, antagonistic. Their only result was to exacerbate Jewish nationalism and encourage, in reaction against the brutalities of Greek administrators, that notion of a Messianic hope which was to be the basis of the teaching of Jesus. But Hellenism and Judaism had other, different contacts. At Antioch, at Tarsus (the birthplace of St. Paul), at Alexandria (where towards the end of the second century the Old Testament had been translated into Greek), at Delos (where the ruins of a Jewish synagogue have been discovered), the Jews learned to know Greeks other than administrators and soldiers. Judaism in its turn came to be penetrated by this cosmopolitan spirit which had formerly been so completely foreign to it, yet which was to become one of the essential elements in the spread of Christianity.

It may be asked if it is worth while in these days for a cultured person to learn about the political history of a small nation whose economic development was so different from ours, one which never had a stable political framework, whose existence was merely one long internecine conflict between jealous cities and ephemeral states. There is certainly something frustrating in the spectacle of the Greeks almost succeeding, again and again, in constructing for themselves an organisation which would have allowed them to develop into a vast and solid state, without ever being able quite to realise it in a durable fashion. But surely it is a far from profitless task to study these attempts, to search for the causes of these failures, to realise that perhaps the whole destiny of the Greek world might have been altered if only Athens in the fifth century had paid more attention to public education, or had sincerely applied the representative principle in her relations with allied cities; or if the Achaean League had evolved a better military legislation or developed much more public spirit.

Above all one must be struck by the fact that this study is not merely of antiquarian or historical interest, but that the political forms and tendencies which are familiar to us in our modern world are already clearly

displayed in Greek history. In the internal affairs of states we see exemplified monarchy, aristocracy of birth or of money, democracies of various
types; in the international relations between states we see a passionate
nationalism; a vigorous but crude imperialism; the dream (actually realised
for a few years) of the conquest and organisation of the known world; a
federalism which, had it learned to perfect itself, might well have proved
the salvation of Greece; and finally the spirit of cosmopolitanism and
human brotherhood. It is certainly no matter of indifference to be able to
observe these forms of social organisation and these political tendencies
confronting one another, in the story of a people so intellectually close to
ourselves. For we find them all again in our modern world, and on the
outcome of these forms and tendencies depends without doubt the future
of our civilisation.

SELECTIVE BIBLIOGRAPHY

by

D. J. MOSLEY, Ph.D.
Department of Ancient History, University of Sheffield

For those who may wish to find other accounts and interpretations, or to pursue further information on various topics the following bibliography is appended.

It has been considered more convenient to arrange the bibliography according to topical divisions, since the book is composed of a large number of chapters, of which some are related and some are quite short. Such a procedure is to some extent arbitrary since many works overlap in their scope and the divisions themselves may not be ideal, but the titles of the books listed should be found to be indicative of their contents. For the convenience of readers of the English edition of this book all the works listed below are those which have been written in, or translated into, English. In the first section works are listed according to the comprehensiveness of their scope, in the other sections according to the alphabetical order of authors.

No attempt has been made to list ancient authorities and collections of source material, since the reader will probably wish to seek more information in the secondary works listed below and thereby gain access to the sources.

HISTORICAL AND REFERENCE WORKS

The Oxford Classical Dictionary. 1949.

HARVEY, P. (Ed.). *The Oxford Companion to Classical Literature.* 1937.

The Cambridge Ancient History. (Vols. I and II rev. 1961-). 1923-39.

SCULLARD, H. H. & VAN DER HEYDEN, A. A. M. *Atlas of the Classical World.* 1959.

GROTE, G. *A History of Greece.* (12 Vols., New Ed.).

BURY, J. B. *A History of Greece to the Death of Alexander the Great.* (3rd Ed., rev. R. Meiggs). 1951.

HAMMOND, N. G. L. *A History of Greece to 322 B.C.* 1959.

STARR, C. G. *The Origins of Greek Civilization.* 1962.

LAISTNER, M. L. W. *History of the Greek World 479-323 B.C.* (3rd Ed.). 1957.

CARY, M. *History of the Greek World 323-146 B.C.* (2nd Ed.). 1951.

BURN, A. R. *The Lyric Age of Greece.* 1960.

    Persia and the Greeks. 1962.

    Alexander the Great and the Hellenistic Monarchies. 1947.

GENERAL WORKS

BONNARD, A. *Greek Civilization from the Iliad to the Parthenon.* (Trans. A. Lytton Sells). 1957.

BOWRA, C. M. *The Greek Experience.* 1957.

CARY, M. *The Geographic Background of Greek and Roman History.* 1949.

COOK, J. M. *The Greeks in Ionia and the East.* 1962.

COOK, R. M. *The Greeks till Alexander.* 1961.

LLOYD-JONES, H. (Ed.). *The Greeks.* 1962.

MYRES, J. L. *Who Were the Greeks?* 1930.

PAGE, D. L. *History and the Homeric Iliad.* 1959.

TARN, W. W. & GRIFFITH, G. T. *Hellenistic Civilisation.* (3rd Ed.). 1952.

TOYNBEE, A. J. *Hellenism: The History of a Civilization.* 1959.

WEBSTER, T. B. L. *From Mycenae to Homer.* 1958.

WOODHEAD, A. G. *The Greeks in the West.* 1962.

ZIMMERN, A. *The Greek Commonwealth: Politics and Economics in Fifth Century Athens.* (5th Ed.). 1931.

ZSCHIETZSCHMANN, W. *Hellas and Rome: The Classical World in Pictures.* 1959.

POLITICAL

AGARD, W. R. *What Democracy Meant to the Greeks.* 1942. Reprinted, 1960.

ANDREWES, A. *The Greek Tyrants.* 1956.

BARKER, E. *Greek Political Theory.* (5th Ed.). 1960.

EHRENBERG, V. *The Greek State.* 1960.

GLOTZ, G. *The Greek City and its Institutions.* (Trans. N. Mallinson). 1929.

JONES, A. H. M. *Athenian Democracy.* 1957.

MICHELL, H. *Sparta.* 1952.

SINCLAIR, T. A. *A History of Greek Political Thought.* 1952.

URE, P. N. *The Origin of Tyranny.* 1922.

SOCIAL AND ECONOMIC ORGANISATION

FINLEY, M. I. *The World of Odysseus.* 1956.

GLOTZ, G. *Ancient Greece at Work.* (Trans. M. R. Dobie). 1926.

HASEBROEK, J. *Trade and Politics in Ancient Greece.* (Trans. L. M. Frazer & D. C. MacGregor). 1933.

JONES, J. W. *Law and Legal Theory of the Greeks.* 1956.

MICHELL, H. *The Economics of Ancient Greece.* (2nd Ed.). 1957.

MIREAUX, E. *Daily Life in the Time of Homer.* (Trans. I. Sells). 1959.

QUENNEL, M. & C. H. B. *Everyday Things in Archaic Greece.* 1931.
Everyday Things in Classical Greece. 1932.

ROSTOVTZEV, M. I. *The Social and Economic History of the Hellenistic World.* (3 Vols.). 1953.

THOMSON, G. *Studies in Ancient Society: The Prehistoric Aegean* (New Ed.). 1954.

WASON, M. O. *Class Struggles in Ancient Greece.* 1947.

LITERATURE

ARNOTT, P. D. *An Introduction to the Greek Theatre.* 1959.

BURY, J. B. *The Ancient Greek Historians.* 1958.

KENNEDY, G. *The Art of Persuasion in Greece.* 1963.

KENYON, F. G. *Books and Readers in Ancient Greece and Rome.* (2nd Ed.). 1951.

KITTO, H. D. F. *Greek Tragedy.* (2nd Ed.). 1950.

KÖRTE, A. *Hellenistic Poetry* (Trans. M. Hadas & J. Hammer). 1929.

NORWOOD, G. *Greek Comedy.* 1931.

ROSE, H. J. *A Handbook of Greek Literature.* (4th Ed.). 1961.

RELIGION AND PHILOSOPHY

ARMSTRONG, A. M. *An Introduction to Ancient Philosophy.* (3rd Ed.). 1957.

CLAGETT, M. *Greek Science in Antiquity.* 1957.

CORNFORD, F. M. *From Religion to Philosophy.* 1912.

DODDS, E. R. *The Greeks and the Irrational.* 1951.

GUTHRIE, W. K. C. *The Greek Philosophers.* 1950.

> *The Greeks and their Gods.* 1954.

> *In the Beginning.* 1957.

JAEGER, W. *Paideia: The Ideals of Greek Culture.* (Trans. G. Highet). 1939.

MARROU, H. I. *A History of Education in Antiquity.* (Trans. by G. Lamb). 1956.

NILSSON, M. P. *A History of Greek Religion.* (2nd Ed. Trans. J. Fielden). 1949.

> *Greek Popular Religion.* 1947.

NOCK, A. D. *Conversion: The Old and the New in Religion from Alexander the Great to Augustine of Hippo.* 1933.

PEARSON, L. *Popular Ethics in Ancient Greece.* 1962.

ROSE, H. J. *A Handbook of Greek Mythology.* (6th Ed.). 1958.

SAMBURSKY, S. *The Physical World of the Greeks.* 1956.

SNELL, B. *The Discovery of the Mind.* (Trans. T. G. Rosenmeyer). 1953.

ART AND ARCHITECTURE

COOK, R. M. *Greek Painted Pottery.* 1960.

CORBETT, P. E. *The Sculpture of the Parthenon.* 1959.

LAWRENCE, A. W. *Greek Architecture.* 1957.

LULLIES, R. & HIRMER, M. *Greek Sculpture.* 1957.

PLOMMER, H. *Ancient and Classical Architecture.* 1956.

RICHTER, G. M. A. *Handbook of Greek Art.* 1959.

SELTMAN, C. *A Book of Greek Coins.* 1952.

WYCHERLEY, R. E. *How the Greeks Built Cities.* (2nd. Ed.). 1962.

OTHER TOPICS

ADCOCK, F. E. *Greek and Macedonian Art of War.* 1957.

GARDINER, E. N. *Athletics of the Ancient World.* 1955.

TARN, W. W. *Hellenistic Military and Naval Developments.* 1930.

CHRONOLOGICAL TABLE

Neolithic settlements at various points in continental Greece and on the Asiatic coast.

3rd millennium B.C. Some agricultural areas, such as Boeotia, and especially Thessaly, become quite thickly populated. The people of these areas practise a primitive agriculture, are aware of wheat and the fig-tree, but not of the vine or olive.

Late 4th to late 2nd millennium. Civilisation flourishes in Crete and the Aegean isles.

Beginning of 2nd millennium. Several fortified towns in Greece and Asia Minor.

Early 2nd millennium. Cretan civilisation at its peak.

2nd millennium. Indo-European tribes move in, and establish themselves in the south of the Balkan peninsula, in the plains of Macedonia, in the islands of the Aegean, and along the western coasts of Asia Minor.

The Danube basin is an important metallurgical centre, producing objects in copper and bronze (and later in iron) unknown to the Minoan civilisation, but forming an indispensable part of Greek life.

c. 1700	Destruction of the palaces of Knossos and Phaistos.
c. 1400	End of Cretan supremacy. Destruction of Knossos.
c. 1400–1200	Culmination of Mycenaean civilisation.
c. 1200	Siege of Troy.

Decay of Mycenaean culture.

Greek-speaking Dorian immigrants in 11th century, followed by migrations of those displaced to coastal regions of Asia Minor.

c. 800   Homer – formation of the *Iliad* and *Odyssey*.

c. 750 onwards (8th-6th centuries). Colonial expansion.

c. 800–700   Formation of the Scythian kingdom in southern Russia.

8th–7th centuries. Unification of Attica under Athens.

Wars between Sparta and Messene.

Introduction of coined money in Asia Minor. Words and terms begin to appear – such as *Hellanodikai* – which imply the common bonds between Greek peoples.

c. 710   Hesiod.

End of 7th century. Lydian hegemony in Asia Minor.

7th–6th centuries. Age of revolution – social revolutions in Greece.

c. 690   Cimmerian hordes invade Asia Minor.

c. 650   They enter Lydia, rout the army of Gyges, king of Lydia, take
                Sardis, and threaten the Greek cities of Ionia. But Gyges's suc-
                cessors rebuild Lydia.

                Loss of political power by the king at Athens.

c. 594–593   Solon appointed 'archon and reconciler' to terminate civil strife in
                Athens.

6th century   Peloponnesian League. Sparta begins to attract attention by the
                stability and peculiar features of her organisation.

                The 6th century is a period of remarkable intellectual activity –
                in law, ethics, science, art, and religion. But this brilliant civilisation
                is founded on the small individual autonomous city. There are
                few ideas of economic, political, or even military unity.

561–527 (with two gaps). Peisistratus tyrant of Athens.

6th–4th centuries. Magnificent development of Athens.

546   Sardis is captured by the Persians, and all the Greek coastal towns
                of Asia Minor fall into the hands of Cyrus, king of the Persians.

539   The fall of the Babylonian Empire secures for Cyrus the additional
                support of the Phoenician fleets.

527   Death of Peisistratus.

527–510   Hippias (son of Peisistratus) tyrant of Athens. Hipparchus (younger
                brother of Hippias) acts as patron of literature and art, while
                assisting Hippias with the government.

525   Cambyses, son of Cyrus, subdues Egypt.

512   Darius invades Scythia, by a combined land and sea operation.
                Owing to the Scythians' scorched earth policy, this fails. The
                Ionian cities threaten revolt, but this is suppressed; Darius subdues
                the peoples of Thrace, and demands homage from Amyntas, king
                of Macedon.

508   Constitution of Cleisthenes, based on *trittyes*, *demes*, a new
                Boulê.

506   The Athenians defeat the infantry of the Boeotian League and the
                cavalry of Chalcis. The Assembly of the Peloponnesian League
                gathers at Sparta.

500–499   Ionian Revolt, headed by Aristagoras.

498   In the spring of 498 the Ionian forces sack Sardis.

500–480   The chief Greek cities of Sicily all came under one dynasty, and
                this federation becomes a formidable military power.

491–0   Expedition of Mardonius to punish Athens and Eretria for their
                support of the Ionian revolt. This fleet is destroyed by a storm off
                Mount Athos, and his land forces are severely beaten by Thracian
                tribes.

490   Persian forces under Datis and Artaphernes invade central Greece,
                and pillage Eretria.
                ✕ Marathon.

486	Darius dies, and is succeeded by Xerxes.
c. 485 onwards.	Aeschylus's plays.
485	The discovery of rich silver lode at Mount Laurium leads to a
480	financial expansion in Athens. By 480 the Athenians have built well over 100 triremes, thus becoming the most powerful maritime city in the Hellenic world.
484	Herodotus born.
480	Persian troops cross the Hellespont in vast numbers.
	Themistocles appointed commander of the Athenian fleet.
	⚔ Artemisium.
	⚔ Thermopylae.
	⚔ Salamis.
480	The Plataeans take an active part in opposition to Xerxes.
480	Euripides born.
479	The Persian army of occupation under Mardonius remains in Thessaly, and devastates Attica in the spring of 479.
	⚔ Plataea. The Persian army under Mardonius defeated, thus assuring the freedom of Greece.
	⚔ Mycale. The Greek fleet under Leotychidas wins a decisive naval victory over the Persians.
	The Carthaginians invade Sicily under Hamilcar, and are completely routed.
468	⚔ Eurymedon. Greek triremes under Cimon destroy the Phoenician fleet off the coast of Pamphylia.
461	Cimon ostracised.
460	Thucydides born.
457	Athenian conquest of Boeotia.
454	Disastrous loss of the Athenian fleet in Egypt.
	The treasury of the great Delian League is moved from Delos to the Acropolis. The Athenians begin to use treasury funds for the city's building programme and internal expenses, without imposing additional taxation on Athenian citizens.
450–449	The Athenians defeat the Phoenicians in two battles off Cyprus. Death of Cimon on this expedition.
450 et seq.	Building activities on the Acropolis at Athens.
447–432	The great temple of Athens is erected, later to be renamed the Parthenon.
446	A Peloponnesian army invades Attica, and encamps at Eleusis.
445	Pericles offers peace, and a thirty years' convention is agreed.
c. 441	Sophocles's *Antigone*.
440	Samos – one of the leading members of the Confederacy of Delos
439	– rebels, and is joined by Byzantium. Revolt suppressed by an Athenian fleet under Pericles, after a nine-months siege. A democratic régime is established there.

438	Phidias creates an enormous statue of Athena in gold and ivory, which is placed in the *cella* of the Parthenon; and another of Zeus a few years later, which is placed in his temple at Olympia.
433	The fleets of Corinth and Corcyra clash near the southern tip of Corcyra, which is saved from invasion by the intervention of Athenian triremes.
432–429	Potidaea revolts, is captured after a two-year siege, and resettled from Athens.
431	The Peloponnesian War begins.
430	Second Peloponnesian invasion of Attica. Plague breaks out in the Piraeus and Athens.
429	Pericles dies of the plague, his effective place being taken by Cleon.
429	The Peloponnesians lay siege to Plataea.
428	The isle of Lesbos revolts, and is admitted to the Peloponnesian League.
427	Plataea's garrison surrender, and all are butchered.
425	The Athenians send help to Sicily. On the way there, Demosthenes takes Pylos, capturing three hundred surviving Spartans. They fortify it, and hold it against Spartan attempts to dislodge them.
426 *et seq.*	Aristophanes's comedies.
422	The Athenians are routed at ✕ Amphipolis, both Cleon and Brasidas are killed.
421	Peace of Nicias.
418	✕ Mantinea. The Argives and Mantineans defeat the Spartans.
415	The Athenians send another expedition to Sicily, under Alcibiades, Nicias, and Lamachus.
414	Alcibiades is recalled to stand trial for impiety. He escapes into voluntary exile.
414	They try to take Syracuse, which is relieved by Sparta at the instigation of Alcibiades.
	The Athenians eventually withdraw from Syracuse, after abandoning their fleet in the Great Harbour, and the rearguard under Demosthenes is massacred.
413	Sparta again invades Attica and occupies Decelea, thus cutting the supply-line from Euboea to Athens.
412	The Athenians substitute an import duty for tribute from subject cities.
	Tissaphernes and Pharnabazus, satraps of Lydia and Phrygia, conclude an alliance with Sparta, with the object of destroying the Athenian Empire.
412–411	The Athenians desperately rebuild their fleet.
411	The Council of Four Hundred comes into power in Athens in June, and is overthrown in September.

409	A huge Carthaginian army invades Sicily, and captures Selinus and Himera.
407	Alcibiades is elected a *strategos*, and returns to Athens in triumph. He sails for Ionia in command of 100 triremes.
	The Carthaginians take Agrigentum (Sicily).
	Dionysius assumes tyrannical powers in Syracuse.
	Gela is taken by the Carthaginians.
	✕ Arginusae: Conon wins a naval victory over the Spartans under Callicratides.
406	✕ Mytilene. This unexpected Athenian success is not exploited.
405	✕ Aegospotami: Lysander destroys the last Athenian squadron.
404	The Athenians surrender. The Long Walls are pulled down. End of the Athenian Empire. Seven hundred Lacedaemonian soldiers garrison the Acropolis.
	An oligarchical government of thirty members is then imposed on the Athenians, known as 'The Thirty'. They distinguish themselves by their monstrous cruelty.
404–403	Thrasybulus siezes the fortress of Phyle, on the frontier between Boeotia and Attica, and occupies the Piraeus. (✕ Munychia.) The Thirty take refuge in Eleusis, and are deposed.
401	Expedition of Cyrus, son of Darius II, in an attempt to win the throne of Persia from his brother, Artaxerxes II, with the help of Greek mercenaries.
	✕ Cunaxa – Cyrus killed. His Asiatic troops disperse, but the Greek mercenaries make the famous return described in Xenophon's *Anabasis*.
400–397	Tissaphernes tries to reconquer Ionia, but fails, and the Spartans come to the protection of the Greek cities.
399	Socrates is tried and condemned.
399 *et seq.*	Plato attempts to establish a theory of morals – the moral reformation of the individual, based on a rational conception of the universe.
398–397	Dionysius is forced to evacuate all western Sicily.
396	The Peloponnesian towns send a relieving fleet to Sicily, and Dionysius destroys most of the Carthaginian fleet in a surprise attack on the Great Harbour.
396–395	Brilliant Campaign of Agesilaus in Phrygia and Lydia. He defeats Tissaphernes at Susa and in Paphlagonia.
395	Revolt of Rhodes. Conon drives out the Lacedaemonian garrison.
395–394	Athens, Thebes, Corinth, Argos, form an alliance against Sparta. Agesilaus is recalled from Asia.
394	Allies are defeated at ✕ Corinth and ✕ Coronea.
	✕ Cnidus. All the towns of Asia Minor and the Cyclades (except the Hellespont) expel their Lacedaemonian garrisons.
	Long Walls reconstructed, with the help of Persian gold.

393	A Carthaginian expedition to Sicily is defeated.
389	The Athenian fleet, under Thrasybulus, re-establishes the Athenian supremacy in the northern Aegean.
390–388	Iphicrates defeats the Spartans at Corinth and the Chersonese. Dionysius gains control of the Straits of Messina.
388	Lysias the orator warns the Greeks at the Olympic festival of the dangers from Persia and Sicily, and urges Greek unity.
387–386	Tiribazus summons representatives from the Greeks. The King's Peace (Peace of Antalcidas). Persia supports Sparta.
386	Spartans seize Mantinea, destroy it, and disperse the inhabitants into five outlying townships.
382	The Spartans seize the Theban citadel of Cadmea.
381	Panegyric Speech of Isocrates – urges unity.
380 et seq.	Dionysius attempts to drive the Carthaginians out of Sicily.
379	The Lacedaemonian garrison is driven out of the Cadmea, in Thebes.
	⚔ Cabala in western Sicily. The Syracusans win a great victory against the Carthaginians. ⚔ Cronion in Sicily. The situation reversed. Dionysius suffers grievous loss.
378	Second Athenian Naval Confederacy is directed against Sparta.
378 et seq.	Thebes reforms the old Boeotian League, with seven 'boeotarchs'.
376	The strategos Chabrias defeats the Spartans at ⚔ Naxos.
375	Most of the towns of Chalcidice and Thrace are brought back to the Athenian alliance.
374	Sparta asks for peace.
374–373	Sparta attacks Corcyra and Zacynthus, and is driven back.
372	Jason of Pherae is master of Thessaly.
	Peace Conference at Sparta. Renewal of the King's Peace.
	Epaminondas defeats Sparta at ⚔ Leuctra.
370	Epaminondas invades Laconia.
	Jason of Pherae is assassinated.
369	Epaminondas invades the Peloponnese again.
368	Alexander II of Macedon is murdered.
	Epaminondas invades Thessaly.
367	Death of Dionysius of Syracuse.
366	Epaminondas invades Achaea.
	The Greeks compete for Persian aid.
	The satraps Datames and Ariobarzanes rise in revolt.
	Thebes gains Persian support, but fails to impose terms on the Greeks.
366–359	Revolt of the satraps of Asia Minor, incited and supported by the Spartans.
362	Epaminondas invades the Peloponnese again. ⚔ Mantinea. Epaminondas killed. End of Theban hopes.

359	Philip of Macedon takes the title of King, and seizes Amphipolis.
358	Artaxerxes III (Ochus) ascends the throne of Persia.
357	Chios, Rhodes, Cos, and Byzantium revolt from Athens, at the instigation of Mausolus.
	Iphicrates and Timotheus defeated at Chios.
356	Dion's victory over Dionysius the Younger in the port of Syracuse.
356–354	Philomelus, the Phocian commander in the Third Sacred War, seizes Delphi. In autumn 355 he uses temple funds to raise an army of 10,000 men. He defeats the Thessalians, but in late 354 he is defeated and killed, and succeeded by Onomarchus and Phayllus.
356	Dion is assassinated.
	Dionysius the Younger returns to Syracuse.
355	Philip of Macedon marches into Thessaly, and is twice defeated.
356–355	Athens recognises the independence of Chios, Rhodes, Cos, and Byzantium.
353	Philip reappears in Thessaly, and defeats Onomarchus near Pherae, uniting Thessaly under the hegemony of Macedon. He is turned back at Thermopylae, and is prevented from attacking Phocis.
352	The Athenian fleet is now increased in strength under the inspiration of Eubulus.
351	Philip forces Cersobleptes into an alliance.
349	Philip advances into Chalcidice.
348	Athens recognises the independence of Euboea.
	All the towns of Chalcidice are incorporated into Macedonia.
346	The Peace of Philocrates leaves only Boeotia between Athens and the advanced Macedonian activities.
c. 345	Philip concludes a treaty of alliance with Artaxerxes Ochus, who has at last re-established the kingdom of the great Darius in its entirety.
	The enemies of Dionysius in Syracuse appeal to Corinth for help.
	Timoleon sails for Sicily, captures Syracuse, and exiles Dionysius.
343–342	Philip offers Athens various conciliatory measures, but all his efforts come to nothing in face of the unshakable opposition of the patriotic party, inspired by Demosthenes.
342	Cersobleptes is dethroned, and his kindgom of the Odrysae becomes a Macedonian province.
341	Timoleon defeats the Carthaginians on the River Crimisus in eastern Sicily.
341–340	Great Athenian military successes.
339	Philip occupies Elatea, thus commanding the road to the Boeotian Plain, bringing about an alliance between Athens and Thebes.
338	The Macedonians march into Locris, annihilate the allied troops, and capture Amphissa.

338 ⚔ Chaeronea. Philip defeats the Athenians and Thebans, thus establishing Macedonian supremacy in Greece. Alexander excels himself in the battle.

The Second Athenian Naval Confederacy and the Boeotian Confederation are both suppressed.

Philip founds the League of Corinth, and compels states to join. Macedonian garrisons are planted at key points.

Artaxerxes Ochus is murdered.

337 Philip despatches 10,000 men under Parmenio beyond the Hellespont.

336 Philip of Macedon is assassinated.

Alexander marches into Thessaly, Boeotia, Corinth.

335 Alexander mounts a punitive expedition against rebellious Illyria, and pushes through to the Danube.

334 Alexander places Macedon under the regency of Antipater, crosses the Hellespont, and lands his troops (c. 40,000) in the Troad.

⚔ Granicus. Alexander's first great victory over Darius III.

⚔ Issus.

332 Alexander is welcomed in Egypt as a liberator. He visits the shrine of Ammon Ra in Libya.

331 ⚔ Gaugamela. Rout and massacre of the Persian army.

Alexander enters Babylon and Susa without having to strike another blow.

King Agis II of Sparta leads a revolt against the Macedonian forces of occupation, with Persian support, but is defeated and killed at ⚔ Megalopolis.

330 Murder of Darius. Revolt of Bessus.

329 Alexander crosses the Hindu Kush into Bactria.

329–328 Conquest of Sogdiana and Bactria.

327 Alexander descends through the valley of the Kabul towards the Indus.

326 He marches into the Punjab.

⚔ Hydaspes. He defeats Porus (Paurava), who is allowed to retain his kingdom, which Alexander proceeds to enlarge.

He plans his return journey via the Indus and the Persian Gulf.

325 He reaches the mouth of the Indus.

324 Back in Susa.

Harpalus, Alexander's treasurer, flees to Athens with 5,000 talents and 6,000 mercenaries.

323 Death of Alexander.

Abolition of democracy at Athens, compelled by the Macedonians.

319 Death of Antipater, who is succeeded by Polyperchon.

318–317 Antigonus sends Cassander into Greece. Athens submits, and agrees to the re-establishment of a plutocratic constitution.

319	The Carthaginians give military command to Agathocles, who becomes master of Syracuse after two days' hard street fighting.
317	Eumenes is betrayed to Antigonus, who has him executed.
316	Cassander rebuilds Thebes, and clearly intends to rule Macedonia (and Greece) for his own benefit.
314–313	War is general throughout Greece and Asia Minor.
313	The authority of Agathocles is recognised throughout eastern Sicily, except Messene and Agrigentum.
312	An Egyptian army under Ptolemy and Seleucus enters Syria. Demetrius, sent against them by his father Antigonus, is soundly beaten. Seleucus returns to Babylon.
311	Antigonus reaches agreement on the partition of Alexander's Empire with Lysimachus and Ptolemy. All Greek cities obtain freedom and autonomy.
311	A powerful Carthaginian expedition lands on the promontory of Ecnomos under Hamilcar and defeats Agathocles, who loses all his territory except Syracuse itself.
310–309	Agathocles captures Tunis and lays siege to Carthage, mastering almost all Carthaginian Libya.
307	Agathocles deserts his troops and returns hastily to Sicily.
	Demetrius, sent by Antigonus, appears off the Piraeus with 200 ships and enters Athens in triumph.
	Demetrius Poliorcetes sets out from the Piraeus with 163 ships to attack Ptolemy I in Cyprus.
	⚔ Salamis (Cyprus).
306	Antigonus and his son Demetrius Poliorcetes fail in a combined land and sea operation against Egypt.
305	Demetrius lays siege to Rhodes.
304	Agathocles takes the title of King of Syracuse.
303	He wages a successful campaign in the Peloponnese.
302	The revived League of Corinth nominates Demetrius as General-in-Chief of the confederate Greek armies.
301	⚔ Ipsus. Antigonus and Demetrius are defeated by Lysimachus and Seleucus. Antigonus is killed.
298	Alliance through marriage between Seleucus and Demetrius.
296–294	Siege of Athens by Seleucus I (Nicator). A Macedonian garrison is established at Munychia.
	Demetrius is King of Macedon.
293	Boeotia rebels – revolt quelled.
291	Boeotia rebels again. Demetrius lays siege to Thebes, and takes it.
	Demetrius invades Thrace.
289	Demetrius invades Epirus.
	Pyrrhus invades Macedon.
289	Death of Agathocles. His empire disintegrates.

288	Pyrrhus and Lysimachus invade Macedonia. Demetrius flees.
287	Demetrius sets sail for Asia.
285	Pyrrhus concludes a secret treaty with Antigonus Gonatas, Son of Demetrius.
283	Death of Ptolemy I.
282	Death of Demetrius.
	A Roman flotilla sails into the Gulf of Tarentum.
280	Pyrrhus disembarks in Italy, at the head of 20,000 Epirots and Greeks.
	✄ Heraclea. Pyrrhus defeats a Roman army under Valerius Laevinus.
279–278	Three bands of Celts push south, one towards Thrace, the other two through Illyria towards Macedonia.
	Ptolemy Ceraunus defeated and killed.
	The Celts reach Delphi. They cross Thessaly and Macedon.
279–276	Pyrrhus relieves Syracuse, and proceeds to clear Sicily of Carthaginian garrisons, except Lilybaeum.
279–274	Hordes of Galatae (Gallic and Celtic tribes) invade Greece, cross the Hellespont, and ravage the coasts of Aeolis and Ionia. They
275	are defeated by Antiochus in an indecisive battle in 275.
278	The Carthaginians blockade Syracuse by land and sea.
277	Antigonus Gonatas defeats the Celts.
276	Antigonus is established in Macedonia. Pyrrhus is busy in Italy.
275	Pyrrhus returns to Macedonia, leaving a garrison at Tarentum, bitterly incensed against the Greek rulers, who had given him no help.
274	War breaks out between Egypt and Syria.
274–272	Pyrrhus defeats Antigonus on his own ground. He crosses Aetolia and invades the Peloponnese, but returns north.
273	He again makes himself master of Macedon.
272	Is killed in a riot at Argos.
266	The surrender of the Messapians assures Roman rule over the whole of *Magna Graecia* (the Greek city-states of south Italy).
265	Antigonus lays siege to Athens.
265 *et seq.*	Rome, now the most powerful state in Italy, begins to come in contact with Carthaginian interests in the western Mediterranean and with the Hellenistic world in the east.
264	Antigonus defeats the Spartans near Corinth.
262	The Spartan army is again beaten, by Aristodemus, tyrant of Megalopolis.
	Antiochus I is beaten by the Pergamene dynasty near Sardis.
261	Athens capitulates.
259	Antiochus II concludes an alliance with Macedonia.
255	Bactria becomes an independent kingdom.

255	Diodotus, Satrap of Bactria, turns his province into an independent princedom.
	The Parthian Empire is established, and continues to grow until (under Mithridates I and II) it extends to the Euphrates, Caspian, Indus, and Indian Ocean.
	⚔ Andros. Antigonus defeats the Egyptian fleet.
c. 245–241	Agis IV of Sparta attempts to carry out reforms, but is assassinated.
243	Aratus seizes Acro-Corinth – Antigonus thus loses the key to the Peloponnese.
242	Cancellation of mortgages in Sparta.
241	Troops of the Achaean and Aetolian Leagues are defeated near Corinth.
	End of First Punic War – Sicily is ceded to Rome.
	Northern Syria is returned to Seleucus by treaty. Ptolemy is given possession of Ephesus and Seleucia-Pieria at the Gates of Antioch.
239	Death of Antigonus Gonatas, leaving the throne to his son, Demetrius.
c. 237	Cleomenes III becomes King of Sparta, and follows the example of Agis IV in attempting to restore the old Spartan constitution.
235	Aratus concludes a treaty of alliance with the Aetolians.
	Central Greece and most of the Peloponnese form a vast group of coalitions all hostile to Macedon.
234	Revolution changes the monarchy of Epirus into a republic.
231–227	Cleomenes carries out reforms in Sparta.
230	Rome sends an embassy to Illyria, whose Queen Teuta has a legate assassinated.
230–229	Argos joins the Achaean League.
229	Demetrius dies after a battle against the Dardanians.
229–228	Seleucus II defeats his brother Antiochus Hierax several times at Ancyra and in Asia Minor.
	A Roman naval expedition relieves Epidamnus, and recaptures Corcyra from Illyria.
	Antiochus surrenders to Ptolemy III.
227	He escapes and goes to Thrace, where he is killed.
	Aratus is defeated under the walls of Megalopolis.
226	Seleucus II dies.
226–224	Cleomenes captures Argos and Corinth.
	Aratus negotiates realistically with Antigonus Doson of Macedonia.
224	'General Alliance' between Macedonia, the Boeotians, Phocians, Thessalians, Epirots, and Acarnanians, leaving Cleomenes isolated in the Peloponnese.

222	Antigonus Doson marches into Laconia, and defeats Sparta (Cleomenes III) at ✗ Sellasia.
221	Death of Antigonus Doson. Antiochus III defeats Molon in Mesopotamia.
220	An Aetolian detachment enters the Peloponnese and invades Messenia, who appeals to the Achaeans for help. Aratus intercepts the Aetolians, and is soundly beaten. Suicide of Cleomenes in Egypt.
219	Lycurgus invades Argolis.
219	Philip V of Macedonia marches into Aetolia, but is recalled home by an Aetolian and Dardanian invasion of Macedonia.
219–218	Philip reappears in the Peloponnese with 6,000 troops.
218	He crosses the Gulf of Corinth, and penetrates into Aetolia as far as Thermos. He advances on Sparta. He clears Macedonia of Dardanians, returns to Aetolia, and takes Phthiotis.
217	The Assembly of the Aetolian League, meeting at Naupactus, agrees with Philip and Aratus to return to the *status quo*. ✗ Raphia. Antiochus is defeated by the Egyptians, and loses Coele Syria.
216	✗ Cannae. Philip of Macedon concludes an alliance with Hannibal with the object of eradicating Roman influence east of the Adriatic.
215–214	Philip invades the Peloponnese and ravages the countryside, thus uniting against him the Aetolians, Spartiates, Messanians, and Eleans, and angering the Achaeans.
212	The Praetor Marcus Laevinus concludes a treaty with the Aetolians. The war between Rome and Carthage thus becomes a 'world war', involving states in Africa, Italy, Greece, and Asia.
211	Antiochus compels the king of Armenia to acknowledge his authority.
210–205	Antiochus undertakes a great expedition to impose his overlordship on the kings of Parthia and Bactria. He renews relations with the rajahs of the Punjab.
208	Philopoemen of Megalopolis becomes *strategos* of the Achaeans, and raises a splendid army of nearly 20,000 men. He defeats the Spartans at Tegea, and advances as far as Sparta.
205	Peace Treaty of Phoenice.
202	Philip invades Thrace, captures and sacks Abydos in 200. ✗ Zama in North Africa – Hannibal defeated by Scipio. End of Second Punic War.
201	Philip seizes Samos. Antiochus invades Syria.

201–200	Embassies from Egypt, Rhodes, and Pergamum meet in Italy, and seek Roman intervention against Philip.
	Alliance between Philip and Antiochus.
201–200	Antiochus is occupied in the conquest of Coele Syria.
	The Romans invade Macedon under the proconsul Sulpicius Galba.
199	Roman victory over Philip in the region of the lakes.
198	Abortive conference at Nicaea. War resumed.
	Antiochus conquers Palestine and Coele Syria.
197	The Consul Flamininus invades Thessaly. ✗ Cynoscephalae results in a severe defeat for Philip.
	The Macedonians are beaten by the Achaeans in Corinth, and by the men of Rhodes in Caria.
	Peace convention.
196	Flamininus proclaims unrestricted freedom for all cities and states recently liberated.
	End of Macedonian domination.
196 and 192	Protracted negotiations between Antiochus and Rome.
192	The Aetolians seize Demetrias. Antiochus crosses into Greece.
191	Antiochus is defeated by the Romans at Thermopylae, and compelled to return to Asia.
190	✗ Magnesia. Antiochus is defeated by a Roman army of c. 30,000 troops under Lucius and Publius Scipio.
188	Antiochus sues for peace.
187	The Achaean League under Philopoemen at first forms an alliance (later retracted) with Ptolemy V.
179	Death of Philip V of Macedonia, succeeded by his son, Perseus, who re-establishes good relations throughout Greece.
177	Eumenes goes to Rome to denounce Perseus.
171	Rome invades Macedonia for the third time.
169	Antiochus invades the Nile Delta, but is ordered by Rome to evacuate Egypt.
168	✗ Pydna. Perseus is defeated by Lucius Aemilius Paullus.
167	Antiochus enters Jerusalem by force for the second time, and violates the temple of Zion.
166	Rome forbids for a time the working of the gold and silver mines in Macedon.
	Delos is returned to the Athenians.
160	Death of Eumenes II.
148	Andriscus of Macedon is defeated by the Romans under Q. Caecilius Metellus at Pydna.
	Macedonia is turned into a Roman province, under a praetor, and has to pay tribute.

146   Critolaus is defeated at Scarpheia. Diaeus defeated by Mummius, the successor to Metellus.

            Corinth sacked and completely destroyed. The states and cities of Greece are all put under effective control of the Roman governor of Macedonia.

141   The Parthians penetrate as far as Babylonia. Demetrius V is beaten by them and taken prisoner.

133   Death of Attalus III, son of Eumenes II, and successor to Attalus II. He bequeaths his dominions, which include almost the whole of western Asia Minor, to the Roman People. At this time the Pergamene kingdom includes almost the whole of Western Asia Minor.

INDEX

GREEK HISTORY AND LITERATURE IN
NORTON PAPERBOUND EDITIONS